Hollywood Harmony

The Oxford Music/Media Series

Daniel Goldmark, Series Editor

oxford
music/media series

Hollywood Harmony

MUSICAL WONDER AND THE SOUND OF CINEMA

FRANK LEHMAN

Oxford University Press is a department of the University of Oxford. It furthers
the University's objective of excellence in research, scholarship, and education
by publishing worldwide. Oxford is a registered trade mark of Oxford University
Press in the UK and certain other countries.

Published in the United States of America by Oxford University Press
198 Madison Avenue, New York, NY 10016, United States of America.

Library of Congress Cataloging-in-Publication Data
Names: Lehman, Frank, author.
Title: Hollywood harmony : musical wonder and the sound of cinema / Frank Lehman.
Description: New York, NY : Oxford University Press, [2018] |
Series: Oxford music/media series | Includes bibliographical references and index.
Identifiers: LCCN 2017041303 (print) | LCCN 2017041598 (ebook) |
ISBN 9780190606411 (updf) | ISBN 9780190606428 (epub) | ISBN 9780190606435 (oso) |
ISBN 9780190606398 (cloth : alk. paper) | ISBN 9780190606404 (pbk. : alk. paper)
Subjects: LCSH: Motion picture music—United States—Analysis, appreciation.
Classification: LCC ML2075 (ebook) | LCC ML2075 .L38 2018 (print) | DDC 781.5/420973—dc23
LC record available at https://lccn.loc.gov/2017041303

This volume is published with the generous support of the AMS 75 PAYS Endowment
of the American Musicological Society, funded in part by the National Endowment for
the Humanities and the Andrew W. Mellon Foundation.

Contents

Acknowledgments

This book is the culmination of a lifetime of interest in film music, one that could never have reached this point without the encouragement and assistance of colleagues, friends, and family. During the early stages of this project, film music theory was still not a large or well-defined discipline, and I must acknowledge the leap of faith it took for my mentors at Harvard University to approve of and steer along my work. Suzannah Clark, Chris Hasty, and especially my endlessly supportive doctoral advisor, Alex Rehding, offered everything an eager but naive young academic could need—feedback, encouragement, opportunity, and professional camaraderie. As I worked toward my PhD, I was fortunate to have guidance from a veritable all-star lineup of scholars, including Carolyn Abbate, Kofi Agawu, Daniel Albright, Richard Beaudoin, James Hoberman, Thomas Forrest Kelly, Fred Lerdahl, Sindhu Revuluri, Christoph Wolff, and the late Allen Forte; one could not ask for a more inspiring group of intellectual models. And for making every visit to the Harvard Music Department a joy (including a few nostalgic stopovers in 2017), I thank Lesley Bannatyne, Kaye Denny, Eva Kim, Nancy Shafman, Jean Moncrieff, Karen Rynne, and Charles Stillman.

What in retrospect seems like an inevitable path into academia was in fact the result of countless little shoves from my extraordinary professors at Brown University—among them, I owe profound gratitude to Paul Austerlitz, Katherine Bergeron, Arlene Cole, David Josephson, Paul Phillips, Butch Rovan, Shep Shapiro, Michael Steinberg, and Jeff Todd Titon. My undergraduate advisor, James Baker, deserves special thanks, not only for turning me on to music theory in the first place, but turning on a whole *generation* of my friends and classmates, who now study and teach music at the highest levels across the country, thanks to the inspiring example he set.

My time at Tufts University has been nothing short of a blessing. I have received continuous support and encouragement for this project from my colleagues in the Department of Music and the School of Arts and Sciences at large. The pages of this book are full of small insights and minor epiphanies I have gained through the many stimulating conversations I have had with every member of the faculty here, especially Joseph Auner, Alessandra Campana, Stephan Pennington, and Janet Schmalfeldt. I have gleaned inspiration from colleagues from every corner of the university, including from Nancy Bauer, Bárbara Brizuela, Jane Bernstein, Julia Cavallaro, Jimena Codina, James Glaser, Charles Inouye, Richard Jankowsky, Lucille Jones, Jamie Kirsch, Paul Lehrman, David Locke, Martin Marks, John McDonald, Michael McLaughlin, Melinda Latour O'Brien, William O'Hara, Aniruddh Patel, Johnny Redmond, Michael Rogan, Joel LaRue Smith, and Danna Solomon. The student body at Tufts, both at the undergraduate and master's level, has also proven an invaluable stimulus to my own thinking, particularly for a seminar I convened in Spring 2016 on multimedia analysis—together, Joe Annicchiarico, Erik Broess, Megan Connolly, Michelle Connor, Stephanie Evans, Kendall Winter, Abbie Rienzo, Allie McIntosh, and Cole Swanson found ways to challenge my own thinking and introduce me to many texts and approaches I would not have encountered otherwise.

When I first began researching film music, I felt as if I were the lone explorer in a vast and daunting landscape. How lucky I was to be quickly disabused of this notion, as I soon found my way into a vibrant (and, hearteningly, ever-growing) community of scholars within the fields of music theory, film music studies, and American musicology. It was an honor to find early support from those I considered luminaries and pathfinders in this discipline, especially from Scott Murphy and David Neumeyer. For their diverse contributions and assorted forms of inspiration, I would additionally like to acknowledge Emilio Audissino, Andrew Aziz, Janet Bourne, Matthew Bribitzer-Stull, James Buhler, Ed Buller, Juan Chattah, Richard Cohn, Michael Ducharme, Grace Edgar, Erik Heine, Craig Lysy, Karoly Mazak, Brooke McCorkle, Matthew McDonald, Stephen Meyer, Drew Nobile, Chelsea Oden, Steven Rahn, Nicholas Reyland, Mark Richards, William Rosar, Tom Schneller, Charles Smith, Willem Strank, and Bill Wrobel.

Writing can be a lonely process, and I spent many hours working on this manuscript with only my feline accomplice, Hector—a rotund tabby cat whose shock of orange fur resembles that of his namesake composer—for company. So it with special appreciation that I acknowledge the members of my Skype writing group, four friends and colleagues who lent their critical eyes to countless drafts scarcely more than a stream of consciousness peppered with neo-Riemannian symbols, and their sympathetic ears to many a bewailing of writer's block. For their patience and fellowship, I owe so much to Elizabeth Craft, Louis Epstein, Hannah Lewis, and Matt Mugmon. My feeling of gratitude also extends to members of my PhD cohort who continued offering insight and inspiration long after graduation—Will Cheng, Michael Heller, Tom Lin, John McKay, Luci Mok, Rowland Moseley, and Meredith Schweig.

Throughout the writing of *Hollywood Harmony*, I have benefited from the institutional support of a host of scholarly societies and organizations, including the Society for American Music, Music and the Moving Image, the New England Conference of Music Theorists, and the Newbury Faculty Fellowship. My research was supported by a pair of generous subventions, one from the Society for Music Theory, and the Claire and Barry Brook Endowment of the American Musicological Society, funded in part by the National Endowment for the Humanities and the Andrew W. Mellon Foundation. The fact that these institutions saw value in this project gives me hope that scholars and musicians of many stripes—theorists, historians, composers—will find something of interest within these pages.

Oxford University Press has been a dream to work with at every stage of the publishing process. From the moment first I sat down with the tireless and supernaturally kind (and superhumanly attentive) General Editor Norm Hirschy to discuss my proposal, I knew I wanted OUP to be *Hollywood Harmony*'s home. I also lucked out with Daniel Goldmark as Music/Multimedia Series Editor, and I consider it a great honor to have found my way into a book series shared with so many of my film musicological idols. To the anonymous reviews of my initial manuscript—thank you for pulling no punches. Your feedback was invaluable and incisive (and voluminous!), and there is not a paragraph in the final book that does not reflect some positive change you directly inspired. Thank you to Kendall Winter for expertly assembling this book's index. I am grateful to the superb editorial work of Leslie Safford, and the dedicated efforts from the entire Production Team at OUP and Newgen Knowledge Works, especially Janani Thiruvalluvar, my project manager.

For stoking my curiosity from an early age, for always supporting my faddish hobbies, and, especially, for cultivating in me a lifelong passion for music, I will never be able to thank my mother and father, Diana and William, enough. And for my brother, John, I admit leaching from you more than a few interests—notably, considering their prominence in this study, *Star Wars* and *The Lord of the Rings*. But the greatest obsession I've parasitized from you is obviously birding. As someone now willing to get up at 2AM and drive 200 miles to see the tiny silhouette of a warbler or hear the faint whimper of a thrush, all I can say is—I'm sorry if I ever made fun of you as a kid for your peculiar love of all things avian. I get it now.

To my wife, my best friend, my academic role model, and my fellow pop-culture obsessive, Kasi Conley: thank you for your loving companionship. We have been together for almost exactly as long as this book has been gestating. From the biggest life decisions to the smallest gestures of kindness and encouragement, any success I have had since we met in 2009 I owe to you.

I dedicate this book to my daughter, Margaret. Margie, you are the greatest wonder in my life.

Abbreviations, Orthography, and Examples

Abbreviations

GENERAL

CP	Common Practice
ET	Equal Temperament
FOTR	*The Fellowship of the Rings*
ic(*n*)	Interval Class (*n*)
ITPRA	Imagination/Tension/Prediction/Response/Appraisal (after Huron 2006)
LOTR	*The Lord of the Rings*
NRO	Neo-Riemannian Operator
NRT	Neo-Riemannian Theory
OST	Original Soundtrack Album
ROTK	*The Return of the King*
TTPC	Triadic-Tonal Progression Class
TTT	*The Two Towers*

SCALES AND COLLECTIONS

maj	Major
min	Minor
lyd	Lydian
mix	Mixolydian
dor	Dorian
aeol	Aeolian (Natural Minor)
phryg	Phrygian
acous	Acoustic (Lydian Dominant)
mel-min	Melodic Minor
diat	Diatonic

chrom   Chromatic
hex   Hexatonic
oct   Octatonic (Diminished)
wt   Whole Tone

CADENCES

PAC   Perfect Authentic Cadence (e.g., V⇨I)
IAC   Imperfect Authentic Cadence (e.g., V⁶⇨I)
HC   Half-Cadence (e.g., ii⇨V)
DC   Deceptive Cadence (e.g., V⇨vi)
PC   Plagal Cadence (e.g., IV⇨I; ii°⁷⇨I)
MC   Modal Cadence (e.g., ♭VII⇨I; ♭II⇨I)
CC   Chromatic Cadence (e.g., ♭vi⇨I; ♯IV⇨I)
CMC   Chromatically Modulating Cadence (e.g., V⇨I/♯III)

TRANSFORMATIONS (FULL INVENTORY GIVEN IN CHAPTER 2)

$\mathbf{T}_n$ Transpose by n
P   Parallel
L   Leading-Tone Exchange (*Leittonwechsel*)
R   Relative
S   Slide
N   Near Fifth (*Nebenverwandt*)
F   Far Fifth
H   Hexatonic Pole
D   Dominant
I   Identity

Orthography

Hollywood Harmony adheres to the general analytic orthography developed in Lewin (1987). The transformations employed herein are detailed in Chapter 2 and follow the nomenclatural precedents of Lewin (1987) and Hyer (1995). Transformations are distinguished in prose and diagrams by bold abbreviated operators (e.g., **PL·D**). Left-to-right transformational orthography is used unless otherwise noted. The dot (·) symbol entails composition of separate operations, and may be used both to imply a specific subdivision of a compound transformation and to ease reading of potentially confusing mixtures of different algebraic groups.

Analysis of harmonic function adheres to the norms of standard American-style Roman numerals, though for the sake of simplicity these will often be the barest possible descriptions of a given harmonic span's function; the Roman nu-meral analyses, in other words, are also reductive. Schenkerian analytic method-ology is intermittently employed and uses the general techniques laid out in Forte and Gilbert (1982). Scientific pitch notation is used to indicate the octave of a pitch. For the titles of film score excerpts, the name of the track from the original soundtrack is generally used, rather than the more difficult to ascertain cue-sheet names (e.g., "Main Title" instead of "1m1").

Specific elements of analytic nomenclature include the following:

CM, Cm	C major, minor chord (in prose, score diagrams)
C, c	C major, minor chord (in transformation diagrams)
C^7	C dominant seventh chord
C major	C major key/tonic
C_x	Sonority built on x-collection or mode. (e.g., C_{oct} = C octatonic sonority)
$\frac{Cm}{A\flat}$	Slash-chord (C minor over A♭ bass)
⇨	Progression (e.g., CM⇨Gm)
⇔	Oscillatory Progression
pc	Pitch Class
scale$_{x,y}$	Symmetrical scale (e.g., oct, wt) featuring pcs x and y.
(xyz)	Set in prime form
{xyz}	Ordered set
$f(x)$	Transformation f on x
f_1/f_2	Alternate interpretation between transformations f_1 and f_2.
f(M) or f(m)	Transformation on major or minor triad

Examples: Transcriptions

All film music analyses in *Hollywood Harmony* are the result of my own personal transcriptions. These examples are rendered in accordance with the dictates of fair use in the United States Copyright Act, Section 107, and are included solely for analytical purposes. Where a passage of music is presented for an example, it is analyzed with interpretive information (such as harmonic labels, prolongational stems and slurs, and screen-action indicators). Examples are reduced for max-imum clarity and often with simplification of register, instrumentation, and sometimes of specific chordal voicing and polyphonic lines as well. Only the por-tions of a cue relevant to written analyses are reproduced. The possibility exists for transcription error, particularly in cases of rhythmically vague and dissonant material; I take extreme care to ensure accuracy, but nevertheless assume respon-sibility for any misinterpretations that result from transcriptive fallibility.

About the Companion Website

www.oup.com/us/hollywoodharmony

A companion website accompanies *Hollywood Harmony*. This site includes audio clips of all the primary musical examples discussed in this book. Additionally, any updates or errata will be posted to this website.

Readers are encouraged to peruse these recordings, which are signaled within the text by the symbol ▶. Sound clips are drawn from Original Soundtrack Albums when available, or recorded directly from the film when commercial CD releases are unavailable. All clips are only partial representations of the scores they stem from, and are limited in duration and scope so as to adhere to Fair Use guidelines.

The companion website also features additional score examples for passages of music mentioned in passing in *Hollywood Harmony*. This includes transcriptions for all film cues discussed in Chapter 2: Altered and Heightened Realities and Chapter 6: The Cadence of Film Music.

Introduction

Figure I.1 Horner, Universal Studios Logo.

Hollywood Signs and Wonders

Today's filmgoers are bathed in music well before a movie even begins. Product commercials, behind-the-scenes promos, sneak previews, and film trailers are paraded out during the preludial "Coming Attractions" segment, each featuring carefully crafted musical accompaniment. Employing in miniature many of the same expressive and technical resources of movie scoring at large, these "pre-show entertainments" make up the first stage in the inherently musical experience of filmgoing. And since the birth of the Studio Era in the 1930s, one component in particular—the logo—has welcomed audiences into the sound world of Hollywood.

These are not just unusually grandiloquent advertising jingles; the pithy fanfares and evocative harmonies of logo themes are calculated to call up associations and build expectations about filmgoing itself.[1] Figure 0.1 (▶) offers one such utterance that audiences between 1990 and 1999 were likely to hear as the theater lights dimmed. James Horner's seven-measure logo for Universal Studios is a paratext, a work that delineates formal and generic boundaries but sits outside the text itself (Genette 1997). The message conveyed by Horner's musical miniature is at once both bluntly informative and artfully suggestive. It serves as a sonic brand, celebratorily proclaiming the company that is responsible for bringing a film to its audience. But it also fulfills an equally important, if somewhat covert, symbolic function. This logo and others like it prepare spectators to surrender fully to worlds soon to be conjured on screen. In concert with grand corporate typefaces and monumental graphical designs, the logo theme offers a sonic sample of larger-than-life spectacle, albeit a spectacle safely enclosed within a brief, neatly bound package.

Horner's broadly arching theme and comforting consonance promises cinematic wonders to come, but it also points backward in time. It embeds its listener within a romanticized history of cinematic experience, a history with a communal, generation-spanning dimension as well as a personal one (as the listener is likely be already familiar with the piece, or at least its style). Logo themes are acute manifestations of a nostalgizing strain in mainstream Hollywood, with music serving as what Caryl Flinn calls "a kind of conduit to connect listeners . . . to an idealized past, offering . . . the promise of a retrieval of lost utopian coherence" (1992: 50).

The musical style of a logo theme tends to be quite generic and may have very little to do tonally (in both senses) with the actual film about to appear. Alfred Newman's boisterously old-fashioned 20th Century Fox fanfare accomplishes essentially the same task when it precedes the harrowing *12 Years a Slave* in 2013 as it did upon its inaugural annunciation with the dramatic comedy *The Bowery* in 1933.[2] In fact, the more out of date the logo's music, the better it may fulfill its nostalgic and communalizing purposes.[3] As Leo Braudy observes, "like every icon, modern and ancient, the Hollywood sign has both a physical and metaphysical life, reaching beyond itself to unspecified wonders in an invisible world of potential and possibility" (2011: 4). Braudy speaks of the literal Hollywood sign that stretches across the Santa Monica Mountains, but he could as easily be referring to the golden letters of the 20th Century Fox emblem, or the roaring lion of Metro-Goldwyn-Mayer, or the splashy red comic book panels of Marvel Studios. Logos, and their meticulously constructed musical themes, are devised to sell *the movies*, not any one movie in particular.

Horner's little composition encapsulates some of the recurrent technical traits of logo themes as a formal archetype (and the sound of Hollywood as a musical ideal). Common features of these paratexts include arresting and cumulatively expanded orchestration, upward-arching melodies, and a sustained crescendo in volume. They tend to be heavily end weighted, speaking a rhetoric of culmination and arrival rather than departure or progress. Temporal constraints obviate full melodic forms such as periods or sentences, with very few exceptions.[4] During the apex of the Studio Era, logos were not always treated as self-contained musical statements; rather, they were composed so as to enable a smooth transition directly into the main credits. Max Steiner's tonally open-ended music for the original Warner Brothers Shield Logo (1937), for example, acts like a musical interrobang, forcefully grabbing attention but purposefully eschewing syntactic closure. This open-endedness allows the subsequent film score proper to determine musical mood and meaning. When logos *do* end, the ringing assertion of the final, almost invariably major triad is all important. In some cases, overall harmonic substance may consist of little more than a single sustained chord—Horner beats this commonplace by having three.[5] Bipartite structure of a sort is often present even where there is minimal harmonic momentum, in the form of pre- and post-cadential segmentation. Musical desire is piqued and swiftly satisfied, enacting a tonal microcosm of the comfortably delivered pleasures of mainstream filmmaking.[6]

The seven measures of Horner's theme fall into two sections, with the first four bars setting up a melody that stresses consonant intervals and chord tones, and the final four lingering on a chord of resolution. No gesture, no matter how small, is wasted. The initial melodic fourth, for example, opens up the tonal space around G, importing the peremptory, heraldic melodic connotations of beginning with a rising perfect interval while softening their impact with gentle syncopation and supple orchestration. The mode is, crucially, not simply major, but rather a scalar alternative that has come to connote wonder and magic. Though no form of the fourth scale degree (aka $\hat{4}$, or "fa") is present in the melody, the rocking oscillation of G and A major triads underneath establishes an unvarnished lydian mode, bright and inviting and distinctively "Hollywood."[7] While the glittering texture might signal "the movies" quite strongly, the structural and affective crux of the piece is assuredly the modulation that takes place in m. 5. Beginning in the key of G, Horner's logo swerves upward by a major third to B major, where the theme's lydian chords continue to lap tenderly before settling on the final tonic chord. Major-third progressions like this one are endemic to modern studio logos, and to film music in general. Ending up in a key signature four sharps richer than you started in is an example of a tried-and-true tonal trope, a musical convention capable of taking on countless guises and narratival functions.

Despite involving a shift between keys with dissimilar pitch content (four rotations on the circle of fifths), the key change in Horner's theme is quite smooth, prepared in a way almost as to sound inevitable. The progression GM⇨AM⇨BM in mm. 4–5 even finds a way to behave both as a modulation and a cadence. In a more harmonically "traditional" piece, the initial vacillation between G and A might signal a maneuver toward G's dominant, D major; in that case, C♯ would act as a pivot pitch, an applied leading tone to the root of the dominant. Yet the theme adheres to a different sort of musical logic: not one defined by the functional impulse of the diatonic-fifth progression, but rather by factors like modal coloration and chromatic surprise.[8] If anything, in Horner's pervasively lydian tonal space, the note C♯ implies upward resolution into D♯, not D♮. Since G can proceed to A major, the reasoning goes, why not repeat the relationship and have A major go to B major (and B to C♯ and so on)? Shifting upward in this manner thus produces a modal cadence through a popular—and conspicuously dominant-avoiding—♭VI⇨♭VII⇨I routine. So common, in fact, is this cadential progression in film music that it assumes the status of a harmonic default for certain composers. For Horner to conclude his theme with a simple V⇨I would no longer fit with the cinematic idiom it inhabits. It would not be wondrous enough![9]

It should be evident from analyzing a piece even as slight as the Universal Logo that, in Hollywood, harmony is a deeply expressive resource, able to conjure magical worlds and plant utopic expectations. Pieces like Horner's theme are musical metonyms. They are able to exemplify a certain "sounds like film music" quality without technically being non-diegetic underscore, and they accomplish this metaphorical status in large part through the resources of tonality—and especially chromaticism. To really understand how this process works, we need the tools of music theory.

***

It was in the late 1980s that Claudia Gorbman's seminal book *Unheard Melodies* asked the simple question "what is music doing in the movies, and how does it do it?" (1987: 2). Gorbman's study helped give birth to academic film musicology, and the approach she took—drawing from history, semiology, and psychoanalysis—was to reflect an intellectual eclecticism that has, as much as anything can, come to define the field. What was an initially unhurried flow of scholarship has now turned into a torrent. Scholars interested in music for multimedia will find it exhilaratingly difficult to keep up with the surge of books, journals, and conferences dedicated to the topic. Many of these sources offer novel and increasingly interdisciplinary perspectives on the inner workings of film music. No longer can we bemoan that movie music is somehow neglected by the scholarly community.

As film music studies continue to effloresce, we find no shortage of analysis. Questions of musical style, structure, and perception cannot help arising as soon as one begins exploring this sonic territory, so much of which remains unmapped. And, increasingly, this discourse is flowing from people with significant technical expertise in the construction of music: composers, orchestrators, musicologists, and music theorists.[10] Yet much remains to be done. While film music analysis is widespread, systematic and sustained analysis that is fully conversant with the tools of music theory is still a work in progress.

It is significant that the field of film musicology found its bearings at the same time that New Musicology leveled its most strenuous (and mostly warranted) critiques of music theory. Often, these critiques centered on the discipline's tendency toward formalistic and sometimes totalizing modes of inquiry. Thankfully, music theory as a field is more inclusive and less attracted to pure formalism in the twenty-first century than it was in the twentieth. Warnings against misapplication of grand theoretical paradigms have been heeded by many theorists, particularly in their embrace of non-canonical repertoires. Nevertheless, scholars coming from a non-musicological background may still feel the jargon and disciplinary insiderhood of music theory to be a barrier toward engagement, even if they are otherwise favorably disposed to style study, close reading, and systematization. Of course, sheer specialization and difficulty—perceived or otherwise—have hardly prevented other, often equally demanding, scholarly metalanguages such as semiology and post-structuralism from contributing decisively to film music studies. If music theory is to play a greater role within the field, it must thus commit to a delicate balancing act, adapting and presenting its findings in a way consonant with the transdisciplinary nature of film music studies, but without sacrificing sophistication for the sake of accessibility.

Just as jazz, popular, and non-Western musics have become well-established features within the landscape of music theory, film music has achieved a measure of disciplinary stability. Much of the crucial music-theoretical groundwork has already been laid. In America, a large share of this work has been done by theorists like David Neumeyer, Ronald Rodman, James Buhler, and Scott Murphy, whose voices resound at various points in this study. It has been an especially tricky foundation to build, compared to what is required of other new repertoires, and for several reasons. Film requires a number of adjustments to the theoretical expectations that hold in almost every other analytical canon. But such differences hold the promise for fresh thinking, unburdened by long-hardened methodological paradigms. Neumeyer considers the cinematic repertoire to be a potential shot in the arm for the larger field of music theory:

> Film places music in a new aesthetic environment that offers new opportunities to test theories of musical listening, hierarchical structure, or formal and tonal organization. It may also nudge music scholars into confronting more systematically and regularly some (admittedly complex) problems of intertextuality . . . as well as the impact of social and ideological constraints on both compositional design and aesthetic judgments. The insights gained can surely feed back into our understandings of concert and stage music in the later nineteenth and twentieth centuries. (1990: 14)

Not that this feedback will necessarily be painless at first. Those used to studying elite art music repertoires must grapple with film's imperatives for emotional directness and accessibility. Those who expect self-contained, stable musical objects and attendant "absolute" forms of musical logic will be frustrated by film music's subordination to a larger text and the resultant (sometimes quite radical) state of material contingency. And those who hold fast to the modernist doctrine that the highest measure of analytical worthiness is technical complexity and/or novelty will surely balk at film music's inclination toward conventionalization and retrospection. (However, it should be said that, in its continual hunt for expressive devices, Hollywood could be surprisingly ahead of its time in presenting audiences with new musical idioms.) If these factors serve as pretexts for shunning a repertoire, they reflect nothing so much as the "prejudices and bad habits" that Theodor Adorno and Hanns Eisler diagnose in their polemical 1947 evaluation of Classical Hollywood—and they suffer from much the same misguided imposition of values from one repertoire to another.

Throughout its history, film music has been a site for development and transformation of many styles, including some seemingly abandoned by the mainstreams of art music as they struck out for more revolutionary pastures. This contributes to the first of three central arguments of this book: *Far from reaching a terminal apex with the music of late Romantics like Strauss and Mahler, chromaticism using consonant triads witnessed expansion and innovation in cinematic repertoires that went far beyond what was imaginable in the "long" nineteenth century, and this expansion was made possible specifically because of the aesthetic goals and constraints of the medium of film.*

For but one example to illustrate this point, consider an idea from Hans Zimmer's *Inception* (2010) score. Zimmer introduces a striking four-chord progression, $Gm \Rightarrow G\flat M_3^6 \Rightarrow E\flat M \Rightarrow C\flat M^{Ma7}$, which gradually becomes thematic—one might call it *leitharmonic*—over the course of the film.[11] The progression is by no means complicated, but that does not mean it lacks complexity.[12] Two things immediately leap out about the idea (about which I have more to say in Chapter 4). First is its treatment in the film as a module: endlessly repeatable, rhythmically distensible, and tonally adjustable, as required according to momentary editorial and visual need. Second, there is the theme's harmonic grammar, which is centric (G minor is always our home base) but without reference to standard diatonic functionality. Indeed, the logic of chord-to-chord-succession here is at once expressive rather than "structural"—try to appreciate the sheer *weirdness* of the initial shift from Gm to G♭M!—and at the same time based on some interesting patterns, like the retention of a B♭ common tone and an embedded major-third cycle. This progression is entirely characteristic of the way modern film composers approach their material, and it does not quite sound like anything that came out of the nineteenth century or, indeed, the concert halls of the twentieth.

I do not want to belabor this compare/contrast approach to film musical style. Indeed, analysts would do well to investigate the repertoire on its own terms. Film music must be heard as an integral part of a complex multimedia whole and a larger cultural cinematic practice, rather than just as an offshoot of one preexisting stylistic tributary or another. With its distinctive compositional demands, film offers paths for creativity and innovation that have attracted many of the twentieth and twenty-first century's preeminent musical voices. Part of what makes the repertoire so *analytically* remarkable is its very contingency. The difficulty of acquiring urtextual printed scores, for example, deters us from lapsing into bad habits of abstruse and *Augenmusik*-obsessed formalism. At the same time it encourages other forms of active engagement, such as through transcription and concentrated audiovisual interpretation. Film focuses attention on musical characteristics native to multimedia and forces the analyst to address what kinds of compositional choices really matter in cinematic perception. Designing the appropriate tools for understanding film music's many idioms and behaviors is a difficult undertaking, one far too broad to be but partially accomplished here. But, for such a vital and influential form of musical expression, it is owed nothing less from music theorists.

The chief practical aim of *Hollywood Harmony* is to demonstrate what the discipline of music theory has to offer film music studies. Just as importantly, and in Neumeyer's spirit, I hope to make good on some of the promise of scholarly reciprocity; that is, what the movies can do for music theory. Though this book is limited in its scope to a single sub-corpus (studio produced, widely released American sound film) and a single musical parameter (chromatic harmony), it is my aim to demonstrate theory's more general ability to elucidate the workings of motion-picture music.[13] Investigating one small but emblematic corner of an artistic practice ought not be read as downplaying the need for analysis of other styles, eras, or national and cultural filmmaking schools. Focusing on Hollywood is a tactic that I believe will lead to greater analytical illumination than were I to take on the entirety of a medium. For composers and scholars curious about technical answers to Gorbman's questions, I hope this study provides a model for analysis that can be imported and adjusted to suit personal projects. For readers already theoretically inclined, I hope *Hollywood Harmony* inspires you to wonder. Wonder "what is music doing here?" "How is it accomplishing its aims?" And "how can I shed light on its many puzzles and marvels?"

Scope

Many musicians will be familiar with the phrase "sounds like film music." Few have thought to seriously unpack this frequently uttered refrain, however. What sounding-like-film-music means can vary a great deal, depending on who is asking and which filmmaking era and corpus they are assuming. It may refer to many levels of musical discourse, from the sweepingly general ("it's bold, emotionally direct symphonic music") to the exceedingly particular ("it's this specific scale-degree inflection in this peculiar phrasal location"). William Rosar has investigated the nature of this sound from a film musicological perspective.[14] He affirms the existence of a movie music style while admitting a certain resistance to clean definition: "Despite all its stylistic variability through-out the decades—whether the often cited 'late Romantic' style or passing trends in musical fashion—there remains a film music *sound*, elusive though that may be to define" (2002a: 3–4). The disuse of Romantic techniques in most every other currently composed musical style (excepting some musical theater and a select few guises of contemporary concert music) supports Rosar's intuition about the singularity of the film music sound. But he is also right about its irreducibility; even a casual survey of music for motion pictures will reveal that a voracious eclecticism of styles has been present since the craft's inception at the turn of the twentieth century. Aesthetic heterogeneity is particularly evident in contemporary soundtracks and may be the defining feature of our present scoring practice (Wierzbicki 2009: 209–227). There are in fact *many* ways in which a piece may sound as though it emanated from a movie theater—sufficiently many that defining the "film music sound" in a categorical fashion will inevitably be too essentializing.

By constraining my corpus to Hollywood symphonic scoring, and my analytical focus to harmony, I hope to cut the putative "film music sound" down to a more manageable topic: the compositional and aesthetic features of a small but highly characteristic facet of American film. Early on, I propose a set of "Hollywood Tonal Practices" to be described and refined throughout the course of this book. Like timbre, texture, tempo, and all other musical parameters active in film music, *pitch design*—the stuff of chords, scales, progressions, and keys—has the ability to structure filmic expectations. Pitch design is especially good at conveying *style topics*. These are particles of culturally encoded signification, defined by intrinsic musical characteristics and capable of enforcing or reinforcing certain meanings (Neumeyer and Buhler 2001: 23–26; Mirka 2014: 1–59). Tonal style topics may be quite broad, such as the use of non-resolving sevenths to imbue a scene with the markers of jazz and its attendant "jazzy" associations. But just as easily, they can be highly particular. Take, for example, an isolated i⇒♭vi$_3^6$ progression, often used to connote mystery and villainy in film music; indeed, it is rare to find an instance of that progression in contemporary film *without* sinister significatory content.[15] The heavy reliance on such tonal style topics is one way in which the cinematic approach to pitch design is distinctive. But no attribute of cinematic tonality is more important than its status as a purely dependent parameter within a larger text. Unlike virtually every other musical genre (including music from comparable spheres like opera, melodrama, and musical theater), tonality is in service of, and sometimes completely subordinated to, a larger multimedia object. This relationship leads to my second thesis: *pitch design is enlisted in film for its expressive and associative powers over its unifying structural capabilities; as a result, analysis should focus on tonality as a constructive parameter that is interdependent with narrative, visuals, and editing.* This expressive imperative has profound ramifications for musical analysis.

My corpus consists almost exclusively of original music composed for mainstream American films from the Sound Era onward, and on a prominent but partial component from within that practice. Pinning down the harmonic character of Classical Hollywood is my initial goal. "Classical" here refers to both a historical periodization (cinema from the 1930s through roughly 1950s) and an umbrella for the set of conventions established in the wide-release studio films during that era. Classical films are typified by continuity editing, conventional and linear narratives, and actors-as-"stars."[16] Classical Hollywood is musically distinct from an alternative paradigm that dominated the 1960s through 1970s. While exceptions abound, post–Studio Era (approximately 1960s through mid-1970s) scoring involves use of less music (and less *originally* composed music) than its forerunners, and it increasingly turns to popular and rock idioms. By contrast, Classical scoring uses specially written music for large orchestras and leans heavily on the techniques of central European art music. Classical Hollywood is where we find a model for the big, bombastic stuff: the dazzling fanfares, the luscious string themes, and other sounds still associated with that catch-all term for enjoyable momentousness, the "epic."

A resurgence of orchestral scoring in the 1970s helped reintroduce many of the conventions of this earlier era—albeit now loaded with sufficiently distinct elements (like synthesizers) and new influences (like minimalism) to require a different label. The period that film historians refer to as "New Hollywood" (mid-1970s onward), marked by the birth of the high-concept blockbuster financial model, draws from earlier scoring models but is even more inclined toward stylistic pluralism, far surpassing the token inclusion of vernacular or ethnic styles in scores from the 1930s through the 1950s.[17] New Hollywood scoring also has a greater tolerance for repetition and/or thematic inactivity (and, indeed, athematicism) than its precursors. In the hands of some composers, particularly those coming from pop/rock backgrounds, it can seem to have greater contrapuntal and orchestrational simplicity than similar mainstream soundtracks from earlier decades; at the same time, contemporary scoring often evinces a greater inventiveness of timbre and instrumentation, especially where electronics are involved. This creativity is perhaps epitomized in the subtle harmonies and restrained textures of a Thomas Newman score, to name one of the most widely emulated composers in today's movie theaters. Contemporary scoring practice further boasts an approach to spotting that is more pliable in relation to editorial decisions (by virtue of digital editing and scoring). At the same time, it is less reliant upon either conspicuous or artfully integrated "mickey-mousing"—a form of tight audiovisual synchronization characteristic of animated films and live-action composers like Max Steiner prone to symphonic pantomime.

Though there will be many occasions to visit pre-1970s scores, particularly in Chapters 1 and 6, most case studies in this book are drawn from the New Hollywood era, with special emphasis on figures like Jerry Goldsmith and John Williams, whose compositional voices were essential in setting today's cinematic tonal expectations. This focus on New Hollywood is partly the product of recency bias: my goal is to help listeners understand film scoring practices better, and newer examples naturally come closer to illustrating contemporary trends. But there is a methodological and historical justification as well. As film matured as a medium, composers started moving away from nineteenth-century music as a direct stylistic influence—and, at the same time, they began referring inward, to other film music, for their models. The shift is gradual and uneven, but over many decades, default harmonic materials began to change. In particular, the reliance on old Romantic standby chords, especially sevenths (most emblematically the diminished and half-diminished seventh) declined after the Classical Hollywood era. Modern film music is more uniformly triadic, less polyphonic, and less diatonically beholden than its predecessors. Furthermore, the sorts of nonfunctional chromaticism that were generally used as one-off special effects in Classical scores are more stylistically normalized in recent film music, to the point that long, discursive progressions with no tonic in sight become common (if never expressively unmarked). This trait makes New Hollywood film, on balance, more amenable to the analytical methodology I develop over the course of this book.[18]

Investigating the various strains that flow into a Hollywood "tonal practice" constitutes one of the major new contributions of this project. Of special interest will be triadic chromaticism, and the issues of tonal space and analytical representation that attend it. Triadic chromaticism may be defined as the use of consonant triads in progressions not strictly governed by the accustomed habits of diatonic tonality. It is thus distinguished from other forms of chromaticism based on different processes and procedures, such as quartal harmony or atonal counterpoint.[19] Concentration on this harmonic style has the effect of narrowing my corpus considerably, onto dramas and fantastical films that more frequently exhibit chromatic style topics than other genres, like romantic comedy or biopics. Though themes and title music are at times treated, the majority of analytical attention is directed to non-diegetic underscore. I consider the cue to be the fundamental unit of film musical form, the span of musical time in which harmony has the greatest ability to sculpt mood and structure narrative. In focusing on the role of chromaticism, my investigations repeatedly return to a special musical aesthetic that I characterize as *wonderment*. This is the pleasurable sense of awe and exhilaration that comes from perceiving something exceeding the frames of normal everyday experience, yet without a threat to the one's sense of physical or psychic security. The third central argument of *Hollywood Harmony* concerns the interaction of this aesthetic with the strongest forms of triadic chromaticism, what theorist Richard Cohn (2012: xiv) calls "pantriadic" tonality: a thorough negation of tonal norms of centricity, diatonicity, and functionality. *Pantriadic harmony is a potent style topic, used throughout film history to represent and sometimes elicit the affect of wonderment.*

Approach

The approach taken within *Hollywood Harmony* focuses on what Gorbman calls "pure" musical codes—in other words, details of musical structure and syntax. But I strive not to lose sight of her other two, equally important axes of meaning: cultural musical codes (extra-textual associations and expectations) and cinematic musical codes (intertextual formal and associative relationships, such as diegesis, congruency, synchronization, and so on) (1987: 12–13). Wherever possible, I augment standard musical analytical tools to incorporate narrative information. My attitude might loosely be characterized as (neo)formalist, insofar as I take as my object of study the film score as a text, and the stylistic and technical markers of the Hollywood-style tonality this text embodies. These elements require a degree of formalized explication.[20] At the same time, my approach welcomes various forms of external knowledge. Wherever it is helpful, I draw on historical context in order to better demonstrate compositional norms and deviations, and psychological context to illustrate the way in which music elicits emotional responses and influences cinematic temporality.[21] Issues that exceed the scope of pure formal description bear increasingly on my investigations in Chapters 4 through 6, with their emphasis on hermeneutics and aesthetic categories such as dread and sublimity.

A diverse set of analytical tools befits the stylistic eclecticism that is the hallmark of Hollywood's approach to harmony. Throughout, I make use of conventional theoretical devices when useful; these include Roman-numeral analysis for centric chord progressions, form-functional labels for themes and cadences, and Schenkerian technologies for pitch design on a large scale. Starting in Chapter 5, I also begin incorporating models from music psychology, particularly as they pertain to the subjective experience of musical expectation. Though I strive for transparency in analytical prose and diagrams, a full explication of each of these systems is beyond the scope of *Hollywood Harmony*; readers are invited to consult any of the fine texts on music theory (some of which are now online and open access) for introduction to these topics. Readers can consult a short orthographical key on page xi for important theoretical nomenclature.

Because chromaticism and so-called pantriadic music in particular is a central concern of this book, I devote Chapters 2 and 3 to a user-friendly introduction to transformation theory, the triadic guise of which has come to be called "neo-Riemannian theory" (or NRT). This system, which owes much to the work of theorist David Lewin, holds numerous advantages in approaching Hollywood film music. Not least of these is its relative freshness, having been formulated at roughly the same time as film music studies (and in the context of the same New Musicological critiques that cautioned against dogmatically formalistic approaches). While it is powered by the machinery of abstract algebra, at its heart the theoretical mechanism of transformation theory is motivated by a simple *conceptual* dichotomy. This dichotomy pertains to how we understand musical relationships: either as static and object-like intervals, or dynamic and predicate-like transformations. The intervallic perspective, which Lewin suggests was a default among theorists for centuries, approaches musical relationships with the attitude of a passive witness, measuring out distances between discrete objects (1987: 158–159). The transformational perspective, by contrast, treats these relationships as processes and characteristic actions that the music, and/or an engaged auditor, continuously enacts in some way. Whether these actions are performed, discovered, posited, or intended depends largely on the analysts' preference and their assumptions concerning listener psychology.

When imported to film music analysis, the Lewinian transformational stance ensures that precedence is given to the harmonic *gestures* that power meaning and the dramatic structures that emerge out of them in time. NRT is less a methodological monolith than a confederation of interconnected perspectives and devices, united by a commitment to Lewin's transformational attitude. Though developed largely in an effort to understand the refractory sorts of chromaticism that run through nineteenth-century art music, in many ways, NRT's priorities render it *more* suitable for certain genres of film music than its originally intended repertoire of Schubert and Wagner. From Chapter 2 onward, I make use of the lexicon of triadic transformations and the networks that convey their relationships. However, in the interest of clarity, I strive to use neo-Riemannian techniques only where they elucidate musical features that more informal analytical prose cannot. Ideally, the music will drive the theorizing, not the other way around.

Organization

The overall trajectory of *Hollywood Harmony* is from style to theory to close reading. Chapter 1 and the first half of Chapter 2 lay the groundwork for understanding tonality in general in American film and the stylistic traits of cinematic pantriadic harmony in particular. Chapters 3 and 4 focus on the technical and interpretive bases of NRT, introducing a set of tools and priorities for music analysis. The final two chapters are more oriented toward questions of tonal hermeneutics—how we can approach film scores as case studies, as texts-to-be-interpreted—and they widen their methodological purview to include perspectives from outside music and film theory.

Chapter 1, "Tonal Practices," outlines a series of conventions involving pitch design that both constrain musical-meaning making in film and enable its unique effects. Part of understanding how harmony works in film requires the specification of its stylistic wellsprings; a portion of the chapter is therefore given to the idiom of late Romanticism in European art music, and to the ways in which film music conforms to and differs from that model. This section is followed by a discussion of three vital aspects of American cinematic tonality: subordination, immediacy, and referentiality. Along the way, I draw in musical examples from an expansive set of filmmaking eras and styles, which range from the early days of the Sound Era to more contemporary sounds. It is also here that I begin constructing an interpretive methodology that draws from approaches as diverse as leitmotivic, atonal, Schenkerian, and audiovisual modes of analysis. Stylistic eclecticism, I hold, mandates analytical pluralism.

Continuing the investigation of how tonal relations can "mean" within a film score, I turn to the linked issues of expressivity and transformation in Chapter 2. I begin with a treatment of "pump-up modulations"—stepwise changes of key that are used to increase dramatic intensity and keep listeners on their toes. This practice, which has its roots in Wagnerian music drama, serves as a test case through which a working theory of tonal expressivity may be formulated, a theory in which intrinsic and extrinsic musical factors collaborate to form all sorts of rich combinatorial meanings. Modulation, which by its very nature conveys a sense of active musical change, is also a perfect entry point into the subject of tonal transformation—the philosophical underpinning of NRT and a useful perspective with which to approach music in a multimedia setting. The second half of Chapter 2 fleshes out the topic of pantriadic harmony and makes a case for studying it from a transformational perspective. I provide a clear definition of pantriadic harmony, offer a tentative aesthetics for the style, and describe three common guises of pantriadicism—absolute progressions, sequences, and discursive chromaticism—which all tend to occur close to the musical surface.

Chapter 3, "Neo-Riemannian Theory at the Movies," takes the plunge into the methodology of triadic transformation theory. It is here that I set up the principles and procedures of NRT, including the transformational inventory that I draw from through the rest of the book. In the process, I touch on important methodological issues like harmonic combinatoriality (interpreting one progression in terms of others); parsimony (moving between triads with smooth counterpoint); tonal agnosticism (bracketing questions of tonal/functional prolongation); and spatiality (suggesting distance and relatedness in an abstract musical space). I give special attention to the associative dimensions of specific triadic transformations here, including a short study of two progressions—T_6 and **S**—beloved by film composers. A pair of step-by-step analyses from *Waltz with Bashir* and *Batman* are presented as straightforward and difficult cases for neo-Riemannian techniques, respectively. The chapter concludes with the introduction of tonal space visualizations, such as the *Tonnetz* and transformation networks, again with a pair of case studies (*The Da Vinci Code* and *Scott of the Antarctic*) used to exemplify theoretical concepts.

Whereas Chapter 3 provides tools for analysis, Chapter 4 offers a whistle-stop tour of a host of interpretive questions and issues that arise in the investigation of chromatic film music. I identify five important topics in neo-Riemannian analyses, each of which has ramifications for the structure and expressivity of film music: contextuality, distance, voice leading, equivalence, and patterning. Each of these subjects is illustrated with a variety of examples drawn from a generically diverse assemblage of movies. Along the way, I pause to explore the distinctive pantriadic style of Bernard Herrmann, and the way in which tonality can create motivic connections within a single movie or even between multiple movies. I offer a few new technical resources and theoretical expansions here, such as an informal model for evaluating inter-triadic distance. Admittedly, some of these tools may be of greater interest to card-carrying music theorists than to the average reader; I present them merely as analytical options—some intuitive, others more esoteric, none strictly necessary for a full understanding of this repertoire. Regardless of the increased technicality of my approach, the overall focus shifts from theory to analysis in Chapter 4. Accordingly, an increasing emphasis is placed on hermeneutics—how we can "read" these movies and their narratives through harmony.

Chapter 5, "Pantriadic Aesthetics," swings open the door to questions of cultural and psychological significance. I provide an in-depth exploration of that most characteristic affect for triadic chromaticism: wonderment. Here, I draw from music history and literary theory as well as psychology and cognitive neuroscience. Particular emphasis is placed on David Huron's theory of musical expectation, which is used to explain two subcategories of wonder—awe and frisson—that play a huge role in common guises of film chromaticism. Awe and frisson have distinct temporal profiles, which lead me to consider the effects that pantriadic harmony can have on cinematic time perception. Rather than skipping across a wide number of film genres, I center my discussion here on a single case study, Howard Shore's music for *The Lord of the Rings* trilogy, in the process locating ways to integrate two traditionally separate analytical approaches: transformation networks and Huron's cognitive model of musical expectation.

Though chromatic harmony is fully capable of signifying wonderment on its own, many paradigmatic usages in film bring nonfunctional progressions into close contact with more conventional tonal styles and procedures. Chapter 6, "Harmonious Interactions," considers the interaction of diatonic and chromatic syntaxes in Hollywood scoring contexts; in doing so, this chapter offers something of a more unified theory of triadic tonality in film, which I hope will stimulate further research into styles of music not covered within this book. In the manner of Dmitri Tymoczko (2011a), I propose a model of "triadic tonality space" that includes three axes: diatonicity, centricity, and functionality. I go on to show how the various vertices of this conceptual space harbor persistent associations in mainstream film music, including at both the thematic and cue level. I argue that many forms of wonder-evoking harmony involve a motion *through* triadic tonality space, particularly vacillations between the poles of functional-centric diatonicism (the ideal Schenkerian style) and nonfunctional/non-centric chromaticism (the ideal neo-Riemannian style). A cinematically well-established example of this is the chromatically modulating cadence (CMC), which is particularly familiar in the film music of John Williams and his soundalikes. The dialectic between idioms has been mined for its connotative power by composers wishing to portray the numinous, and a variety of examples drawn from films that dramatize what I call the "beatific sublime" are examined closely. A final case study, from Alfred Newman's *Song of Bernadette*, serves as a capstone not only to the chapter's concern with tonal interactions, but also every other theoretical and aesthetic issue raised over the course of the book as a whole. I close with a reconsideration of *The Lord of the Rings*, its ending in particular, and a word on future prospects for film music analysis.

1

Tonal Practices

"Sounds Like Film Music"

The hero swoops in to the sound of a brash major fanfare . . . A screechingly dissonant stinger announces the arrival of the villain . . . A bold modulation hurtles across tonal space, just as the camera pans over a fantastic new landscape. An expanding cluster chord gradually engulfs the soundtrack, promising the demise of the terrified victims . . . A long-building dominant seventh resolves at long last, the moment lovers finally kiss. . . .

These musical gestures could have come from almost any period of film history. Their meanings will be instantly intelligible to experienced moviegoers, despite relying on some of the most abstract seeming of compositional resources: pitch relationships, chord successions, and tonal idioms. When someone refers to a piece as "sounding like film music," the characteristic that makes it distinguishingly cinematic is very often its treatment of pitch. Musical style topics as outwardly dissimilar as the jump-scare stinger chord and the amorously delayed cadence owe their effectiveness to a common process: the transformation of tonality into a potent expressive device.

Tonality, which I take to include both small-scale details of harmony and long-range matters of prolongation and key, is capable of profoundly sculpting the way we perceive the movies. If film is an apparatus designed to transport the filmgoer, it is hard to imagine that apparatus functioning smoothly without the aid of tonal design. Handled correctly, tonality can perform any and all of the music track's many customary functions, from maintaining continuity to deepening characterization to delivering commentary. This power derives first and foremost from a set of binaries built deep into the way tonality—and Western common-practice tonality in particular—is structured: tension and release, distance and proximity, strangeness and familiarity, disunity and coherence. By themselves, these distinctions are expressively neutral, and it is up to a huge assemblage of cultural codes and conventions to direct this primal tonal matter toward specific cinematic goals. Of course, pitch design is only one of many musical parameters capable of generating meaning and in many cases may be a less relevant factor than aspects like rhythm or instrumentation. Yet the hierarchical and deeply systematized nature of Western pitch organization gives it some special advantages.

Robust associations can grow out of the smallest of deviations from diatonic norms, and these elements make possible some incredible feats of significatory shorthand. Take modality, for example. With nothing more than an inflected scale degree—say, ♯4 or ♭7̂—a film composer can instantly connote an entire society, its history and geography, perhaps even the emotional relation the viewer is meant to feel towards it. Figure 1.1 illustrates this with a tune that smacks of "the cinematic." When Erich Wolfgang Korngold uses the pitches A♯ (♯4̂) and D♮ (♭7̂) in his theme to *The Prince and the Pauper* (1937, ▶)), he conjures up a certain modal ethos—a touch of lydian to suggest youthful energy and optimism, a dash of mixolydian to evoke the folksy (and specifically English) days of yore.

Compare with the composition with which we began this study: James Horner's lydian logo for Universal studios (Figure 0.1). When Horner concludes his theme with a characteristically "Hollywood" modulatory cadence from G to B major, that same well of diatonic/chromatic meaning is being drawn from, and to a similar effect. These harmonic codes stick. The semiotic particulars of Horner's progression may be different from Korngold's—childlike awe instead of brash energy, cinematic nostalgia instead of Tudor-era antiquity—but the same associative buttons are being pressed, the same heartstrings plucked. As we will discover throughout *Hollywood Harmony*, it is the collaboration of these kinds of intrinsic properties with a suite of extrinsic connotations that lends tonality such a formidable ability to *mean* in the movies.

Much of the expressive richness of Hollywood's harmonic language stems from its assimilation of many idioms. This mix is easy to hear today, when over the course of a single film one might detect pitch-organizational principles drawn from, say, the mid-twentieth-century avant-garde, Middle Eastern folk, and contemporary electronic dance music. Yet no style's shadow looms quite so large over American cinema as European Romanticism. If there is a concrete set of techniques behind the phrase "sounds like film music," the harmonic language of Wagner, Tchaikovsky, and Liszt is a good place to start looking. As I begin to inspect the role of triadic chromaticism in later chapters, I will adopt an analytic tool—neo-Riemannian theory (NRT)—that was devised specifically to grapple with nineteenth-century art-music repertoires. Yet while this tonal parlance is a symptomatic and meaning-saturated element of Hollywood scoring, it is

Figure 1.1 Korngold, *The Prince and the Pauper*, Main Theme.

ultimately but one facet of a musical practice that is by its very nature eclectic. Since the advent of film scoring, screen composers have been voracious in their absorption, adaptation, and invention of harmonic idioms. The imperative to contribute the most fitting possible musical voice for a film requires a conversancy with many styles, and a good film composer must be a chameleon.

Film places demands on music that are unlike those impressed upon virtually any other genre. Out of these compositional challenges have emerged a host of harmonic quirks that are typical of cinematic tonality, but uncommon or highly marked in most other styles. Some of these characteristics, like the proclivity for chromaticism, are clearly an inheritance of Romantic and Impressionist practices. But as filmmaking matured and the sound of the movies began diverging from its models, we find more truly endemic harmonic procedures. For example, there is the "slide" progression (**S** for short), which we will have occasion to explore in depth in Chapter 3. Slide is a rare and terrifically pregnant motion in nineteenth-century repertoires; transformations of its sort, like CM⇔C♯m, are a once-in-a-symphony kind of occurrence for Schubert or Brahms. Yet **S** becomes a common (if still expressively potent) "word" in the vocabulary of contemporary film composers, as evident in the important motivic function it serves in films as generically diverse as *The Sixth Sense* (horror), *Inception* (sci-fi thriller), and *A Beautiful Mind* (biopic/psychodrama).

Could the identification and theorization of particles like **S** constitute a meaningful elucidation of the phrase "sounds like film music"? Or, to pose the question in a more far-reaching way: does the totality of distinctive tonal behaviors in American film music add up to a genuine tonal practice—a set of harmonic conventions that persist through a broad period and that are readily intelligible to most listeners?[1] In an important sense, the answer to this question is a categorical "no." After all, what could possibly unite the disparate styles of a Golden Age icon like Max Steiner and a modern crossover group like Daft Punk? Pointing to a shared triadic progression like **S** or any set of comparable procedures is trivial, hardly enough to synthesize a practice out of a century's worth of film music. For sure, the vocabulary of Romanticism furnishes *some* of the harmonic habits of Steiner and Daft Punk. And it still manages to drive its chord-to-chord, key-to-key syntax in some compositional subidioms, notably music for fantasy and science fiction cinema. But even the most widespread of harmonic routines are not so rigidly enforced across eras (or genres) as to constitute a monolithic "Hollywood Tonal Practice," something we can define stably or succinctly. The landscape of American film is spotted with too many compositional methods to accommodate such clean reductions. Whether or not we recognize the instinctive rightness of "sounds like film music" in certain cases, there is ultimately no *one* Hollywood tonal practice that the phrase uniquely specifies.

What makes film music an attractive corpus for analysis is not simply the existence of a repository of shared harmonic strategies and their concomitant significatory powers. Rather, it is the way in which constraints *native* to the medium of film tend to elicit those musical strategies in the first place. An alternative conception of "practice," from film theory instead of music history, is of greater use to us here. As film theorists David Bordwell, Janet Staiger, and Kristin Thompson define it, a film practice is a coherent and unified combination of formal and stylistic conventions, crucially *along with* the conditions of creation that enable and limit those conventions.[2] A film music practice, therefore, is a collection of customs and associations that enables the telling of properly behaved stories, *plus* the circumstances of production that standardize them. Elements of the "Hollywood Sound" certainly can include tonal styles and harmonic formulas. But the Bordwellian conception of a practice also folds in broader creative and practical considerations. It reminds us that a stylistic endowment (such as from Romanticism) is not sufficient to guarantee musical meaning. Without some sort of conventionalized production system, which for Bordwell et al. is the Classical Hollywood machine, creative choices cannot become expressive norms.

In *Hollywood Harmony*, I am most interested in the formal and stylistic aspect of scoring practice. I am less focused the details of production—the vagaries of spotting, orchestration, editing, and other factors that might play into a process-based or "poietic" analysis. But this is not to say that practical circumstance will not inform the investigations herein. Quite the contrary—it behooves analysts of film to remember the many constraints that influence the creative process in general, and cinematic tonality in particular, carefully concealed from view though they often are.

Music is no privileged object within mainstream filmmaking, and we see the conditions of its creation manifested in a number of significant ways throughout Hollywood history. Rarely is the score entirely the product of a single creative voice. Authorship is often spread out among arrangers, editors, music directors, orchestrators, and (more often than one might realize) multiple composers.[3] Temp tracks may steer choices of style and key, while tight deadlines tend to preclude overarching tonal designs. Competing sound effects and dialogue may diminish music's salience massively. In some situations, whole sections of a cue, including seemingly obligatory tonal goals, are dialed down in volume, transplanted, or excised. Studio pressures and audience expectations reduce room for experimentation, limiting forays into challenging idioms except in generically sanctioned circumstances. The background of the composers themselves—their exposure to preexisting film music, their performing chops, their relationships with sound designers, etc.—is immensely important in shaping what tonal strategies one can expect in a movie theater. And always, dramatic exigency guides harmonic decision-making.

The chief goal of this chapter is to formulate a set of analytical categories that reflect the plurality of film music, its irreducibility to a single tonal style, and its dependency on medium-determined conditions of creation. To that end, I propose three wide-ranging Hollywood tonal practices.

1. **Subordination**: The score's contingency with respect to the larger filmic text
2. **Immediacy**: The tendency for film music to rely on immediate gestures for expressive impact. Entails two sub-practices:
   2a. **Surface Orientation**: The shortening of music's attention span
   2b. **Short Prolongational Horizon**: The absence of a need for tight, tonally closed forms and corresponding lack of tension resulting from non-monotonal design
3. **Referentiality**: The elevation of tonality's rhetorical and allusive qualities

Though in many ways enmeshed with procedures of Romantic harmony, these three tendencies also occur within many other tonal idioms and are strictly independent of any one film era or genre. Immediacy can be a feature of atonal music based on non-repetition. Tonal referentiality informs many polystylistic and postmodern styles. And subordination is an essential trait of melodrama, musical theater, radio drama, and opera. But together, I argue, these three practices define the coordinates of the "sound" of the movies in a manner that is deeper, more revealing for analysis, than the mere listing of specific harmonic idiosyncrasies like Slide or $\sharp\hat{4}$.

The rest of this chapter falls in two parts. The first outlines the pertinent harmonic characteristics of Romanticism, those that were carried over so enthusiastically into film scores during the birth of the Sound Era. In addition to grounding the three tonal practices in a specific stylistic context, the clear delineation of Romantic tonality will help highlight the continuities and differences between concert and film scoring conventions. I will turn again to Korngold—the film composer most committed to the stylistic values of Romanticism, and whose film scores best exemplify this heady aesthetic.

The second portion of the chapter offers a tour through each of the three practices listed above. In anticipation of my treatment of chromaticism in subsequent chapters, I emphasize the close, sometimes micro-level harmonic analysis of underscore. I illustrate the various guises these tonal practices take through a series of analytical vignettes from a diverse assortment of film composers, a few drawn within the Classical Hollywood stylistic sphere and others representative of more modern directions in scoring.

The Romantic Inheritance

It is taken as almost an axiom that American film scoring is a stylistic product of the nineteenth century, and the direct inheritor of many of the tropes that typify musical Romanticism.[4] Classical Hollywood, with its expansive orchestras and sweeping themes, appears especially beholden to this earlier era of musical composition.[5] In the case of Post-Classical and New Hollywood scoring practices, those Romantic echoes are filtered through the voices of earlier generations of film composers, and in some cases the "original" stylistic influence may be replaced by references to earlier references, throwbacks to throwbacks. Directly imprinted or not, the telltale fingerprints of the nineteenth century are nevertheless easy to discern in many modern scores.[6] The impression left by European art music, especially on early sound film, is quite deep, though not all influence came from high-cultural venues like the symphony or opera. Musical theater and melodrama, for instance, furnished essential precedents for many of American film music's most characteristic techniques, some of which, like intermittency and the dependence on style topics, feed directly into various Hollywood tonal practices.[7] Furthermore, the traces of "popular" tonality—added sixths, pentatonic scales, blues progressions, etc.—are also quite evident in films in the 1930s and 1940s, especially within movie themes.[8]

Of special relevance to this study is the intimate linkage of American scoring styles with the tonal proclivities of *late* Romanticism, which for our purposes is defined not by chronology, but an "extended" harmonic syntax that builds on and diverges from the more heavily regulated common practice as exemplified in the music of the late eighteenth century. And while this extended idiom is hardly the only one that flows into movie music, it poses the most difficult questions for analysis and contributes most substantially to the tonal habits of Hollywood. Indeed, it is not an exaggeration to regard American film scoring as the arm of the "long" nineteenth century that stretched furthest into the twentieth.

It was during the height of the Studio Era (roughly 1930 to 1950) when extended tonality became a stylistic default. Music departments, eager to incorporate sonic codes that fit the overall model of cinematic mass appeal and intelligibility, happily absorbed the hyper-expressive ethos of late Romantic concert and stage music. In terms of training and sensibility, more than a few film composers were already situated within the same artistic line as luminaries like Puccini, Rachmaninoff, and Strauss. Among this formative scoring generation was a group of composers who came to exert an outsized influence: continental émigrés and exiles who brought with them an idiom steeped in the dramatic styles of fin-de-siècle Europe.[9] Most were also fluent in the vocabularies of popular music, with a considerable proportion having a background in radio or theater.[10] The languages of the tone poem, melodrama, and opera were consistent reference points for the scores most emblematic of the early Sound Era: *Captain Blood* (Korngold, 1935), *Gone with the Wind* (Steiner, 1939), *Wuthering Heights* (Newman, 1939), *Rebecca* (Waxman, 1940), *Spellbound* (Rózsa, 1945), to name a few. The devotedly Romantic style evinced in these scores lagged behind trends in contemporary art music, whose shifts toward tonal and formal dissolution took some time to be widely incorporated into mainstream film.[11] But it is precisely in this respect that music of Classical Hollywood, as well as implicitly retrospective music from the twenty-first century, gains its significatory power. For the lush and extroverted sound of late Romanticism is itself deeply referential.[12] Then and now, it signifies sentiment, magic, and above all nostalgia—a nostalgia for the elusive and universalized pastness that the Hollywood apparatus was cunningly devised to intimate.[13]

Eschewing the modernist gravitation toward non-repetitive, non-lyrical forms, film music in the Classical Hollywood Era enlists "the transcendence of melody," as Kathryn Kalinak (1992: 101) puts it, as its basic structural and semiotic building block. Memorable and topically rich themes are stated in full during main and end titles and are subjected to fragmentation and rearrangement within underscore. The typical cue has a form based on succession: a series of thematic modules, stitched together by modulations, sequencing, and special effects like ostinati, stingers, and pitch plateaus.[14] Definitive versions of themes, such as may appear within climactic cues, are typically tonally closed. Less intrusive underscore, on the other hand, often deliberately withholds harmonic closure. As wall-to-wall scoring became increasingly common in the 1930s, techniques such as phrasal elision and cadential evasion helped to instill a perpetual feeling of forward momentum. The pliability of Romantic tonality was thus able to accomplish several structural objectives simultaneously. It could churn forth narrative tension constantly, it could mask inadequacies of early recording technology, and it helped cover up the formal gaps and artifices that continuity-editing vigorously strives to efface.[15]

Sonority is a particularly important component of the film music sound. Many musical habits that irresistibly call to mind Hollywood's Golden Age result from composers' appetite for sonorous intensification, as accomplished through mode mixture, chromatic predominants, pedal complexes, and elaborate chordal substitutions. Following Wagnerian and Impressionist precedents, progressions and sometimes chords themselves were to be savored for their own sake, without need for motivic development, contrapuntal intricacy, or long-range structural implications. This penchant for "sensuous" harmony receives a huge boost from Bernard Herrmann's high-profile scores, beginning in the 1940s, and is further ingrained in New Hollywood with its assimilation of minimalist and later ambient styles.[16]

Triadic consonance was and remains the norm, though dissonance without resolution is partially normalized within some subidioms, notably cinematic appropriations of jazz. Dissonance was also sanctioned within genres like thrillers and film noir. These genres spurred the development of the non-thematic cue, constructed through the direct succession of tonal effects, without the need for themes.[17] In a similarly strategic fashion, nascent atonality could, when subject matter permitted, selectively run riot. The prototypical case of this is Steiner's almost unrelentingly cacophonous score to 1933's *King Kong*. But regardless of how the scales are tipped, some form of intrinsic tonal tension through a consonance/dissonance distinction is nevertheless stringently retained in Classical Hollywood, irrespective of genre.[18] By the 1950s, composers like Alex North and Leonard Rosenman were writing pervasively dissonant scores in settings not dictated by generic expectation, like historical and domestic drama (e.g., *Viva Zapata* and *East of Eden*). Nevertheless, pockets of pure triadic harmony often remain as reminders of an acutely absent norm. Even the rise of sound-design-based soundtracks such as pioneered by David Lynch in *Eraserhead* (1977) have not dislodged consonance's primacy in mainstream cinema, or the lingering grasp of Romanticism on the ears of filmgoers.

The reliance on the consonance/dissonance binary and the prevalence of functionally tonal themes is what film music historian Mervyn Cooke has in mind when he alludes to the "indestructibly tonal" facade of Classical Hollywood (2008: 78). Yet the very same cues that bear these sturdily tonal themes in isolation often engender no small amount of consternation for analysts as soon as their attention lifts above the most local of harmonic levels. Extended tonality encompasses procedures that unseat the primacy of a single key across long spans of musical time. Sometimes taken to constitute a veritable "Second" tonal practice, the various elements of extended tonality were imported with great regularity into film music. Ten of these traits are summarized in Table 1.1. To demonstrate the continuity with Romantic styles, examples are taken from the Classical Hollywood Era for each trait, though any of them can be located in scores that are more recent as well.[19] Crucially, all involve chromaticism, or the undermining of diatonic monotonality, in some form.

The final three attributes in Table 1.1 involve key design on a gross scale. Directional (8), paired (9), and symbolic (10) forms of tonality all require at least cue-length durations to emerge, and may even act across an entire film score.[20] It is safe to surmise that they necessitate a measure of compositional intentionality (and effort) to implement. Perhaps unsurprisingly, these types of large-scale tonal design have received a proportionately larger amount of attention in the film theoretical literature, particularly in the form of studies from theorists David Neumeyer and Ronald Rodman.[21] But because I contend that harmonic meaning is at its most powerful at the musical surface, these three components of the extended tonal toolbox are relegated to the sidelines for the rest of this study.

Chromaticism is an essential feature of all ten attributes. It is truly remarkable just how thoroughly chromaticism came to infuse Classical and Post-Classical film music, especially when it is compared to nearly any other commonly heard twentieth/twenty-first-century musical genre. It did not have to be this way; diatonicism alone is equipped with enough expressive nuance to suit most dramatic multimedia. The techniques in Table 1.1 should be understood as arising from, but not always being unique to, nineteenth-century art music. Not all chromaticism in film owes to the Romantic extended practice. Once assimilated into the "Hollywood Sound," jazz in particular offered its own chromatic enrichments. Nevertheless, these devices all owe some of their significatory potential to their markedness against the norms of diatonicism.[22] Chromaticism, as Cooke notes, is "instantly perceived as exotic or 'other'" in many cinematic contexts (2008: 78). But chromatic material can suggest much more than undifferentiated

Table 1.1 **Elements of Extended Romantic Tonal Practice**

Trait	Example
1. **Absolute Progressions**: Harmonic succession justified by intrinsic quality	L. Stevens, *War of the Worlds* Several cues showcasing oscillations between DM and A♭M triads
2. **Linear Chromaticism**: Tonal intensification through counterpoint, dissonance, smooth voice leading	F. Waxman, *Rebecca* Main theme drenched with chromatic counterpoint and characteristic subdominant chords like Cdim$^{♭7 ⇨ ♭7}$
3. **Manipulation of Dominant-Tonic Polarity**: Avoidance or intensification of V chord; use of deceptive and modal cadences	M. Rózsa, *Ben Hur* Several cues structured around modal cadences like v⇨I and ♭VII⇨I
4. **Ambiguous/Nonfunctional Progressions**: Absence of clear syntactical implications for chord successions	A. Newman, *The Robe* Crucifixion theme based on chromatic mediant and semitonal relations around Cm tonic
5. **Intraphrasal Chromaticism**: Destabilizing progressions within, not outside, thematic units	R. Webb, *Sinbad the Sailor* Main theme built on chromatic progression DM⇨F♯m⇨B♭M⇨EM⇨CM⇨E♭M⇨DM
6. **Harmonic Sequences/Cycles**: Iterated harmonic patterns, especially driven by chromatic intervals	E. W. Korngold, *The Sea Hawk* Lyrical theme based on rotations around major-third cycle of B/G/E♭
7. **Constant Modulation** and **Cadential Denial**: Keys not given sufficient time to establish long-range prolongations	D. Tiomkin, *High Noon* Climax goes through numerous keys, dissonant passages, definitively cadences on G♭M only once hero has triumphed
8. **Directional Tonality**: Beginning in one key and ending in another	H. Stothart, *Maytime* Key scheme with C representing the hero and D the heroine, meeting halfway at conclusion in D♭
9. **Tonal Pairing**: Two keys in juxtaposition or alternation, or fused together to form a "double tonic complex."	B. Herrmann *The Trouble with Harry*: Double tonic complex between E♭ and G
10. **Symbolic Tonality**: Keys justified by programmatic or descriptive associations	M. Steiner, *Mildred Pierce* Key scheme with character dynamics represented by relationships between numerous tonics

otherness, connoting in the right contexts childlike wonder, divine terror, or fevered eroticism.

Korngoldian Splendor

As the composer whose opulently Romantic style outshone that of almost all his peers (in the film industry or otherwise), Erich Wolfgang Korngold exemplifies the extended chromatic style at its heaving apex. From the rollicking Lisztian modulations of his first full score, the swashbuckler *Captain Blood* (1935) to the seemingly never-ending lyrical themes for his last, the melodrama *Escape Me Never* (1945), Korngold's effortless mastery over the elements of extended tonality suffuse all nineteen of his Hollywood forays. Though his lavish music exemplifies the Romantic bent of Studio Era scoring, Korngold's output was actually atypical in a few instructive respects. He did make use of cue sheets and click tracks, but is better known for improvising at the piano while watching the rough edit of a film.[23] Compared to the sometimes frenzied pointillism of his contemporary Steiner, Korngold's cues are longer-breathed, conceived in what Neumeyer calls "bolder, broad-brush operatic style" (2010: 128). Though Korngold was an adept harmonic colorist, his scores admit the influence of basically no other idiom beyond swooning Viennese Romanticism, token nods to ethnic styles for local flavor notwithstanding. There is none of the jazz-influenced harmony that sometimes shades the work of Steiner, or the nervous splashes of modernism that mark Franz Waxman's scores.[24] Furthermore, the relationship between Korngold's film and concert oeuvres was exceptionally fluid, full of self-borrowings and adaptations in both directions (Van Der Lek and Swithinbank, 1994). As a result, some of his film music is itself *already* late Romantic concert music in both sound and sentiment.

Figure 1.2 offers a reduced transcription of a passage from Korngold's score *The Adventures of Robin Hood* (1938, 1:18:15, ⊙). The music accompanies a discussion between Maid Marian (Olivia de Havilland) and her nurse about the feeling of being in love. Unbeknownst to them, Robin (Errol Flynn) looks on from Marian's chamber window. The excerpt presents a full statement of the film's love theme; this music is as harmonically sumptuous—and stylistically anachronous for pre-Modern Britain!—as anything from *Tristan und Isolde*. As was commonplace for Korngold, the theme was not originally inspired by the film it came to occupy. In this case, it was one of several passages reworked into *Robin Hood* from the 1919 concert overture, *Sursum Corda* (particularly material at rehearsals 17 and 41).[25]

Despite his atypical scoring methods, Korngold was capable of adroit mickeymousing, and inspiration from sources external to the film itself never interfered with his ability to synchronize tightly to image. In the case of the *Robin Hood* scene, there is only a modest correspondence of musical gesture with the topics of Marian's dialogue. Korngold paints the action with expansive strokes, manipulating register and tonal stability relative to the home key of B major. The

Figure 1.2 Korngold, *The Adventures of Robin Hood*, "Love Theme."

single significant audiovisual accent is the cut that reveals Robin Hood, matched with the tonic arrival at m. 18. To achieve this effect, Korngold made his most dramatic alteration to the original *Sursum Corda* theme, which lacks tonic-securing cadences. Everything following m. 12 is material new to *Robin Hood*, comprising an extended cadential motion back to the starting key.[26] Overall, the love theme's tonal rovings are not directly motivated by dramatic incident. Rather, they are built into Korngold's voluptuous style, contingent at least partly on the shape of preexisting, similarly amorous music from *Sursum Corda*.

As is typical for movies from the Hayes Code era, Marion's scene is decorous in its visuals and dialogue. But a great deal of erotic energy is smuggled in with a music track laden with sexual style topics. This sort of sublimation is enacted, in a fashion, through the relationship between Korngold's melody and harmony. The melodic line in Korngold's cue is, for a love theme, fairly chaste: largely diatonic, sparing with dissonant intervals, and projecting an unsullied B-pentatonic scale for the first nine measures. The accompanimental substratum is where most of the aromatic chromaticism takes place, with its sinuous semitonal lines and polymorphously resolving dominant sevenths. From mm. 10–16, the urge to visit new tonal regions steers nearly all pitch content, far more so than the melodic trajectory, which is content to convey simple chord tones, peaking successively on F#5, C6, and finally F♮6.

It is difficult to enumerate every last one the extended tonal fingerprints detectable in this excerpt, so immersed it is in the late Romantic style. A partial list includes the following: chordal enrichments (e.g., the $\frac{F\sharp7}{D}$ harmony at m. 9); functional ambiguities (e.g., D♭M in m. 14); chromatic linear processes (e.g., the wedge in m. 13); surprising progressions (e.g., the enharmonic slip from $V^7/C \Rightarrow V^6_4/B$ at mm. 15–16), and longer-range destabilizing routines (e.g., a host of implied keys and distant tonicizations). The tonal remoteness of the theme's various regions is underlined by highly contrasting textures and dynamics on a measure-to-measure level, much of which must be attributed to the efforts of Korngold's inspired orchestrator, Hugo Friedhofer. These markers of distance and disparity help engender a feeling of breathless expectancy, not unlike the physical sensation of love that Marian's nurse describes. "When he's with you," she explains, "your legs are as weak as water . . . when he looks at you, do you feel a prickly feeling, like goosey pimples running all up and down your spine?" This description matches what psychologists call *frisson*, and as we will see in Chapter 5, it is an important aesthetic goal for film composition, too. Frisson involves chills and gooseflesh and can be elicited through unexpected harmonies, dynamic shifts, and other devices based on surprising contrast. In characteristically maximizing style, Korngold is not content with producing just one instance of that "prickly feeling." He piles on the frisson-inducing harmonic moves, swerving first to A♭ major, then C, then D♭, each exceeding its predecessor in registral expanse and orchestrational richness.

Explaining Korngold's swift chromatic realignments in terms of Roman numerals is difficult and at times even unworkable. Indeed, the awkwardness with which this passage and similar ones respond to functional analysis is a major reason for adoption of the transformational perspective that I describe in the next chapter. Yet, for all its tonal wanderlust, the theme is strictly monotonal, landing squarely back in the key of B major, in which it began. Despite the passage's ambiguous chromaticism and modulatory zeal, the prevailing impression is not one of anxiety. Rather, the major chords at mm. 9, 11, and 13 are oases of shimmering calm, their tonal remoteness from B major tempered by softly glowing orchestration and an abeyance of linear activity. The eroticism of Korngold's music lies more in its tonal hedonism than in Wagnerian perpetual denial. His love theme for *Robin Hood* relishes sound for its own sake, and frisson-inducing chromatic progressions for their sensual luminosity.

Subordination

Korngold's mannered style, perfectly natural when emanating from the silver screen, would sound out of place in virtually any other venue for new music during the twentieth century. Yet his effusive scores ultimately represent but one sound of American cinema, and a rather extreme one at that. For all their stylistic similarities, late Romantic and Hollywood ways of navigating tonal space are dissimilar in a number of fundamental ways. Overemphasizing the indebtedness of film music to precedents in European art music can hobble our analytical project before it hit its stride. It also encourages a kind of unenlightening game of spot-the-influence, an activity with little explanatory usefulness. American film music is a distinctive art form and demands a distinctive analytical perspective. The first and most important step is recognizing the subordination that tonality in film music is constitutionally subject to.

According to composer Leonard Rosenman, "music for films has all the ingredients that real music has—counterpoint, orchestration, voice-leading, bass line—but it doesn't have the primary ingredient that separates music from non-music. The propulsion is not by musical ideas but by literary ideas" (quoted in Evans 1975: 266).[27] Rosenman presents film music as sitting on the disadvantaged side of an either/or situation. Though the basic resources of a score are no different from any other (implicitly Western) style, the decisions on how to arrange them are not based on the logic of an autonomous musical form, but that of a governing text.[28] Rosenman's notion of "non-music" is more than a little hyperbolic, and the line between "pure" and literary motivation in music has never been enforced with great stringency in *any* genre.[29] Though atypical of Hollywood practice, many famous scores were written at least in part independently of the demands of spotting and synchronization. And even a piece with as twisty an origin as Korngold's *Robin Hood* is still, by any reasonable definition, film music, despite an initial "propulsion" by largely non-programmatic considerations. Exaggeration or not, Rosenman's principle nevertheless points to an essential aspect of film scoring practice: when tonality serves an active role in making meaning, it does so primarily as an expressive, not structural, parameter.

The justification of tonal design through practical exigency places film in a tradition that includes opera and musical theater. Verdi, for example, was known to transpose arias for the convenience of his singers, even in operas with symbolic key schemes.[30] Examples of transposition for the sake of performative expediency are not unheard of in film, particularly when singing is a factor. For instance, Rodman (1998: 138) notes a case of a vocal-range-necessitated transposition that impacted Herbert Stothart's network of keys in *The Wizard of Oz*. Yet film music's brand of dependency is more thoroughgoing than opera's, more built into the medium it supports. Manipulations of tonality far beyond the occasional stepwise transposition routinely arise from simple pragmatic, often editorial needs. Tonal choices that might seem arbitrary or even "non-musical" in another repertoire in film may be fully justified on film (and even celebrated, after the fact, on soundtrack albums).

John Williams's contribution to the *Star Wars* franchise offers some striking illustrations of the subordinated status of film tonality. Despite its obvious debts to Wagnerian music drama, Williams's music for the triple trilogy includes instances of cinematically run-of-the-mill tonal subordination that would strike the ears of nineteenth-century audiences as stunning breaches of harmonic coherency.[31] The opening and closing cues in several of the movies are contorted with abrupt modulations in order to fit the tonally fixed credits music. Incipient leitharmonies and symbolic keys are introduced in one film, only to be abandoned in later entries.[32] Quite often, material is cut from its original scene, only to be tracked or spliced into new and unexpected places. Sometimes this editorial transplantation can completely alter or disrupt the harmonic course of a sequence.[33] None of this is to say that the music of *Star Wars* is haphazardly constructed. Rather, it suggests that any responsible analysis of Williams's scores—and by extension others composed under similar pressures—ought to concede that tonal choices are not *as* essential or form generative as they are in other repertoires.

Tonal subordination is at its most immediately apparent in cases of "mickey-mousing." [34] In the most extreme forms of this approach, each chord, progression, and even pitch hinges on and reinforces what happens on screen. The quintessential examples of mickey-mousing can be found in animation, especially from cartoon virtuosi Carl Stalling and Scott Bradley. In concert music, listeners and analysts are accustomed to tonality as an architectonic force, something that governs long swathes of musical time and, in a sense, justifies its own significance. Pitch design through mickey-mousing, by contrast, is a dependent phenomenon, drawing its meaning from what it does for the larger text.

We might suppose that the exaggerated volatility of cartoon scoring represents a special case for cinematic tonality, and harmony is usually not so subservient to the whims of narrative. Yet even in contexts in which tonality's freedom from textual minutiae is maximized, harmonic organization is often steered by broader dramatic considerations such as mood or characterization. This organization is particularly true in cases of audiovisual counterpoint, in which the incongruence of visual and musical information has a strong significatory capacity. When Hannibal Lecter slays his victims to the sounds of Bach's "Goldberg" Variations (*Silence of the Lambs*, 1991), the Baroque harmonic language, far from being some incidental attribute that comes along for the violent ride, is wholly implicated in the scene's generation of meaning. Well-behaved major-mode diatonicism suggests order, elegance, and control; its presence during a scene of horror in *Silence of the Lambs* brutally ironizes the proceedings on screen and twists the original tone of Bach into something bizarre, even fiendish. Many less obtrusive instances of audiovisual counterpoint rely just as much on tonal incongruity for signifying purposes.

Between the poles of audiovisual counterpoint and mickey-mousing lies what Fred Karlin and Rayburn Wright (2004: 154) call "playing through the drama."[35] Music in this approach—the norm for many composers—adheres to a scene's narrative arc and editorial landmarks but avoids assiduous tailoring of its every detail to instantaneous changes on screen. Closely connected is the idea of the flowing and logical "long line," which some commentators have treated as an aspect of film music bearing unusually high artistic priority. The value of the long line finds its most outspoken proponent in film music theorist Alfred Cochran. Cochran argues that truly successful cues bear specific and deliberate formal organization that operates at multiple hierarchical levels, occasionally in a manner that may "transcend" filmic form itself, "at times, in wonderful ways" (1990: 69–70).

Cochran's veneration for long lines and "over-all" scoring has much to do with his idiosyncratic Schenkerian analyses and cannot be taken as a uniform gauge of music's effectiveness or aesthetic value within cinematic contexts.[36] However, his glorification of music taken on its own terms, not the film's, points to an interesting dilemma facing film score analysts. With music written within Karlin's playing-through paradigm, the moment-to-moment particulars of tonal design may, in a sense, be unmotivated, constituting cinematic excess. As formulated by Kristin Thompson (2004 [1981]), excess results from artistic decisions that do not impact the telling of the film's unifying narrative. In music, these decisions need not only consist in arbitrary details but could also be grounded in structural customs, such as the need to follow an antecedent phrase with a consequent. In general, the less intrusive, more "inaudible" the underscore, the more carefully the analyst must weigh attributing importance to tonal decisions. Poor indeed would be a reading that strove to discern some profound meaning for every last note, even for the most punctiliously mickey-moused cue. Nevertheless, even music that bears all the hallmarks of excess on a local level is bound to host other harmonic characteristics that contribute to a *holistic* form of expressivity. Perhaps a cue's cadences do not align with narrative events, but its major mode still brightens the prevailing mood. Perhaps no one single chromatic progression attaches to a cut within a montage, but the overall sensation of continuous modulation lends a seething affect to the sequence. Excess is not an escape clause for the interpretation of tonality in film, only a caveat.

In order for us to grapple with tonal contingency, several analytical practices must be adopted. The presence of audiovisual accents—important coincidences of multiple sensory streams, such as occur when cadences and stingers synchronize with narrative shifts or editorial cuts—should be indicated clearly.[37] Pertinent visual and sonic events can be represented above the musical score, although this addition can easily lead to clutter, and such information is generally more easily conveyed in prose. One should pay special attention to what Michel Chion (1994: 190, and 2000: 214) calls "audiovisual phrasing": the way in which temporal structures in both music and visuals collaborate to organize a scene and give it a distinctive sense of progress and durationality. Finally, analysts should not feel pressure to discover every possible interesting or subtle musical detail. Rather, they should locate that which, to a sensitive listener, might bear on an interpretation of the larger text.

To see this contingency-cognizant approach in action, we might consider some of Leonard Rosenman's own music. Contrary to the composer's attestations, Rosenman's scoring is often conceived in remarkably well-developed musical paragraphs (albeit with a much higher dose of experimental harmony than was typical for the era).[38] His predilection for through-composed underscore brings certain aspects of sonic subordination into unusually sharp relief. Figure 1.3 presents a reduced excerpt from Rosenman's score to *Rebel without a Cause* (1955, 1:27:35, ▶). The passage comes from a lengthy cue accompanying the long-anticipated kiss between Jim (James Dean) and Judy (Natalie Wood), followed with an abrupt segue to the discovery of their friend Plato (Sal Mineo) by a group of murderous ruffians. Text annotations describe dramatic developments, with arrows indicating audiovisual accents of note.

Rosenman's cue typifies the push and pull of competing musical instincts in Hollywood underscore. On one hand, we can observe the playing-through paradigm with its long-breathed musical phrases; on the other, a targeted use of harmonic devices for immediate expressive ends, the hallmarks of mickey-mousing. At the beginning of the excerpt, Rosenman grants Jim and Judy a full statement of their love theme, replete with a perfect authentic cadence (PAC) in C major. This scoring is done without any of the kinds of alterations, truncations, or interruptions that often steer theme-based underscore. No disruptions, that is, save for the dialing down of music during a snippet of dialogue, which renders inaudible a few bass pitches (most notably B♭2 in m. 2). Though a fairly inconsequential absence, the obscuring of that note does deprive the listener of some of the goal-directed motion to C in the bass, and the basis for the flavorful ♭VII[13](♯11) chord that B♭ supports.

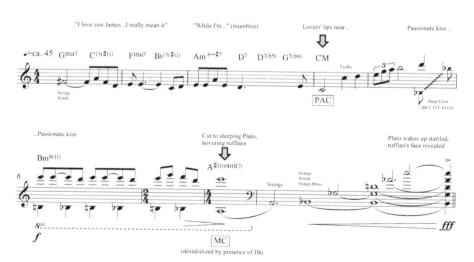

Figure 1.3 Rosenman, *Rebel without a Cause*, "Kiss and Aftermath."

The real climax of the scene (mm. 5–7) garners a flashy new harmonic gesture. With the love theme already completed at m. 4, Rosenman telegraphs the moment of passion with an orchestral swell on a secondary theme. The harmonic support for this climax is a functionally ambiguous Bmin^9 chord (ultimately resolving as ii^9 of the unanticipated key of A major). Meanwhile, the connective tissue between the completed love theme and the kiss progression is slight but efficient. First, an unaccompanied melodic ascent from E5 to E6 creates a suspenseful pitch plateau. Secondly, a whole-tone harp glissando at the edge of m. 5 magnifies the sense of anticipation. More extreme in its reliance on dramatic rather than musical logic is the sudden swing in tone and harmonic language at m. 8 and onward. Rosenman denies full cadential closure for A major by stressing a dissonant pitch (D♯) within the chord. Soon thereafter he erects one of his trademark pyramidal stinger chords over B♭2, banishing any lingering memory of diatonic placidity.

If the music for this sequence owes its local tonal details to dramatic constraints, it also reveals a few cunning ways in which Rosenman stays one step ahead of the action. The love theme, despite its languid pace, wraps things up a bit prematurely, moments before Jim and Judy actually kiss, thus virtually ensuring that a bigger, more physical payoff than simple amorous dialogue is yet to arrive. The destabilization of the cadential chord at m. 8—what ought to have been the most contented sonority in the cue!—hints at the catastrophe to befall Plato seconds away before he is awakened. The faintly tense B♭2 in mm. 6–7 was initially excusable as a chromatic passing tone to A, but it rears its head in an aggressive way a few measures later, where it acts as the foundation of the dissonant stinger.

Rosenman's most subtle touch involves another, more concealed return of the tonally repressed. The whole-tone glissando at m. 5 insinuates a small element of tonal disorientation at the instant of the kiss. This hint of harmonic unease portends both the poignant B♭-E♮ outer-voice interval at mm. 6–7 and, more frightfully, its verticalization in the form of the whole-tone pentachord of m. 11 (also with B♭-E♮ outer voices). With carefully wrought details such as these, Rosenman turns music's narrative subordination into an asset. The soundtrack seems to be actively driving the narrative forward, even if it is, ultimately, entirely beholden to it.

Immediacy

The composing out of Rosenman's whole-tone sonority takes place within a window of just five measures. Longer-term harmonic narratives do sometimes emerge in film music, but short-range effects are far more characteristic. As noted by Robert Nelson, an early analyst of the Hollywood harmonic style, film music is "overwhelmingly coloristic in its intention and effect" (1946: 57). For Nelson, "coloristic" means associative, unobtrusive, and expedient.[39] Once again, there is a parallel to be drawn with Romantic practices. While monumentality of scope is a definite nineteenth-centuryism, so too is miniaturization. The constant flow of small motives and atomized gestures that constitutes Wagnerian "endless melody" finds a second home in Hollywood scoring. Often, the compression that we observed in *Rebel without a Cause* leads to a modular style, in which short musical ideas are chained together and repeated or shuffled.[40] This modularity is one contributor to the feeling film underscore sometimes has of simultaneous eventfulness and terseness—*impatience*, in other words.[41] The temporally and tonally pliable idiom that results from "thinking small" in this way proves exceptionally useful, especially where editorial demands might disrupt otherwise through-composed forms. Because filmgoer attention is constantly split between multiple streams of visual and sonic information, the most salient perceptual and organizational information tends to lie along the score's surface or shallow middle ground—not, I argue, along more rarefied structural levels or intricately laid key schemes. Local events, like striking sonorities, modulations, or cadences, are the real seats of tonal expressivity.[42]

The conflicting duty toward short-term cinematic temporality and longer-range "pure" musical temporality is a tension that surfaces throughout discourses on film musical aesthetics. Some have reaffirmed the potency of long-range planning, while others rule it out categorically.[43] The critic Hans Keller, for example, rated film music's ability to install unity across a film as one of its most essential responsibilities. Keller enjoined composers to justify their choices of key carefully, "because the episodical character of widely separated entries [film cues] has to be counteracted by ever-alert methods of unification" (2006 [1955]: 82). More recently, music theorist Tahirih Motazedian has made a strong case for examining film-spanning key relationships, which she suggests are "far more prevalent than scholars have previously anticipated" (2016: 34). She finds evidence for systematic tonal design in numerous film soundtracks, particularly those hailing from fastidious directors like Anthony Minghella and Wes Anderson. While we cannot therefore dismiss tonal design out of hand, long-range tonal connectivity should nevertheless be treated more as an aesthetic opportunity than a practical default—and certainly not a precondition for artistic coherence.[44]

The more dominant attitude toward film tonality is epitomized in the highly informal but nevertheless codified "fifteen second" rule. This principle, which implies a commitment to the experiential surface, rather than background, of film structure, was formulated by Leonid Sabaneev in his trade book, *Music for the Film* (1935). Sabaneev was particularly concerned with the impact of music on viewer attention. For example, he implored composers not to make use of overly complex harmony or counterpoint during crucial dialogue scenes. The crux of Sabaneev's "rule" is the contention that tonal relations do not retain perceptual power over a gulf of fifteen seconds of silence. Therefore, he holds, composers should feel no obligation to relate one cue to its close neighbors in any harmonic respect. On the other hand (as Claudia Gorbman paraphrases), "if the gap has lasted less than the requisite time, the new cue must start in the same key (or a closely related one)" (1987: 90).

Composers in Sabaneev's time were just beginning to invent stable scoring principles for sound films, especially with continuous and dialogue-sensitive underscore in mind. Sabaneev's principle reflects an attitude toward scoring still under the influence of Silent Era practices, where rapid selection of typically monotonal stock cues was a norm. The fifteen-second rule's prohibition of distant keys between proximal cues precludes most chromatic relationships, even though they may be apt signifiers for surprising or uncanny filmic events—or, just as likely, amount to unnoticed and unimpactful harmonic epiphenomena. Indeed, we find this "rule" frequently honored in the breach, even in early Studio Era scores. Sabaneev's kernel of insight lies in his realization that a filmgoer's divided attention places a high responsibility on the musical surface, while necessarily removing some tonal expectations once the memory of that surface has faded.[45]

As analysts of film music, we should not shy away from elevating brief tonal phenomena to form-generative status, even if this attitude countervails the structuralist "behind the scenes" instinct possessed by many music theorists. As we turn increasingly to pantriadic chromaticism in subsequent chapters, we will see that neo-Riemannian techniques offer advantages over more traditional methods such as Schenkerian analysis. For the time being, it is worth inspecting a cue in which form does not depend on transformations between triads, but rather abrupt changes of sonority and tonal collection.

Figure 1.4 offers a reduction of a thirty-second micro-cue from Henry Mancini's *Charade* (1963, 1:35:50, ▶). Late in the film, the protagonist Reggie (Audrey Hepburn) discovers the corpse of one of her mysterious pursuers. Mancini scores the horrific revelation with four harmonic gestures that are closely synchronized with stages of the onscreen action. None of the melodic constituents recur elsewhere in the score, though its harmonic content closely mirrors music from an earlier discovery of another dead body (1:07:30). A cue of such a fragmentary nature might have puzzled Keller and Sabaneev, as it relies on immediate effect instead of cumulative musical development.[46] Yet "Reggie's Discovery" is keenly effective film music, and it demonstrates the value that composers like Mancini placed on economical surface changes over long-range tonal planning.

Mancini had an excellent instinct for manipulating the relative prominence of music amid other sonic information. Here, the aggressive foregrounding of the initial stinger injects Reggie's discovery with a jolt of musical adrenaline. This

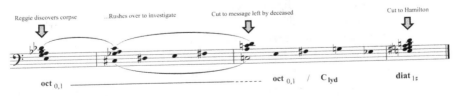

Figure 1.4 Mancini, *Charade*, "Reggie's Discovery."

reaction is followed by a lingering, terrified freeze response. The cue's first component is a diminished-seventh-based stinger (set class 01369), and the second a stretching out of the parent octatonic collection with an ominously crawling bass line. A third harmonic idea pits a similar scalar fragment against a pedal C♯, matching Reggie's discovery of a cryptic message left by the deceased. The final component is an unresolved cluster chord, drawn from the 1♯ diatonic collection. This soft and faintly genteel sonority synchronizes with a cut to the character Hamilton (Walter Matthau), who answers Reggie's panicked phone call while shaving in his well-appointed bathroom. Two harmonic threads give the short cue an element of consistency that might have garnered tentative approval from Keller: the persistence of E♭3 through each of the cue's four stages and the emphasis on the <0,1> octatonic collection throughout much of its duration. Nevertheless, the overriding impression is of discontinuity, surprise, and incompletion, all deftly induced by Mancini's tonal materials to manufacture a feeling of shock and revulsion.

By privileging harmonic gestures according to their dramatic efficaciousness rather than structural necessity, music like Mancini's gives the impression of impatience. This shortness of attention span lends some scores, particularly those of the Classical Hollywood Era, a feeling not unlike the churning "musical prose" attributed to composers like Brahms, Scriabin, and Schoenberg.[47] Liberated from four-square, symmetrical theme structures, film music in the most "prosaic" mode takes on a discursive and variegated aspect, sending its motifs through unpredictably contrasting contexts, sometimes latching onto audiovisual accents, sometimes changing simply for the sake of change. The motivations for this malleability are quite different from those of the late Romantic repertoire. Rare are instances of Hollywood scoring wholly devoid of the "padding and empty repetition" that Schoenberg decried as antithetical to his idea of musical prose (2010 [1947]: 415). Tonal attention span in film is not steered by an underlying drive for developing variation, even though some scores by Rosenman may approach this Schoenbergian ideal. Rather, it is a function of dramatic and editorial pace, and thus asymmetrical musical units are hugely useful.[48]

Because tonal choices in film derive from cinematic imperatives, cues can bear a very short tonal horizon without implying atonality. A striking harmonic motion may be stated and never recur, having served its expressive purpose without need of corroboration. Indeed, for some composers, a version of the fifteen-second rule seems in place *within* a cue; we see this method particularly in the constantly modulating music of figures like Alfred Newman and Danny Elfman. This is not to say that the particulars of a briefly visited key are ever wholly arbitrary. But composers and listeners rarely feel obliged to justify musical changes by an appeal to an intrinsic musical logic, whether common-practice formal customs or the rigors of developing variation. Far from disrupting continuity editing, the rapidity of tonal change and the avoidance of cadences or closed melodic units typical of Classical Hollywood Era scoring allows a supple responsiveness to drama that smoothes gaps and effaces the music's own presence. Analysis should reflect this approach by attending not only to the details of synchronization, but the grosser implications of tonal impatience in manufacturing and sustaining a certain mood or characterization.

With the analytical issues posed by subordination and immediacy now established, it is worth examining the style of the composer I earlier compared to Korngold: Max Steiner. Steiner's enormously influential wall-to-wall style of dramatic accompaniment often evinces the kind of short attention span that went on to become standard for much Classical Hollywood scoring. Even passages of eerie stasis in Steiner's music, like the "Boat in the Fog" sequence from *King Kong*, find a way to host an ever-changing variety of sonority types and tonal centers. Gorbman observes a "formlessness and fragmentary nature" in Steiner's scores, in which "music often sacrifices its musical coherence to effects gained in coordinating with diegetic action" (1987: 97). Coherence is among musical musicology's most loaded terms, and one that is—to an extent theorists are often hesitant to admit—in the ear of the beholder. We are better served by specifying *what* in Steiner's music renders it so distinct from other tonal styles. And while Steineresque harmonic coruscation, full of Romantic harmonic style topics and clichés, is apt to sound pointedly out of date today, the principle of tonal non-corroboration remains just as much in place in contemporary soundtracks.

The ten-minute cue that Steiner uses to introduce the heroine of *Now Voyager* (1942) bears a sprawling tonal design. Charlotte's (Bette Davis) musical introduction is diverse not only in the keys it touches on but also in the harmonic devices employed to prevent monotony from setting in. Figure 1.5 represents the maneuvers that occur during the cue's first four minutes (7:05–12:15, ▶), from Charlotte's first interactions with her psychiatrist, Dr. Jaquith (Claude Rains), to the beginning of a lengthy flashback sequence.[49] Double bars indicate the ends of leitmotivic modules, while stems and slurs convey (strictly local) harmonic dependencies and voice-leading connections. No fewer than seventeen changes of tonal center take place during this span. These shifts are accomplished without cadential reinforcement in all but three cases, the most notable of which is the stretched-out IAC that ushers us into Charlotte's bedroom. Until the definitive statement of the "Voyager Theme" (at the excerpt's end), no key is allowed to remain seated all the way through to the conclusion of a thematic module.

Steiner's yearningly contra-cadential style, if we may borrow a term that David Huron (2006: 334–339) applies to Wagner, is one of many techniques he uses to keep up harmonic momentum. Others include shifts of mode, the use of stingers that trail off with pitch plateaus, intensificatory rising stepwise sequences, passages of standing on the dominant, and leitmotifs with built-in chromatic trajectories. Because so much of the cue's bustling affect stems from these surface processes, my analysis avoids reducing all of the activity that sits atop the key-flailing bass line. Note that even in this partial analysis, some elements of overarching harmonic design appear: the keys of A and C are emphasized more than others, and certain progressions take on motivic significance. Nevertheless, it

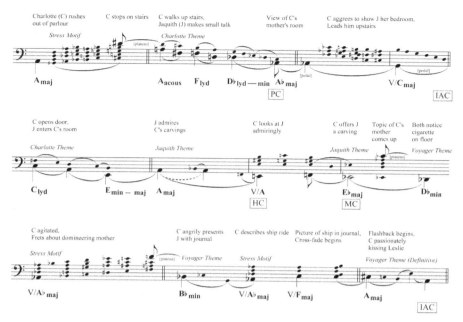

Figure 1.5 Steiner, *Now Voyager*, "Charlotte Meets Jaquith."

would be wrong to interpret Steiner's cue as working out a multiple-tonic complex, or even necessarily remembering its own tonal habitations from minutes before. The central impetus here is tonal change for its own sake, as a way of conveying the constant shifts in emotional tone registered by Charlotte.[50]

Besides matching minute details of onscreen action with a surplus of musical gesticulations, Steiner's hyper-responsive scoring helps paint character psychology. Much of the cue adheres to a pattern of vacillation in stability, swinging between harmony that is held back in some way (as with the protracted dominant pedals) and harmony that rushes forward without an obvious tonal destination. The tonal unpredictability mirrors the difficulty that the perpetually unfazed Jaquith has in assessing Charlotte's state of mind, which alternates between shyness and bluster. It is telling that the only telegraphed and unambiguous points of tonal arrival correspond to moments in which Charlotte opens up: literally, in the case of the reveal of her room at 8:52, and figuratively with the flashback to her earlier adventures at the conclusion of the segment.

It is tempting to read the superheated approach Steiner takes as a kind of harmonic style topic, a way of coding a certain Hollywood notion of hysterical femininity into the score's tonal fabric. In a few cases, Steiner's music overplays a sense of feverishness, as when Charlotte's anxious but muted dialogue about her mother garners an ascending sequence straight out of *Tristan und Isolde*. For Gorbman, Steiner's propensity for clipping his musical thoughts is "closely linked with the 'melodramatic spirit'—a desire to externalize and explicate all inflections of action" (1987: 97).[51] Being a seminal entry in established genre of the woman's film, *Now Voyager* does emphasize the heightened emotionality and tumultuous inner lives of its (mostly female) characters. However, Steiner's tonally impatient style is hardly limited to women's films, and indeed it is a characteristic of some scene archetypes, like action sequences, that are often brimming with masculine-coded musical topics. The larger takeaway to draw from this cue is that whatever Steiner sacrifices in terms of musical coherence, he more than makes up for with the gains of expressivity and sensitivity to character dynamics.

Prolongation

In recognizing the importance that harmonic impatience plays in film music, we should not dismiss the constructive power of its seeming antithesis: tonal prolongation. The idea of prolongation comes from the work of German theorist Heinrich Schenker, for whom simple contrapuntal procedures came together to generate the fundamental tonal structure of a piece.[52] However, modern usage is considerably looser toward the term, frequently admitting the use of both of linear procedures and abstract diatonic functions like "dominant" to establish a tonal center. Prolongation allows a tonic to govern spans of arbitrary duration, directing pitch materials toward a goal, effective even when that goal is not literally sounding.[53] Because it is often associated with structure rather than expression or rhetoric, prolongation would seem an odd category to impose on film music analysis. But in fact there is a great deal of expressive potential in subtly playing with prolongational implications.

To see how a fairly "well-behaved" case of tonal prolongation can shape the flow of a scene, consider "The Picnic" from Miklós Rózsa's score to *Spellbound* (1945, 21:30, ▶). Occurring near the beginning of the film, Rózsa's pastorale accompanies an outdoor stroll between the clinical Dr. Petersen (Ingrid Bergman) and the romantic Dr. Edwardes (Gregory Peck). Most of the sequence is dedicated to light philosophical banter on matters of love, poetry, and psychiatry. A slight obstacle in the couple's way brings about a momentary change of topic and tonic. The discussion shifts to the beauty of the landscape (though one can tell Edwardes is thinking of something else), and the cue ends with a cut to another location. Mostly written in an "overall" style, Rózsa's music has few overt audiovisual synch points. Compared to the febrile music of Steiner, the cue is more reliant on a leisurely melody—the main love theme—and a single, diatonically sustained key. This construction makes conventional linear analysis a suitable interpretive lens.[54] A Schenkerian middle-ground sketch is provided in Figure 1.6, illustrating the essential arc of the two-minute cue.[55]

In most respects, Rózsa's cue adheres nicely to Schenkerian structural conventions. "The Picnic" falls into a ternary form that prolongs D major. The first section encompasses the antecedent phrase of the love theme, charting out a

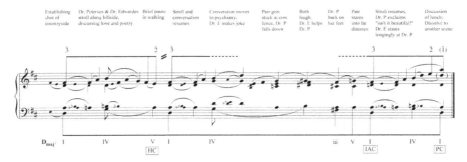

Figure 1.6 Rózsa, *Spellbound*, "The Picnic."

$\hat{3}$-line based on F♯4. This melodic edifice is interrupted, in standard fashion for a parallel period, on $\hat{2}$ at a half-cadence, which is elegantly synchronized with the moment the two doctors briefly pause their walk. The contrasting middle section is more tonally digressive, as befits the more active and playful tone of the scene once Edwardes has cracked a joke and Petersen has tumbled through a fence. Ultimately, however, it can comfortably be read as a contrapuntal expansion of the underlying tonic through its tonicized subdominant. Rózsa continues hinting at new keys as soon as the barrier of the cow fence is standing in the pair's way, reaching a harmonic far-out point of B major for when Petersen trips. This key area can be understood as a tonicized upper third of the subdominant G major, and the whole section as a symmetrically prolonged melodic neighbor motion, from F♯4⇨G4⇨G♯4⇨G♮4⇨F♯4. Once Petersen is back on her feet, Rózsa begins to wend his way back to D, liquidating the chromatic G♯, and securing the original key and $\hat{3}$ *Kopfton* with an elided imperfect authentic cadence.

A few spots in "The Picnic" challenge Schenkerian priorities, albeit only slightly. For example, there is the effect of the prolonged seventh and added sixth chords in the middle section, and the parallel octaves from E to D at the cue's introduction (not to mention Rózsa's idiolectical fondness for parallel intervals in surface voice leading). However, it is only at the end of cue where the Schenkerian analytical machinery begins to show signs of malfunctioning. Rózsa does not provide the cue with a definitive PAC that captures $\hat{1}$ in the main structural register via a dominant-to-tonic motion. Rather, the truncated statement of the love theme's consequent phrase that begins when Petersen exclaims "isn't it beautiful" concludes with a stretched-out, modally mixed plagal cadence (PC). This cadence produces only $\hat{1}$ in an implied inner voice, while the actual concluding pitch is A5 ($\hat{5}$). Despite being resolutely monotonal and diatonically functional throughout, "The Picnic" lacks a completely coherent *Urlinie*. The effect at the cue's conclusion—highly characteristic of Hollywood underscore—is of simultaneous tonal closure and melodic open-endedness. Indeed, in many soundtracks, true structural PACs are absent in non-diegetic music until the very concluding measures of the finale or end credits.

The prolongational idiosyncrasies of Rózsa's cue have to do with the way that tonality is earned—that is, whether or not it is a product of what Neumeyer (1998: 103) characterizes as "an overarching, teleological, hierarchical" plan.[56] It is in this regard that film music is often most unlike its precedents in Romantic concert music, as well as other twentieth-century styles like Debussyian impressionism in which key is a more nebulous entity. In film, dramatic effect determines what is earned and what is not. As we have already seen in *Now Voyager*, musical impatience can have a large impact on the way keys are established and sustained. While tonal centers are very often unambiguously prolonged—sometimes with improbable tenacity, as in rock and minimalist-inspired scores—monotonality is *not* a requirement in film music. Crucially, its abeyance does not automatically represent an inherent structural problem or tension as it might in late Romantic repertoires.

Last-minute key changes potentially outrageous in any other genre routinely take place with the minimum of fanfare in Hollywood. Figure 1.7 gives one such example, the final ten measures of Max Steiner's score to the pulpy supernatural adventure film *She* (1935, 1:41:30, ▶). The movie ends with an astonishingly abrupt modulation, totally unmotivated by prolongational logic, earned only in the sense that it produces a jolt of surprise for the movie's last few frames. This concluding passage is preceded by almost a half hour's worth of wall-to-wall scoring in the protean style we have already encountered from Steiner. It is in that context that we arrive at the long-anticipated final cadence.

The climactic statement of the film's love theme (mm. 1–4), accompanying the heroine's parting words about love and domesticity, provides the first area of clearly functional harmony heard in a very long time. A dominant-pedal chord in D♭ major resolves exactly as one might wish for a movie with a big, happy, conservative ending: with a totally unambiguous PAC, $\hat{5}\Rightarrow\hat{1}$ in the bass dutifully supporting $\hat{3}\Rightarrow(\flat\hat{3})\Rightarrow\hat{2}\Rightarrow\hat{1}$ in the melody. The screen fades to black, and at m. 5, Steiner begins to set up one of those key-reinforcing codettas one often finds in Romantic finales. Yet this post-cadential affirmation of D♭ major turns out to be a ruse: the ascending melodic line in m. 6 rapidly turns chromatic, and with

Figure 1.7 Steiner, *She*, Finale.

whiplash speed, Steiner modulates to the distantly related key of E major, effecting an overall transposition of the tonic by a minor third. This unanticipated—in fact, unanticipatable—new key is confirmed with a brassy (and stereotypically "old Hollywood") modally mixed PC [iv⇨ii°⁷⇨I], synchronized with the arrival of the words "The End" on screen. E major then garners its *own* post-cadential codetta, with the film's danger theme given the final word in the bass. Arriving as it does at the formal moment one would expect greatest closure and tonal security, there is essentially no narratival or visual motivation for Steiner's modulation away from D♭. Its justification is instead expressive and temporal, born out of a desire to capture a sense of weirdness and impetuous adventure, one last thrill for the audience who came to the theater in expectation of impossible sights and sounds.

Steiner's big finish in *She* is a radical example of the undermining of monotonality. But it also illustrates a more generally loose attitude toward single-key prolongation in film music. Composers from the Classical Hollywood Era onward have never felt an obligation to end a cue in the same key as it began, or a duty to project a tonic on a middle-ground level, as we have already seen in several cases. Rather than a universal trait of Hollywood film music, prolonged monotonality, or the omission thereof, is an effect available to the composer for associative purposes, and secondarily if at all for its coherence-generating potential.

Theodor Adorno and Hanns Eisler came to essentially the same conclusion while observing an ironic (and to them unfavorable) similarity to the modernist dissolution of tonality in film music. In a passage from *Composing for the Films*, they state the following:

> [Film] tonality remains one of single sounds and their most primitive sequences. The necessity of following cues, and of producing harmonic effects without regard for the requirement of harmonic development, obviously does not permit of really balanced modulation, broad, well-planned harmonic canvases; in brief, real tonality in the sense of the disposition of functional harmony over long stretches . . . according to the prevailing practice, while the separate chords are banal and over-familiar, their interrelation is quite anarchistic and for the most part completely meaningless (2007 [1947] : 123n2)

The reasoning here is needlessly dismissive of the possibility of harmonic design in film cues and scores. Tonal planning on the level of the cue is clearly extremely common (c.f. *Spellbound*'s "Picnic"), particularly with monotonally minded composers like John Barry or Ennio Morricone.[57] Planning on the level of the film, on the other hand, is "rare and precious, representing the exception to the rule, rather than a widespread trend," as Motazedian notes (2016: 194).

The really problematic aspect of Adorno and Eisler's position is that they castigate film harmonic relationships as being "anarchistic" and "meaningless" compared to some chimerical "real tonality." The ascription of harmonic anarchy suggests that a composer could write a random succession of chords and expect it to be as successful a cue as one that was constructed deliberately. The imputation of "meaninglessness" is even more bizarre. It should be apparent from *She*, and indeed every cue we will consider, that these relationships—coherent by misplaced Adornian standards or not—are often the *primary* vessels for musical meaning through their associative connotations. This primacy is true even where not justified by tonal or immediate visual-dramatic incident. Analysis should be less concerned with the sheer fact of prolongational disruption than with the expressive nuance that comes from choosing a new key or a particular modulatory strategy over the alternatives.

Adorno and Eisler's final evaluation, that "requirements of the motion picture" free composers from the no longer relevant needs of monotonal key preservation, is true enough. Less earned tonality than their "well-planned harmonic canvases" is also possible, and is in fact the norm in many cues. Yet the associative forcefulness of a strongly projected tonal center does not necessitate that composers expand their vocabulary beyond "single sounds and their most primitive sequences." A doggedly monotonal cue might be used for the affective quality of inescapability or resolve. Conversely, a flailingly unstable cue could signify a continual change of dramatic situation.

Importantly, the fast-and-loose attitude toward monotonal prolongation does not make film music non-tonal, nor does it preclude it from drawing from the norms of diatonic functional harmony. It does suggest, however, that maintenance of a single key, rather than being an unmarked default, can be itself expressive. An artful example of this expressivity—one particularly emblematic of contemporary minimalist-informed scoring styles—can be seen in Terence Blanchard's score to *25th Hour* (2002). Figure 1.8 reproduces just a sliver of a lengthy cue (45:05–50:33, ▶) that plays during a scene in which two characters, Frank (Barry Pepper) and Jacob (Phillip Seymour Hoffman) discuss the fate of their soon to be incarcerated friend. This conversation takes place in Barry's apartment, an upscale Manhattan high-rise that overlooks the ruins of the then recently destroyed World Trade Centers. Their whole exchange takes place in front of a window, with Ground Zero acting as their backdrop.

Figure 1.8 Blanchard, *25th Hour*, "Ground Zero."

For nearly five minutes, Blanchard holds fast to a dark and unvarying C minor. This key, which in its impassivity holds the listener captive, is emphasized through both high and low C♯ pedals. The cue is texturally diverse, creating waves of intensity through alternating strings, wordless Middle Eastern male vocals, and, eventually, a battery of bagpipes and snare drums. These waves replace audiovisual synch points for the majority of the passage; for example, the change in texture at m. 8 of Figure 1.8 corresponds with a pronounced darkening of Frank and Jacob's conversation. A few of these episodes touch on modal inflections of C minor, but throughout, the $\hat{5} \Leftrightarrow \hat{\flat 6}$ eighth-note ostinato and its companion tonic pedal refuse to loosen their grip. The scene is one uninterrupted shot, and while the conversation between Frank and Jacob drifts from the devastation to their relationship with their criminal friend, the music remains fixed in its tonal gaze. Blanchard's unflinchingly prolonged C minor conveys a trauma much deeper and more universal than the interpersonal concerns of a pair of New Yorkers. There is no room for the consolations of "earned" diatonic tonality here.

Referentiality

The terrible resonance of Blanchard's "Ground Zero" stems from its unwillingness to deviate from a single, pitilessly prolonged object of musical reference. The ability for pitches to absorb and project such associative significance is the final, and perhaps most important, Hollywood tonal practice. Tonal referentiality can take many forms. I have alluded to a handful of studies from theorists like Rodman and Motazedian that find choices of key to be, like leitmotifs, connected with a filmic character or idea. Symbolic tonality like this does not, however, appear to be a widespread practice, and the consistency of application (and salience to listeners) is an unsettled question.[58] A procedure related to symbolic tonality, easier to reconcile with normal film perception, is the use of tonality to mark specific textual functions like beginnings and endings. For example, a composer might differentiate contrasting sections of a movie by assigning one key to extra-diegetic material (such as main/end credits), and another set of keys to the proceedings of the main action. Similarly, tonality may clarify the structure of films with complexly interwoven narrative levels (e.g., multiple intercut stories, nonlinear editing, and flashbacks).[59] Key networks like these, which articulate levels of the diegesis, allow analysts to propose long-range tonal designs without necessitating great demands on filmgoer attentiveness. Indeed, the robustness of film-spanning associative key schemes may actually *benefit* from the music track's discontinuous, mediated nature, since tonal centers will more likely be heard in relation to one another than as integral parts within an overall tonic prolongation, an idea I will explore with greater psychological nuance in Chapter 5. Yet in spite of their analytical attractions, long-range referential designs are still less

Figure 1.9 Goldsmith, *Escape from the Planet of the Apes*, Main Title.

common or influential than associative techniques that heed the demands of
the musical surface. Taking advantage of the semiotic power possessed by specific triadic progressions is one method that we will devote more attention to in
coming analyses. But, by way of concluding this chapter on broad tonal practices,
let us consider the form of referentiality in which tonal idiom *itself* becomes the
signifier.

Consider the octatonic collection (set class 8-28, or [0134679T]). This specific
arrangement of pitches is invested with all manner of associations in Hollywood,
much of it by way of Romantic and Modern repertoires. Twentieth-century
Russian music in particular is often suffused with octatonic spices, though the
collection's associative ties with the magical and primordial date back a century
earlier, to music of Glinka and Rimsky Korsakov (Taruskin 1985, Frymoyer 2016).
One may easily discern shades of Stravinsky's "Symphony in Three Movements"
in Goldsmith's main title to *Escape from the Planet of the Apes* (1971, ▶), shown in
Figure 1.9. In this excerpt, every pitch in the cue derives from the <0,1> octatonic
collection. Characteristic octatonic touches include the minor-third-emphasizing
bass line, the semitone/whole-tone alternating horn melody, and the oscillation
of tritonally related seventh chords in the winds. The <0,1> octatonic scale is a
referential collection here in two ways: it furnishes the pitch material for the entire passage, and it acts to direct the listener to a well-established set of generic
and affective associations. Goldsmith's main title thus recasts Stravinskian poly-
rhythmic octatonicism as a kind of thrashing, primitivistic disco track, taking an
ancestral aesthetic and remixing it with a 1970s groove.[60]

Collections like the octatonic rarely occur in isolation, removed from other
"referential" tonal idioms. Indeed, their significatory power is strengthened by
contact and contrast by other scales and styles. (Goldsmith's main title, for example, alternates between weird octatonic harmonies and more urbane dorian
materials.) Composer Lalo Schifrin describes a hypothetical situation that requires calculated shifting of harmonic styles:

> Let's say that you are in a very dramatic scene in which the most hor-
> rible conflict is coming between good and evil, and evil is winning . . . if
> you have to go from something that is tonal, because it's kind of neutral,

pleasant, or pastoral, and all of a sudden something starts becoming dis-
turbed . . . you start using the modes of limited transposition until it
finally becomes very disturbing, and that gets you into the twelve tones.
(cited in Brown [1994: 317]).

Schifrin endorses the use of a tonal idiom itself as a style topic.[61] The harmonic
syntax of late Romanticism was already pluralistic to a limited extent; composers like Mahler and Busoni frequently recruited differing idioms (chromatic
musical prose, modal folk melodies, diatonic fanfares, etc.) for both expressive and formal purposes. Film harmony, however, is *intrinsically* plural, able
at all times to draw from and hybridize eclectic practices. This hybridization
is not practiced arbitrarily, but always in a referential fashion, with the harmonic mannerisms of different styles justified by their ability to elicit cultural
associations.

The deployment of various tonal styles in succession is what we might call
"meta-tonal design." It is an effective method for responding to shifts in dramatic
tone and subject. The associations attached to broad styles tend to be more stable
within (and across) films than those that fasten to semantic units of a limited
scope, like keys or chords. Design through tonal idiom has the advantage of being
aurally obvious. The consistent encodedness of divergent styles ensures that an
analyst need not grapple with matters of relevance or audibility and may leap
right into more productive investigation. In fact, we should be wary of any interpretive angle that minimizes meta-tonal design, particularly if it presumes that
keys and key relations are the basic articulators of harmonic meaning.

Meta-tonal design operates equally well at surface and background levels of
film form. We saw the former in the shift from functional diatonicism to atonality in *Rebel without a Cause*. In Rosenman's scores, this kind of play between
stable and unstable tonal languages furnishes a productive tension that can run
through entire films. David Shire is another composer who brings together competing idioms for highly expressive effect. For instance, his contribution to *The
Conversation* (1974) juxtaposes monotonal jazz harmony with a host of subcuta-
neously unnerving (and wholly atonal) methods, including electronic manipulation and extended piano techniques. This approach is entirely apt for a film about
a loner surveillance expert and recreational saxophonist who falls victim to crip-
pling paranoia (Chattah 2015).

Even comparatively conservative composers will tailor tonal polystylism for
dramatic effect. In John Williams's *Empire of the Sun* (1987) five distinct tonal dialects reflect different aspects of the child protagonist's experience: diatonicism for
domestic life, modality for religion, pantriadicism for wonder, atonality for anxiety and psychic disintegration, and pentatonicism for Asian local flavor. In some
cues, like the centerpiece "Cadillac of the Skies," the protagonist's words collide,
and the music cycles through the tonal extremes in order to convey the buzzing
confusion that besets his unstable world.

For David Neumeyer and James Buhler, the promotion of tonality's referential powers in film is the result of a concomitant draining away of music's functional potency.

> Film composers . . . [since the 1920s are] faced with a number of overlapping and potentially conflicting models for tonal design: the unified hierarchical schemes of instrumental music, simple "chaining" of key regions (as in popular theater such as operetta), the seemingly radical disunity of the fifteen second rule, and such later 19th-century practices as associative tonality (key symbolism) and double-tonic complexes. Composers' choices were further complicated by [general musical discontinuity, lack of ultimate control over spotting, use of source music, and post-recording editing and mixing]. Given these constraints . . . it seems reasonable to assume that any large-scale tonal designs found in film scores will be abstract and symbolic rather than functional. (2001: 26–27).

In framing the movement toward associativity as an upshot of extended harmonic procedures and partly the subordinate, discontinuous nature of film music, Neumeyer and Buhler sum up many of the Hollywood tonal practices I expound on in this chapter. They argue that the power of common-practice functional tonality over the course of a film is compromised, and its potential constructive capacities are necessarily shifted to referential tasks.

Nearly all theorists recognize an abundance of obstacles to an approach to film music analysis that does not take referentiality into account. But these obstacles have wider implications than the pragmatic and prescriptive barriers described by Adorno/Eisler and Sabaneev. Treating tonality as a referential resource absolves analysts from some of the more problematic issues in soundtrack hermeneutics—tracing long-range linear prolongations in light of the fifteen-second rule, making excuses for imperfectly followed symbolic key schemes, and so on. More importantly for us, it lifts some of the interpretive baggage of "nonfunctionality" from chromaticism, allowing analysts instead to focus on more germane transformational and expressive aspects of nondiatonic progressions.

As we proceed, I devote more attention to the densely chromatic style of fantastic cinema and less to the workings of prolongational monotonality. It is with pantriadicism where the tampering of tonal prolongation and its attendant elevation of harmonic referentiality has the most palpable implications for hearing and analysis. Especially in styles that emphasize thematic and leitmotivic fragments, modulations may be rife, but stable keys elusive or established by nontraditional means (that is, not through dominants). This unpredictability is one of the major differences between Classical and New Hollywood practice, even where both employ basically Romantic tonal styles on their surface. We saw, for instance, that in

Now Voyager, the numerous dominants still point unambiguously to their tonics, even if the target keys are rarely secured with cadences. In more recent styles, however, dominant-based tonal syntax often gives way to more contextually defined strategies of navigating tonal space.

Though an unparalleled diversity of musical styles (and thus tonal idioms) defines the film oeuvre of John Williams, his vibrant scores for films like *Indiana Jones, Jurassic Park*, and *Harry Potter* are in many ways direct revivifications of Steiner and Korngold's soupy chromatic language. Few active film composers besides Williams regularly write with the harmonic sophistication or mastery (or, perhaps, mannerism) that once typified the Golden Age of film scoring. But while the sparing, minimal harmonic activity of Blanchard's *25th Hour* is more typical of scoring practices of the new millennium, the Williamsesque approach to tonal drama—intense, complex, and unpredictable—continues to be represented in blockbusters and mega-franchise American movies.

Action and suspense cues from John Williams exhibit the new forms of the cinematic chromatic practice starkly, with an abundance of non-diatonic relationships populating the musical surface, and V⇨I motions being saved for truly exceptional moments. Buhler compares Williams's leitmotivic and modulation-reliant approach to other musical processes, like sonata form, that rely equally heavily on thematic work. In his final assessment, Buhler finds this style of film composition to be at risk of a kind of incoherency, as it appears to lack immanent or structurally motivated thematic/tonal development. "The music nervously flits from one key to another with little sense to the overall progression other than the theme constantly sound fresh" (2000: 53–54). To equate coherence with certain kinds of musical teleology (invariably imported from discourses surrounding concert music) is a questionable stance, if not an unfamiliar one. But the bigger problem here is simply that critiques like Buhler's, accurate and necessary though they are, rarely prompt any actual in-depth tonal analysis of the music in question. Doing so may reveal other kinds of coherence—or at least elucidate the ways in which film scoring is materially dissimilar from putative models in late Romantic art music. For that reason, I conclude this chapter on broad tonal practices by briefly inspecting a sequence that points toward different kinds of analytical strategies to use for this style.

The cue "Faking the Code" from *Return of the Jedi* (1983, 52:00, ▶) accompanies a suspenseful scene wherein the protagonists attempt to pass their ship undetected through an Imperial military blockade. Like many sequences in modern blockbuster films, this one has a brisk editorial rhythm (fifty-one shots over 278 seconds) and is full of intercutting between locales, which lends itself to tonally active underscore. Figure 1.10 offers a bass-only reduction of the succession of keys. During its four-minute duration, Williams flies through no fewer than twenty-six briefly tonicized keys, giving the average tonic a duration of a mere 9.5 seconds (about one key every other new shot).[62]

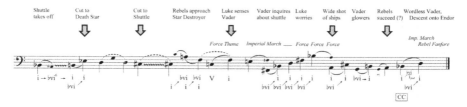

Figure 1.10 Williams, *Return of the Jedi*, "Faking the Code."

Every last key here is in a minor mode, producing a special tonal idiom we will come to recognize as *intensified minor pantriadicism*. Not a single inter-thematic diatonic progression appears in "Faking the Code." In fact, very few multi-chord progressions take place *within* prolonged keys either, save for a few ♭vi⇔i motions that amount to references to the franchise's famous "Imperial March." Generally, step progressions and major-third cycles steer the constantly fluctuating tonal surface. Keys are too briefly articulated to become referential in and of themselves. The D minor at timestamp 53:34, for example, is not meaningfully "the same" D minor that appears at 54:15, or the one that concludes the cue a minute later. However, D minor's flanking in each instance by chromatic minor-third relations *is* a meaningful similarity relation and is most likely heard as both motivic and coherence granting. The general absence of lengthy slurs in Figure 1.10 represents the difficulty in assigning any tonal regions hierarchical priority. The cue's single dominant-to-tonic bass motion (CM⇨Fm) is tellingly attached to the introduction of a leitmotif that belongs to the protagonists: the "Force Theme." Though functional in a local context, this is arguably a case of harmonic mention rather than use. It is the V⇨i progression's meta-tonal symbolic power that motivates its placement at that moment in the cue, not the fact that it "completes" any one musical thought.

Buhler observes that harmony plays both a motivic and an ideological role in the *Star Wars* scores, with diatonicism and modality associating with the heroes, while nonfunctional—but crucially *centric*—chromaticism linked rigidly to the villains (ibid: 44–40). Apart from its strikingly narrow, perhaps "anarchistic" prolongational horizon, "Faking the Code" builds up nervous anxiety by basing nearly every inter-key modulation on one of these chromatic progressions. This approach signals to the viewer that the cautious optimism of the heroes at this stage is ill founded. In *Return of the Jedi*, and many scores of similar fantastic aspirations, musical referentiality relies on a play of tonal styles and often resides in association-laden progressions themselves. What we need in order to truly unlock this cue and others like it is a new methodology, one capable of characterizing these sinisterly allusive harmonic moves without misapplying functional expectations. For that, we must explore more fully the topic of pantriadic chromaticism in cinema, and introduce a few new analytical tools.

2

Expression and Transformation

Tonality as Drama

Much of our understanding of how chromatic harmony works in narrative-driven contexts stems from the study of opera. Just as film composition has continuously drawn from nineteenth-century operatic practices, film musicology has imported some of its vocabulary and its analytical priorities from studies of this repertoire. This chapter falls in roughly two halves, exploring a pair of concepts that hail from opera studies—expressive tonality and pantriadic chromaticism. These twin tonal procedures inform my rationale for using a particular analytical perspective—neo-Riemannian theory—for the rest of this book. Emphasizing expressive and pantriadic tonality as a component of the "Hollywood sound" will inevitably steer my attention onto certain harmonic features and away from others. The turn toward the musical surface, a direction I advocated implicitly in the previous chapter, will become even more pronounced as we move forward.

As with many aspects of modern musical culture, the shadow of Richard Wagner looms over both the theoretical concepts I plan on exploring herein. The film musicological debt to Wagner is vast, as already evident in the various "extended" devices that I enumerated in Table 1.1.[1] Of those techniques, the final three—directional, paired, and symbolic tonality—were first described by the music theorist Robert Bailey. In his groundbreaking studies of Wagner's operas, Bailey addressed how it was possible for tonality to organize what were at the time the longest uninterrupted spans of music in Western culture.[2] Bailey revealed that tonal design, far from serving a purely formal role, could take on dramaturgical and mythopoetic power in works like *Tristan und Isolde* and the *Ring* cycle. Wagner's keys, like his leitmotifs, are storytelling devices, capable of accruing meaning, guiding the listener through complex narratives, and controlling "larger structural units than ever before." (1977: 60) And while few movie soundtracks have ever been knit together with key schemes of Wagnerian scope or systematicity, Bailey's central analytical insight is no less applicable to film: tonality *is* drama.[3]

The nature of pitch organization in Wagner has relevance to film music analysis for an additional reason, beyond the linkage of keys with the "poetic idea."

The sumptuous chromaticism of his mature operas proved exceptionally influential for subsequent generations of dramatically minded composers. One aspect of Wagnerian chromaticism in particular was to secure a permanent place in the language of film scores: *pantriadicism*. Put succinctly, pantriadicism is the succession of consonant triads without reference to diatonic scales, functions, or centers. Admittedly, the roots of this "pantriadic" idiom hardly originated with Wagner. There exist plentiful precedents from other central European Romantics (especially Schubert and Liszt), as well as distinct but parallel branches of pantriadic innovation throughout the nineteenth century (especially from Russia, and Rimsky-Korsakov in particular).[4] Neither can it be said that the idiom stopped growing after Wagner's last opera, *Parsifal* premiered in 1882. Indeed, film music, along with strains of jazz and progressive rock, features expansions of triadic chromaticism well beyond what Wagner and his heirs imagined.[5] And yet nothing so epitomizes the pantriadic style as the chromatic centerpieces of mature music dramas from the "dread mage of Bayreuth"—a few of which are rendered in Figure 2.1: Elsa's octatonic dream in *Lohengrin*, the Wanderer's enigmatic leitmotif from *Siegfried*, and Kundry's uncanny expi(r)ation at the end of *Parsifal*. Each of these moments is steeped with a sense of otherness, which Wagner tapped to suggest matters magical and mysterious. Chromaticism's potency stems here, as ever, from its markedness against the norm of diatonicism, and Wagner's pantriadic trances seem to swirl with unusual tonal urges and expectations. It is practically movie music *avant la lettre*, intensely expressive and overflowing with affect.

Because they breach the boundaries of diatonic syntax, pantriadic passages have proven both refractory and irresistible as subjects of investigation. Attempts to understand their inner workings have spurred a number of original music-theoretical systems.[6] Most relevant of these to *Hollywood Harmony* is neo-Riemannian theory (NRT): the triad-focused offshoot of a larger school of

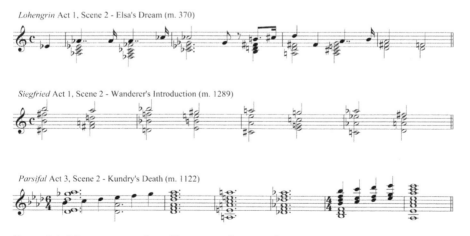

Figure 2.1 Wagner, examples of "cinematic" pantriadicism.

thought called transformation theory. Neo-Riemannian approaches were initially devised to navigate the waters of nineteenth-century chromaticism, particularly those places where other methods ran up against analytical rocks. The value of NRT to the study of film music is manifold, but one huge asset is its sensitivity to tonal change *as such*. NRT treats chord progressions as the foremost conveyors of harmonic structure—and thus, for our purposes, communicators of tonal drama. As I argue throughout the rest of this book, NRT offers a way of thinking that heeds the imperatives of film composition underlined in Chapter 1: subordination, referentiality, and especially immediacy.

We will have occasion to explore the machinery of NRT at length in the next chapter. But before diving headlong into methodological nuts and bolts, I intend to spend this chapter introducing, sometimes indirectly, the core concepts and concerns of NRT. In the sections that follow, I set up the way tonality can be expressive in film music, how this expressivity ties into the notion of tonal transformation, and what it all has to do with this strange and thorny style of pantriadicism. I begin this exploration, perhaps a little perversely, with a pitch collection and a transformation that NRT has generally steered clear of: the whole-tone scale and the step progression. It is impossible to discuss filmic chromaticism without examining the former, and doing so will help prepare my investigation into both tonal expression and pantriadic aesthetics. The latter requires a bit more special justification. I contend that step progressions are easily hearable and ostensibly straightforward examples of what transformation theory is really all about—the power of a tonal change to reorient the listener. Conveniently enough, analyzing step progressions also pulls in Robert Bailey's work on Wagner, namely his notion of *expressive tonality*. At the midpoint of this chapter I recalibrate this category so that it applies more broadly than Bailey originally envisioned. But as we transition from discussing filmic tonality in a general sense to the narrower domain of pantriadic chromaticism, it will be worthwhile to also consider the concept at face value.

Whole-Tone Dreams

Chromaticism in cinema is remarkably, almost effortlessly expressive. Part of this expressivity is the product of music's semantic absorptiveness in general, its "stickiness" in Carolyn Abbate's memorable formulation (2004: 523–524). Music has the ability to soak up the meanings of its visual and narratival counterparts, and to exude its own messages in turn, as even the most random of music/visual substitution exercises will affirm. But many guises of chromatic harmony arrive onto the soundtrack already pumped full of expressive content, ready to insist on releasing their particular flavors of meaningfulness, regardless of what is taking place on screen. Chromaticism, after all, is the great foil to diatonic tonality, the indelibly marked tonal other whose power to enrich and disrupt is essential to the fundamental flow of Western harmony. Many of the specific semiotic targets of chromaticism were standardized in the nineteenth century: exotic lands, erotic experiences, magical encounters, and so on. But even now, a century after the alleged "emancipation of dissonance"—and two centuries after the first stirrings of "extended tonality"—cinematic chromaticism overflows with significatory potential.

Hollywood stylistic standardization renders some chromatic habits utter cliché, while leaving others to await discovery or revival. Consider one particularly vivid example: the whole-tone scale and its associated collection, <02468T>. Part of the collection's attraction is its oddly restricted character, with only two forms of the six-note scale being possible: C-D-E-F♯-G♯-B♭; and C♯-D♯-F-G-A-B. See Figure 2.2 for a depiction of this collection. Whole-tone harmony may be thought of either as a product of an interval cycle (repeated major seconds) or as a fusion of other sonorities (two distinct augmented <048> triads, two distinct <024> trichords, or three distinct <06> tritones). This pitch resource turns out to be the source of one of cinema's hoariest style topics. For most of the Classical Hollywood Era, whole-tone derived harmony stood as a near-obligatory signifier of dreams. The swirling music that ushers in dream sequences in Waxman's *Rebecca* (12:20) and Rózsa's *Spellbound* (1:22:15) are paradigm cases of this chromatic special effect.[7] In these and other prototypical instances, the whole-tone scale is projected as a solid, non-progressing wash of harmony. Any sense of internal energy is generated not by the collection itself, but by equally conventional timbral and textural touches like harp glissandi and murky orchestration.[8]

Like many symmetrical pitch collections, the whole-tone scale draws much of its cinematic resonance from influential Russian compositions from the nineteenth century and French works from the early twentieth. A perceptive listener during the early Sound Era may have drawn a connection between the scale's usage in James Dietrich's score for *The Mummy* (1932) with the rippling whole-tone orchestral interludes in Rimsky-Korsakov's *Sadko* or Debussy's *Pelléas et Mélisande*. However, the average twenty-first century cinemagoer is more likely to understand whole-tone harmony in terms of film and television precedents (including many parodic uses) than its late Romantic origins. Today, its impact has been dulled by overuse and caricature, and outright employments are rare. Even so, though the ubiquity of other, closely related pitch resources, like the hybrid whole-tone/major hexachord (C-D-E-F♯-G-A♭) that behaves leitharmonically in Hans Zimmer's *Interstellar* score (2014), suggests that the collection still retains

wt 0,2   2   2   2   2   2   Caug Daug   {024} {68T}   {06} {28} {4T}   C Fr+6   D Fr+6

Figure 2.2 Whole-Tone Collection.

its ability to connote liminality, and to do so in a sincere, not necessarily self-referential or parodistic way.

The expressive legibility of the whole-tone scale speaks to a persistence in cultural memory that verges on fetishization. Yet the collection's floating associations (in both senses of floating) would never have persisted were it not for something somehow intrinsic to the harmonic resource that was poised for expressive activation. On this point, one might entertain a loose analogy with linguistics. Harmonic style topics like the whole-tone collection more closely resemble onomatopoeia than the empty, arbitrary signifiers of classical semiotics. Figuratively speaking, whole-tone harmony *sounds* dreamlike. The relevant intrinsic morphological traits include the collection's symmetry (manifesting in symmetrical subsets like the augmented triad and French sixth chord); intervallic homogeneity (note its unique interval vector, <060603>); and inadmission of consonant triads. These traits stand in radical contrast with diatonic norms. Together they all but annul tonal hierarchy and position finding, and thus map with ease onto expressive states of weightlessness, disorientation, and hypnogogia.

Sweeping harp or celesta glissandi notwithstanding, whole-tone harmony often gives an impression of motionlessness, a sound offered to the ear as a tonal block, unwilling or unable to progress forward. So strong is the associative bond between the whole-tone collection and the idea of liminality that it even retains its expressive quality when frozen solid, icily concretized into the form of a wall of static harmony—or even a diegetic sound effect. The strictly non-musical sound of the transporter in *Star Trek* (original series and onward) consists in a synthesized whole-tone cluster, subtly alluding to this specific harmonic topic every time someone "beams" aboard the Starship Enterprise. This is an exaggerated example of a more general aspect of tonal expressivity: certain pitch resources suggest meaning primarily through their *vertical* constitution, that is, as pure sonority. We see this tendency most vividly illustrated by film musical tropes that arrest the listener's attention and affix it on anxious sonorities. We have already observed many examples of such tropes: chord clusters, pyramid chords, and stingers—pervasive harmonic topics all marked by an intensely dissonant makeup, often brought out by aggressive or unnerving orchestration.

However, a harmonic object hardly needs to be dissonant in order to signify directly: pure triads and even naked intervals may suffice if sustained in such a way that makes their acoustic surfaces the primary point of salience (the reader might think back to the prolonged "C minor-ness" of Blanchard's *25th Hour*). The effectiveness of these sorts of topics in stems first and foremost from their sound-as-such, what Daniel Harrison terms their "sensuous" quality, their feeling of "mass and substance," there to be "savored, appreciated, and even caressed . . ." (2011: 553). Yet for all the condensed tonal suggestiveness of such musical objects, it also matters deeply how one progresses *into* or *out of* these more vertical harmonic topics. Whole-tone stingers, for example, work by generating a stark contrast with their immediate surroundings. But the tonal indeterminacy of whole-tone harmony also allows it to flow smoothly, even imperceptibly, into and out of other, more stably defined pitch regions. Whole-tone chord clusters and pyramids work best when assembled piecemeal, one note added at a time until the effect is ear-splittingly dissonant (think back to Rosenman's *Rebel without a Cause*). In order to keep up with changes in action, film tonality must be dynamic rather than inert. Even in the case of the most immobile and "sensuous" seeming sonorities, expressivity is always bound up with the changes undergone *between* harmonic objects. And no other form of harmonic change is more obvious—or expressively powerful—than modulation.

Pump-Up Schemes

According to Bailey, expressive tonality arises whenever "a passage is transposed up to underscore intensification, or shifted down to indicate relaxation . . . usually by a semitone or whole tone" (1977: 51).[9] We see expressive tonality in the way the three successive renditions of the "Song to Venus" in Act I of Wagner's *Tannhäuser* climb from D♭ to D♮ to E♭, "heightening the anguish" of the eponymous character's plea. Unlike conventional modulations, stepwise shifts lack harmonic mediation, rarely involving "pivot" chords to smooth the movement from one area to another. Bailey identifies expressive tonality as an outgrowth of sequencing techniques, the likes of which are customary in the development sections of instrumental music. To this characterization we might add a non-modulatory precedent: the deceptive cadence (e.g., V⇨VI at a phrase boundary), wherein intervallic directionality and surprise similarly contribute to tonal expressivity. In all three cases, upward motion calls to mind effort, strain, and working against gravity; downward motion suggests sagging, sighing, or giving way to gravitational forces.

For Bailey, the defining manifestation of expressive tonality is the stepwise modulation, which is to say transposition of a key by interval class (ic) 1 or 2. More formally, we can treat any tonal motion as the result of a musical transformation—a specific action performed on one musical idea to yield another. The standard shorthand for transposition is T_n, where T stands for transposition and n for the number of semitones by which the target sonority/key is shifted. These notations will be T_1 and T_2 for upward stepwise transpositions by minor and major second, and their inverses, T_{-1} and T_{-2}, for downward shifts. (Triadic transformations usually assume octave equivalence, meaning that downward motions by step may also be described by T_{10} and T_{11}, though this notation loses the handy sense of directionality.) Note that expressive modulations in Bailey's sense tend to involve verbatim transplantation, and thus are *mode-preserving* transpositions. Modal invariance is quite important for the affect of such procedures, as it entails maintaining the major/minor valence of the transposed unit while the music is thrust wholesale into a new space. (If we wish to account for a modally varied transposition—say, Cm⇨D♭M—we will need to append the mode-flipping operation, **P**, to the transformation.).

Scholars following Bailey have shown expressive tonality to be a feature of a host of other musical styles. Applications have been found for early Romantic instrumental music, Italian opera, Broadway song, and pop/rock, to name a few genres.[10] The ubiquity of transposition-based expressive modulation in film music, on the other hand, has gone largely unnoted. With care, modulations driven by ic1 or ic2 (half and whole steps) can provide for some potent dramatic effects, even when the tonics of the transposed keys are separated by intervening material.

Take, for example, Mark Isham's cue for an exhilarating scene in *Fly Away Home* (1996, 52:30, ▶). Isham's locally diatonic but quick-to-modulate music accompanies a montage in which a father and his daughter train gaggle of orphaned Canada Geese to take flight. Stepwise rising bass lines are a recurrent linear element of the cue, urging it constantly skyward. For the scene's conclusion, Isham modulates up from F major to G major (a T_2 transformation). However, rather than connecting I/G directly with I/F, Isham first transposes an active but non-cadential progression [I^6⇨IV⇨I^6_4⇨vi] into the new key. He then pauses on G major's dominant, and only after several seconds have elapsed does he finally unveil a G-major chord in all its root-position glory.

Figure 2.3 summarizes the tonal design of the concluding two minutes of this cue. The shift from F to G is emphasized with a new symbol—the directed black arrow—which is a mainstay of transformational analysis. As indicated in the diagram, the substages of Isham's modulations are carefully timed to sync with the dramatic action, such that with each step closer to G major, the audience feels that those goslings are a bit closer to lifting off. With the deferred arrival of each new key, Isham combines a feeling of surprise, anticipation, and eventual release. Weddings of shock and expectation in this manner are hugely important to expressive chromaticism in film, though I defer full exploration of the psychological mechanisms involved until Chapter 5.

Step modulations as (relatively) understated as Isham's are not what theorists generally have in mind when they invoke expressive tonality. Attention instead tends to fall on *direct* transposition, a technique whose power lies, arguably, in

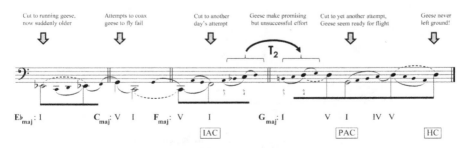

Figure 2.3 Isham, *Fly Away Home*, "Goose Chase."

its crudity. For contemporary listeners, expressive tonality's most familiar guise is assuredly the well-worn but fabulously effective formula wherein the final chorus of a popular song suddenly jumps up a key—a jolting effect that has been dubbed, among other things, a "pump-up" or "gearshift modulation"[11] Even in pop music, these transpositions have an inherently dramatic quality that cannot help suggesting a certain theatrical flair.[12] Given that film music is about controlling the ebb and flow of tension, it is no surprise that film composers have used pump-up modulations to communicate rising intensity since the very first moving images were set to music. Arguably, the original film score, Camille Saint-Säens's music for *L'Assassinat du duc Guise* (1908), is already full of these modulations. The most notable "gearshift" occurs in the transition from the film's third to fourth tableau. In a terrifically melodramatic twist, Saint-Säens veers from F major to F♯ minor (T_1P) at the moment an intertitle announces the titular duke is about to meet his sticky end. Early film music is replete with such reminders of the continuity between mature film-scoring practices and their precedents in nineteenth-century instrumental and theatrical music.[13]

Expressive tonality proves an even more useful technique in sound film, where its bluntness is an asset for scenes in which loud sound effects threaten to swamp the soundtrack. Figure 2.4 (▶) offers two examples that illustrate this point. In the middle of the electrifying creation sequence in *The Bride of Frankenstein* (1935, 1:08:05) (Figure 2.4a), Franz Waxman hauls the film's twisted love theme up from E to F♯ major. This modulation is accomplished over deafeningly loud sound effects—so clamorous that the listener will barely be able to assimilate any musical information other than that a modulation has taken place. Nearly eighty

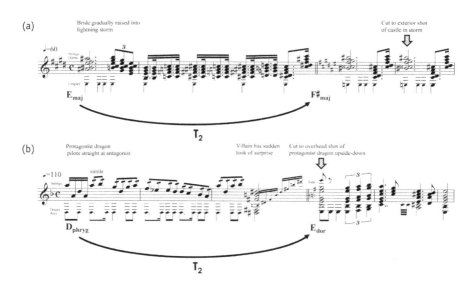

Figure 2.4 Two cinematic pump-up modulations: (a) Waxman, *The Bride of Frankenstein*, "Creation Scene"; (b) Powell, *How to Train Your Dragon 2*, "Toothless Found."

years later, John Powell plays the same T_2-driven trick for the climax of *How to Train Your Dragon 2* (2014, 1:23:48). At the moment the villain realizes he has lost track of the wyrm-riding protagonist, Powell surges the orchestra up a key, from D to E. This shift takes place after a full minute of uninterrupted D-dorian/phrygian (Figure 2.4b). In both *Frankenstein* and *Dragon* examples, an additional characteristic device is at work: a conspicuous upward melodic motion that anticipates a subsequent upward motion between tonal regions. In Powell's cue, this effect is accomplished by a sudden arpeggiated flurry on the dominant of E, while Waxman's features a more steady semitonal process that fills in the space between $\hat{5}$/E and $\hat{5}$/F♯.

Music theorist Patrick McCreless notes that expressive modulations in the nineteenth century rarely rely on pitch alone for their affective impact. Composers "articulate and dramatize the leap out of diatonic space with techniques from the arsenal of rhetoric and gesture: changes of dynamics, orchestration, texture, and rhythmic flow; pregnant silences; and the like" (1996: 90) Cinematic pump-ups bear out the importance of these non-harmonic parameters. For example, wedding a key change to a surprising rhythmic transformation can amplify the affective impact of both. Consider the way David Arnold drives home a shift from outdoor to indoor peril during the opening chase in *Casino Royale* (2006, 16:50).[14] The change in geography marks entry into a new, more claustrophobic phase of James Bond's pursuit and is accompanied with a metric modulation from a simple triple rhythm (♪=172 in 3/4) in E minor to a compound duple pattern in F♯ minor (♪=230 in 6/8).[15] The effect is disorienting, bracing, and expressively perfect for the virtuosically staged action scene.

Repetition is another surefire strategy for underlining an expressive modulation. If one stepwise shift injects an isolated dose of tension to a scene, then several chained together can generate a climb in emotional intensity whose predictability translates into a feeling of inexorability. This is a manifestation of a more general principle. Maximization of expressivity by reiteration of a certain type of progression is a common procedure in film music, which I designate from now on by the modifier *intensified*. So, for example, **intensified transpositional chromaticism** describes the way that a passage based on iterated stepwise transformations is more than the sum of its parts, affectively speaking.

Intensified transpositional chromaticism is like a game of tonal one-upsmanship: how much higher do you think this climb can go before collapsing? John Williams has proven partial to the procedure, employing it to memorable effect during the various action set pieces of the *Indiana Jones* franchise.[16] At the climax of *Raiders of the Lost Ark*'s (1981, 1:26:55, ▶) desert chase, for example, Williams drives his octatonic villain motif up a transpositional ramp from B♭ to C, C♯, D, and finally E♭. Figure 2.4c captures the trajectory of this nail-biting sequence. Each tonal gearshift is timed to coincide with a new stage of the hero's ordeal. This tight modulatory ballet persists right up to the moment Jones achieves his goal, at which point a rendition of his heroic leitmotif transforms E♭ octatonic

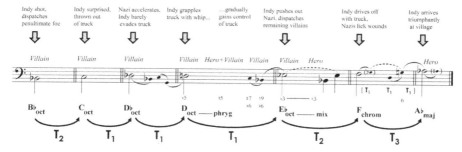

Figure 2.4c Williams, *Raiders of the Lost Ark*, "Desert Chase."

into the brighter realm of E♭ mixolydian. Williams' use of expressive modulation here—always coordinated with increasing volume, tempo, and orchestrational density—actively *produces* the tension of the set piece. It even goes so far to ensure a mounting level of excitement when the level of threat against the hero strictly *decreases* as he closes in on his goal. On this tonal thrill ride, Williams has no intention of providing rest for the weary.

The modulatory details differ substantially in these examples of expressive tonality. Isham's tonics in *Fly Away Home* never directly touch. Throughout the *Frankenstein* sequence, Waxman holds onto a low E pedal point that softens the impact of stepwise transposition in the higher registers. Powell includes a tiny applied dominant to the new key that makes the tonal shift in *Dragon* even more propulsive. Arnold ends the first key in *Casino Royale* on a dissonant stinger and commences the next region with a complex percussive texture. And Williams cranks the transpositional gear in *Raiders* as many times as possible within the time given. Yet across all five examples, the expressive effect of rising excitement and intensity is essentially identical, as is the concomitant "forgetting" of the structural ramifications of initial key almost immediately after the modulation takes place.

No, they are not pinnacles of harmonic subtlety. Yet these harmonic devices deliver an immediate impact few other techniques could accomplish. And they accomplish this impact by strategically breaking through the bounds of diatonic tonality. As Walter Everett observes, "often, the [step] modulation appears arbitrary and shallow but takes on a life of its own; once it starts, it seems unstoppable." (1997: 151) Intricate counterpoint, complex progressions, carefully prepared modulations—these devices are well and good when audiovisual circumstance permits the foregrounding of musical detail. But technical refinement does a film composer little good when the scene being scored is overstuffed with other, more aggressive forms of stimuli. Sometimes, only a mannerism as broad as a pump-up modulation can cut through cacophony to even register as a distinctly audible musical event.

Musical Expressivity

Pump-up modulation, transposition, gearshifting—these descriptions are all ways of getting at the essential transformational character of tonal change. Steven Rings, one of the foremost neo-Riemannian theorists, defines a transformation as "[an] action that move[s] musical entities or configurations along or that transform them into other, related entities or configurations" (2011b: 24). A transformation is an energetic idea, a way of getting from one place to another. Transposition is just one type of transformation, a member within a larger taxonomy that shall be detailed in the next chapter. Regardless of their specific classification or behavior, transformations serve as the primary bearers of harmonic expressivity in a great deal of film music. One might fairly counter that other aspects of pitch design, such as modality and cadential placement, are comparably capable of influencing the affective flow of a cue. Yet two essential features of film underscore—the demand for instant referentiality and the lessened need for structural coherence—elevate the prominence of moments of transformation, rendering them perhaps the most representatively *cinematic* harmonic processes of all.

Understanding harmony as a dynamic process is an explanatorily powerful way to approach film music, but it does require a shift of perspective for those used to thinking of pitch design in terms of static entities such as chords, scales, and keys. To help make this concept more intuitive, let us remain with the topic of expressive transposition a little longer. As the examples we have already encountered demonstrate, stepwise shifts of tonal center have enormous utility for screen composers. Transformations by intervals of a semi- or whole-tone provide a potent and fast-acting source of emotion, be it intensity, anxiety, or amazement. Nor are $T_{1/2}$ transformations necessarily just short-term gambits; they can also influence a film on a broader level, being able to drive narrative momentum forward, swing a scene in a new direction, or signal crucial turning points in the plot.

Expressive tonality in Bailey's sense hinges on a linkage between an aspect of pitch design (step modulation) and an affective quality (generally, subjective tension). The ability for a harmonic gesture to stir emotion in this way raises two general questions. First, exactly where does the expressive content in such transformations come from? Second, should Bailey's notion of expressivity be limited to tonal shifts of the pump-up (or down) variety? The arguments from the previous chapter should signal that the answer to the latter question will be a decisive "no." But before we leap to that conclusion and what it means for analysis, it will pay to tackle the first question. For even with stock techniques, the source of tonal expressivity turns out to be a complex issue, involving a thick mixture of contributing factors and a wide landscape of theories about musical emotion and connotation.[17]

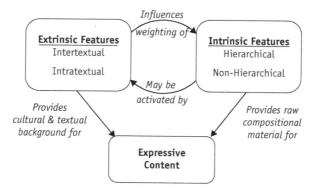

Figure 2.5 Schematic network for musical expressivity.

One way to clear the fog is to differentiate **extrinsic** and **intrinsic** factors in harmonic expressivity.[18] This bifurcated way of conceptualizing musical expressivity is something I already introduced informally with the earlier discussion of whole-tone harmony, but it deserves a more systematic treatment here. Extrinsic features are of a cultural origin and involve signifying systems originating both within (intratextual) and without (intertextual) a given film. Intrinsic features, by contrast, operate through the structural and psychological constraints of a given musical system; they may encompass both hierarchical factors like tonal distance and non-hierarchical factors like voice-leading smoothness. Rudimentary though this extrinsic/intrinsic binary may seem, it is powerful enough to produce an explanatory framework for harmonic associativity generally, and various triadic progressions in particular. Figure 2.5 offers a schematic representation of this model, the terms and behavior of which will be clarified presently. Inspired by similar networks developed by Lawrence Zbikowski and Nicholas Cook, the graph shows a relationship of mutual influence and interaction between extrinsic and intrinsic musical domains as they blend to form expressive content.[19]

EXTRINSIC MEANING

Extrinsic (or extramusical) factors are matters of convention. Music psychologist Annabel Cohen defines them simply as "associations," meanings that "relate to the external world" (2014: 102–105).They include all the ways in which a musical idea has been set up at an *intra*textual level, within a given text: what emotions or situations the idea is coupled with, where and when it occurs, its role within a larger narrative, and so on. Intratextual information includes everything within a film that singles out a specific musical gesture for special meaningfulness.

Figure 2.6 Silvestri, *The Abyss*, intratextual clarification of **F** progression: (a) Main Title; (b) "Bud on the Ledge."

For a demonstration, consider the oscillation between C♯M and G♯m that marks the climax of Alan Silvestri's opening credits for *The Abyss* (1989, 0:24, ▶), reproduced in Figure 2.6a. At this early stage in the film, the modally mixed fifth progression (designated as **F**, for "far fifth") is expressively underdetermined. We do not know what it means within the context of *The Abyss*, what it signifies, or how we should react toward it. After a long absence, Silvestri revives the triadic pairing during the film's final act, shown in Figure 2.6b. In the cue "Bud on the Ledge" (1:58:36) he integrates the progression, now between B♭M and Fm, into the hymn-like choral theme; from this point, the modally mixed fifth progression attaches to an immense alien spacecraft and the ability of its strange race to determine the fate of humanity. The **F** transformation thus becomes a signifier of extraterrestrial awe and power. This strictly intratextual clarification, what Matthew Bribitzer-Stull (2015: 4) calls "accumulative association," ensures that the harmonic transformation's latent capacity for cuing wonderment is fully realized.[20]

Of course, this abyssal progression is never heard completely free of cultural associations, even upon its first "unassigned" rendition. Silvestri most likely chose the **F** transformation because of its history in *other* film music in which it suggests adventure and objects of vast astonishment, particularly of oceanic origin (see Chapter 4, n26). In general, signification within a work itself is enriched by and made more legible through a musical idea's *inter*textual contexts. A peculiar sonority, for instance, may be closely tied with a specific affect within a single composer's oeuvre. Such is the case with Bernard Herrmann's famous "irrational" major-minor seventh chord in Hitchcock's films (Brown 1994: 148–174). Restricted and self-contained intertextual networks reward intimate familiarity and insider knowledge, but those are rarely the primary goals for Hollywood film music. More characteristically, the tendrils of intertextual expressivity stretch far—through multiple eras of filmmaking history—and wide—across many film genres and scoring styles. Extrinsic factors tend to be embedded within dense tangles of historical precedent, of which the average listener (or even composer) might not be actively aware. Nevertheless, conscious recognition is not a prerequisite for basic stylistic competency. Filmgoers need only be sufficiently registered with a musical convention and its affiliated styles for that convention to effectively work its expressive magic.[21] Appreciating the way T_2 ratchets up intensity in *Casino Royale* does not mean retracing its associative origins back to, say, Act I of *Tannhäuser* (or, indeed, *Indiana Jones* or *L'Assassinat* or any one gearshifting pop song for that matter).[22] All that is required is prior exposure to *any* texts in which the harmonic-expressive convention is utilized in a clear and memorable way. And in the unlikely case that listeners truly have never heard a given convention before, they may begin to determine its significance by digging into its internal structure.

INTRINSIC MEANING

While extrinsic factors infuse a harmonic gesture with meaning by reaching out to a wider practice, intrinsic factors reside within the gesture itself. They rely on the way overall tonal systems define and delimit musical possibilities and, relatedly, the cognitive dispositions through which harmonic gestures are filtered. Listeners use a variety of metrics to judge aspects like harmonic relatedness, tension, and function, and with the right calibration, such gauges can easily be mapped onto all manner of expressive states. To take a non-chromatic example, let us examine the descending-fifth motion. By virtue of its basis in a consonant interval and its centrality to key articulation in common-practice tonality, a simple T_5 transformation (as in V⇒I) is able to cue affects including—but not limited to—resolution, closure, attainment, strength, and normalcy. Intrinsic factors may also resemble symbolic content, through what Nicholas Cook (1998: 78) calls an "enabling similarity" between differing media.[23] The coiled-up potential energy of a diminished seventh chord, the youthful brightness of the lydian $\hat{\sharp}4$, the alien quality of a tritonal progression—these all rely on mapping internal characteristics (unresolved dissonance, upward chromatic alteration, and diatonic estrangement, respectively) onto emotional states.

Consider again the stepwise tonal transformation, now conceived of as a vessel for various *intrinsic* contributors to expressivity. Bailey identifies the central affect of step modulations as being that of tension and release. This expressive quality appears to reside in three separate varieties of tension: (1) tension as pitch height; (2) tension as psychoacoustic dissonance; and (3) tension as subversion of tonal norms. The first two criteria are immediate "raw" facets of the sonic signal, while the last criterion is hierarchical in nature, dependent upon a network of cognitive preferences and relationships. The non-hierarchical criteria are generally easier to pin down. Across many musical styles, high pitches are linked with an increased sense of energy and mental arousal. This is a natural association (if a largely metaphorical and culturally conditioned one), considering the strain required to produce higher-energy sounds, the sensitivity of the ear to stimuli in the frequency range of screams, and so on.[24] Lower pitch levels, conversely, seem to correspond across styles to a cooler and calmer—if not necessarily positively valenced—affect.[25] Relative dissonance further explains why transpositions by strictly larger intervals, like a third, fifth, or octave, are not usually comparably tense. Semi- and whole-tones rank high on subjectively evaluated scales of dissonance, as corresponds with their more complex frequency ratios, even in just intonation (16:15 and 9:8, respectively). Gestures that are founded on interval class 1 or 2 can thus sound rough, unpleasing, or unresolved—both in the horizontal domain, as chords, dyads, and simultaneities, and in the vertical domain, as melodic lines, progressions, and so on.[26]

Not just any instance of a step progression will sound inherently tense, of course. To understand why some transformations are affectively potent and others neutral, we need to appreciate how they fit into the hierarchical system of functional tonality. Mode-preserving stepwise modulations are distant and/or unusual according to several metrics that reflect the way listeners parse common-practice music. These measurements include proximity along the circle of fifths, the presence or absence of common tones, and the statistical occurrence of various inter- and intra-key progressions. More generally, we expect key changes to be earned through normative processes like well-telegraphed cadences, pivot chords, and so on. When a composer suddenly picks up a theme and deposits it a step higher, these expectations are violated, thus flagging the event for attention and signaling that harmonic business as usual has been suspended. A sizable chunk of the expressivity of Bailey's expressive tonality therefore hinges on the markedness of any and all stylistically uncommon and hierarchically destabilizing tonal gestures.

Cohen (2014: 103–111) observes that in visual multimedia, congruency between internal musical structure and visual information leads to many artistically desirable results: strengthened emotional and semantic associations, increased engagement, and heightened memory for plot details.[27] Structural elements of a progression that "fit" visual or narratival information can reinforce their meanings, while those that conspicuously fail to fit may nuance or subvert them. But internal musical structure is rarely "independent of connections to the world," as Cohen suggests is possible. (2014: 105). Many intrinsic factors also have a hefty cultural component, the affective differentiation of major and minor being one obvious example. All intrinsic factors have at least the *potential* to become culturally loaded. The harmonic destabilization wrought by stepwise modulations, for example, owes to the way musicians have consistently used them in intensity-producing contexts, producing a kind of musical bandwagon effect. Culture and structure are opposite poles of an easily traversable scale, a continuum along which meaning is dynamically generated.[28] Musical structures are never innately possessed of particular meanings; rather, as Cook argues, they have "the potential for special meanings to emerge under special circumstances." (2001: 180). It is ultimately up to the composer to activate some intrinsic associative factors and downplay others to achieve a desired expressive effect.

By way of summarizing the past few paragraphs, Figure 2.7 presents a network for the various intrinsic and extrinsic factors that feed into pump-up modulations.

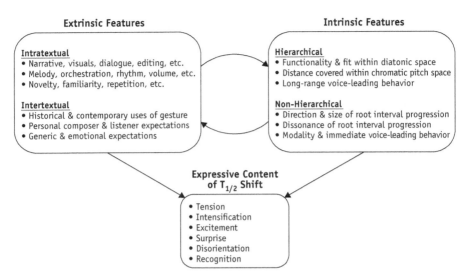

Extrinsic Features   **Intrinsic Features**

Intratextual
• Narrative, visuals, dialogue, editing, etc.
• Melody, orchestration, rhythm, volume, etc.
• Novelty, familiarity, repetition, etc.

Intertextual
• Historical & contemporary uses of gesture
• Personal composer & listener expectations
• Generic & emotional expectations

Hierarchical
• Functionality & fit within diatonic space
• Distance covered within chromatic pitch space
• Long-range voice-leading behavior

Non-Hierarchical
• Direction & size of root interval progression
• Dissonance of root interval progression
• Modality & immediate voice-leading behavior

**Expressive Content
of T$_{1/2}$ Shift**

• Tension
• Intensification
• Excitement
• Surprise
• Disorientation
• Recognition

Figure 2.7 Schematic network for **T**$_{1/2}$ expressive content.

Though the **T$_{1/2}$**-based shift is the only tonal gesture for which I supply such a graph, it is a valuable exercise for readers to devise similar diagrams on their own for the chromatic collections and absolute progressions to come.

***

At this point, it may seem curious that we are still talking about step progressions. Bailey's definition of expressive tonality implies that step relations are uniquely privileged purveyors of tonal tension and release. Yet with so many axes of meaning for even simple triadic harmony to slide along, it feels odd to reserve the label "expressive" for one modulatory procedure, and odder still to affix to it only one continuum of expressivity.[29] The sheer number of extrinsic/contextual and intrinsic/structural influences that flow into an expressive gesture means that it is easy to come by counterexamples. For example, what do we make of the nail-biting climax of Williams's score to *Jaws 2* (1978, 1:55:55)? The cue, entitled "The Big Jolt," houses a rare intensificatory "pump-down" modulation. At the moment of greatest intensity, right as the shark barrels toward the protagonists, the key slings *down* from D♮ to D♭. This **T$_{-1}$** trajectory is neither a subversion nor an exception that proves the rule. The D⇨D♭ shift sounds appropriately terrifying when it occurs, and it does nothing to relieve pent-up harmonic stress. Examples of similar "misbehaving" harmonic significations are rife. And while they do not interfere with the basic soundness of the model presented in Figure 2.5, they do caution against hasty one-to-one ascriptions of musical structure to meaning.[30]

It is not only that inclusion of pump-down modulations suggests widening the scope of expressive tonality. Transpositions of material by intervals *other* than whole and half steps are often called upon to manufacture tension. Tritones and minor thirds—characteristic intervals of the octatonic collection—appear particularly favored for this end. A perfectly customary instance of stepwise intensification occurs in Miklós Rózsa's score *El Cid* (1961, 2:40:45), when the key clambers up from B_{phryg} to C_{min} to D_{oct} in order to mark the meeting of armies in a massive battle. Yet one need only observe the incredible density of modulations elsewhere in the scene (many of them built from minor thirds) to know that other species of transposition are just as capable of generating tension. Furthermore, incessantly modulating action cues like *El Cid*'s demonstrate that tonal change *as such* is itself often expressive of tension. We must acknowledge that any harmonic shift—stepwise, diatonic, chromatic, or otherwise—is capable of generating tension by simple dint of offering something new to the ear. The expressive antithesis of a pump-up modulation, therefore, is not a "pump-down" modulation, but tonal stasis, an unchanging fixity of key.

A generalization of expressive tonality is overdue. Any aspect of pitch design in film—even static monotonality—has the potential to be expressive. What concerns us from here on out is the special sort of tonal expressivity that occurs when harmonic areas succeed one another because something in their relationship bears expressive content. These areas could be chords, keys (as for Bailey), or even more broadly, tonal idioms themselves, like modality or dodecaphony. Crucially, the relationship that spawns this form of expressivity is *transformational*, which is to say it depends on a feeling of active, dynamic change on the musical surface. Transformational analysis, correspondingly, focuses on the details of such changes, such as the particular character of progressions or the placement of modulations. This kind of expressive power rests on the listener's ability to interpret harmonic motions, rather than absolute keys, as principle conveyors of meaning. Keys matter insofar as they facilitate islands of tonal stability or fill in nodes within transformational networks. Nevertheless, I maintain that for a cue to begin in, say, G as opposed to any of the eleven other alternatives, is largely irrelevant to the immediate experience of film music. But if that cue proceeds to hold onto G diatonically, or peppers it with chromatic mediants, or modulates to F♯—those are matters of great consequence.

Generalized expressive tonality is thus distinguished from prolongational tonality, which treats successive harmonic regions as cogs within the larger regulative mechanism of monotonality. And since the specific keys involved in expressive tonality do not really matter, expressive tonality also differs from various forms of symbolic tonality that justify key successions through the connotations of individual regions. Transformational expressivity is efficient and immediate, making it well suited to acting in concert with evocative and imaginative visuals. And no musical style finds itself recruited for these ends more often in film than pantriadicism.

Pantriadic Chromaticism

The sorts of stepwise transformations we have focused on for much of this chapter are by definition "chromatic." That is to say, shifts between like-moded keys will necessarily feature or imply tonal fields of more than seven diatonic pitches, often quite a lot more. Yet expressive modulations by $T_{1/2}$ are just one manifestation of a much larger harmonic style that is based on chromatic relationships between triads. The idiom has garnered many labels from theorists and critics, some of which are apt, others analytical dead ends: nonfunctional chromaticism, coloristic harmony, wandering tonality, polytonality, polymodality, triadic atonality, triadic post-tonality, and so on. The term that I prefer and employ from this point forward is **pantriadic chromaticism** (or pantriadicism for short). Compared to other labels, pantriadic chromaticism is theoretically exacting, but it is also inclusive enough to suit a style whose forms are numerous and sometimes fuzzily related with other ways of exploring tonal space.[31]

Pantriadic chromaticism is a principle of pitch organization in which the musical surface is primarily made up of consonant (major and minor) triads, while diatonic functional norms are not in operation. Right away, emphasis on pure triads distinguishes this idiom from other chromatic styles that partake of complex sonorities or that bury their consonant infrastructures under layers of discordant polyphony. Unlike other forms of expressive chromaticism, pantriadicism is largely nondependent on vertical dissonance. However, this does not mean the music is "tonal," at least in any traditional sense. Because diatonic tonality is a complex and hierarchical phenomenon, the harmonic conventions violated in pantriadicism are tricky to disentangle from one another—in fact, they might even be mutually implicative. Nevertheless, we can identify three norms that pantriadic chromaticism definitely lacks:

1. **Nondiatonicity:** *Pantriadicism avoids close adherence to a single diatonic collection, or near-diatonic collections like the harmonic minor scale, blues scale, etc.*
2. **Noncentricity:** *Pantriadicism lacks syntactically unambiguous projections of a single key center across more than a few chords.*
3. **Nonfunctionality:** *Pantriadicism eschews diatonic functional routines, including fifth motions, cadences, and the tonal phrase model.*

These three criteria offer more descriptive precision than other, potentially misleading formulations like "any chord can follow any other chord."[32] Admittedly, they give more of a picture of what pantriadic chromaticism is *not* than what it is. But even having purely negative attributes at our disposal is useful, as they enable us to notice expressions of the style in context.

While it may be common as a tonal idiom in Hollywood film scoring, pantriadic harmony hardly ever persists across an entire movie's score. Pantriadicism may be likened to a musical special effect, reserved for moments of increased excitement

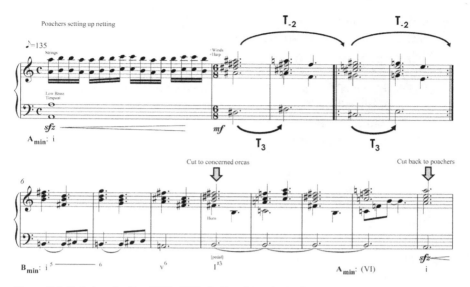

Figure 2.8 Poledouris, *Free Willy*, "Whale Poaching Scene."

or intensified feeling.[33] Composers like Basil Poledouris, who feel comfortable moving between multiple musical styles, often phase in and out of pantriadic harmony freely, as he does, for example, throughout his scores for films like *Robocop* and *The Hunt for Red October*. The passage analyzed in Figure 2.8, from Poledouris's soundtrack for *Free Willy* (1993, 2:35, ▶), provides a concrete demonstration of the three defining (non)features of pantriadic harmony, and how this idiom can behave as a special effect.

Poledouris's cue accompanies a group of whalers as they prepare to capture a pod of killer whales. The excerpted music is particularly illustrative of pantriadic practice because its chromatic patches are set apart from areas of more conventional diatonic and monotonal syntax. Furthermore, unlike the pump-up modulations we have already examined, the interesting harmony occurs within phrase boundaries (intraphrasally) rather than along their fringes. The key of A minor frames the segment but is not in any true sense prolonged by it. Only a small portion—mm. 6–9—adheres to a single diatonic collection, B minor, and this area feels like an island of stability within the cue's otherwise murky waters. The material that establishes the menace of the poachers (mm. 2–7) is thoroughly pantriadic. The abrupt cessation of Roman numerals after the first measure is meant to illustrate how diatonic functionality and centricity is cast into doubt with the arrival of D♯ minor. For example, the second chord in the sequence, F♯ minor, could be heard as fulfilling several distinct functions, some mundane, others truly bizarre: i/F♯m, ♭iii/D♯m, iv/C♯m, or even ♯vi/Am. Whether or not this intrusion of harmonic multistability means that Poledouris has suddenly gone fully atonal is largely an issue of semantics, hinging on one's definition of tonality.

At the risk of getting too far ahead of ourselves, let us stay for the moment non-committal on this question—tonally agnostic, so to speak.

While the gravitational tug of monotonality is indisputably weakened in the *Free Willy* cue, other forces are nevertheless at work in organizing harmony. With the aid of a linear-intervallic sequence in mm. 2–5, Poledouris slips keylessly down from D♯ to C♯, landing finally on B minor. This shift is indicated in the analysis with over-arching T_{-2} transformations. Between each leg of the descent sits an intervening third relation, smoothing the landings and injecting further harmonic mystery into the proceedings.[34] A progression like this, by chromatic third, is perhaps the most stereotypically cinematic of all pantriadic procedures. (Readers might have seen them referred to as "chromatic mediants," though I avoid that label, which suggests the diatonic functional notion of a mediant chord, unless musical context clearly commends it.) Meanwhile, the tritonal oscillation that begins at m. 9 imparts a modicum of measure-to-measure predictability, even as it dismantles all hopes that B major might garner standard functional articulation. The undulations of B and F lend a wondrous aspect to a shot of the alarmed orcas, but soon all is ceded back to the dark realm of A minor, recaptured with an unanticipated but diatonically assimilable resolution (retrospectively VI/$\hat{2}_{pedal}$⇨i). The scene's cetacean protagonists are in trouble, and Poledouris's insecure harmonies make sure we in the audience are warned, too.

Though necessary to define pantriadicism, the conditions of nondiatonicism, noncentricity, and nonfunctionality should not be treated as definitional straitjackets. The border between pantriadic chromaticism and other tonal idioms can be porous, able to blur into pandiatonicism, tethered chromaticism, and other styles I detail in later chapters. Pantriadicism sits at one extreme along a smooth continuum whose other pole is functional diatonic monotonality. Some of the more stereotypical "nonfunctional" chromatic transformations we have witnessed are perfectly capable of operating within the arena of goal-driven monotonal syntax. Major-third relationships between major triads, for example, arise naturally through progressions like I⇨V/vi, IV⇨V/V, and ♭III⇨V. (These are true chromatic mediants.) However, pantriadic chromaticism of the most robust sort tends to work against the functional potential of such intertriadic moves. The anchoring effect of tonal gravity can be instantly undercut by simple strategies like oscillation, unusual phrase and harmonic rhythms, or the accumulation of multiple mediants—forces all present in the Poledouris example.

While pantriadic harmony's preferred state might be of entropic keylessness, under certain conditions even the most twisting of chromatic passages can accommodate fleeting points of tonal reference, which may be accomplished through transformational strategies as well as the brute forces of repetition or duration.[35] A tiny moment in George Auric's score for *Roman Holiday* (1953, 13:30) provides a glimpse of triadic chromaticism that fortifies a key rather than disrupting it. As Audrey Hepburn finds herself within an opulent hall of mirrors, Auric interrupts the larger cue's sneaky tone with a shimmering chain of root-position major triads, BM⇨EM⇨CM⇨DM⇨BM. The sequence is pantriadic inasmuch as it lacks traditional diatonic progressions, which it pointedly shuns in favor of a few "magical" chromatic third transformations. But this is still a far cry from triadic atonality. B-centricity is achieved—or more accurately, asserted—by virtue of the passage's brevity and the B-major bookends that lie on its either side.

Like any other tonal practice, pantriadicism relies on a number of its own conventionalized pitch collections and routines. The familiarity of some of these procedures to the ears of filmgoers can verge on a very loose sort of syntax. Scott Murphy (2014a: 489–490) describes how certain triadic transformations that might seem intrinsically ambiguous out of context are nevertheless deployed in such a way that one triad acquires more tonic weighting than the other. This process could be called stylistic disambiguation. For example, for any CM⇔A♭M type oscillation, all other things being equal, the first chord is more often heard as a stable point of reference than the reverse in American film scores. If musical contexts are strong enough to support functional hearing, then a pairing of C and A♭ is probably heard as tonic and chromatic submediant (♭VI), rather than chromatic mediant (III♯) and tonic, respectively—an effect that, as Murphy notes, is particularly strong when the chords occur intraphrasally, "within a formal unit instead . . . spanning formal units" (2014a: 490). (Exactly this relationship may be found in Silvestri's score to *The Abyss*—n.b. n 20.) Small discrepancies in weighting can thus give rise to larger patterns of usage, and from them the effect of stylistic disambiguation. These harmonic statistics can give sufficiently exposed listeners something to latch onto and form expectations about, even in the absence of traditional tonal hierarchies. The degree of congruency, of perceptual "rightness," is reinforced wherever the filmic forces of narrative cuing and audiovisual synchronization provide strong justification for otherwise unusual musical decisions. As a result, pantriadic chromaticism can feel, if not truly *inevitable* in the sense of diatonic tonality, then at least sometimes fairly predictable.

Altered and Heightened Realities

Earlier in this chapter, I discussed individual transformations such as $\mathbf{T_{1/2}}$ and $\mathbf{F}$ as vessels of expressive content. Pantriadic harmony as an *overall* style may itself be recruited in a similar way, as a harmonic gestalt, over and above any single progression. The expressive associations of this gestalt are consistently applied and received in film, enough so as to speak of an aesthetics of pantriadicism. Richard Cohn, chief theorist of the pantriadic style, has noted its connection with "altered and heightened realities" in the music of the nineteenth century (2012: x). That this aesthetic remains largely intact since the style was imported from Wagner, Debussy, and company is a testament to the enduring markedness of chromaticism. While some scholars have a habit of labeling any nonfunctional harmony as "coloristic" regardless of its structure or behavior, in this case the adjective is fairly apt.[36] Pantriadic harmony glows; it puts the "chroma" in chromaticism.[37] In the hands of countless film composers, it has been the tonal idiom of choice for the weird and wonderful. This all-purpose alterity is used to fulfill four closely related aesthetic needs, all of which involve situations outside the realm of everyday reality: intensification, fantasy, unusual psychology, and sublimity.

1. **Intensification**: We have already seen evidence of the efficaciousness of pantriadic intensification, namely in the knack of chromatic transformations like T_1 and T_2 for ramping up energy and narrative significance beyond what can be produced within diatonic space. Wholesale shifts of key easily accomplish this effect, as with, for instance, the swing from IV/C to I_3^6/E in the midst of a rousing battle speech in Patrick Doyle's *Henry V* (1989, 1:32:19). In this case, the change of harmonic hue follows immediately on the heels of a plagal half-cadence, a local stepwise shift that helps effect a larger-scale modulation by chromatic major third. More so than the particular details of one progression type or another, however, it is the innate changeability of chromaticism—its capacity to subvert expectations and disrupt hierarchies—that makes it perennially attractive as an intensificatory strategy. While we have mostly encountered examples of this aesthetic by way of modulations, more extended progressions can capture the feeling as well. For example, Hans Zimmer recruits a pantriadic sequence [Dm⇒B♭M⇒Fm⇒D♭M⇒E♭m⇒BM⇒Dm] several times through in the *Dark Knight* trilogy (2005–2012) to imply escalation of insurmountable threats.

Chromatic intensification can also add a heightening effect to otherwise realistic events. In Rachel Portman's score for the romantic comedy *Only You* (1994), pantriadic chromaticism is used to lend a larger-than-life, almost mystical quality to the central relationship between Faith (Marisa Tomei) and Peter (Robert Downey Jr.). Portman prepares Faith and Peter's first kiss (53:45) with a steadily rising diatonic line, A5-B5-C6-D6-E6, which is supported by a chromatic chord progression scored with ethereal high strings, DM/A⇒Bm/F♯⇒FM/A⇒Dm/A⇒EM. The passage is both cadential and modulatory in character. Portman smoothly leads away from D major while simultaneously clinching E major as a new tonic— a key that is confirmed right away with a statement of the film's love theme, heard as Faith and Peter give in to their passion. This procedure, of preparing a big thematic statement with a chromatic cadence, is a trope in Hollywood film scoring and will be explored at greater length in Chapters 5 and 6.

2. **Fantasy**: Pantriadic harmony can seem phantasmagoric, as though steered by its own arcane will, rather than by human hands.[38] It is naturally allied with the fantastic, a category which encompasses all sorts of tropes employed constantly in imaginative films: strange settings, mysterious characters, miraculous events, and especially magic and the supernatural. Music in the fantastic vein plays upon the incongruity of chromatic progressions against the backdrop of functional, "natural" syntax. It encourages a stance of hesitation when it comes to deciding between "rational" (tonal, functional) and "irrational" (atonal, chaotic) explanations.[39]

In special cases, fantastic chromaticism may also intimate the *uncanny*, that sensation of spooky familiarity for which film composers often turn to certain dependably strange transformations like **S** (e.g., CM⇔C♯m) and **H** (e.g., CM⇔A♭m). A clear instance of uncanny pantriadicism can be seen in the opening progression from Alexandre Desplat's 2007 score to *The Golden Compass*: [Gm⇔AM⇨F M⇨D♭m⇨FM⇨A♭m⇨Bm⇨A♭M⇨Bm⇨E♭m]. These arcane transformations, not a single successive pair of which fits into any diatonic collection, accompany a disclosure of a hidden magical reality that lurks just behind our own. A similar intimation of otherworldly influence is made through the harmonies that underlie Jon Brion's waltz from *Magnolia* (1999): [Fm⇨E♭m⇨Adim⇨D♭m⇨Gdim⇨A♭m⇨ E♭M . . .]. The serpentine melody and high degree of surface dissonance in its harmonization add even more to the theme's distinctly off-kilter quality, perfectly in line with the inexplicable interconnections that are drawn across the film's out of balance and fallen world.

The potential for uncanniness is amplified when triadic chromaticism takes root in genres and styles where it is not accustomed, such as in popular idioms or diegetic music. Both forms of estrangement are at work in a source cue by David Lynch and Dean Hurley in 2017's *Twin Peaks: The Return* (Part 8, 28:40) in which a phonograph plays a hybrid of industrial ambient music and slinky 1930s instrumental jazz. The record cycles through a glacially paced chordal succession with almost no functional or teleological foundation: Am⇨Em⇨Bm⇨G♯m⇨Em$^{7(♭5)}$⇨Cdim⇨G♯m⇨Em, and so on. The scene accompanied by this music is similarly static and obscure, consisting of four minutes of barely edited footage of a mysterious room within a mysterious tower inhabited by mysterious occupants. The primary effect of Lynch's cue is dislocation. The music has enough trappings of familiar jazz to evoke standard generic associations concerning time period, sexuality, cosmopolitanism, social status, and so forth. But its aimless, looping pantriadic structure works to contradict—or at least confuse—the clean cinematic connotations of jazz, rendering cryptic what is normally semiotically clear, surreal what is often filmically coded as "realistic."

3. **Atypical psychology**: The uncanny potential of pantriadicism has also tied it to portrayals of altered mental states. Surveying a number of well-known scores, including *Spellbound, Lost Weekend, Vertigo,* and *Freaks,* Michael Long extrapolates a trope of "chromatic psychosis" in which "the subconscious, neurotic, or psychotic is . . . rendered by a classical inscribed signature effect for expressive madness: the sudden manifestation of unprepared, nonfunctional chromaticism" (2008: 160–161). This style topic—which for Long also includes devices like the theremin glissando and other strange timbres—also is exploited for less pathological conditions, such as meditation, out-of-body experiences, and oneiric frames of mind.

In early twenty-first century cinema, pantriadicism seems to have also attached to desirable states of heightened cognitive activity, such as creativity, problem solving, and intense intellection. For example, James Horner makes use of a variety of chromatic cells (e.g., CM⇨Em⇨E♭M) in *A Beautiful Mind* (2001) to paint the interior life of schizophrenic math genius John Nash; roving pantriadicism captures both Nash's febrile creativity and his teetering grasp on reality (Eaton

2008: 162–178 and 2014; and Lehman 2013b).[40] Traditionally, altered states of consciousness have been evoked through disorienting chromatic collections like the hexatonic and whole-tone scale. And while some of the sonorities associated with these collections, like the augmented triad, are symmetrical (and thus not ideally modeled by neo-Riemannian operations), they can nevertheless help spawn tonal spaces in which pantriadic harmony emerges.[41]

4. **Sublimity**: Of all the expressive uses of pantriadicism, the sublime is most directly linked to the idea of chromaticism-as-special-effect. Sublimity is the feeling evoked by things vast and incomprehensible and is thus well matched with pantriadicism, with its ability to suggest large tonal distances and structurally ambiguous spaces. The sublime is among the most heavily theorized concepts in aesthetic philosophy and is often split into substates and subcategories. Depending on its presentation, sublime stimuli may inspire dread, confusion, wonderment, and divinity—the last two being the focus of Chapter 5 and 6, respectively. Although its most stereotypical evocations in film music involve mammoth orchestral forces blasting away at fortissimo dynamics, quieter examples of pantriadic sublimity are not rare. The composer Vangelis's atmospheric cue for a flight over futuristic Los Angeles in *Bladerunner* (1982, 9:50) includes a quiet and gradually paced exploration of the space around E major, E♭ major, and C major. The awe-inspiring music includes numerous surface-level embellishments of these tonal regions, but at no point do they hew to any single diatonic collection.

In practice, all four of these aesthetic buttons are often pressed at the same time for maximum weirdness. Elmer Bernstein's score for *Ghostbusters* (1984) abounds with examples of pantriadic harmony fulfilling these various expressive ends simultaneously. The malevolent god Gozer garners music that alternates between pantriadic and non-triadic whole-tone harmony. The short passage in Figure 2.9 accompanies a scene late in the movie (1:22:35, ▶), wherein Gozer takes psychic hold of two unlucky characters. Bernstein's music manages to represent the dreamy state of the possessed protagonists, the awesome spectacle of Gozer's arrival, and the snowballing supernatural craziness of the film's climax. The reduction includes a glimpse of the music that comes before and after this pantriadic passage as well—harmonically immobilized material in E♭$_{wt}$ and A$_{dor}$,

Figure 2.9 Bernstein, *Ghostbusters*, "Summoning Gozer."

respectively. Transformational arrows link the chords—all root position—according to the interval between their bass notes.

The top melodic line of this progression is actually not all that chromatic—mm. 2–4 make use of only white notes, and the addition of the chromatic G♯ and B♭ in m. 5 could conceivably fit into a modally enriched scale like F major/minor. The harmonization, however, tells a different, more demonic story. Note the proliferation of devilish tritones between triads—four T_6s in all—each obliterating the tonal claim of the chord that preceded it. Lest the tritonal cascade grow too predictable, Bernstein varies the transpositional interval between each two-chord pair: in order, we hear T_7, T_4, T_9, and finally T_{11}. Only one of these non-tritonal transformations—the T_7 from A♭ to E♭—is even conceivably diatonic as a relationship between two major triads. The chromatic bass line that unspools beneath this progression produces two interlocking semitonal wedges—a slippery D3-E♭3-D♭3-E♮3 on the strong beats and a slithery A♭2-A♮2-G♮2-B♭2 on the weak ones.

With all these tonal signifiers for awe and intensity and *weirdness* blaring away, the score is at distinct risk of taking itself too seriously. And it is here that Bernstein's musical wit serves him well. At m. 6 of the example, the cataclysmic chorale instantly reverts to a spunky and oblivious A-dorian theme—the moment the camera cuts away from Gozer's supernatural lightshow and onto the four ghost-busting protagonists, plodding up a stairway to confront him. The shift of tone, from the incredible to the insouciant, makes it seem as though the harmonic catastrophe of the previous four measures were happening on an entirely different planet.

Back to the Surface

Although the expressive aims of pantriadic chromaticism are often abundantly clear, finding a suitably systematic method for analyzing the style is less straightforward. Pantriadicism is a boundary idiom, belonging neither to common-practice tonality nor to full-blown atonality. Accordingly, it tends to chafe against frameworks like Schenkerian and pc-set theory that are devised for uncomplicated instances of one or the other.[42] This intransigence often flares up when one attempts to distinguish between a chord and a key, ordinarily a clear-cut matter in functional tonality.

Take the short passage in Figure 2.10 from Jerry Goldsmith's *Alien* (1979, 13:39, ▶)), a score unafraid to indulge in extravagant triadic chromaticism—that is, when not otherwise occupied with purely atonal horrors. The progression in question accompanies a tense landing sequence early in the film and seems to channel some of the weirdest pantriadic energies from Scriabin and Vaughan Williams. Is the D major in m. 2 the segment's initial tonic? If so, does that mean the subsequent A♭ minor is heard as some obscure chromaticized function with relation to D? Or vice versa? Are we hearing a string of four modulations and five autonomous keys, each one its own tonic? Or a succession of pure, floating sound, no one triad more or less centric than the last? Must we choose?

Figure 2.10 Goldsmith, *Alien*, "Landing Sequence."

Without the aid of cadences or prolongational counterpoint to lock down tonics, music in this style can seem to squirm nervously across tonal space. Over the course of just a few measures, pantriadic patches may career through ostensibly incompatible modes of hearing, moving from "totally atonal" to "constantly modulating" to "every chord is its own tonic." Like any source of musical ambiguity, the chord/key quandary is suffused with expressive potential. But ambiguity can also become something of a distraction, an analyst's problem more than a cinemagoer's one. When our attention is fixated on resolving unanswerable questions like "which side of this tritonal oscillation has more claim to tonicity?" we risk running in interpretive circles, overlooking other matters more pertinent to the experience of harmony in film. This confusion is one of the chief justifications for tonal agnosticism, and a great advantage of the neo-Riemannian methodology insofar as it allows bracketing of such questions. The "Landing" from *Alien* illustrates this point. While from the standpoint of chord/key analysis, the music might seem intensely ambiguous, disjointed, and even illogical, from a transformational basis it is elegantly and quite perceptibly organized. (At this stage, the reader might feel comfortable analyzing the modal and transpositional relationships between successive triads. What, if any, pattern emerges?)

The chord/key issue often boils down to a question of scale: over what range does a particular triad establish its influence? Pantriadicism can, at least in principle, operate over arbitrarily long musical spans. The cue from *Now, Voyager* analyzed in Chapter 1, for instance, is typical in the way its region-to-region motions are unpredictable and thoroughly chromatic. Those same nonfunctional, noncentric forces that steer the musical middle ground in Steiner's music are arguably operative at an even deeper level in *Now, Voyager*, given the symbolic key scheme that governs the score as a whole. Transformational analysis is still a viable entry point for examining tonal design at these gross scales. However, the sacrifice of aural immediacy that often comes with inspecting tonality from a bird's-eye view must be justified by explanatory fruits greater than mere demonstration of "cohesion" or "unity."

There remains a good reason that most transformational analyses cleave rather staunchly to patches rather than whole pieces: pantriadic harmony is a creature of the musical surface. By their very nature musical "special effects," instances of triadic chromaticism are often limited to short spans. The cue remains the space in which sustained compositional discourse in film takes place, where harmonic choices of perceptible scope may shade and guide the narrative. But pantriadic harmony has a habit of blurring tonal hierarchies and disrupting unities. In doing so, it effectively narrows our harmonic perspective—already shortened by the formal and temporal exigencies of film underscore—onto the experiential surface or, at most, shallow middle ground. Those levels, I maintain, are where chromatic harmony's expressive impact is greatest and its structural ramifications most interesting.

Here, then, is another advantage of neo-Riemannian analysis: its facility with and indeed preference for dealing with the musical surface in all its sensuous, unruly complexity.[43] This is something of a reversal of normal value systems in music theory. The surface has long sat, as Robert Fink and others have noted, on the disprivileged side of the surface/depth binary.[44] Celebrating the aesthetic riches of the surface does not mean we must discount the possibility of *anything* operating on more rarefied levels of cinematic experience. Nor should the deprioritization of hierarchy be taken as a repudiation of formalism *tout court*.[45] But before leaping into speculative and arcane (if fascinating) formal readings of film underscore, it seems wise to develop a theoretical vocabulary tailored to those aspects of film music that hit the hardest. To that end, let us establish how pantriadicism actually emerges on the musical surface.

Pantriadic Forms

ABSOLUTE PROGRESSIONS

Pantriadic harmony is not a homogeneous style; rather, it assumes a number of interconnected but differentiable forms. Sometimes, nothing more than a single progression between two triads suffices to dissolve a cue's diatonic, centric, and functional fortifications. Such on-the-spot applications of chromaticism may be enormously salient events in underscore; the more isolated and detached from surrounding tonal context a triadic transformation seems, the greater its expressive potential. A heavily underlined interchordal motion may be understood as an **absolute progression** (AP): a harmonic relationship whose meaning is taken solely on its own, immediate terms. The idea originates with the German theorist Ernst Kurth, who, in his attempt to grapple with Wagnerian chromaticism, noticed that certain harmonic successions stuck out of their surrounding contexts, vibrant and unmediated. Kurth saw such progressions as being justified by their "sonic appeal as such . . . [by] the unique effect of connecting two harmonies"—not, as is normally expected, through their emplacement within a larger regulative tonal framework (Kurth, Rothfarb [trans.] 1991: 121).[46]

Besides pure isolation, what enables intertriadic progressions to sound as if they existed in the middle of a tonal vacuum? Scott Murphy explains that absolute hearing may arise when a chordal pairing "is atypical—for example, the two triads cannot fit within a diatonic collection—or when the juxtaposition avoids participating in a larger harmonic trajectory but self-encapsulates somehow, often through undulation" of two triads (2014a: 484). To those conditions for harmonic self-sufficiency we might add the following: contrapuntal and melodic simplicity; textural uniformity; long duration; phrasal segregation and dynamic emphasis; and coincidence with important visual or narratival events. The unifying feature of these compositional choices is that they siphon interest *away* from distracting musical processes so that the particular progression between triads is flagged for greater than normal attention.

If we focus on the intrinsic quality of a progression, certain absolute progressions easily fulfill the three criteria of pantriadic harmony. However, an AP on its own is not pantriadic. Some may truly be able to "annihilate" tonality in one fell chord change, such as claimed by theorist Ernö Lendvai and corroborated by Cohn with respect to the hexatonic pole relation (e.g., CM⇔A♭m).[47] Yet, given the right sort of emphasis, a sense of centricity may still linger in even the most unassimilable-seeming progressions. Nor must an AP even necessarily be chromatic: diatonic progressions can be used to this effect as well. Indeed, the clearest example we have encountered yet of an absolute progression is Silvestri's initial use of the perfectly diatonic **F** transformation in *The Abyss*. This example illustrates a common procedure by which APs arise in film music: **chordal oscillation**, in which the music swings back and forth between two triads. Note how in Silvestri's usage, all musical parameters appear coordinated to draw maximum emphasis onto the C♯M⇔G♯m transformation. The music's volume, range, and orchestration swell for the big annunciation of that oscillation, collectively screaming, "Pay attention to this harmony!" At the same time, Silvestri strips away any linear complexity, which is irrelevant to the progression's "sonic appeal as such." The simple, blocky chordal undulation does away with any melodic or contrapuntal distractions, leaving behind only a pure, ringing repetition of what will eventually become an important *leitharmonie*.

This is not to say oscillations cannot also be integrated into perfectly grammatical themes; Bear McCreary's memorably uneasy main theme for *10 Cloverfield Lane* (2016), for example, revolves entirely around a chromatic undulation of Em⇔C♯m and its transpositions. Yet oscillation on its own cannot clarify which chord in a two-triad pair is more stable. By continually swaying between two fixed harmonic objects, oscillatory progressions can, however, counteract some of the centrifugal tendency of pantriadic progressions. Imagine a binary star system in comparison to a single sun; chordal oscillations exert a more complex and dynamic sort of harmonic gravity on the listener than a solitary tonic does, but they are still capable of holding a larger (tonal, expectational) structure in place.

SEQUENCES AND CYCLES

Though their ability to seize a listener's attention is undeniable, absolute progressions on their own are not the purest representatives of pantriadic chromaticism, inasmuch as two triads alone can cover no more than half (six pitch classes) of the chromatic universe. Other pantriadic procedures involve multiple triads linked in extended musical thoughts. **Chromatic sequences,** in which tonality is steered by the reiteration of one or more transformational cells, were historically among the first ways that composers experimented with nonfunctional, noncentric harmony. The heavily chromatic portion of the aforementioned cue from *Free Willy* is a good demonstration of this principle. Poledouris's sequence adheres to a <+m3, –P4> root-interval pattern, which, after just two iterations, has visited ten out of twelve pitch classes.

An even more exotic chromatic sequence may be found in Lorne Balfe's score for *Lego Batman* (2017, 0:38:00). Here, a rapid spin around chromatic space (Dm⇨D♭M⇨Fm⇨EM⇨G♯m⇨GM⇨Bm⇨B♭M⇨Dm) follows a <–m2, +M3> interval pattern, with modal alternation with each chord. In neo-Riemannian terms, this amounts to an **S·L** cycle, an unusual but symptomatically "filmic" way of producing an overall <+m3> third sequence (Lehman 2013b: 7–8). The spiraling profusion of atypically juxtaposed triads is perfectly suited to Robin's geeky exuberance in discovering the Batcave, while a pair of flanking third motions around "tonic" D Major (DM⇔ B♭M and FM⇔DM) provide more sturdy, but no less pantriadic bookends.

A special sort of pattern arises from **interval cycles,** in which a *single* interval serves as the sole transformational impetus behind a musical span—often but not necessarily sequential.[48] These cycles generate highly symmetrical pitch collections, useful as "off switches" for tonal gravity. The whole-tone collection, for instance, may be thought of as the product of an interval cycle that iterates major seconds. When combined with the mode-shift transformation (**P**) on consonant triads, major- and minor-third cycles in particular can be produced with the added benefit of extremely tight voice leading. Smooth cycles like these provide a sense of transformational and textural uniformity amidst modal variety. This effect can be desirable to film composers who seek ear-catching but not anarchic pantriadic progressions. Lengthy cycles are the harmonic equivalent of the barbershop-pole illusion, always spinning in one direction yet never seeming to progress anywhere.

Two interval cycles, and the scales they generate, are of particular importance to film music. We have already encountered the **octatonic scale** on several occasions, including *Raiders of the Lost* Ark, *El Cid,* and *Escape from the Planet of the Apes.* It is based on a minor-third <m3, m3> interval cycle that divides the octave up symmetrically. The octatonic scale can be conceptualized in a variety of other ways:

- As a scalar alternation of half steps and whole steps
- As a union of any two diminished seventh chords
- As a product of three **T3** transformations
- As a product of three chained **P**arallel and **R**elative transformations

Figure 2.11 provides a handful of representations of the octatonic scale, including a symmetrical scale, a union of diminished chords, and chord cycle. As an abstract pitch collection, the octatonic can be represented by the set class 8-28

Figure 2.11 Octatonic collection.

Figure 2.12 Hexatonic collection.

[0134679T], a grouping that emphasizes semitones, minor thirds, and tritones. Eight consonant triads pop out of the collection, a parallel major/minor pair pegged to each note of a fully diminished seventh chord. Other tertian sonorities that emerge from the octatonic scale include the diminished triad, dominant seventh, half-diminished seventh, and minor-seventh chords. There are only three unique octatonic scales, and they can be differentiated by the unique pitch classes they feature: $oct_{0,1}$, $oct_{0,2}$, and $oct_{1,2}$. Note that, while there are four perfect fifths with which to build the collection's eight triadic subsets, there are no perfect fifths available *between* triads, meaning the basic functional motion of diatonic tonality, Dominant, is not available in octatonic music. As a result of this intervallic disposition, octatonic sonorities and progressions have a spiky, bracing quality, well suited to scenes of tension and excitement.

The six-note **hexatonic scale** can be described in similar terms, and Figure 2.12 provides an analogous guide to its construction. Hexatonic harmony results from a major-third <M3, M3> interval cycle, and heavily features that interval, along with m2s and m6s (and their enharmonic counterparts, d3 and A5). Like the octatonic scale, it can be interpreted in several ways:

- As a scalar alternation of half-steps and minor thirds/augmented seconds
- As a union of two semitonally adjacent augmented triads
- As a product of three **T4** transformations
- As a product of three chained **P**arallel and **L**eading-Tone transformations

The scale's distinctively gapped, exotic-sounding quality derives from its ic1-ic3 interval pattern. The four possible hexatonic scales ($hex_{0,1}$, $hex_{1,2}$, $hex_{2,3}$, and $hex_{3,4}$) each support six triads, two each per note of an augmented triad. Other associated sonorities include the augmented triad, major-seventh, minor-major seventh, and augmented-major seventh chord. Like the octatonic scale, the hexatonic scale precludes root motion by fifth and thus the ability to assert diatonic functionality. Its affiliation with the augmented chord and chromatic mediant relationships has lent the collection long-standing associations with disorientation, wonderment, and the supernatural; indeed, Michael Friedman dubs the associated set class 6-20 [014589] the "magic hexachord" (1990).

Figures 2.13 and 2.14 provide illustrations of both of these collections from the music of Jerry Goldsmith—a composer second perhaps only to Bernard Herrmann in terms of a long-running fascination with pantriadic harmony. The passage in Figure 2.13 accompanies a scene in *Total Recall* (1990, 1:20:15, ▶) in which the amnesiac protagonist's memories are accessed by a mind-reading alien. The creature repeats a mantra "open your mind," which is exactly what Goldsmith's hypnotic music asks of the listener. The larger cue from which this ten-chord progression stems is thoroughly octatonic, featuring increasingly fervent downward minor-third cycles in different octatonic collections. This specific portion of the cue sits in $oct_{0,2}$ and is flanked by nearly identical third cycles in $oct_{0,1}$. During the course of this cycle, all eight triads of the $oct_{0,2}$ collection are eventually visited— Dm, DM, Bm, BM, G♯m, A♭M, Fm, FM—though Goldsmith takes a few transformational shortcuts to retain sequential variety. Instead of using transposition (T_n) to analyze the passage, the excerpt's triadic transformations are described with neo-Riemannian operators and compounds. An intrepid reader might consult the next chapter for a formal description of **P** and **R**. For now it is sufficient to describe why these labels are warranted: the cycle is impelled by extremely tight

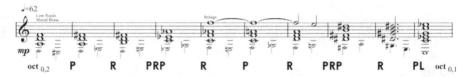

Figure 2.13 Goldsmith, *Total Recall*, "The Mutant."

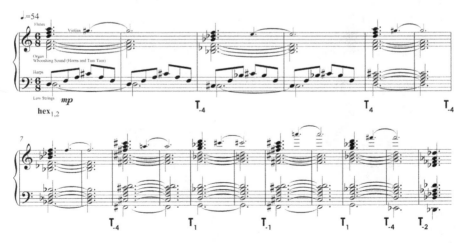

Figure 2.14 Goldsmith, *Star Trek: The Motion Picture*, "The Cloud."

voice leading and individual pitch displacements, rather than wholesale chordal shifts.

Goldsmith's score to *Star Trek: The Motion Picture* (1977) is suffused to an extraordinary degree with nonfunctional chromaticism, and the centerpiece cue "The Cloud" (56:39–1:00:32, ⊙) is its most sustained presentation of this idiom.[49] Figure 2.14 presents a reduction of the first seventeen measures of this bravura sequence, which sees Captain Kirk and crew pilot the *Enterprise* into a massive energy cloud. The visual design of this fearful cosmic entity is marked by hexagonal symmetries and apertures. And while likely an accidental synchronicity, Goldsmith's music too is peppered with six-sided symmetries of its own through its recourse to the hexatonic scale. With an opening clearly inspired by Herrmann's similarly hexatonic prelude to *Vertigo*, "The Cloud" charts out the space created by the $hex_{1,2}$ scale, first oscillating between Dm^{Ma7} and $B\flat m$ ($T_{+/-4}$), then moving down another rung of the cycle to $F\sharp m$. This second leg of the musical paragraph, from mm. 9–17, is less confined to the original hexatonic scale, however. $F\sharp m$ alternates with its upper semitonal neighbor, Gm, rather than its T_{-4}-twin, Dm. And instead of settling back onto Dm where the cue began, Goldsmith "cadences" via T_{-2} onto its lower semitonal neighbor, $D\flat m$—a close, but inexact doppelgänger of the cue's harmonic entry point. The passage thus gives the outward impression of being a perfect major-third cycle, but in actuality it manages to surreptitiously land in new, alien territory.

Though I have arrayed these two examples to showcase octatonic and hexatonic cycles, it is worth reiterating that neither is *purely* based on those respective pitch collections. The *Star Trek* example's departures from $hex_{1,2}$ are more evident, but *Total Recall* also makes use of non-$oct_{0,1}$ pitch classes in its creeping bass line. Given the uniformity of both scales (and, in the hex-collection's case, limited number of available pitches), it should not be surprising that composers often enrich passages with extra-scalar pitches, even if the prevailing impression is still one of scalar consistency. It is in this somewhat counterintuitive sense that the $E\flat$ in m. 2 of "The Mutant" or the $G\sharp$ in m. 1 of "The Cloud" are "chromatic" pitches: they are decorative, inherently less stable, and potentially more expressively marked than their intra-scalar counterparts.

DISCURSIVE CHROMATICISM

Lengthy pantriadic passages that do not adhere to regular sequential or cyclical patterns may be placed into the broad category of *discursive chromaticism*. To see a manifestation of discursive chromaticism in action, let us pick up where we left off at the end of Chapter 1, with a tense cue from John Williams's score to *Return of the Jedi*. In my earlier analysis of "Faking the Code," I glossed over a short introductory passage between the initial $B\flat$ and $E\flat$ chords in which the key/chord issue is strongly in play (⊙). Figure 2.15 expands what happens during this twenty-second span, which sees the heroes departing the Rebel Fleet to embark on their dangerous mission. Because the passage is athematic,

Figure 2.15 Williams, *Return of the Jedi*, Opening of "Faking the Code."

we can observe the harmonic effects of pantriadicism in an unusually unadulterated state, free from the formal expectations of the franchise's well-learned leitmotifs.

These six measures go out of their way to deny the listener any of the predictable comforts of functional tonality. The transformational vocabulary is limited to chromatic moves, with five shifts by major third and three by minor second mode flip. The density of these nondiatonic transformations means that the chromatic aggregate is completed, almost trivially, over the course of the progression. But chromatic saturation does not imply that the passage is a random triadic free-for-all. The consistency of move types between these melodically unraveled triads imparts a feeling of dread logic, and the passage's bookending T_4s—associatively pungent transformations in *Star Wars*—lend it an odd sense of balance as well. If any stop along this tonal journey is felt to be more stable than its neighbors, it is the result of secondary, non-hierarchical factors like duration and triadic inversion—examples of what theorist of music cognition Fred Lerdahl calls "salience conditions" (2001: 320). The opening B♭ minor is barely established as a region before being liquidated by the digressive activity beginning in m. 2. From that point forward, Williams journeys from one dark triad to the next in a series of wilting downshifts, nearly all of which contain one or more drooping semitones. Though there is no single tonic to unify these six measures, there is a unified affect: a sinking feeling that with every successive triad, the situation grows more dire.

While the harmonic logic of "Faking the Code" rests on the local alternation of T_1 and T_4-transformations, other, more holistic factors contribute to its expressive content as well. One distinguishing aspect is its voice leading. Observe that the majority of chords progress to one another as a unit, retaining the same inversion, register, and spacing. Voices always move in the same direction and by the same intervallic increment, lessening the impression of non-independence of musical lines. This procedure is commonly known as **parallel voice leading** (or **planing**) and, unlike other means for generating pantriadic harmony, is more an importation from Debussyan Impressionist harmony than Wagnerian Romanticism.[50] Planing is widespread in certain strains of film scoring—especially varieties that privilege stepwise motion, and thus direct transposition, from chord to chord. Stephen Meyer points out that the use of parallel chords is prevalent in scores for historical epic films, particularly those from Miklós Rózsa such as *Quo Vadis* and *Ben Hur* (2015: 81–82, 153). Meyer argues that planing in those contexts is used to connote antiquity (by its association with venerable traditions like parallel organum), authenticity (by evoking certain modal and folk practices), and strength (by the uniform, massed voice leading). Planing need not be chromatic; indeed, much of Rózsa's "imperial style" is actually grounded in diatonic church modes. Even so, parallel treatment of triads will quickly slip into pantriadic territory if the modal quality of individual triads remains invariant. However, despite its propensity for producing nonfunctional progressions, parallel voice leading is not the driving force behind most forms of pantriadic chromaticism; our exploration of displacement and inversion-based neo-Riemannian transformations in the next chapter will make this clear.

Another significant aspect of pitch design in Williams's "Faking the Code" is *modal* consistency. When nearly every chord in a progression is minor, a tremendous magnification of the negative emotional valence of individual triads takes place. The effect of **intensified minor chromaticism** is to engulf an entire passage in the dark associations usually pegged to a singular harmonic object, multiplying the expressive power of the ever sullen minor triad. Intensified minor chromaticism is associated with threats and evils beyond human understanding, particularly when the composer is exploiting tritonal transformations, synonymous with diabolism for centuries. The gothic flavor of this procedure makes it a prized trope in horror scoring, particularly from the 1980s onward. Intensified minor chromaticism forms the basis of themes from *The Fog* (John Carpenter), *The Evil Dead* (Joseph DoLuca), *The Ninth Gate* (Wojciech Kilar), *Hellraiser* (Christopher Young), *Hellboy* (Marco Beltrami), *Young Frankenstein* (John Morris), and *Dracula: Dead and Loving It* (Hummie Mann). That the last two examples are satires rather than straight horror films testifies to associative strength—parodistic appropriation of a musical trope being the surest indicator that it has achieved widespread generic legibility.

Slightly less common in film music but equally unnatural by the standards of functional harmony is **intensified major chromaticism**, which prioritizes the motion between major triads in nondiatonic relationships. This species of pantriadicism has somewhat more varied expressive capacities than its minor cousin, able in some contexts to sound sublimely threatening, as we have witnessed with "Gozer" from *Ghostbusters*, for example.[51] More often, however, the affect of this "hyper-major" idiom is one overexposed brightness and overoptimistic enthusiasm, making it well matched to moments of giddy triumph or enchantment. Intensified major chromaticism in Hollywood is often closely tied to lydian harmony, specifically progressions of the type [CM⇔DM]. We have already seen this refulgent idiom in James Horner's logo theme for Universal Studios, in which every chord seems to garner its own T_2-related chromatic neighbor. Indeed, intensified major chromaticism is one of the most immediately identifiable of the composer's many distinctive "Hornerisms," appearing in similar guises but suiting different dramatic ends in films like *Star Trek II*

("Genesis Countdown"), *Aliens* ("Resolution and Hyperspace"), *The Rocketeer* ("To the Rescue"), *Sneakers* ("The Escape"), *Apollo 13* ("Reentry"), *Titanic* ("Take Her to Sea, Mr. Murdoch"), and *The Amazing Spiderman* ("Becoming Spiderman"). Purging all minor chords from one's vocabulary may seem like a blunt way to achieve a positive musical affect. Yet harmonic overkill like this has been an indisputably effective tool for Horner and other composers who have few compunctions about emotional blatancy.

Modal consistency produces a stable affect, an expressive gestalt based on the fixed quality of the constituent sonorities. In other ways, however, intensified major/minor chromaticism exemplifies the fundamentally transformational character of pantriadic harmony. The effect in "Faking the Code," for instance, does not revolve around one key or chord in particular, nor does it rely on the hierarchical networks that focal chords tend to erect around themselves. Instead, the ear traces a pulsing, shifting journey taken by an initial sonority, a gradual process of metamorphosis more structurally and expressively salient than the pitch identity of any one of the momentary locations along the way. Nowhere is this restless quality more evident than **mixed chromaticism**, which is any form of triadic chromaticism that includes both major and minor triads and that does not adhere to a set sequential or cyclical pattern. This is the pantriadic style best modeled by NRT, and the one we will examine closely in the coming chapter. Suffice it to say, mixed chromaticism fits many subject matters, including all four of the pantriadic aesthetics enumerated in the previous section. It is especially well suited to fantastic montage sequences, where it can provide a form of sustained eventfulness—continuity through transformation—to counteract the dispersive effects of rapid cuts and shifts in spatial or temporal perspective.

***

My insistence on the dynamical character of pantriadic music does not entail that functional diatonic music does not also have a critical transformational aspect. Nor do I mean to suggest that there are not subtle gradations in harmonic weighting at work in even the most tonally amorphous pantriadic patches. Taking into account metrical, durational, and contrapuntal information, one could still analyze most of the passages we have examined in terms of (weakly) differentiated stable/superordinate and embellishmental/subordinate harmonies. Analysis along these lines could even result in serviceable prolongational reductions. Nevertheless, pantriadic tonal spaces encourage a listening strategy that is *primarily* transformational. We do not navigate extensive passages of pantriadic harmony by fruitlessly hunting for a tonic that lurks hidden behind the musical surface. Rather, we tune in to the unique relational quality between chords, whether at an immediate level as with absolute progressions or in terms of an expressive gestalt like with discursive forms of chromaticism.

Over the course of this chapter, I have proposed that harmonic change is an essential expressive resource for film composition, and as a consequence, the idea of musical transformation should be foremost among our analytical priorities in investigating this repertoire. I identified a small but highly "cinematic" style, pantriadic chromaticism—a tonal idiom whose colorful associations and syntactical slipperiness grants it a high expressive potential, and whose varied manifestations will occupy us for the remainder of this book. Though I have already traced out at a transformational methodology, the next chapter will be devoted to the technical apparatus of NRT and its application to film music. It can be easy to become lost in the details of nomenclature and the charms of systematization. Let us not lose sight of targets of film-score analysis beyond pure musical structure: matters of an affective, narratival, stylistic, and—of course—audiovisual nature. These concerns shall remain in the background, even as we dive headfirst into neo-Riemannian theory.

3

Neo-Riemannian Theory at the Movies

Theoretical Background

There is a strain in musicology that holds pantriadic chromaticism to be, at its heart, anomalous. On this view, pantriadicism subverts normative functional tonality but does not offer a systematic tonal practice in its place. It is a daub of harmonic color, a phenomenon of the musical surface whose disruptiveness lends it expressive power but not coherence. Suzannah Clark, noting the persistence of this attitude in the reception of Franz Schubert's music, cautions us not to use the inherent otherness of chromaticism as an excuse to abandon analytical precision. The otherworldliness of, for example, the hexatonic pole relation (e.g., CM⇨A♭m) ought not imply "that the theoretical explanation needs to match the sound, or that we need to be kept in the dark" (2011b: 202). Rather, it should be a call to action, a spur to invent new and more inclusive forms of coherence, for "music theory to catch up with the musicological imagination." Clark claims that providing a theoretical account of an uncanny harmonic effect no more divests it of wonder than does explaining a good magic trick. Indeed, it offers a new form of wonder, the kind that arises from deeper understanding. The theoretical lacuna located around chromaticism can, Clark argues, be filled (in part) with the tools of neo-Riemannian theory. And it is therefore to the nuts and bolts of this system that we now turn.

The goal of this chapter is to take the three issues previously described in mostly abstract terms—expressivity, transformation, and pantriadicism—and develop from them the methodology of neo-Riemannian theory. In the following pages I hope to provide a user-friendly introduction to the NRT toolkit. Admittedly, neo-Riemannian techniques alone cannot fully describe how we parse triadic chromaticism in film, either unconsciously as passive viewers or actively as close readers. But when it comes to providing a way of thinking about the "*ars pantriadica*" on its own terms—not as a distorted form of tonality or a transitional step on route to atonality—no framework is more illuminating, no approach more able to open our minds to broader issues of musical coherence and expressivity.

NRT helps articulate many aspects of how chromatic harmony operates in film. But there remains a curious tension innate to filmic pantriadicism that makes the idiom resist theorization: it is at once (a) clichéd and well-understood and

(b) intrinsically challenging and disruptive. The comprehensibility of pantriadic harmony resides in a strategic feeling of tonal ambiguity, a kind of easily intelligible form of musical unintelligibility. This is not as paradoxical as it sounds. Plenty of other cinematic techniques, like jump cuts and nonlinear editing, are inherently unruly, but become understood after sufficient exposure. Pantriadicism's "weirdness" nevertheless does lead to a tricky question: can we make sense of this music without at the same time stripping it of its disruptiveness, its intended feeling of difference?[1] It is my belief that NRT can thread this needle, largely thanks to its transformational nature and its eclectic collection of analytical tools. I sketched some of these assets in the previous chapter and now expand on them more thoroughly.

NRT revolves around a fundamental conceptual dichotomy, first formulated by music theorist David Lewin.[2] Lewin proposed two modes of understanding musical relationships: the **interval**, which is discrete and object-like; and the **transformation**, which is dynamic and predicate-like. The intervallic perspective approaches musical relationships with the attitude of a passive witness, measuring out distances between discrete objects. The transformational perspective, as we have seen, treats these relationships as processes and actions that the music, and/or an engaged auditor, enact in some way. (Whether these actions are performed, discovered, or imagined depends on the analyst's preference, plus some assumptions concerning listener psychology).[3] Transformational analyses emphasize motion, energy, and action; they invite us to see harmony not as something that is, but something that *does*.[4] When cultivated in the study of film music, this *transformational attitude* ensures precedence is given to the harmonic gestures that power meaning, impart expressivity, and erect dramatic structures in time.

Despite its acceptance into the disciplinary mainstream of music theory, NRT is less a theoretical monolith than a web of interconnected insights and tools, all of which aim to inform the analysis of nonfunctional, noncentric triadic chromaticism. The designation of "Riemannian" stems from Lewin's revival of a cluster of ideas originating from the theorist Hugo Riemann (1849–1919), and nineteenth-century German music theory more generally. Especially relevant to Lewin was Riemann's interest in formalizing the relationships between triads. During his long career, Riemann put forth a number of systems for analyzing triadic harmony. One such system revolved around his basic tonal functions, which we now take almost for granted in modern music theory: the tonic, dominant, and subdominant. In Riemann's scheme, these tonal pillars could be subjected to an assortment of alterations based on small pitch displacements, without the chord's underlying tonal identity changing. The resulting alterations ("apparent consonances," in Riemann's lingo) allow for aberrant chords to be related to a more paradigmatic tonal function. For example, a D♭ major triad in the key of C might be interpreted as an altered form of the minor subdominant, with D♭ a semitonal substitute for the chordal fifth of the iv chord, C♮. That minor subdominant, in turn, is the product of a displacement of the normally natural sixth scale degree, A♭ for A♮. Strange, nondiatonic sonorities may thus be tamed, treated as modified and displaced variations of an underlying tonal pillar.[5]

Despite the relational quality of these descriptions, they remained for Riemann adjectives *for* chords, rather than actions performed upon them. However, Riemann also proposed a different system, the *Harmonieschritte* (harmonic steps), which had a more patently transformational character. Like the apparent consonances, this system could result in elaborate, pseudo-algebraic labels for chords, but the emphasis is more clearly on the relationship *between* triads rather than the identity of one triad within the context of a given key. These relationships are based not so much on pitch displacement as on transposition by root interval (chiefly by fifths and major thirds) and inversion (chiefly by flipping the direction a triad was built from its root, either up or down).[6] Sticking with the example of a CM to D♭M progression, Riemann's account for the chromatic chord is *Gegenleittonschritt* (counter-leading-tone step). This term derives not from a step relationship as the German label suggests, but a conjunction of a mode-flipping fifth transformation (yielding an intermediary Fm, like before) and then a downward major third. The combinatorial potential of these operations is high, enabling the listener another means of relating extremely distant tonal regions to one another in a rational and systematic way.[7]

Lewin's innovation was to take a number of the Riemannian non-transformational functional displacements and treat them *as if* they were *Harmonieschritte*— that is, as actions on a chord, rather than intrinsic properties of a chord. This change in perspective thereby infuses a useful, if inert, system of relating triads with transformational energy. Three displacements, adapted into a group of transformations, have become synonymous with neo-Riemannian theory: **L**, **P**, and **R**. I formally define these neo-Riemannian operations (NROs) in the next section, but for now it is worth noting that they can be thought of as actions that displace a single pitch by one or two semitones. **L** turns C major into E minor and vice versa (swapping the pitch C for B). **P** flips a triad's mode, transforming C major into C minor (swapping E♮ for E♭). And **R** takes us from C major to A minor (exchanging G for A).[8] Relevant to Lewin's project is the fact that these three transformations do not alter the underlying function of a triad. For example, applying **L**, **P**, or **R** to a F-major triad in the key of C does not change the chord's essential subdominant function. The resulting chords of Am, Fm, and Dm are all syntactically, if not sonically—and certainly not qualitatively—interchangeable.

The functional implications of these neo-Riemannian operations retreated in importance as more people began exploring this new theory. Further refinements to the neo-Riemannian system of relations came from scholars like Brian Hyer, Henry Klumpenhouwer, and Richard Cohn, who continued Lewin's project of actualizing the transformational potential of Riemann's labeling system.[9] They accomplished this project by (a) laying out the algebraic group structure formed by these transformations, and (b) more explicitly wiping away the need for functional tonal context. This process makes NRT quite distinct from its function-obsessed paleo-Riemannian predecessor. As Nora Engebretsen (2011: 355) observes, modern neo-Riemannian theorists "retain names associated with Riemann's function theory" while adopting the mindset of the *Harmonieschritte*, describing "only local relationships between chords, saying nothing about the meaning of those chords within a key."

While listeners of all sorts of music are already aurally well accustomed to these transformations, the act of providing them with an explicit name and a system for combining them is tremendously useful. The neo-Riemannian lexicon makes recognizing triadic transformations easier; it assists in relating diverse harmonic phenomena (or distinguishing superficially similar phenomena); and it invites all sorts of larger-scale textual and stylistic explorations, which we will embark on shortly. However, despite serving as neo-Riemannian's unofficial emblems, **L**, **P**, and **R** do not represent all that the theory is interested in, nor must they be recruited in order for an analysis to be neo-Riemannian in spirit. NRT, as expanded and codified over the course of the 1990s and 2000s, involves a number of conceptual priorities that together render it highly useful for the analysis of pantriadic film music. These attributes also distinguish it from other theories of "Second Practice" tonality, such as tonal pairing or chromaticized diatonicism, which we encountered back in Chapter 1. The five traits outlined below, inspired by a similar list by Cohn (1998) all relate in some way back to the shift in perspective from intervallic to transformational thinking.

Combinatoriality: A well-defined group of triadic transformations like **L**, **P**, and **R** can model any conceivable relation between the twenty-four major and minor triads. (In fact, **L** and **R** alone are sufficient.) By themselves, these *unary* transformations assume the status of NRT's harmonic atoms. More complex progressions can be provided with unary labels, or they can be "built" out of these atoms, resulting in transformational *compounds* of varying length and intricacy. Repeating compound transformations can generate harmonic cycles and the pitch collections (e.g., hexatonic, octatonic) associated with them.

Parsimony: The neo-Riemannian transformations privilege progressions with smooth, incremental voice leading and retained common tones. **L**, **P**, and **R** all hold two pitch classes (pcs) fixed while shifting the remaining pc by no more than a major second. The NROs are the only progressions that can do so, and accordingly they are esteemed highly in a repertoire in which harmonic shifts—and so some argue, harmonic coherence—are accomplished with parsimonious voice leading.[10] The emphasis on parsimony also alerts the analyst to instances of linear *roughness*, which may arise through complex progressions lacking common tones, but also from abstractly parsimonious progressions in cases in which literal voice leading is disjunct rather than smooth.

Contextuality: Neo-Riemannian transformations are context-sensitive, with differing transformations able to convey differing interpretations of the same harmonic event. The individual members of the **LPR** group possess another, more mathematical kind of context dependency; they act in equal and opposite ways on triads of opposing mode. This "dualistic" symmetry allows, for example, for apparently different-sounding progressions to be treated in a highly specific sense as equivalent.[11] Other transformations, including all transpositions, are by contrast less contextually driven, responding in the same way to major and minor triads.

Tonal Agnosticism: As actions on pitch classes rather than diatonically specified scale steps, the NROs are noncommittal with regard to both tonal function and enharmonic spelling. This agnosticism frees the analyst from some of the stumbling blocks inherent in studying pantriadic chromaticism, such as the way functional theories can break down when swamped with symmetrical progressions, enharmonic paradoxes, and ambiguous tonal centers.[12] Tonal agnosticism does not so much repudiate the existence of stable pitch centers as it brackets the issue, allowing analysts to concentrate on other interesting aspects of harmony without distraction.

Spatiality: Triadic transformations can model how listeners traverse tonal space, allowing the analyst to represent harmonic progressions visually in such a way that reveals interesting structural or perceptual features. Tonal geometries can be used for a variety of purposes, including representing musical pathways, calculating intertriadic distances, and discovering musical patterns. A predetermined geometry may be determined by the iteration of a number of operations, which grants it consistency and generalizability. Alternatively, the music being analyzed may itself determine the shape of a network; though more ad hoc, such diagrams are often more visually elegant and better at reflecting the transformational particularities of a specific piece.

Taken together, these features provide a framework for approaching cinematic chromaticism. The highly formal nature of some of these tools should not dissuade more critically oriented readers, however. A good neo-Riemannian analysis is neither a statement about the group structure of a set of operations, nor the presence of tight voice leading, nor the path taken within tonal space. Least of all is it a rote application of transformational labels. Rather, NRT provides a means for characterizing the harmonic relations that a listener experiences, or might wish to entertain, while parsing a musical text. Every transformation label amounts to an *interpretation* of a musical event. NRT's richest resource lies in how it enables events to be read in terms of others, as part of a network of musical potentialities. It allows the characterization of relationships readily apparent, and the discovery of relationships buried but significant.

Triadic Transformations in Theory

Triadic transformations are the basic words in neo-Riemannian theory's vocabulary. Having a precise language for triadic progressions saves us from the under-descriptive catch-alls that frequently afflict discussions of chromatic repertoires—ideas like the evocative but non-explanatory adjective "coloristic" or the far too loosely applied notion of polytonality.[13] Particularly problematic is the term "unrelated" when it is used to describe any unconventional succession of keys or chords. Smuggled in by this descriptor is the erroneous assumption that only diatonic intervals can serve as yardsticks for meaningful tonal relationships.[14] However, what seems genuinely erratic or unrelated by diatonic logic can exhibit just as sturdy a logic by other relational parameters.

The inventory of transformations employed for the rest of this book is presented in Table 3.1. The supplementary Table 3.2 illustrates each transformation using the smoothest possible voice leading, once on C major and once on C minor. Even readers already familiar with the standard neo-Riemannian nomenclature

Table 3.1 **Triadic transformations**

	Transformation	Action on CM/Cm	Definition
Basic	T_n	$T_2(CM) = DM$ $T_2(Cm) = Dm$	Transpose by *n*-many semitones
	Parallel	P(CM) = Cm P(Cm) = CM	Go to parallel major/minor
	Leading Tone	L(CM) = Em L(Cm) = A♭M	Go to leading-tone exchange major/minor
	Relative	R(CM) = Am R(Cm) = E♭M	Go to relative major/minor
Derived	Slide	S(CM) = C♯m S(Cm) = BM	Go to triad with same third ($\hat{3}$)
	Near Fifth	N(CM) = Fm N(Cm) = GM	Go to fifth-related triad where common tone is $\hat{1}$ of major triad/$\hat{5}$ of minor triad
	Far Fifth	F(CM) = Gm F(Cm) = FM	Go to fifth-related triad where common tone is $\hat{5}$ of major triad/$\hat{1}$ of minor triad
	Hexatonic Pole	H(CM) = A♭m H(Cm) = EM	Go to hexatonic pole
	Dominant	D(CM) = FM D(Cm) = Fm	Go to triad of same mode down a perfect fifth
Supplemental	Identity	I (CM) = CM I (Cm) = Cm	Leave triad unchanged
	$f'(x)$	D′(CM) = GM D′(Cm) = Gm	Inverse form of transformation.
	$fg(x)$	LSP(CM) = E♭m LSP(Cm) = AM	Compose multiple transformations in left-right order
	$f \cdot g(x)$	L·SP(CM) = E♭m L·SP(Cm) = AM	Emphasize or clarify a particular subdivision of a compound transformation
	$\sim\!f$	$\sim$LP(CM) ≈ EM^{Ma7} $\sim$LP(Cm) ≈ A♭m^{Ma7}	Fuzzy transformation, where input and/or output chords are not pure triads

Table 3.2 **Triadic transformations on C major and C minor**

Action on Major Triad

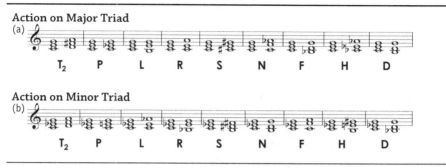

| | T_2 | P | L | R | S | N | F | H | D |

Action on Minor Triad

| | T_2 | P | L | R | S | N | F | H | D |

should spend some time with this chart, as there are a few idiosyncrasies specific to *Hollywood Harmony*. For true newcomers, it is worth memorizing, playing, and seeking out all of these progressions.

Table 3.1's first column presents the name and symbol that stands for each transformation, and the second column demonstrates how it acts on a sample triad. The third column provides the simplest definition possible for each transformation. Note that these are not necessarily the most mathematically elegant definitions. Triadic transformations may be defined in a variety of ways, and differing characterizations will capture differing relational qualities. Generally, definitional criteria for triadic transformations involve root progressions and the presence of common and displaced tones, but they can also be described, somewhat less intuitively, as inversions about fixed pitches or dyads.

The inventory is organized into three families of transformations: basic, derived, and supplemental. The first four entries fall within the basic family and constitute the most atomic types of transformations. First is the transposition operation T_n, which acts on all three triadic pitches simultaneously and treats major and minor triads in the same way. As we have seen, transposition is at play whenever a cue's tonal center moves up or down by step. The T_n operation also proves useful in accounting for ambiguous modal progressions, parallel voice leading, and repetitions of the same thematic material at differing pitch levels. When transpositions are tinted by a change in mode, such as happens with the filmically commonplace progression Cm⇒DM, T_n can be appended with a P operation. For example, T_2P(Cm) = DM.

The other three basic transformations are the canonical neo-Riemannian operations (NROs) introduced a few paragraphs earlier: **P**, **L**, and **R**. The *Parallel* operation **P** reverses a triad's mode. By shifting a triad's third by chromatic semitone, **P** will always technically be chromatic within a diatonic context, even though the triadic root remains fixed. The *Relative* transformation **R** takes a triad to what, in a functional setting, would be considered its relative major/ minor cousin—a chord rooted a minor third away. This change involves moving one voice by a whole step, making it slightly "rougher" than the other two, consummately smooth, basic NROs. The *Leading Tone* transformation **L** may be less familiar for English-speaking musicians, but it describes a move similar to its counterpart, **R**. With **L**, one pitch moves by semitone to produce a chord a major third away.[15] It is worth re-emphasizing that, while the terms parallel, relative, and leading tone might be used in diatonic theories to refer to specific scale degrees or chords, those functional echoes are relics of earlier modes of thinking and can be ignored (or, perhaps better, bracketed). The NROs presume no fixed point of tonal reference; whether acting on a major or minor triad, **P**, **L**, and **R** say nothing of which side of the progression bears more tonal stability. This looseness is in keeping with the overarching tonal agnosticism of neo-Riemannian analysis.

Together, the basic NROs capture the three unique ways one can get from one consonant triad to another by moving one pitch by step. Voice-leading parsimony is thus implied between the pitch classes of NRO-related triads, though smoothness might or might not be realized in a specific musical texture.[16] The NROs represent minimally complex ways of navigating tonal space when our yardstick is voice leading and common-tone retention. Because of this capability, and the fact that they can be chained to form more complicated compound transformations, the NROs serve as a useful way of gauging harmonic proximity/distance. Transformational complexity can thus be added to our preexisting intuitions about tonal distance as, for example, a function of intervallic span, complexity of frequency ratios, and relatedness to a contextual tonal center.

The next family in Table 3.1 includes derived NROs, which, like the canonical NROs, all yield triads of the opposite mode of the input triad. The "derived" aspect of these particular transformations stems from the fact that they may be defined, if one wishes, in terms of compounds of the basic operators.[17] However, there are good reasons for assigning these progressions unary labels. **S**, **N**, and **F**, in addition to being common and highly distinctive progressions in Hollywood, can be thought of as mirror images of **P**, **L**, and **R**.[18] For example, where **P** preserves a triad's fifth (ic5) and shifts its third ($\hat{3}$) by semitone, *Slide* (**S**) preserves the third and shifts its fifth by semitone.[19] **N** and **F** work analogously, although one must use an admittedly peculiar definition of triadic root in order to define the preserved scale degree. It is easiest to think of *Near Fifth* (**N**) as the comparatively smooth mode-flipping fifth relation, the one that nudges two voices in parallel by semitone. *Far Fifth* (**F**), by contrast, is the comparatively rough fifth relation, moving the two unfixed pitches by whole tone.[20] **H**, the *Hexatonic Pole,* is a rare but extensively theorized progression, and has to it a marked quality that ensures it leaps out of almost any context.[21] It may defined in terms of simpler operations (as **LPL** or **PLP**) or, alternatively, as the transformation that takes a triad to the M3-related chord with which it shares *no* common tones.

One last derived progression is a nod to Riemann's original functional conception of triadic interrelationships: *Dominant* (**D**). This transformation is defined as the operation that takes a chord to its tonic in the manner of a V⇨I or v⇨i resolution. It is algebraically equivalent to $\mathbf{T_5}$ but implies a functional resolution while transposition merely describes upward or downward motion.[22] Note that, in a system I have touted as being tonally agnostic, $\mathbf{D}$ is the inventory's sole functional operator. Its inclusion is justified because it is *the* fundamental progression of diatonic tonality and has a way of showing up even in the most digressive pantriadic patches.[23] The interface of functional and nonfunctional chromaticism will be dealt with in a sustained way in the final chapter.[24] Until then, the reader is asked to accept that the oddball $\mathbf{D}$ behaves differently from the way that standard NROs do. $\mathbf{D}$ is unique in possessing a sense of what Steven Rings (2011b) calls harmonic intentionality; the $\mathbf{D}$ominant transformation "points" toward a tonic and to the broader harmonic hierarchy that tonality implies. Along with $\mathbf{T}_n$, $\mathbf{D}$ is also non-dualistic, meaning it acts in the same way for triads of both modes. Compare the behavior of the dualistic neo-Riemannian operators: L, for example, takes a major triad up to the minor triad sitting an M3 above it, while it does the exact opposite for a minor triad, sending it *down* an M3. This behavior is part of the reason that the NROs are *contextual*, producing equal but opposite effects on input triads of differing mode.

A third family of supplementary relations in Table 3.1 includes a few formally necessary transformations like the identity (**I**) and inverse (′) operations, the latter of which is chiefly useful for transmuting $\mathbf{D}$ into $\mathbf{D'}$, meaning "go *to* the dominant." This portion of the inventory also describes how transformations are combined. Any single unary operation can be joined with another to form a *compound*, thereby describing a more complex move across tonal space. Normally, compound transformations will be written without gaps, as with the ternary compound **LSP**. Because NROs are not commutative, it is important to read these in the correct order, as acting on triad from left to right, Given **LSP**, for instance, perform **L** first, then **S**, then **P**. On occasion, it may be useful to demarcate subdivisions within a more complex transformation. In those cases, the algebraic symbol for composition (the dot "·" symbol) is employed. **LS·P**, for example, achieves the same result as **LSP**, but the orthography implies that **LS** groups separately from **P**. This notation may be useful to illustrate if, for example, **LS** is a motivic transformation in a score, and at some point it is subjected to a variation involving an additional shift of mode (**P**).

The final supplementary component of our inventory is the symbol ~, which indicates that the attached progression is a *fuzzy transformation*. Fuzzy transformations are required because, however appealing pure triadic harmony is to many film composers, other sorts of sonorities find their way into pantriadic textures all the time: incomplete triads, diminished and augmented triads, seventh chords, chords with suspensions, polychords, and so on.[25] In some cases, reducing out the non-triadic components so that only an abstracted pure triad remains (a "*Klang,*" in neo-Riemannian terms) represents an acceptably small tampering with the harmonic content of a passage, and no special labels will be employed. However, for cases in which those components are sonically essential, I use the ~ symbol to denote a *strictly informal* degree of fuzziness, and the affected transformation still operates on the underlying triadic subsets within the specified chords. For example, an **~LP** transformation could take a C-major triad to an E-major^{Ma7} chord, or, just as consistently, C major^{Ma7} to E major.[26]

One of the benefits of the transformational inventory I have presented is that it shrinks the universe of triadic progressions down to a manageable number. Progressions that are superficially dissimilar, like CM⇨AM and E♭m⇨F♯m, can be collapsed into a single category defined by some important commonality. All the NROs are **involutions**, meaning that they are their own inverse, returning to the input triad after two applications; this characteristic is in contrast to all transpositions except T_0 and T_6, and many, but not all, compound transformations. The fact that a single transformation can describe progression backward and forward in this way makes the NROs well tailored for analyzing chordal oscillations between triads of opposite mode. This is a hugely widespread practice in Hollywood, no doubt because modal contrast equals affective contrast, and oscillatory progressions are capable of delivering such contrasts efficiently and repeatedly.

Occasionally, the transformational apparatus can get in the way of the simplest explanations of chromatic harmony. For example, the NROs privilege progressions between modally mismatched triads, while rendering progressions between like-moded triads more transformationally complex—even, as is often the case with absolute progressions, when they sound indivisible in context. (It may also be desirable to describe modally mismatched progressions that are complex according to the NROs, like, say, **PRPRL**, in simpler terms.) There is utility in separating out "major" and "minor" versions of dualistic progressions, particularly when one is describing absolute progressions or *leitharmonies* with strong extramusical associations. One can envision scenarios in which it is *not* advantageous to conflate, say, a motivic CM⇨AM-type transformation with its dualistically equivalent E♭m⇨F♯m motion, even though both can be analyzed as **RP** compounds.

Transformation theorists have found a variety of ways of addressing these issues. One approach is to craft a system that grants every pairing of triads a unique label. This is the strategy taken by Scott Murphy in his own (2014a) study of transformation theory and film music.[27] Murphy's triadic-tonal progression classes (TTPCs) account for every conceivable intertriadic relation—all forty-eight of them—with a simple and economical description.[28] Murphy's framework has advantages and trade-offs. Unlike the NROs, Murphy's TTPCs are defined in terms of centricity, with one of the chords in a two-triad progression counting as "more tonic" than the other. This characteristic makes the TTCPs adept at describing chromatic transformations when one of the triads feels comparatively stable, and the TTCPs can therefore help distinguish patterns of differential weighting of certain progressions across film idioms.

At the same time, the TTPCs lose the tonally agnostic quality of the neo-Riemannian operators. Because they provide each progression a unique name, the TTPCs work best at characterizing absolute progressions, but they fare less well in extended pantriadic passages. As Murphy acknowledges, the TTPCs are not true transformations: they describe a class of musical objects and thus do not really "act" on triads. This limitation means they cannot be deployed in the same combinatorial fashion as the NROs. Murphy's TTPCs provide a simple and uniform way of describing inter-triadic relationships, but this elegance comes at the expense of some of the explanatory power and analytical flexibility of **L**, **P**, **R**, and company.

Another answer to the potential shortcomings of neo-Riemannian analysis is proposed by Richard Cohn. Cohn challenges the assumption that compound transformation labels necessarily imply mediation. He suggests instead that a transformation like **LP** can represent a "unitary Gestalt whose name happens to have two syllables" (2012: 30).[29] This attitude is embodied by his decision to assign the hexatonic pole relation the **H** label, rather than **LPL** or **PLP**; one can see that Cohn views the **LPR** group as being useful but not entirely required to characterize intertriadic relationships. Still, something is undoubtedly lost when all transformations are reduced to unary progressions—chiefly, the algebraically built-in metrics of distance, and the ability to interpret complex transformations contextually.

My solution to the issues that motivated Murphy and Cohn's alternative systems is a compromise. In certain cases, I might refer to the application of a transformation f to a triad of a specific mode: f(M) for major or f(m) for minor. Thus, all CM⇨AM-type progressions may be described by **RP**(M), and all E♭m⇨F♯m-type progressions by **RP**(m).[30] This description restores modal specificity without implying tonicity and can be useful for conveying like-moded progressions as being, in a sense, "unitary Gestalts." Just like Murphy's TTPCs, these are no longer true transformations; they act in only one direction, and need to be paired with their reversed forms to capture oscillations.

In general, my preference is not to add additional machinery to the neo-Riemannian apparatus, but rather to acknowledge that, like any theory, it is necessarily reductive and cannot convey all aspects of music with perfect fidelity. It is better to let NRT tell its own analytical story and to rely on prose and diagrams to fill out a more holistic picture of how a musical passage works. Though having labels aids analysts in noticing the occurrence of certain progressions more readily, triadic transformations are not an end in themselves. It is incumbent upon analysts to decide from among the various different operations and compounds at their disposal, to determine what interpretation this or that particular progression suggests in context. Then the analysts must impute meaning into the patterns they play out in actual music, just as one would for other descriptive vocabularies, like diatonic Roman numerals or pc sets. This richer, more interpretive stage is of course the most rewarding part of any music analysis.

Triadic Transformations in Context

EXAMPLES FROM ELLIOT GOLDENTHAL

With the technical background of neo-Riemannian theory now established, we can return to analyzing film music. The next few pages display Table 3.3. Each row is populated with a musical excerpt by Elliot Goldenthal (▶) that illustrates one of the triadic transformations. Only the identity (**I**) operation is omitted, as it is usually a trivial transformation to depict in an analysis.[31] As much as possible, I have chosen moments that accompany a striking visual image or dramatic event. The passages are transcribed in such a way that the pertinent operation always occurs between measures 2 and 3. (In a few cases, this choice leads to some creative re-barring or re-metering). Some of the examples include multiple iterations of the transformation being highlighted, or a series of interesting chromatic progressions beyond the showcased operator; readers are encouraged to play through each and to see if they can assign transformational labels to anything not already indicated.

I have assembled this transformational menagerie from Goldenthal's oeuvre for a few reasons beyond simple consistency. Despite the limited extent of his filmic output, Goldenthal has been one of Hollywood's most dependably chromatic composers, with a special taste for ear-catching pantriadic harmony. Goldenthal's compositional craftsmanship is exceptional, his orchestrations particularly inventive. But when it comes to triadic chromaticism, he often eschews complex counterpoint, busy melodies, and densely active textures. This restraint brings his triadic transformations into high relief, making them unusually affecting in context and useful for study when taken in isolation. The foregrounding of pure triads distinguishes the eclectic Goldenthal from his similarly polystylistic mentor, John Corigliano, another (much less frequent) film composer whose music also skirts tonal boundaries but less often presents triadic transformations so nakedly. Stylistically, Goldenthal's chromaticism draws more heavily from German late Romantic models, with strong echoes from Mahler, Strauss, and early Schoenberg.

Most of Goldenthal's scores, even those for non-fantastical films like *Michael Collins* (1996), positively swirl with triads in unusual relationships. At the same time, the hallmarks of functional diatonicism—especially V⇔I motions—can be astonishingly scarce. One instance of fairly conventional diatonic syntax is the (minor) **D**ominant that occurs within in an expansive lament in his score to *Public Enemies* (2009). More typical, however, are examples like the merely functionally allusive **N** progression in *Demolition Man* (1993). In this excerpt, the near-fifth relation is flanked by destabilizing chromatic moves (**PRP** and **PRPR**) and supports a melodic line driven by a semitonal descent. A passages like this one raises the question of where to place Goldenthal's music along the spectrum of tonal idioms. The composer attests that he holds no "differentiation in my head between tonal and atonal; I either hear melody or I hear sonority" (Wherry: 2003). This claim seems odd when one takes into account only the

Table 3.3 **Triadic transformations in the scores of Elliot Goldenthal**

Film, Transformation, and Description	Progression
Final Fantasy (1:05:45)	
T_6 (Am) = E♭m	
Giant spirit monster looms over soldier, who resigns herself to her imminent death	
Titus (0:07:30)	
P(DM) = Dm	
Ceremonial war choreography concludes; general removes mask	
Alien[3] (1:47:15)	
L(DM) = F♯m	
Heroine prepares to sacrifice self into giant vat of molten metal	
Michael Collins (0:03:20)	
R(Am) = CM	
Somber street scene of aftermath of failed 1916 Dublin uprising	
Sphere (0:33:34)	
S(Fm) = EM	
Scientists marvel at impossible, glimmering sphere	

(continued)

Table 3.3 **Continued**

Film, Transformation, and Description	Progression
Demolition Man	
(1:37:50)	
N(F♯m) = CM	
Villain schemes about creating perfect society right before betrayal by henchmen	
Cobb	
(1:34:40)	
F(F♯M) = C♯m	
Ty Cobb travels to Georgia to meet estranged daughter	
Interview with the Vampire (1:08:45)	
H(BM) = Gm	
New Orleans consumed in inferno as protagonists escape by boat.	
Public Enemies	
(1:43:00)	
D(F♯m) = Bm	
Dillinger's moll Frechette is arrested	

Pet Sematary

(0:02:40)

$\mathbf{LP}(\text{Em}) = \text{Cm}$

Opening credits, scene of creepy ramshackle cemetery, Steven King's name

A Time to Kill

(0:53:20)

$\mathbf{F}(\text{F}\sharp\text{M}) = \mathbf{P\cdot LR}(\text{F}\sharp\text{M})$

$= \text{Bm}$

Imprisoned vigilante has conversation with wife.

Batman Forever

(1:22:26)

$\sim\!\mathbf{T_6P}(\text{D}^{7(\flat 9)}) \approx \text{A}\flat\text{m}^{\text{add6}}$

Batman and love interest have nighttime romantic liaison.

rampaging Pendereckisms (incontrovertible atonality) or stirring adagios (incontrovertible diatonic tonality) that turn up in Goldenthal's filmography. But considering the pervasive, terrifically "chordy" brand of nondiatonic, noncentric, nonfunctional harmony typified by these excerpts, it is clear that Goldenthal's pantriadicism fits accurately into the strange space "between tonal and atonal."

ASSOCIATIVITY OF NEO-RIEMANNIAN TRANSFORMATIONS

In addition to illustrating the sound of the neo-Riemannian transformations, the cues in Table 3.3 exemplify the associative content of these progressions. While it is not my intention to provide a thorough guide to the cinematic associations of every intertriadic progression—they are too many, and too semiotically changeable—a few quick generalizations can nevertheless be drawn. Hollywood, after all, prizes accessibility and legibility, and Elliot Goldenthal's chromatic progressions, for all their power and craftsmanship, trade in some very well-established expressive conventions. I provide an extremely cursory overview of the bulk of the triadic relations, followed by a more in-depth exploration of two of the most arresting of the lot, T_6 and S.[32]

Goldenthal's use of the Parallel progression to shift from D major and minor in *Titus* (1999) draws on that transformation's connotations of duality and opposition. In this particular case, **P** provides an early suggestion of the two sides to the title character's fractured personality—honor and barbarity, eloquence and insanity. Compared to **P**, the affect of the Leading Tone operation is more determined by the modal quality of the input triad. L(M) is frequently tied to a feeling of sadness and loss, as evidenced by a study from Murphy on the progression (2014b). The undulation between DM and F♯m in the example from *Alien³* draws on L(M)'s bittersweet disposition, with Goldenthal's music providing a preemptive elegy for Ripley as she prepares to sacrifice herself. While similarly capable of expressing both delicate sentiment and profound loss, L(m) is more often tied to matters of mythic significance in Hollywood, a connotation to which we will return in Chapter 5.[33] Compared to the other NROs, the Relative progression is too familiar a diatonic functional progression to shoulder particularly robust associations for either of its modal guises. However, in the right settings it conveys a feeling of authenticity, resolve, and seriousness, as demonstrated in the *Michael Collins* excerpt.

The Near Fifth progression can conjure up an alluringly exotic feeling—an association no doubt linked to the $\hat{5}$–$\hat{6}$ modal mixture the transformation strongly implies, which has a tradition, especially in Romantic era music, of connoting non-European cultures. The delicate orchestration surrounding this transformation in *Demolition Man* suits the villain's conceit of a pure society with "the beauty of a flawless pearl," all imperfections of human conflict polished away. The similarly allusive Far Fifth transformation has a variety of associations—nature, ominous portent, depth, venerability, vastness. Goldenthal's autumnal music for *Cobb* (1994) seems particularly inspired by the music of Strauss, with the nexus source for the undulating **F** progression being the expansive opening to the early tone poem, *Aus Italien*.[34]

Two hexatonic progressions, **Hexatonic Pole** and **LP/PL**, are heavily freighted with extramusical associations in Hollywood. As the most tonally extreme transformation involving major thirds, **H** has a long history of intimating catastrophe, death, and transcendence. It is progression with one foot in the grave, so to speak. Cohn (2004) characterizes the relation's affect as "uncanny" in the sense theorized by Ernst Jentsch (1995 [1906]) and Sigmund Freud (2003 [1921]): the eerie, paradoxical familiarity that can accompany seemingly unfamiliar phenomena. The clash of BM and Gm that occurs during a city-consuming conflagration in *Interview with the Vampire* (1994) draws more on the catastrophic connotations of the progression than its uncanniness, though considering the film's undead *dramatis personae*, Goldenthal's progression remains generically appropriate.

Though less chromatic than its polar cousin, **LP/PL** has perhaps the most emphatic and consistent expressive content of all triadic progressions in film, though its connotations are more strongly constrained by mode than many other transformations. The major version, **LP(M)**, is a favored device for suggesting amazement, both as a floating pantriadic progression or as a tonally tethered I⇒III♯. Its expansive and bright quality owes to the upward root motion and implication of "sharpward" key shift; C major, for example, hosts four fewer sharps than the LP-related E major. The same wondrous connotations hold even more strongly for the reverse form of the transformation, **PL(M)**, whose diatonic correlate is the Romantic dream progression par excellence, I⇒♭VI (Taruskin 2005: III/96). Curiously, neither transformation appears to be a major part of Goldenthal's harmonic idiolect, though examples can be found throughout the work of nearly every other major contemporary film composer.[35]

Both "major" and "minor" versions of the **LP** transformation turn on a feeling of harmonic unnaturalness, a contravention of the accustomed diatonic order in which major-third based progressions like i⇒♭VI or vi⇒IV are commonplace. **PL/LP(M)** exploits the positive potential of this "otherness," swinging the door open to new, utopic worlds. On the other hand, the progression's evil twin, **LP/PL(m)**, bear a strong attraction to the affective "dark side." In his study on the nineteenth-century origins of the transformation and its importation into Hollywood, Matthew Bribitzer-Stull (2012) dubs it the "Tarnhelm progression." His label derives from its prototypical use in Wagner's *Ring*, in which it denotes an evil artifact and maleficent magic in general. Bribitzer-Stull observes the progression's lasting linkage to matters of "mystery, dark magic, the eldritch, and the otherworldly" (2015: 144). It is the tonal calling card of Darth Vader, Voldemort, Gollum, and many other memorable cinematic villains. Goldenthal's deployment of **LP(m)** as part of a i⇒♭vi⁶ motion in *Pet Sematary* (1989) is textbook "Tarnhelm" in its suggestion of spooky, concealed malevolence.[36] Note the characteristic semitonal displacements of the pillars $\hat{1}$ and $\hat{5}$ of the home triad, pitches that are flayed outward in opposite directions, as though being tugged by invisible tonal tendrils of ill intent. Their function as chromatic neighbor notes may be clear, but this linear clarity is at the expense of triadic coherency, as these displaced notes fall on en-harmonically contradictory scale degrees ♭$\hat{6}$ and ♯$\hat{7}$ (or stranger still, ♭$\hat{1}$). **LP(m)** is a tonal corrupting influence, perverting the expected diatonic ♭VI—a precious out-post of major brightness within the dreariness of the natural minor mode—with vile darkness.

TRITONAL TRANSPOSITION

Progressions between triads of the same mode whose roots are related by tritone ($\mathbf{T_6}$) are frequently associated with encounters of an alien or inhuman nature. The interval of the tritone hosts long-standing diabolical connotations that are routinely exploited by film composers, particularly within horror films (and horror comedies), as demonstrated by Janet Halfyard (2010). Maximizing this satanic ambience, the *minor* $\mathbf{T_6}$ progression (or **PRPR[m]**) is a favored tonal trope for conveying threats and evils beyond human understanding. The shift from an A-minor tonic to E♭ minor in Goldenthal's *Final Fantasy* (2001) fits this expressive pattern nicely, functioning as a harmonic death knell for one of the film's soon to be devoured protagonists.

Scott Murphy has shown that the progression between *major* triads a tritone apart (e.g., **PRPR[M]**) has held special fascination for composers working within the genre of science fiction, particularly when the transformation is linked with cosmic spectacles like mysterious planets and awe-inspiring spaceships.[37] For ex-trinsic evidence of this association, Murphy catalogues a variety of uses in and outside Hollywood, including, notably, "Mars" and "Saturn" from Gustav Holst's *The Planets*—a work that serves as a wellspring for several other chromatic ab-solute progressions in film.[38] Murphy argues that $\mathbf{T_6}$'s cosmic vibe owes to four intrinsic factors ripe for mapping onto weird interstellar sights:

1. Remoteness according to intervallic metrics, with the tritone being the longest distance between pitches judged by the standard chromatic-scale generators, ic1 or ic5
2. Remoteness according to overall voice-leading work and voice-leading distance spanned by individual voices
3. Ambivalence due to the tritone's symmetrical bisection of the octave
4. Unfamiliarity from the standpoint of functional tonality, with I⇨♯IV/♭V pro-gressions being as prolongationally inadmissible within standard monotonal hierarchies[39]

Danny Elfman, Hollywood's preeminent purveyor of zaniness, makes use of mod-ally matched tritone progressions frequently in his scores for science-fiction and fantasy films (Halfyard 2010: 24–28). A particularly knowing example can be found in his music for Tim Burton's *Mars Attacks* (1996), a travesty of alien invasion films like *The War of the Worlds* and *The Day the Earth Stood Still*. Along with orchestrational

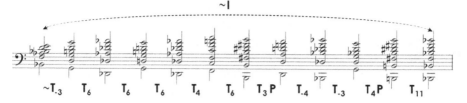

Figure 3.1 Elfman, *Mars Attacks*, "The Landing."

tropes like theremin and wordless choir, Elfman imports aspects of those earlier scores' harmonic language, particularly their abundant T_6 transformations. The most dramatic reference is during "The Landing," when a Martian spacecraft approaches an awestruck crowd. Figure 3.1 supplies a harmonic reduction of the relevant passage (35:00, ▶), along with a simple transpositional analysis. (The excerpt could easily be interpreted with the **PLR** group as well, though I stick with the T_n nomenclature to emphasize T_6's prominent, unary role). As the alien ship comes into view, Elfman transitions from Bb_{lyd}—a region that already emphasizes the tritone interval—to a grand pairing of G major and Db major. These two chords oscillate twice before "modulating" to another tritonal coupling, now between F major and B major. Those triads then meander off into more discursive minor pantriadic harmony, culminating in the recapture of Bb. In no sense has Bb been "prolonged" during this extraterrestrial encounter; yet its recurrence does nevertheless provide a loose sort of bookend to the passage, indicated by an overall ~Identity relation.

SLIDE

Unlike many of the other examples given in Table 3.3, the excerpt from *Sphere* (1998) is quiet and understated. Rather than grabbing listeners by the collar and throttling them with a bombastic collision of triads, Goldenthal's use of **S**lide in "Sphere Discovery" is meant to instill a feeling of hushed amazement. The music accompanies a group of scientists upon their first encounter with the titular glowing globe of unknown origin. When the **S** relation occurs, shuttling F minor to E major, it is not underlined by other musical parameters, as is often the case with absolute progressions. Goldenthal makes hardly any change to the cue's subdued texture, dynamics, or orchestration. And yet the change in harmonic perspective is enormous. The arrival on E major stands as "Sphere Discovery"'s most affectively marked moment, a carefully calculated injection of musical frisson, right as the impossibility of the huge orb sinks in. What is it about this progression that makes it so unusually capable of sending chills down the spine of listeners?

The black sheep within the traditional neo-Riemannian family, **S**lide is a profoundly uncommon transformation in common-practice tonality but becomes surprisingly prevalent in some twentieth- and early-twenty-first-century harmonic dialects (Segall 2011, Lehman 2014a). It has found a truly welcome home in film music, particularly around the turn of the twenty-first century.[40] If a single association can be assigned to this slippery tonal motion, it is ambivalence. The progression has a vigorously unsettled affect, as though it were being wrenched between irreconcilable tonal pulls. On one hand, it can sound "close" according to several intrinsic distance metrics. **S** facilitates a semitonal root motion—literally the nearest any two triads can be, at least as far as simple difference of frequency between chord roots is concerned. It is also a parsimonious transformation, involving only two semitonal displacements and leaving the triadic third in place as a common tone, often treated as an effective axis of inversion, as it is in *Sphere*. And, despite its chromatic nature, **S** is not altogether immiscible with functional tonality. Modally mixed chords based on the same Roman numeral (e.g., vi and ♭VI) quite literally hinge on this oddball progression, as do a few odd but legible progressions like ♭vi⇨V.

At the same time as it can suggest tonal closeness, **S** is capable of communicating great distance. If it powers a modulation, **S** implies a shift of four accidentals to the overall key signature. It likewise requires at the very fewest four turns around the circle of fifths, and at most eight. If derived from the canonical NROs, it is a ternary compound, either **LPR** or **RPL**. It can suggest bizarre, even impossible tonal functions like ♯i or ♭I. And the fact that the third remains a fixed common tone is as much an alienating factor as a familiarizing one, as it draws the radical change of tonal context into high relief. In terms of its intrinsic structure, the progression is therefore something of a tonal paradox.

The way in which **S** is able to imply both proximity and distance accounts for its filmic association with boundary spaces—dream, afterlife, artificial intelligence, virtual reality, and other states in which the border between two fundamentally opposing conditions is straddled. It is a favored transformation of James Newton Howard, who mines its uncanny effect with eyebrow-raising insistence in the contemplative horror movie *The Sixth Sense* (1999, ⏵). Figure 3.2 presents the "densely enigmatic musical sign" that Lloyd Whitesell identifies as the film's main musical motto (2010: 211), here in the guise in which it appears during the movie's main title. A slender melody glides atop the theme's undulating **S**lide progression from G♯m to G♮M. A whiff of acoustic scale-derived dissonance in the second chord is sufficient to prevent a facile ♭ii⇔I tonal interpretation. The motif could just as easily signal i⇔VII♯, or, perhaps absurdly,

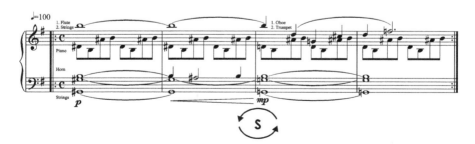

Figure 3.2 Newton Howard, *Sixth Sense*, theme.

i⟺I. The registrally and metrically prominent third, B6, stitches the two harmonies together, insisting upon the eerie shared element between these otherwise starkly contrasted tonal signposts. The thematic kernel hovers unattached to any particular signified through most of the film, suggesting a nagging mystery at the edge of the narrative. It is not until *The Sixth Sense*'s dénouement that the true meaning of this ambivalent *leitharmonie* is disclosed. At that point it is revealed that the ghostly oscillatory progression has been a covert indicator throughout the narrative of the main character's state of undeath—the *ne plus ultra* of boundary states. Slide is a harmonic hint, a clue hidden in plain sight (or, rather, plain sound).

Two Neo-Riemannian Analyses

So far, we have inspected harmonic transformations in isolation, clear absolute progressions that garner a single neo-Riemannian description like **S** or **LP**. As expressively potent as these atoms of harmonic meaning can be, cinematic pantriadicism consists of much more than one-off chord changes. What follows are two short analyses, one straightforward and one more problematic, that demonstrate how transformational analysis can be conducted on discursively pantriadic music.

WALTZ WITH BASHIR

To begin, let us consider a cue that lends itself to the neo-Riemannian methodology quite naturally: "I Swam Out to Sea," from Max Richter's score to the Israeli animated war documentary, *Waltz with Bashir* (2008, 33:38, ▶). Richter's cue accompanies a flashback told by Ronny Dayag, a Israeli veteran who made a harrowing escape during the 1982 Lebanon War. After the rest of his unit is killed in an ambush, Ronny manages to evade enemy detection and swims into the Mediterranean Sea under the cover of darkness, continuing south until being

Figure 3.3　Richter, *Waltz with Bashir*, "I Swam Out to Sea."

rescued by friendly forces. Figure 3.3 displays a reduction of the cue's central harmonic module, specifically the forth and fullest of its five full iterations.

Ronny's escape possesses a dreamlike quality, much of which owes to Richter's hypnotic music, its synthetic timbres churning and bubbling with Phillip Glass–style arpeggios.[41] The steady chord progression on which "I Swam Out to Sea" is based is, in a sense, self-motivated. There is no theme or traditional melody that impels it forward, no overarching harmonic teleology or push for resolution. Admittedly, none of the constituent chords are completely estranged from a hypothetical G-minor tonic—all their roots, for example, belong to the G-minor scale. However, the impression is decidedly not of a conventional prolongation of G. Each individual triad is drawn away from its immediate predecessor by minute voice-leading shifts and displacements, and these small moves add up quickly. Richter's minimalistic module is always drifting away from G, only to be yanked back abruptly to the starting point every eight measures, as if by some sort of irresistible tonal undertow.

This is about as "textbook" pantriadicism as it comes, both in construction and expressive content. Figure 3.4 offers a neo-Riemannian analysis, here presented in a more step-by-step way than I generally adopt, so as to make plain what each transformational label means and how it links up with discrete stages of Richter's tonal journey. "Swam" is reduced down to a three-voice texture that captures the essential polyphonic structure, and only the canonical NROs are needed to account for the cue's harmonic makeup. Text below the entire system conveys the overall chord-to-chord transformations, while the smaller labels and slurs above indicate how each individual voice moves to arrive at the next chord. Every measure contains the literally sounding chord (open note heads), as well as incrementally moving voices (filled note heads), which, while not necessarily heard, are implicit for compound transformations. For instance, the initial change from Gm to E♭m is interpreted as an **LP** transformation, which involves two implicit steps. First, **L** moves the middle voice's D4 up to E♭4, resulting in E♭ major. Secondly, **P** shifts the bass note G3 to G♭3, flipping the chord's modality to E♭ minor. Tracing out the incremental changes implied by a complex progression like this one illustrates why order matters in spelling transformational compounds. Taking the

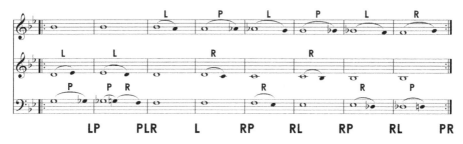

Figure 3.4 Richter, "I Swam Out to Sea," neo-Riemannian analysis.

same starting triad of Gm, for example, and applying **PL** instead of **LP** would result in Bm instead of the desired E♭M.

My analysis of "I Swam Out to Sea" has thus far been purely descriptive. But a bigger question remains: how does Richter's harmony relate to the scene's meaning? The key to the cue's expressive and semantic content lies in its musical uniformity. In describing his experience, Ronny recalls that the sea was "really calm, no waves. I felt calm and at peace. Just me and the sea." This feeling of calm amid incredible danger finds an expressive correlate in the cue's several near-perfect uniformities—transformational characteristics that smooth out harmonic disruptions and impart a sense that the music is flowing freely and naturally, of its own accord. At least four such uniformities are active in Richter's music: parsimony, directionality, modality, and sequential design.

1. *Parsimony*: The way in which Richter realizes this eight-chord progression is maximally smooth at almost every juncture. Every possible common tone is retained and no voice ever moves by anything other than a step. All chord-to-chord motions involve the preservation of at least a single common tone. The sole exception is the seam between mm. 6 and 7, in which the progression's top and middle voices trade pitch classes. This small instance of linear disjunction enables a parsimonious transition back to the initial G-minor chord when the progression restarts (otherwise, the cue would endlessly crawl downward in tessitura).

2. *Directionality*: Not only do the cue's voices always move by step, but they also do so in the same direction—down. This motion creates a sinking effect, what theorists call downshifting, that is perfectly apt for the oceanic setting. Again, there is a single exception: the initial Gm⇨E♭m, which involves one voice moving down by semitone and one up, with a resulting directed voice-leading interval sum of zero.

3. *Modality*: With the exception of the B♭-major chord in m. 3, the "Swam" progression is modally homogeneous, a showcase of intensified minor chromaticism and its capacity to connote shadowy, nocturnal states. This modal uniformity has a secondary effect of ensuring that all but two of the transformations (**PLR** and **L**) involve binary transformations, a feature that is closely related to the way the cue is able to project linear parsimony.

4. *Sequential Design*: "Swam" quickly settles into a repetitive harmonic pattern: a [–P4, +m3] sequence for the last four chords, enabled by the repetition of the cell **RP·RL**. In fact, in terms of transformational operators, the pattern stretches back a bit further—note the –P4 motion embedded within the indirect but comparable move from Gm to Dm. Compressing those together, we have (Gm⇨Dm)⇨(Fm⇨Cm)⇨(E♭m⇨B♭m), a sequence with three iterations. (An intrepid reader might find mapping this progression out in the Tonnetz useful (see "Tonal Space," below), as the [+P4, –m3] pattern is more readily apparent when visualized.)

BATMAN: MASK OF THE PHANTASM

Most pieces do not lend themselves in such an effortless manner to neo-Riemannian analysis as Richter's cue from *Waltz with Bashir*. For a more complex case study, we may turn to the "Caped Crusader." The gothic and at times campy Batman franchise has inspired many composers to turn to expressive chromaticism. An astoundingly thoroughgoing pantriadic passage may be found in Shirley Walker's score to *Batman: Mask of the Phantasm* (1993, 36:30, ▶).[42] Figure 3.5 provides a transcription of the cue "Birth of Batman," heard when Bruce Wayne commits to his vigilante alter ego and dons his iconic cowl for the first time. The excerpt falls into two thematic subsections, first (mm. 1–8) a statement of the family tragedy theme, and second (mm. 9–18) a definitive rendition of Walker's Batman leitmotif. Both are heavily chromatic, though in differing senses. The tragedy theme is resolutely nonfunctional and noncentric, its appoggiaturas and semitonal voice leading reminiscent of some of the more agonized music from

Figure 3.5 Walker, *Batman: Mask of the Phantasm*, "Birth of Batman."

Parsifal. The Batman motif, by contrast, uses triadic transformations to articulate a B♭-minor tonic, a key whose control over the theme persists until the last few measures, which dissolve back into tonal ambiguity.

Part of the difficulty in analyzing this passage is that it employs two different harmonic subidioms in succession—truly unmoored pantriadicism followed by chromatically enriched diatonic tonality. This difference in style might be partially accounted by providing an additional layer of annotations to the second theme (Roman numerals, for example). Yet the question of how to describe the progressions *transformationally* remains. For instance, despite using chromatic chords relative to the key of B♭ (♭v and VI), m. 12 has a clear half-cadential character, almost like a distorted iv⇨V progression. The harmonic logic is temporarily steered by diatonic expectations rather than transformational ones, and thus a different kind of description, T_2P, from that of its surroundings—though this expectation also does not entirely communicate the latent functional implications of the move, either. The issue of whether such mergers of functional and transformational thinking are coherent (or contradictory) is one that has puzzled many theorists, and it will be broached more thoroughly in the final chapter. Two more pressing issues arise from this excerpt, however: non-triadic harmonies and multiple interpretations of the same harmonic transformation.

Although its chief harmonic building block is the consonant triad, Walker's tragedy theme is peppered with seventh chords and dissonant sonorities, none of which lend themselves to simple neo-Riemannian labels. Some, such as the appoggiatura chord that opens m. 7, are clear embellishments of more basic underlying triadic harmonies and may be reduced out. Others, however, are essential to the theme's tonal makeup. Measures 4 through 6 exhibit more dissonant sonorities than they do consonant triads, yet it would be odd to break off a neo-Riemannian analysis for this short span, only to resume once simple triads have begun to dominate the texture once again. A dramatic shift in methodology should be occasioned by a substantial change in the tone and structure of the music, a change that is simply not the case here.

The way around this impasse is to recognize whatever triadic background structures are present in these measures and convey their activity by using fuzzy transformations. The ~**PRP** that ferries D♯m to C7/B♭ in m. 4 does not perfectly describe the behavior of every pitch involved in the transformation: the pitch-class B♭ is effectively cancelled out by the final **P** operation to account for the new C5, even though B♭3 persists in the bass. Yet on its own, **PRP** describes the essentially *triadic* behavior of the top three voices, which moves D♯m smoothly to CM. The following ~**PRP** transformation, also fuzzy, effectively undoes its predecessor by returning to D♯m (enharmonically E♭m). But observe the retention, like before, of a "leftover" note, in this case C5, making the overall chord a C7♭5. Subsequent fuzzy transformations in this excerpt operate in a comparable fashion: pick out an underlying triadic progression, even if it requires waiting for accented dissonances to pass or reducing out non-chord tones where they occur.

A second challenge posed by "Birth of Batman" involves the assignment of transformations. Many of the intertriadic motions in this passage can be described in more than one way. This is not a defect of the methodology—far from it, descriptive multiplicity is among NRT's greatest assets. However, when it comes to making a first analytical pass at a passage, it can be frustrating to have to choose between alternatives, especially where context does not definitively support one option over the other. Already, the first transformation in the excerpt, for instance, raises this issue. Why not label this F♯m⇨B♭M with the specific unary operator for such motions: **H**exatonic Pole? There are, I believe, good reasons for analyzing it as a **PLP** compound instead of **H**. Performing **P**, **L**, and **P** on the upper chord produces the specific inversion and configuration of the upper portion of the chord. More importantly, the progression does not *sound* particularly atomic or unary at this stage: it is the beginning of a lengthy span of discursive pantriadicism, not a one-off absolute progression that asks to be taken on its own terms.

Compare this hexatonic relation to the alternation between A♭M and E♭m at the theme's conclusion. With rhythm stripped down to whole notes and the memory of B♭'s tonicity fading, this chordal oscillation really does sound justified, in Kurth's words, by its "sonic appeal as such." Hence, the use of the unary **F**ar **F**ifth transformation. This unary label can be contrasted with another instance of that same triadic motion in the middle of m. 7. Because the Em⇨BM progression is embedded in a more flowing and ongoing kind of pantriadicism, the shift is analyzed in a dependent way, as **LRP**. Similar lines of reasoning exist behind every other transformational label in the analysis of Walker's cue. On a few occasions when these differing construals are possible and noteworthy, alternative transformations are provided, wrapped inside parentheses. When one conducts a neo-Riemannian analysis, many such choices come down to matters of consistency and personal analytical priorities. Good transformational analysis proceeds neither arbitrarily nor by rote, but rather it involves a constant back and forth between contesting interpretive possibilities. As will become especially clear in the next chapter's section on contextuality, much of this methodology's explanatory power derives from the fact that it can offer different perspectives on the same musical event.

Tonal Space

Thus far, our analyses have been conveyed primarily through a combination of prose description and annotated musical notation. However, a different approach to representing neo-Riemannian findings, one more in keeping with the theory's concern for motion and symmetry, is available: the tonal-space diagram. Tonal space refers to any representation of harmony as occupying an abstract visual domain, and it usually involves a means of indicating distance and connectedness between harmonic "locations."[43] Tonal spaces can represent musical pathways, help calculate distances, and aid in discovering musical patterns. Insofar as they model how listeners comprehend harmonic relationships, tonal spaces are *conceptual spaces*; they may therefore reflect underlying neural or cognitive structures, though this function is not a requirement.[44] Indeed, tonal spaces can be used for a number of analytical purposes, and some of these will suggest different competing visual representations; no single space can ever model every noteworthy aspect of a piece of music. Transformation theorists have at their disposal a number of well-developed devices and strategies to render these conceptual spaces graphically, two of which—the Tonnetz and the transformation network—I will introduce presently.

When one is dealing with pitch relationships, the twin factors of distance and connectedness often imply a particular geometry in which processes such as chord progressions or modulations can be shown to play out. The most familiar of these geometries involve only one or two spatial dimensions. (Some theorists, notably Dmitri Tymoczko, have found uses for spaces with four or even more dimensions.) The circle of fifths exists along a single linear dimension, while the traditional musical staff, with its twin axes of pitch height and chronology, is a two-dimensional space. The geometrical properties of a space are determined by the presence or absence of certain musical equivalencies. For example, octave equivalence constrains the extent of the circle of fifths to a familiar clockface with twelve tonal "hours." But octave equivalence does *not* constrain the musical staff, which could go on forever in either direction (provided an arbitrarily huge number of ledger lines). Likewise, enharmonic equivalence, which holds that differently spelled notes like F♯ and G♭ are representatives of the same sonic entity, is assumed for the circle of fifths, as well as most atonal pitch spaces. Without it—and relatedly the equivalence of equal temperament (ET)—tonal spaces will sprawl out into infinity (Harrison 2002).

Figure 3.6 presents an important space to neo-Riemannian theorists: the *Tonnetz* (tonal network). This graph, which has its origins in eighteenth- and nineteenth-century central European music theory, depicts relationships between consonant triads, and it does so with no assumption of tonal hierarchy or chordal weighting.[45] Each point where lines meet (vertex) represents a named pitch class. These pitches are arrayed along three axes that correspond to different interval cycles. The horizontal axis adheres to an ic5 (perfect fourth/fifth) cycle; the northwest to southeast diagonal to an ic3 (minor third) cycle; and the northeast to southwest diagonal to an ic4 (major third) cycle. The small triangles formed by any three nearby pitches represent consonant triads. Right-side-up triangles are major triads, upside-down ones minor. While not a perfect gauge of interchordal distances, the Tonnetz can be used as an informal way of judging how close or distant two triads are, provided that the criterion of distance is transformational word length (e.g., how many **L**s, **P**s, and **R**s it takes to transform chord-1 into chord-2).[46]

The overall shape of the Tonnetz depends on whether enharmonic equivalence and equal temperament is assumed or not. If enharmonic equivalence and ET are ignored, the grid will stretch on forever in every direction, with note spellings taking on arbitrarily large numbers of accidentals. If instead enharmonic equivalence and ET are accepted, then the space wraps around itself into the finite

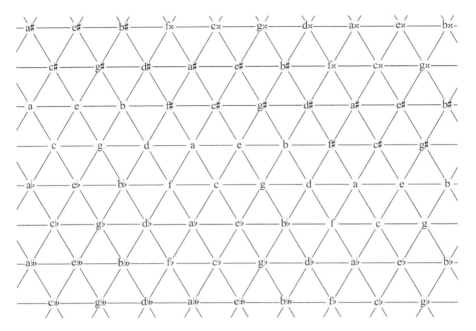

Figure 3.6 Tonnetz, infinite version.

shape of a torus—akin to the surface of a doughnut, geometrically speaking. The version of the grid in Figure 3.6 does *not* assume enharmonic equivalence for two reasons: (1) for the benefit of those not yet familiar with pc notation; and (2) in order to highlight a sense of directionality we often intuitively attribute to tonal space, where "sharpward" corresponds to ascending, brightening motions, and "flatward" corresponds to descending, darker shifts. For all subsequent renderings of the Tonnetz, I employ an enharmonically equivalent version, which is better suited to representing pantriadic chromaticism, where pitch-name distinctions lose the relevance they possessed in functional tonality.

A happy consequence of the Tonnetz being formed by intersecting fifth and third cycles is that adjacent triads are related according to the basic neo-Riemannian operations. This organization helps visualize, among other things, common-tone retention, inversion about stable pitches or intervals, and distance according to **PLR**-type displacements. Figure 3.7 provides two views of the neighborhood surrounding a single C-major triad. The first graph shows C major at the center of a collection of twelve closely related triads, while the second shows that same region as the product of a number of transformations from our neo-Riemannian inventory. Reflecting a triad upon its horizontal axis is equivalent to a **P** operation—note how the two pitches that form its fifth are retained. Moving a triad one triangle to the left or right corresponds to either an **L** or an **R** transformation, depending on the mode of the initial chord.

A number of familiar interval cycles are embedded within the Tonnetz's geometry. Figure 3.8 highlights the ic3, ic4, and ic5 cycles that emerge around a central C-major triad. Iterating **P** and **R** creates the eight-step octatonic cycle along the northeast to southwest diagonal alleyway. Similarly, **P** and **L** generate the six-step

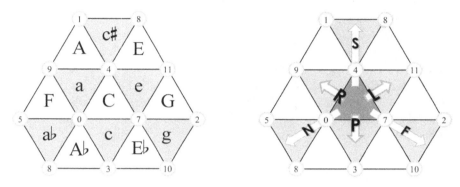

Figure 3.7 *Tonnetz* space around C major: (a) chordal neighborhood; (b) transformational neighborhood.

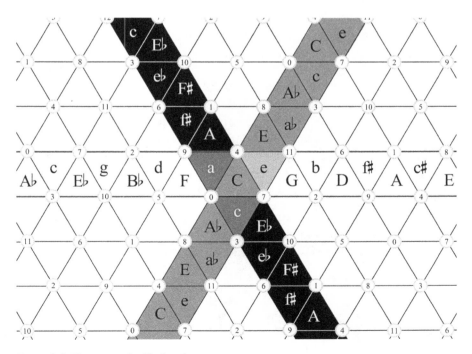

Figure 3.8 *Tonnetz* embedded cycles.

hexatonic cycle along the opposite diagonal. Meanwhile, a chain of repeated **Ls** and **Rs** produces the twelve-step circle of perfect fifths along the horizontal axis. This last cycle has a convenient upshot: all six consonant triads that belong to any one diatonic scale will be grouped contiguously and horizontally parallel with one another (Cohn 2011, 2012: 164–194). Both diatonic passages and cyclical processes therefore leap out of the Tonnetz when one grows to recognize the slivers and alleys they occupy. The presence of these emergent cycles and regions also serves to illustrate the geometrical redundancy of the enharmonically equivalent Tonnetz; note, for example, how the same C-major triad appears several times in the hexatonic diagonal of Figure 3.8. Short of representing this space differently—toroidally, for example, a representation that is confusing when viewed on the printed page—such repetitions are bound to happen. Redundancy might pose a slight graphical inconvenience, but it can also be a way to emphasize different contextual perspectives on seemingly identical triads. Just because two C-major triads share the same frequencies in ET does not mean they must occupy the same local spot in tonal space, as we will see.

THE DA VINCI CODE

One way in which the Tonnetz can aid film music analysis is by revealing the connections between passages with related but outwardly dissimilar musical material. Movie franchises provide some golden opportunities to track such musical connections. Hans Zimmer's music for the "Da Vinci Code" series, which includes *The Da Vinci Code* (2006), *Angels and Demons* (2009), and *Inferno* (2016), offers one such laboratory for inspecting franchise-spanning tonal transformations. The main theme for all three movies is based on a four-chord harmonic module that supports a simple, arching melody. Figure 3.9 offers a melodic reduction of the thematic cell as it appears in the climactic cue of *The Da Vinci Code*, "Chevaliers de Sangreal." At this stage, the chord succession is diatonic and, indeed, a purely white-note affair. However, the long duration of each triad and the absence of dominant-powered cadences grant the succession a nonfunctional, noncentric quality. Zimmer's theme is crafted to sound vaguely modal, rather than traditionally tonal—as befits of the ecclesiastical, esoteric subject matter of the film.

Over the course of the three *Da Vinci Code* movies, this module is subjected to a range of tonal transformations. Figure 3.10 provides a reduction and neo-Riemannian analysis of six such variants (▶). A few large-scale changes are clearly visible from this overview. Most apparent is the tendency toward

Figure 3.9 Zimmer, *Da Vinci Code*, "Chevaliers de Sangreal Theme."

Figure 3.10 Zimmer, *Da Vinci Code*, "Chevaliers Theme" harmonic variants.

increased chromaticism, as evident, for instance, with the replacement of the diatonic **R** transformation with much darker chromatic progressions in the last four examples. However, a number of other patterns are not immediately obvious in the diagram, because of the variable transposition levels and triadic orderings of the six iterations. Thankfully, the Tonnetz can help neutralize these confounding factors.

Table 3.4 shows how each of the six variants of the *Da Vinci* theme fits into the Tonnetz. The diatonicity of the first and second variants is plainly evident in the horizontal and contiguous orientation of each four chord module. The second variant, which is a standard continuation of the main theme and also heard in "Chevaliers de Sangreal," is effected by a simple T_5 transformation of the original cell, shifting the whole module one diatonic "slot" to the left. The third variant, on the other hand, appears in its complete form *only* on the *Da Vinci Code* soundtrack album, not in the film itself. (A partial version does occur at 1:39:50.) And while this unused material cannot inform a typical moviegoer's listening experience, it can help in understanding subsequent harmonic transformations. The progression, Dm⇨F♯m⇨FM⇨Am, contains three out of four of the same chords as the original. Yet the use of **PL** instead of the typical **R** dramatically changes the transformational "shape" of the module, which is no longer confined to the horizontal (i.e., diatonic) plane. The introduction of this chromatic third relation anticipates the more pervasive hexatonic orientation of subsequent thematic transformations.

The fourth and fifth variants, each powered by hexatonic compounds, share the same shape in the Tonnetz—something that may not be obvious in music

Table 3.4 **Zimmer, *Da Vinci Code*, "Chevaliers" theme variants in the *Tonnetz***

Film and Cue	Progression
a. Basic Module	
b. Transposed Module	
c. Partially Chromaticized Module	
d. Fully Chromaticized Module	
e. Fully Chromaticized, Reordered, and Transposed Module	
f. Fully Chromaticized, Reordered, Transposed, and Deconstructed Module	

notation, given their differing pitch content, ordering, and interior transform-ations (**RL** and **SP**, respectively). Note how, while a diatonic spine is still intact in both (Dm⇔Am and Am⇔Em), the overall degree of chordal connectedness is reduced, with triads now only sharing corners, not edges. The final variant, which accompanies a tense conversation in the midst of a swat-team operation in *Angels and Demons*, is most distantly related to the initial diatonic module. Here, only the D-minor starting triad and slow chordal texture remain as vest-iges of the "Chevaliers" theme. However, the Tonnetz representation makes plain how it is descended from the original model by way of the progressive transformations of earlier variants, from which it clearly owes its double **PL** mo-tions. Unlike every other modification of the model, the *Angels and Demons* pro-gression is no longer fully connected on the Tonnetz. The first and second halves of the module share no edges or corners and are separated by a wide spatial gulf. This separation breeds a sense of tonal alienation, chiefly the product of the unprecedentedly complex **SLRP** compound—an appropriately dire-sounding tritonal motion that figuratively "cracks open" the already chromaticized "Chevaliers" motif.

Useful though the Tonnetz is for representing tonal pathways and spaces, it is sometimes advantageous to construct spaces bound by a less rigid geometry. **Transformational networks** have been as important to neo-Riemannians as pre-fabricated chessboards like the Tonnetz and related grids.[47] A transformational network requires two elements: nodes and arrows. Nodes represent harmonic objects and may be filled with specific triads or, in more open-ended cases, left empty. Arrows power the network and provide a description of relevant connec-tions between triadic nodes. Arrows may be bidirectional, which helps convey oscillating progressions and reversible transformations like the unary NROs. Alternatively, one-sided arrows can capture directionality and chronology, while also being able to describe non-reversible transformations.

The number of nodes, the distances between them, and their spatial configura-tion is up to the analyst. Transformation networks normally do not make commit-ments about tonicity, but in cases in which a key center is obvious, the tonic can be indicated with a doubly encircled node (following Rings 2011b). Node/arrow systems can be as simple as a pair of triadic nodes and a single arrow, or as com-plex and spatially byzantine as one can imagine. Transformation networks are ad hoc in a positive sense: while they lose some of the orderliness of the Tonnetz, their ability to capture the peculiarities of a specific piece can more than justify any loss in geometrical generalizability.

A transformation network for the *Da Vinci Code* theme is shown in Figure 3.11. This network models every possible inter-triadic motion between the triads Dm, Am, FM, and CM as a neo-Riemannian transformation, including some path-ways, such as Am⇔FM (**L**) and Dm⇔CM (**RLR**) not taken in any of the varia-tions already cited. While not as systematically constructed as a Tonnetz diagram would be, the network nevertheless does capture aspects of relative distance and

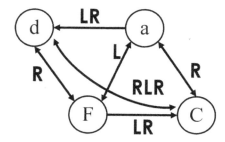

Figure 3.11 Zimmer, *Da Vinci Code*, "Chevaliers Theme," general network.

relatedness through its shape; note, for instance, that arrows for unary transformations are shorter than those for compounds.

Zimmer's work on the *Da Vinci* franchise provides many more examples of passages whose harmonic activity can be described by this network. For example, the first film includes a recurring (1:10:58, 1:53:18) progression [Am⇨CM⇨Dm⇨FM] that, while bearing a different chordal order and dissimilar melody from the main theme, fits snugly into the generative transformational network. The same can be said of less motivic moments, such as a cadence at the end (2:27:20) of the first film, (Dm⇨CM⇨FM⇨CM⇨Dm⇨Am⇨FM), or a progression twenty-three chords long during the climax of *Angels and Demons* (1:47:30), composed exclusively from these four triads in various orders (albeit decorated with occasional nonfunctional sevenths). That all these examples use literally the same chords as the main theme makes their transformational correspondence readily apparent, as all ultimately emerge out of the pseudo-modal, pseudo-minimalist idiom Zimmer employs throughout the series. Even so, the same network in Figure 3.11 can capture related music that uses different transpositional or modal configurations equally well; a tonally generalized "meta-network" for Zimmer's harmonic predilections in this franchise would simply need to empty its nodes of specific triads.

SCOTT OF THE ANTARCTIC

For a demonstration of the usefulness of spatial visualization in the analysis of extremely discursive pantriadicism, let us inspect a cue from Ralph Vaughan Williams's score to *Scott of the Antarctic* (1948). Although it sits outside the New Hollywood mainstream that has occupied us for most of this chapter, Vaughan Williams's music for this film proved highly influential to later American composers like Goldsmith, Shore, and Williams, who drew inspiration from its alien progressions and unearthly textures in their soundtracks for major science-fiction and fantasy movies. Yet the movie's music is also of substantial independent interest for the purposes of neo-Riemannian analysis.

The film, which depicts Sir Robert Scott's ill-destined expedition to the South Pole, is largely forgotten today, but Vaughan Williams's score enjoyed a second life in the concert hall, with large portions being adapted in his Seventh Symphony, *Sinfonia antartica* (1952).[48] The score and symphony both showcase a heavily chromatic main theme, whose twisting modulations seem to represent Scott's trudging progress across the frozen wastes of Antarctica. The theme's definitive statement comes in the cue "Scott Climbs the Glacier," written for a dialogue-free sequence (58:47, ⏵) in which the explorer and his team slowly ascend an icy peak. Figure 3.12 provides a reduction with neo-Riemannian annotations.

The sprawling theme, which is thirty measures long (without repeats) falls into six subphrases, rendered as separate staves in the analysis. Vaughan Williams begins and ends by placing emphasis on G major, though this is not a "key" in any traditional sense. The overall tonal idiom is discursive pantriadicism, with a fixation on chromatic step and third progressions, at the near total exclusion of diatonic-fifth relations. There are many transformationally noteworthy aspects of Vaughan Williams's music—and more still for the thematic transformations it undergoes over the course of the film and symphony—but I will concentrate just on a handful of details especially germane to tonal space analysis.

Figure 3.12 Vaughan Williams, *Scott of the Antarctic*, "Scott Climbs the Glacier."

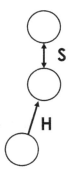

Figure 3.13 Vaughan Williams, *Scott of the Antarctic*, harmonic motif network.

The first four measures set the stage for the rest of the theme in several respects. The melody's ascent from E♭4 to C5—a near whole-tone hexachord—establishes the stepwise motion that will mark the cue from beginning to end. The harmonic progression that undergirds it, E♭m⇨GM⇨A♭m⇨GM, is tailored to nullify any diatonic expectations surrounding its lightly implied "tonic" of G. These first four chords set up what will become an important harmonic motif throughout the cue, represented with a transformational network in Figure 3.13. (The reasons for the unusual vertical orientation will be made clear shortly.) This little network has three triadic nodes, connected by a unidirectional **H**exatonic pole relation (as in E♭m⇨GM) and a bidirectional **S**lide relation (as in GM⇔A♭m). The three-pronged progression occurs, in some guise, five times over the course of the theme, though not every instance is as aurally obvious as the one in mm. 1–4. For seeing how the **H/S** transformational pairing arises, it is best to refer to the Tonnetz, where modified or concealed iterations of the cell leap out.

Table 3.5 provides a Tonnetz representation of the whole theme, split into six stages that correspond to its subphrases. In addition to housing the name of the triad, each triadic node includes an Arabic numeral that indicates at which stage of the journey the triad occurs. (Ideally, the graph would be animated in real time; these ordinal numbers are a compromise, given the limitations of the printed page.) Using this information, one can trace the theme's chronological progress from beginning to end. The motivic **H/S** cell is indicated by a dark halo surrounding triadic triangles, which now can be seen as the origin of the oddly skewed shape of the three-chord network in Figure 3.13.

Following its introduction in the first four measures, **H/S** cell is repeated in an easily recognizable form within mm. 5–7. For the most part, this is a simple T_7 transposition of the cue's opening. But it is not a perfect transposition, as the head motif is cut short, landing on an E♭-minor triad that does not return to its **S**-partner, DM. Observe that the E♭m in m. 7 occupies a *different* spot on the Tonnetz than the one that initiates the whole theme. Despite the appearance of symmetry, there is a good case for not treating these spots as representatives of

Table 3.5 Vaughan Williams, *Scott of the Antarctic*, "Scott Climbs the Glacier" in the *Tonnetz*

Measures	Progression
a. mm. 1–7	
b. mm. 8–13	

(continued)

Table 3.5 **Continued**

Measures	Progression
c. mm. 14–17	
d. mm. 18–21	

Table 3.5 **Continued**

Measures	Progression
e. mm. 22–24	
f. mm. 25–30	

the same harmonic object. $E\flat_{m.1}$ and $E\flat_{m.7}$ serve starkly different harmonic roles within their respective phrases and harmonic modules. The "function" of the initial E♭m is taken over by B♭m in the parallel phrase, while the concluding E♭m acts comparably to the A♭m of the previous phrase. One of the benefits of transformational analysis is that it allows us to make fine-grained distinctions about shifting a tonal intention like this one, without getting hung up on extraneous matters of enharmonic-identity or recurrence.

The next iteration of the **H/S** cell occurs in the second phrase (mm. 9–11) through the progression Am⇨C♯M⇨Dm. Here again the module is clipped at its conclusion, and is further distanced from its original model by being shifted over one measure within its phrasal unit; A minor occurs on the second of four measures instead of the first, and the following two triads are similarly displaced. The transition into the theme's subsequent phrase hosts the fourth appearance of the **H/S** cell, though here the **H** progression is obscured by the repeated interjections of an intervening sonority. Fm progresses to its **H**-partner, AM, but with an interloper, GM, sitting between the two and acting as a passing chord. This relationship, effectively invisible in Figure 3.12, is suddenly obvious when we consult the Tonnetz.

The theme builds to a massive climax, with a twofold ascent up an octatonic ladder (mm. 18–21, 22–34) that mimics the strenuous push of Scott and his men over the unforgiving polar terrain. Vaughan Williams's cue culminates with a fortissimo breakthrough onto GM at m. 27. The final **H/S** cell, which occurs between mm. 25 and 28, ties the theme together by recalling the opening's specific E♭m⇨GM⇔A♭m progression. Yet it is also a return informed by the sorts of transformational modifications the rest of the theme has undergone. The once unary hexatonic progression is again mediated by interstitial material, now *two* passing chords—an inverted D♭ and C♭7—which further thicken the space between E♭m and GM. (In the symphonic revision of this cue, this polar gap is further obscured by a series of lengthy new interpolations.) Yet, with the sight of the glacier's peak in view, we do return at last to well-trodden territory: a ringing repetition of the **S** progression, Vaughan Williams's harmonic emblem of the unfathomable mystery of the Antarctic landscape.

***

Having reached the halfway point in this book, it is worth briefly taking a step back and asking what exactly it means to closely study film music. Arguably, going to the movies turns everyone into a music analyst. The facility with which even an inexperienced cinemagoer can make sense of the busiest of soundtracks is astonishing. Within milliseconds of striking the ear, film audio is broken down and reassembled into meaningful constituents, from simple frequencies to rich timbres to discrete instrumental choirs. We entrain rhythms and metrical hierarchies, form and confirm hypotheses about key, and draw predictions about how themes will proceed based on what we have heard before. What emerges is an independent and coherent stream of musical commentary, one we intuitively understand as coming from a different narrational space than other forms of cinematic audio like sound effects and dialogue. The presence of a moving image makes this perceptual feat even more impressive. We evaluate character psychology according to underscore, activate generic expectations in relation to style topics, and draw inferences about what will happen in the narrative based on what the score is foreshadowing. That for many filmgoers all of this mental activity happens unconsciously, without disrupting immersion, does not diminish just how complex the music analytical tasks in perceiving screen media are. Small wonder then that so much film music is governed by convention and cliché. Any shortcut to audience intelligibility, any method for lifting the cognitive load imposed by the soundtrack, stands to ensure more accessible, semiotically optimized musical storytelling.

This implicit form of music analysis might seem rather starkly opposed to the more active, score-based form of analysis I have advocated for. Close textual reading can reveal many treasures, including hidden patterns and connections never before grasped by listener or even composer. But it is a mistake to think that music analysis must be confined only to recondite matters, its only pleasures stemming from what Carolyn Abbate (2004: 524) dubs the "cryptographic sublime."

In introducing the tools and concerns of neo-Riemannian theory, I hope this chapter has provided a way of articulating some aspects of film music structure and meaning that our unconscious minds are already registering, that we as filmgoers already, in a deep if unexamined sense, "know." My goal has always been to provide readers with a pathway to more active, engaged filmgoing. Far from violently taking one out of the movie, knowing a Slide-progression or an octatonic cycle when one hears it can provide a frisson of recognition and rush of understanding that only deepens appreciation. It is with this possibility for a more profound—indeed more *musical*—way of engaging film in mind that we move on to the next chapter, where close analysis takes center stage.

4

Analyzing Chromaticism in Film

Playing with Transformations

The previous chapter provided us with a box of theoretical tools—transformations, networks, spaces—for understanding cinematic chromaticism. Now, we are in a position to release these implements onto the full diversity of pantriadic styles and techniques. The chief goal of this chapter is show the neo-Riemannian tools in action; to this end, a variety of chromatic cues will be surveyed, all of which share an expressive goal—the representation or elicitation of cinematic wonderment. Our focus is thus now firmly on analysis. My intent, however, is not to treat these cues as pure case studies—that is, as texts that merit close inspection on the basis of their innate aesthetic and cultural worth. Rather, I wish to sketch some interpretive strategies with which one can gain a handle on this repertoire. To that end, I confront a number of challenges that arise routinely in the act of analyzing pantriadic film music. Importantly, the interpretive tactics I propose all make a concerted effort to heed the exigencies of harmonic subordination, immediacy, and referentiality that are defining features of Hollywood's tonal practices.

Organizing this chapter are five parameters that are central to the way we as listeners and filmgoers make sense of triadic chromaticism: **contextuality, distance, voice leading, equivalence,** and **patterning**. At first blush, these may seem sterile and formalistic devices to serve as exciting analytical jumping-off points. But I contend that within each resides the capacity for tremendous expressive meaning. With the parameter of voice leading, for example, intrinsic features like parsimony, toggling, or up/downshifting may conspire to make a passage seem well organized and logical from a structural perspective. At the same time, those characteristics may lend a potent affective quality to a cue, like placidity or strenuousness or upheaval.[1] This interactive, context-dependent form of musical meaning is the driving force of tonal drama in film music.

Composers of screen music tell stories through harmony, and good music analysis spins its own tales, too. To build a convincing narrative of pantriadic music is to convey how a composer plays with chromatic transformations.[2] This idea of "play" is central to this chapter. I urge readers to play whatever they see on the page, and I have made a special effort to convey analytical findings through simplified, easily realizable reductions. On a handful of occasions, I also encourage the readers to try out simple experiments on the piano. Playing these examples and exercises, I hope, will make the power of various transformational parameters vivid, both aurally and tactilely.

Another sense in which "play" is a unifying concept is the idea of free, creative manipulation of musical material. Film composers use pantriadic transformations in imaginative ways to shape our expectations, to direct our attention, and to pluck our heartstrings. The discussions that follow may suggest some novel or, at the very least, efficacious ways of exploiting the possibilities of chromaticism to good dramatic ends. Music analysts, like composers, engage in their own forms of play.[3] They test interpretations, tease out connections and discontinuities, entertain against-the-grain hearings, and generally allow music to steer their imagination. This open, subject-centered approach, comfortable with interpretive multiplicity, is one of the major boons of transformational analysis.[4] Ideally, transformation theory is neither a prescriptive model of musical structure, nor a descriptively neutral way of accounting for musical events. Rather, it is a dynamic and pluralistic way of understanding change in music. It celebrates the possibility that, given a small shift in perspective, the same music can sound totally different.

I hope this chapter will illustrate just how much of an art of interpretation transformational analysis is. Though my five categories alone cannot erect a full hermeneutics of chromatic film music, they are handy as entry points for analysis, even for dealing with the most familiar of chromatic clichés. It may seem odd that, say, a run-of-the-mill chromatic third progression could warrant such attention or provide such an analytical payoff. After all, how mundane, how seemingly self-explanatory are such compositional routines in Hollywood? But the everyday amazements of filmic pantriadicism are positively kaleidoscopic in their potential to reward close inspection.

Contextuality

HARMONIC CONTEXT AND INTERPRETATION

Try the following musical experiment. Go to a piano and play any two consonant triads, one after the other, letting each ring out for three seconds. Make a mental note of the distinctive relationship between these chords. Does it seem as though this pairing could function within a diatonic key? Does the way in which the chords connect feel smooth or rough? Do you sense any strong expressive content in the chordal pairing? How might you imagine it arising in a real piece of music? Finally, can you imagine one or more transformational labels to reflect these qualities?

Now, take those same two chords and play them again, but this time with a three-second-long C-major triad struck both before and after. What has changed? Have they absorbed a new feeling of functional directedness? A clear sense of purpose in prolonging (or disrupting) that initial C chord? Has their expressive content changed accordingly? Do you feel as though you were hearing them purely on their own terms, or instead now with reference to some larger tonal phenomenon?

This little experiment illustrates how context shapes the way we perceive harmony. In conventionally monotonal music, the primary context through which we hear all elements of pitch design will be the tonic itself. When a random pair of chords is flanked by instances of C major, we instinctively search for some way to relate those interior chords to their unvarying bookend—perhaps as (potentially altered) diatonic scale steps, or alternatively as part of some ad hoc linear strategy.[5] But recall what it sounded like to hear just the two chords in isolation. What did they point to? Steven Rings (2011b: 104–106) provides for a term for this effect: tonal intentionality, the sense in which harmonic percepts are directed *toward* something.

In diatonic music, it is typically the tonic that is the thing "pointed to." However, with pantriadic chromaticism, a progression may have no tonic to refer to, and it may not even extend its intentional reach beyond the immediate vicinity of the progression itself. We have encountered some cues that leave the impression that important interchordal motions are detached and isolated, like the first two solo chords in our experiment. In such cases, it is appropriate to resort to the notion of an absolute progression. One way in which transformational analysis can reflect the self-sufficiency of APs is to cast them as unary transformations—that is, indivisible atoms of tonal meaning. Earlier, I selected a number of passages from Goldenthal's film music to exemplify the various neo-Riemannian transformations. These all have an "absolute" sound in their respective contexts, a sound that in turn justifies analysis through of unary labels. Even if our transformational lexicon formally mandates a non-unary description of a progression—say, **LP** for the Em⇨Cm motion in Goldenthal's *Pet Sematary*—we may interpret such compounds in a unary way. That is to say, we may stress the *overall* semantic impact of the transformation over the details of its transformational etymology.

Absolute progressions in film grab our attention as few other musical techniques can. But the sheer vividness of such events should not blind us to the crucial interconnectedness of harmony within larger musical contexts. When heard over appreciable spans of time, pantriadic chromaticism, like any other tonal style, will generate networks of reference and implication that stretch beyond the purview of just one pair of chords. This interconnectedness is the opposite of the Kurthian tonal vacuum. The less that we hear pantriadic harmony as a series of isolated moves, the more it makes sense to interpret chordal transformations in relation to—and in terms of—other transformations.

The way that context dependency shapes our hearing was already suggested in the experiment of placing C major around two arbitrary triads.[6] But there is a vital difference between that form of tonal bookending and the sorts of contextuality that arise in pantriadic music: harmonic interconnectedness need not be in terms of a single chord like a tonic. It may rely on motivic similarities, on previously heard transformations, or on routines like interval cycles or oscillations. Crucially, tonal intentionality can reside in transformations themselves; they too can point to and depend upon one another, in much the same way diatonic scale degrees and chords do in Rings's theory. Where exactly they point all depends on context.

Contextuality is a keystone concept for transformational music theories, and it comes in two varieties. In its algebraic sense, contextuality refers to the way in which transformations are defined in terms of the structure of the sonority they act upon, as opposed to a fixed axis or point.[7] This further entails that the *product* of some transformations depends on the structure of the inputted sonority. Consider again the **LP** transformation. The modal quality of the input triad, not a fixed and specific pitch axis like G♮, determines whether the output triad is major or minor—and similarly whether it lies a M3 above or below its predecessor.

The other important sense of transformational contextuality is less formal but bears arguably deeper relevance to the analysis of film music. Milton Babbitt, aiming to describe atonal works with idiosyncratic forms of compositional organization, formulated contextuality as "the extent to which a piece defines its materials within itself" (1987: 167–168).[8] In other words, the meaning of a musical event hinges on its musical surroundings—what comes before, after, and around it—rather than an already established principle or a priori framework (like functional tonality) that applies broadly to a style or idiom.

Because transformational theories make available many different ways to characterize tonal relationships, any analytical accounts of intertriadic relationships should strive to reflect Babbitt's perceptual sort of context dependency. The choice of a transformation for, say, an Em⇨Cm progression should be based on potential musical and perceptual contexts when one is determining whether it is best described as T_8, **LP**, **NS**, or something more exotic. And the combinatorial nature of transformational theories further facilitates context-dependent analysis. Complex musical maneuvers can be built out of simpler, more direct particles, and large tonal spaces can be spawned by combination and iteration of these basic moves.

Hearing *in terms of* is what we do whenever we propose that a progression is mediated through elided or unheard transformations.[9] The decomposability of any tonal move into some concatenation of harmonic atoms allows the analyst to refer complicated or novel-sounding harmonic events back to simpler or accustomed motions and vice versa. Rings notes that "a given auditor's tonal intentions at any instant are multiple and perhaps partly inchoate, varying in degree of intensity and cognitive mediation. Thus, no single analytical representation can do full justice to our prereflective intentional activity" (2011b: 106). Even in the world of mainstream film scoring, where every affect is overdetermined and every meaning underlined, Rings's contextual openness holds true. This is actually a wonderful thing for analysis. Interpretive under-determination makes possible a robust hermeneutics not unlike that applied to traditional leitmotifs and bears

Figure 4.1 Zimmer and Newton Howard, *Dark Knight* Trilogy, leitharmonic development.

the same potential for charting gross or subtle shifts in dramatic representation across large spans of film time.

Consider what happens across Hans Zimmer and James Newton Howard's music for the *Dark Knight* Trilogy. A leitharmonic idea that spans three films is depicted in Figure 4.1 (▶). In the first installment, *Batman Begins* (2005), the franchise urmotif, D4⇨F4, is initially unharmonized over D minor, thus warranting a simple **Identity** transformation. Later on, as Batman's persona comes into focus, it is harmonized by a major-third progression (Dm⇨B♭M). In this form, it furnishes the basic transformational atom of the series, namely, the **L(m)** transformation (Rahn 2016). Throughout the next movie, *The Dark Knight* (2008), we hear two variants. One is a darkening (Dm⇨B♭m), and the other a more ambiguous change of tint (Dm⇨D♭M).[10] Both clearly derive from the original **L** model and share with each other the introduction of a new pitch, D♭/C♯. The label **L·P** for the former is intuitive. Even though the latter could be described "atomically" with perfect ease by the unary **S** transformation, the more roundabout **L·PR** accounts for Dm⇨D♭M's warping of the originary M3 motion. A similar story can be told of the new, more hopeful Dm⇨FM progression in the final film, *The Dark Knight Rises* (2012); this reharmonization is connected to Batman's implied successor, Robin Blake. In addition to the obvious interpretation as a straight **R** operation, it is useful to think of it as an "undoing" of parent motif's **L**, which can be captured through **L·LR** compound transformation. Perhaps this is a counterintuitive way of hearing such an outwardly simple move, but as a means of indicating its underlying indebtedness to the established **L** model, it is actually fairly apt, dramatically. The accustomed "dark" **L** is still a reference point, but it has receded to the background—inaudible, reconfigured, perhaps even replaced.

PANTRIADICISM IN BERNARD HERRMANN

Before launching into a case study that highlights the nuances of transformational contextuality, an excursus into the pantriadic style of Bernard Herrmann, Hollywood's quintessential chromaticist, is warranted. For it is with Herrmann that we find, for the first time, a composer for whom pantriadicism is not just an excuse for occasional bursts of color, but a truly integral component of a personal harmonic style. It is not that his progressions themselves that are novel. Far from it—any chordal relation that Herrmann employs can be located in a hundred earlier scores from composers like Steiner or Newman, themselves adept and creative weavers of chromatic wonders.[11] What is genuinely new is the way pantriadicism in Herrmann is so utterly naked, proudly uncluttered from competing forms of musical information. Richly scored, lingering collections of nonfunctionally related triads are offered for the filmgoer's delectation, like colorful jewels within a cabinet of chromatic curiosities. This treatment of harmony is a highly influential development, and to this day it marks the way many film composers approach expressive chromaticism.

The paradigmatic Herrmann pantriadic patch features a string of tightly voiced triads, uncrowned by any independent melody and unmoored from any tonal center. In keeping with the composer's taste for the dark and macabre, intensified minor chromaticism is extremely common, while the refulgence of intensified major chromaticism is elusive.[12] Herrmann occasionally enriches his pantriadic textures with other sonorities of tertian origin, ranging in markedness from the nondescript to the positively ear catching. The most famous of the latter category is assuredly what Royal Brown (1994) has labeled the "Hitchcock" chord, a minor triad with major seventh (alternatively the hexatonic set class 4-19) that serves as Herrmann's musical emblem for irrationality.

Though Herrmann's pantriadicism is not restricted to any one genre, it is strongly associated with pulpy and fantastic subject matters. Nonfunctional chordal relationships course through films like *Fahrenheit 451*, *The Day the Earth Stood Still*, and especially Ray Harryhausen's adventure pictures (not to mention many a *Twilight Zone* episode). Yet even when accompanying strictly earthbound sights—as is the case for *The Snows of Mount Kilimanjaro* and all of the famous Hitchcock scores—Herrmannesque chromaticism imbues its scenes with an oneiric, unearthly quality. This reality-heightening potential is already fully exploited in Herrmann's breakout score for *Citizen Kane*; the Rachmaninoff-inspired pantriadic gloom of film's finale in particular elevates the titular magnate's biography to the status of American gothic mythology (Rosar 2001: 103–116).

The clarity of Herrmann's pantriadicism is enabled and reinforced by other aspects of the composer's often remarkably anti-lyrical scoring style. In particular, it is facilitated by (1) his pared-down musical textures and (2) his tendency to organize underscore through duplicable modules.[13] Herrmann's preference for pure sonority and textural uniformity over complex counterpoint lends his triadic progressions an unvarnished quality, which is noticeable, for example in the opening "Prophecy" scene in *Jason and the Argonauts* (1963, 2:15). The cue begins with a bizarre harmonic module [Dm⇔B♭m⇨Dm⇨A♭M$_4^6$⇨E♭m/D], full of creepy tritonal and Tarnhelmic shifts. See Figure 4.2a The progression is conveyed by low woodwinds moving in lockstep homophony throughout, with only the smallest glint of timbral variety provided by the arrival of harp with the module-concluding polychord—not incidentally, an inverted "Hitchcock" chord. Herrmann's idiosyncratic orchestration, and his willingness to use extremely plain textures, have the effect of focusing the ear on the immediate quality of sound, and away from long-range processes. This effect in turn draws the distinctive pantriadic interactions *between* sonorities into high relief wherever they occur.

Herrmann's uncomplicated textures go hand in hand with a "progressions-for-their-own-sake" mentality. At the same time, the composer's reliance upon motivic modules and ostinati to generate large spans of underscore naturally favors nonfunctional content over robustly hierarchical structures or goal-directed themes. A typical occurrence of this almost atemporal style of writing can be found in the "Mushroom Forest" sequence from *Journey to the Center of the Earth* (1959, 1:33:15), shown in Figure 4.2b. Herrmann's music accompanies the discovery of an underground source of amazement and makes use of a handful of pantriadic modules. The main harmonic cell is a six-chord-long tour through a menagerie of tonal wonders, [EM⇨Dm⇨B♭m⇨G♭M⇨E♭M⇨CM⇨EM]. Herrmann's harmonic loop is repeated twice verbatim before the scene moves onto other topics. While E major begins and ends the progression (and is even prepared by a retrospectively functional B-major dominant), it is not prolonged in even the most anemic sense of that word. Each chord is a strange realm unto itself.[14]

(a)

Figure 4.2a Herrmann, *Jason and the Argonauts,* "Prophecy".

(b)

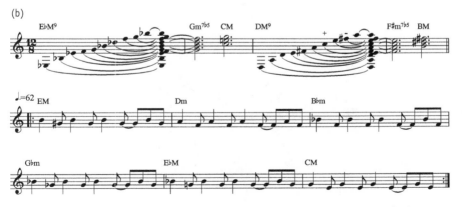

Figure 4.2b Herrmann, *Journey to the Center of the Earth,* "Mushroom Forest".

MYSTERIOUS ISLAND

Pantriadic harmony in Herrmann is both pervasive and systematic. These characteristics create a breeding ground for the sorts of score-specific networks of harmonic reference and implication that repay close analysis. Consider another entry into the composer's library of fantasy scores. Figure 4.3a provides the first few modules of the cue "The Nautilus" from *Mysterious Island* (1961)—a score praised as an "ingenious potpourri" of orchestral colors (Smith 2002 [1991]: 249). This material accompanies a dialogue-free scene (55:35, ▶) in which the castaways discover a submarine, soon revealed to be the property of the legendary Captain Nemo. No prolongation, diatonic or otherwise, is operative. Nor are there any clear cadential goals or telegraphed thematic endpoints. Despite these coherence-thwarting effects, the passage does not feel disordered, largely because the voice leading is smooth and the lexicon of triadic progressions and melodic gestures is limited. Overall, the cue is powered by two parsimonious third relations of differing size and direction (**RP, LP**); together, these enable a 5-6-5 intervallic pattern between outer-voices, and a semitonal descent in both melody and bass.

The analysis offered below the reduction in Figure 4.3a assigns neo-Riemannian transformations to each of the excerpt's triadic moves. While the majority are relatively straightforward third motions, the shift from B♭m to E♭M in mm. 3–4 is analyzed in three separate ways. The explanations offered range in complexity from a simple unary label to a seven-stage compound transformation. What motivates the explosion of possibilities for this one progression, hardly an aspect of the cue that leaps out as especially strange or marked for attention? Each interpretation, I submit, has value, and each tells a different story about how we hear this move depending on our aural frame of reference.

If we are concerned only with the intrinsic, context-divorced sound of these progressions, there is no reason not to describe the switch from B♭ minor to E♭ major in mm. 2–3 as a simple **F** motion, which preserves a B♭ common tone while shifting the triad's major-third interval by semitone. And while too understated to sound like a true absolute progression, the gesture does project a hint of the wondrous quality commonly associated with **F**, a fifth progression that curiously

Figure 4.3a Herrmann, *Mysterious Island*, "The Nautilus."

refuses to assert either of its chords as more "tonic" than the other. The ternary option, **PRL**, on the other hand, makes use of the canonical neo-Riemannian operators (NRO)s. Its virtue is consistency, accounting for the move by using the same incremental operators as the rest of the passage. This approach keeps the analysis's implicit distance metrics and tonal space pathways consistent (which we will explore more in the next section).

That leaves the far more elaborate **PLPR·PLP**—a description absurdly out of proportion, it might seem, with the apparent simplicity of the progression. So, why the complexity? The rationale for this byzantine transformation stems from the *thematic* origination of the harmonies in "The Nautilus." This cue, like many in *Mysterious Island*'s score, is based on a germinal motif first heard in the film's opening credits, and twenty-nine additional times prior to the particular passage in question. The three-chord fanfare, which Herrmann uses to signal fantastic and threatening sights, is shown in Figure 4.3b. Harmonically, the motif consists of two chromatic third motions (**RP** and **LP**) followed by a stepwise return to the initiating triad, after which the pattern is normally repeated. The sheer amount of repetition this fanfare undergoes prior to "The Nautilus" ensures it becomes referential, a little shard of involuntary harmonic memory. The more that Herrmann plays with the fanfare, the more likely that similar but inexactly duplicative melodies, textures, or progressions will be heard in terms of it. Gradually, an expectation forms that that minor triads at the end of any three-chord unit will progress back to the place where the unit began. In Figure 4.3a, this progress can be represented most faithfully by reversing the pattern that got us to the third chord. That is to say, with a **PLPR** compound transformation that literally undoes what came before. (T_9 would also be an apt label, especially considering the block-chord voice leading of each triad, though is less appropriate for the smooth, incremental voice leading of "The Nautilus.")

"The Nautilus" begins with exactly this three-chord pattern. Whatever pathway the third chord will take to the fourth will, I suggest, be perceived in a way that refers to the anticipated first chord in the series. Thus, when the pattern-disrupting E♭-major triad sounds in m. 3 of "The Nautilus," it is through an *unheard* B minor that that unexpected triad should be referred. This is where that bulky explanation of **PLPR·PLP** comes from. It formalizes the sense in which

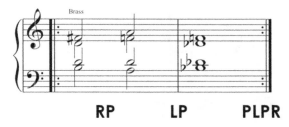

RP   LP   PLPR

Figure 4.3b Herrmann, *Mysterious Island*, three-chord fanfare.

Herrmann's progression must first pass back through Bm to reach its destination of E♭M. The initial step, **PLPR**, is the normative "reversing" transformation from the fanfare. Whether or not we consider Bm to be the tonic of the sequence, it represents a fair anticipation of where Herrmann will head at this stage. The difference between expected and actual destination is represented by the second step, a transformational modification to the missing Bm. This hexatonic polar **PLP** deposits us on E♭M.[15] The complex overall transformation thus captures a subtle but important intentional (in Rings's sense) aspect of this seemingly innocuous motion.

Figure 4.4 produces a network for the entire "Nautilus" cue. The diagram's intent is to encapsulate each sounding and possible progression in terms of the basic harmonic frame established by Herrmann's three-chord fanfare. The shaded triangle consisting of B-, D-, and B♭-minor triads is the motivic basis for the entire cue, and as noted it hails directly from the fanfare. Meanwhile, E♭M and D♯m are attached as harmonic supplements off to the right, with E♭M in particular shown to be auxiliary in nature, not participating in any of the pertinent symmetries of the core network. Directed arrows indicate the path taken during the first three measures, and dotted edges convey implied pathways for the whole cue. Arcing all the way across the network is the monster **PLPR·PLP** compound, which is now more clearly shown as a way of passing back through the initial triad before hitting its E♭M mark. The alternative, more direct, but less motivically informed interpretations of this progression are shown as well: a straight **F** transformation, "as the crow flies," and a mediated **LPR** that takes a transformationally more circuitous route.

Transformation theory is interpretive. However mathematical seeming its tools, it does not provide objective descriptions, but rather it generates "takes" based on ever-shifting frames of auditory reference. Anyone looking for a single, unified answer to how a pantriadic module from *Mysterious Island* works is unlikely to be satisfied with the multiplicity of stories I have told about the move from B♭m to E♭M. Yet multiplicity is inseparable from the notion of transformation.

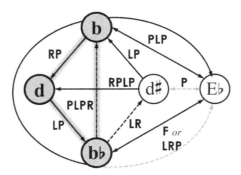

Figure 4.4 Herrmann, *Mysterious Island, general network.*

Transformational accounts of music encourage—even mandate—what Rings calls a "prismatic" analytical outlook, one in which "phenomenologically rich passages are refracted and explored from multiple angles" (2011b: 38). Not every account needs such an extreme (uncharitably, contrived) profusion of explanations. Nevertheless, insisting upon sensitivity to harmonic contextuality ensures that our interpretive refractions do not spread out in every possible, arbitrary direction but stay focused on meaningful and rewarding new ways of hearing.

Distance

MEASURING PANTRIADIC DISTANCE

In the previous chapter, I defined compound transformations as musical moves involving more than one neo-Riemannian operator, given the basic or "unary" members of one's transformational inventory. The ability for NRT's descriptive units to combine in numerous, often interpretively interesting ways, makes transformational analysis *combinatorial* in nature. Besides facilitating the kind of contextual approach I advocated above, this capacity for combinatorial description is behind one of the more useful features of NRT: the linkage of transformational complexity with subjective distance.

The expressive impact of pantriadic film music is wrapped up in the way listeners gauge varying degrees of distance between triads. As analysts, we would like to be able to qualify subjective impressions of harmonic distance in language more precise than "sounding close" or "foreign." Normally, these judgments are grounded in metrics such as key-signature similarity and number of rotations along the circle of fifths. However, without the framework of diatonic tonality to provide these predetermined standards of proximity, transformational analysis must consider alternative measuring sticks for tonal space. Luckily, for assessing the span covered by a triadic transformation there are other means, three of which can easily be determined through neo-Riemannian analysis: voice-leading work, transformational word length, and sounding voice-leading interval.[16]

1. **Voice-leading work** is a measurement of the number of half steps that a transformation's operators cumulatively shift one sonority to arrive at another sonority. As Cohn formulates it, a single unit of voice-leading work is "the motion of one voice by semitone," and it deals with ideally tight—rather than written—voice leading, assuming octave, inversional, and enharmonic equivalence (2011: 6). Thus, in terms of voice-leading work, a given C-major triad is equidistant from any and all voicings and inversions of, say, any E-minor triad, since no matter how it is written, CM and Em will always differ by only one semitone, C and B. The larger the number of semitones involved in a transformation, the more distant it is, according to voice-leading work. Appropriately, tritonal and stepwise transformations tend to have the highest voice-leading work values. It takes a lot

more half steps to shift from, say, CM to F♯M (six semitonal scootches) than from CM to C♯m (just two), even though both are comparably unusual progressions within functional tonality.

2. **Transformational word length** is a measurement of how many discrete stages it takes to generate a given harmonic move; this metric may be compared with the number of mental steps involved in understanding it and is captured analytically by the number of operators within a transformation (Gollin 2000). Thus, simple unary transformations like **L** and **S** have a short word length, while complex compound transformations like **LSRP** and **DPSRN** have much longer word lengths. Aural complexity is thereby related to transformational (indeed, algebraic) complexity. Word length is a function of how one selects and combines one's transformations, and thus it is more subjective and open to interpretation than many other distance metrics.[17] Usefully, when one is using **L**, **P**, and **R** as transformations, word length is the same as distance traveled on the *Tonnetz*. In general, depicting an intertriadic motion by using unary transformations or short compounds implies smaller perceptual spans between the triads, while longer or more convoluted word lengths suggest correspondingly indirect, complex expanses across tonal space.[18]

3. **Sounding voice-leading interval** is a measurement of how far a given musical line travels between chords *as written*, as judged in terms of a diatonic musical interval like m2 or A4—or more abstractly, in terms of semitones or interval classes. The motion of the bass voice in particular is one of the most salient aspects in assessing felt distance in music; think of the difference in quality between a progression in which the bass remains static versus one in which the bass plunges down by a seventh or octave. Unfortunately, sounding linear distance is a feature that is often underrated, even downright ignored, by transformational theories that, in their rush for explanatory parsimony, abstract away from actual voice leading. Nevertheless, it is essential to keep track of how actual voices behave in written music if the subjective experience of distance is something we are truly interested in capturing with fidelity.

THE PERFECT STORM

To see transformational distance, and these three metrics, in action, let us consider two cues in which a sense of space and scope is played with through harmony. Few film composers understand the power of pantriadic harmony to impart a feeling of expanse better than James Horner. In his score for *The Perfect Storm* (2000), Horner uses chromatic progressions to convey the awe-inspiring threat of a once-in-a-century nor'easter. Late in the film (1:35:00, ▶), the crew of a fishing vessel, the *Andrea Gail*, find themselves stranded in the heart of the tempest. As the ship struggles to stay upright atop the heaving sea, Horner unleashes a series of root-position triads, each swelling in density and volume before giving way to the subsequent chord. The effect

Figure 4.5 Horner, *The Perfect Storm*, "The Decision to Turn Around."

is vertiginous, like a series of waves of growing intensity and magnitude, hurtling the listener into new spaces when the biggest tonal motions hit.[19]

Figure 4.5 provides an analysis of this hair-raising sequence. Horner begins with a smooth oscillation of Dm and B♭m (**L**), but soon he disrupts this pattern with visitations to chords related by ternary compounds and increasingly large-sounding bass intervals: first a minor third by **PRP**, then a major third by **PLP**, and finally a tritone by **PRP**. The trajectory from unary to ternary compounds is repeated in a much compressed manner with a global transposition from the initial reference triad of Dm to a new jumping-off point of F♯m; this transition is effected by a loose "cadential" progression launched from C♯M—a shift too functionally muddled to count as a clear-cut V⇨i motion, perhaps, but well described by the smooth **N** operation. (A reasonable case could also be made for **PLR** here, too.) This new section cuts out the chromatic middlemen and leaps straight to another tritonal **RPR** transformation, producing C major. In terms of voice-leading work, transformational complexity, and bass motion, the two tritone shifts are the sequence's "biggest" strides. In a testament to Horner's instinct for tonal mickey-mousing, both **RPR** transformations occur with cuts away from the desperate crew and onto a wide shot of the *Andrea Gail*, battered by the churning Atlantic. Throughout the passage, all three distance metrics are perfectly coordinated with one another: high voice-leading work correlates with high transformational word length correlates with extent of sounding voice-leading interval.

SUPERMAN

The Perfect Storm's pantriadicism has the analytical advantage of involving only root-position triads, cleanly projected and without structurally significant non-chord tones in any voices. But what of chromatic progressions with more complex surfaces? In such situations, it is not always possible to assess intertriadic distance in a simple, mechanical way. Consider the passage from John Williams's score to *Superman* (1978, 38:40, ▶)), displayed in Figure 4.6. The music accompanies the lone Clark Kent (Jeff East) as he explores a strange and astonishing arctic landscape. Out of this desolate waste, the Fortress of Solitude will soon spring.

A few surface-level ornamentations notwithstanding, the F minor that initiates the cue is essentially frozen in place for its first thirty-five seconds. Similarly

Figure 4.6 Williams, *Superman*, "Arctic Expedition."

fixed is the B♭-minor chord that closes out the passage's final fourteen seconds. Otherwise, the rest of the dozen chords involved in this progression are tonally emancipated, unencumbered of any sort of internal prolongation or hierarchy. Yet despite the prevailing sense of tonal vacuum, not every motion between triads feels equally harmonically alien.

The passage's first four harmonies coincide with medium-distance shots of Clark. As if to match the tight visual perspective in this portion of the scene, the transition from Fm to Dm and Am is accomplished by relatively simple binary transformations, first **PR** and then **RL**. Both compounds retain triadic mode and involve only one intermediary chord, FM, increasing their sense of relatedness, especially in conjunction with the immobilized A4 common tone in the bass. A minor gradually builds in volume, and along with a melodic ascent from E5⇨F5⇨G5, matches a newly awestruck look in Clark's eyes.

The object of telegraphed wonder is revealed in the next shot—an impressive matte painting of the sprawling wilderness, synchronized with the arrival on a thickly scored C♯ minor. The progression in the upper voices that matches this cut is a major-third shift, **PL**. As a pure transformation, **PL** is actually less than distant than the previous two harmonic shifts. However, here is where keeping track of literal bass intervals, rather than chordal roots, becomes crucial. Williams does not sustain the same high orchestral tessitura as the previous three chords for C♯m; rather, he plunges the bass down to C♯2. This massive shift of register corresponds to a downward (enharmonic) major-sixth interval, compounded by several octaves; this registral nosedive dramatically increases the move's overall sense of expanse, with change in texture further reinforcing this feeling of harmonic and melodic dislocation. It also turns out to be an important recurring feature, as the next largest bass motion in the progression (D♯4⇨G3) also descends by eight semitones, and also involves C♯m.

The camera returns to Clark through the next five steps of this progression. Williams continues with an alternation of transformations with relatively short and relatively protracted word lengths, as anticipation builds over what the superhero-in-training will remove from his backpack—a magical Kryptonian crystal, it turns out. Fuzzy transformations are required throughout the cue, as Williams's mostly stepwise bass line does not produce triadic chord tones against the majority of the cleanly projected triads in the upper voices. This technique has a simultaneously gluing and wrenching effect on the passage; it grants the music a degree of linear continuity where it counts the most—the bass—but also highlights the alienation of high and low strata, as upper and lower voices in the score have increasingly less to do with one another, especially once contrary motion has come to dominate the cue's outer-voice counterpoint.

The smoothness of the bass thus partially counteracts some of the chromatic strangeness between top-voice chords during this passage. Smooth, that is, until the film's perspective once again dilates to present the entire frozen landscape and another subjectively tremendous transformation synchronizes with the cut. Williams lands now on GM, which is about as far-flung as is possible relative to its immediate predecessor C#m (with a non-chordal D# in the bass). The resulting transformation is the largest: a tritonal ternary compound, requiring a great deal of voice-leading work (six moving semitones), and hosting another gigantic downward (compound) minor-sixth interval in the bass, and conveyed with another full orchestral swell. The tritone relation is soon answered with another big move: a hexatonic pole, **PLP**, to E♭m. Reversing the tendency of increasing distance, however, is the smaller bass motion, tighter voice leading, and steady stepwise descent, shrinking the subjective breadth of the progression considerably. This contracting effect is similarly in place with the concluding (nonfunctional) fifth motion to B♭ minor. Despite a balance of large strides and small steps, the impression left by this passage in its totality is nevertheless one of tremendous tonal change. Harmonically speaking, we are most assuredly not in Kansas anymore.

Voice Leading

The foregoing discussion of distance made use of the concept of voice-leading work as part of the larger goal of determining tonal proximity. However, voice leading is very rarely discussed as an independent *expressive* parameter, perhaps because, unlike other parametric axes such as dissonance/consonance and proximity/remoteness, voice leading does not suggest an obvious lane for dramatic interpretation. Neo-Riemannian methods can redress this neglect, alerting us to ways in which the treatment of multiple musical lines influences emotion and narrative. Common-tone retention and parsimony are prime among voice-leading attributes to which NRT can draw our attention. The degree of smoothness for a given transformation—either sounding literally or idealized between abstract "Klangs"—provides an informal measure of, for a lack of better word, a progression's "effort." This knowledge this can come in handy when one is analyzing the transitions between remote tonal areas. The simple presence of a common-tone connection can soften what may have otherwise been a most bumpy path. Parsimony is an especially useful compositional tool if the individual harmonic waypoints themselves shine with strikingly different colors. Smooth voice leading enables them to be stitched together in such a way that their connections seem delicate, effortless, even magical.

FELLOWSHIP OF THE RING

In one of the earliest allusions to film music's amenability to neo-Riemannian analysis in the music theory literature, Guy Capuzzo turns to the cue "Aniron" from Howard Shore's *The Lord of the Rings: The Fellowship of the Ring* (2002, 1:35:40, ▶). While the focus of his larger project is chromaticism in popular music, Capuzzo uses this passage as an example of voice-leading parsimony, specifically smoothness within chromatic third relations (2004: 196–197). Capuzzo isolates a passage from "Aniron" that accompanies an ominous conversation between characters Aragorn and Arwen, shortly before a scene change that reveals the two are secret lovers. Shore provides a brief chorale to accompany their dialogue, which centers on Aragorn reluctance to assume his kingly birthright. According to Capuzzo, the progression is positively "shot through with chromatic third relations and p parsimony [literally sounded retention of common tones], a few octave doublings and register shifts notwithstanding" (ibid: 196). The relevant portion of "Aniron" is presented in Figure 4.7.

The pervasive third relations that Capuzzo observes in this cue are very much tied up with Shore's contrapuntal procedures. These third relations, chromatic and otherwise, are the product of a pattern of harmonized neighbor motions involving alternation between root-position and inverted chords.[20] During the vocal portion of the passage, starting at m. 11, the melodic line comes to rest on the common tone A♭4/G♯4, while inner voices alternate B3 and C4 (**P**) and E3 and E♭3/D♯3 (**L**).

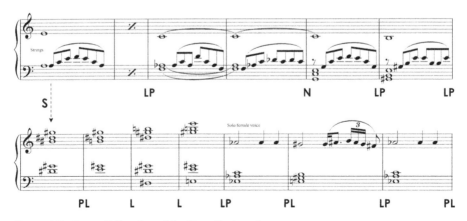

Figure 4.7 Shore, *Fellowship of the Ring*, "Aniron."

This **PL** motion is mirrored in the linkage of A and F minor by **LP** at the cue's onset. The semitonal contrary motion is identical in both cases, with **L** sending E to F and **P** sending A♮ to A♭ in the earlier instance. However, the effect is subtly different due to the absence of common tones in the bass, leaving the implication of linear continuity to the melodic arpeggiations in the cello. Along with the comparatively non-parsimonious transition to C major in second inversion (a textbook instance of **N**), the overall trajectory is from greater contrast between chords to less. By the time m. 8 is reached, the bass voice moves exclusively by semitone.

Shore uses the gradual shift in smoothness to achieve a tranquilizing effect, matching in musical content the move from the weighty realm of kingly responsibility into the private safe haven of Aragorn and Arwen's romance. The relaxation of voice leading is reinforced by the cue's overall harmonic arc, a global **S** from the dark A minor to the softly lit warmth of A♭/G♯ major—shown with the vertical transformation arrow between m. 1 and m. 7. This **S**lide is accomplished indirectly, by a parsimonious recasting of EM as **LP** partner of A♭/G♯M (not, as one might expect in a functional setting, as an unrealized dominant of A minor). But perhaps the most refined transformational touch is how the **LP** shift that brings about the destination key in m. 7 occurs at the exact moment Arwen begins whispering to Aragorn in Elvish instead of speaking in English. It is a model usage of the **LP(M)** progression to suggest otherworldliness and enchantment.

That so much of Hollywood-style chromaticism hews to some form of voice-leading parsimony says as much about the general desire for linear clarity in part writing—or perhaps a composer's tactile affinity for certain routines at keyboard/guitar—as it does the inherent structure of the neo-Riemannian group of transformations. However, film composers have never felt beholden to the strictures of common-practice voice leading: the avoidance of jumpy inner parts, the prohibition of parallel octaves and fifths, and other rules drilled into harmony students. Considerable swathes of many scores from even the most "classically" trained composers may contain nothing but root-position triads, as we have already seen in Horner's *Perfect Storm* music. Blocky planing of chords, transpositional shifts, and invariant chordal inversions are all common occurrences, and their prevalence should steer us away from any reflexive assumption that "smoothness = coherence." Instead, surface roughness ought to be treated as an expressive compositional choice, something to be integrated into analysis, not ignored or reduced away.

For comparatively rough triadic relations, one has the option of casting them as compound transformations, or inventing a unary operation that captures their behavior should tonal context deem them basic or "directly intelligible."[21] Linear smoothness should be evaluated along a continuum that can convey dramatic or symbolic meaning. As witnessed in "Aniron," tightly voice-led passages can map onto states of relaxation or effortlessness, while rough progressions (either complex compounds or bumpily realized NROs) may project effort, tension, or intensification, particularly if triadic mode remains invariant.

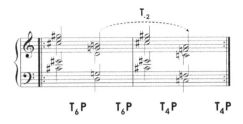

Figure 4.8 Herrmann, *Mysterious Island*, Main Title motif.

The effect need not be understated as it was during Aragorn and Arwen's nocturnal tryst. Consider another motivic cell from Herrmann's *Mysterious Island*, this one from a different section of the main title, reproduced in Figure 4.8 (▶). The octatonic ($\mathbf{T_6P}$, or $\mathbf{RPR}$) and hexatonic ($\mathbf{T_4P}$, or $\mathbf{PLP}$) progressions are already complex by dint of their aggressive renunciation of diatonicism, but Herrmann magnifies the disjunction between each by placing chords in differing octaves and inversions. The effects of transformational word length, voice-leading work, and especially sounding voice leading are united in a shared pursuit of massiveness. In particular, the registral disparities erase any possible trace of latent semitonal voice leading between chords, thereby giving the motif a feeling of enormity and unassimilable otherness.

AVATAR

An extended passage Horner's score to *Avatar* (2008, 3:26, ▶) demonstrates how motion along the spectrum of smooth/rough voice leading can serve formal and expressive ends. Figure 4.9 provides a heavily reduced transcription of a portion of the film's first cue, entitled "You Don't Dream in Cryo," which accompanies an extended arrival sequence that brings the protagonist onto the planet of Pandora. This segment scores Jake's (Sam Worthington) preparations for landing, followed by a panoramic tracking shot of the arrival, with the camera dwelling on images of ecological devastation already wrought by the interplanetary military-industrial complex. The conclusion of the passage matches the dispatching of a military unit onto the strange world's surface. A cursory glance at Horner's music reveals it is about as far from idealized voice-leading smoothness as is possible without sounding successive chords *à la* Herrmann, in different octaves and voicings. Every triad is in root position, even those easily connectable by common tones, and the first fifteen chords are all voice-led by brute transposition, with no attempt to convey contrapuntal independence among interior voices. So much for maximal smoothness.

Measures 1–7 accompany the sight of Jake and company suiting up. This stretch contains both the roughest voice leading and the most thoroughgoing triadic chromaticism, and is a clear case for $\mathbf{T}_n$-type transformational labels over the smooth, combinatorial NROs. Each triadic root relationship follows the mostly third-driven

Figure 4.9 Horner, *Avatar*, "You Don't Dream in Cryo."

melody in doggedly anti-functional fashion. Only the transformations T_3P and $T_{-5}P$ could conceivably occupy a diatonic space. But, surrounded by so many chromatic progressions, they sound as tonally unanchored as everything else. Nevertheless, even within this thicket of parallel voice leading, there are some aspects that lend order to a tonal design that might at first seem rough and anarchic.

Among the first things noticeable from the analysis is the near complete avoidance of transformational repetition. Even as the cue's melody (such as it is) adheres to a roughly predictable contour, the chords that decorate it do not. Just as very few triads are heard repeatedly, only one of the nine intertriadic moves is used on more than one occasion. The repeated move is $T_3(m)$, which by m. 7 lends a faint octatonic feel to the overall progression. Harmonic density amid linear bumpiness is an apt means of reinforcing the anxious affect of the scene. The rigidity of triadic motion aligns with the sequence's threatening tone, one of imposed militarized order. But that order chafes against the in-built apprehension of the tonally ungrounded—and actively parsimony-resistant—progression. Small vacillations in the degree of transformational complexity further contribute to the mood of suspense-despite-regimentation. The most parsimonious transformation, the $T_{-1}P$ within m. 3 (alternatively **S**—the one place an NRO seems justified), is a smooth progression that provides a momentary sigh within the larger bumpy passage. But its calming effect is neutralized by the filmic event with which it coincides: an ancillary character's reference to the threat of death—another nice instance in modern film music of the **Slide** relation associating with ideas of mortality and the uncanny.

The arrival at the next portion of this musical paragraph, mm. 7–9, continues this play with of parsimony and roughness. A $\mathbf{T_4}$ progression at m. 7 initiates the new section, just as it did in m. 1, and corresponds to the opening of a new sight: a scene of ecological devastation on the surface of Pandora. A shot of the denuded landscape is lingered upon, giving Horner a chance to arrest harmonic momentum with a twice-repeated E♭m⇨DM⇨Dm oscillation, driven by **SP**, now with $\mathbf{T_{-1}P}$ as a subsidiary interpretation. This approach creates a more lengthy respite of "smoothness." Yet it continues to also highlight tonal polarization with its repetition of the semitonal major/minor clash of triads.

Measures 10–16 introduce a distinctly different texture and harmonic logic. Here a more active and teleologically driven melody focuses the tonal trajectory into diatonic territory, including (possibly) even the monotonal control of B minor. Horner spins the music first through an **L**-based oscillation, and then through a series of downward diatonic thirds (**L·R·L·R·LR**), reaching all the way to D minor. This final section is smoother by virtue of both transformational simplicity and—crucially—a melody that prominently preserves common tones and melodic motives. So even while the triadic progressions aren't *maximally* smooth (the bass still moves by skips rather than steps), Horner's music provides at last a sense of tonal groundedness, just as Jake's spacecraft lands on terra firma. The downward-chaining of diatonic thirds and the steadily arching melody also suits the increasing sentimentality of the scene, which ends with Jake reminiscing about how "one life ends, another begins." As the ship's crew disembarks on the planet for ethically questionable purposes, ambivalence is once again thrown into the mix with a drawn-out **S**-oscillation with which the musical paragraph concludes. The movie has only just begun, and already the listener has been run through the chromatic ringer several times over.

Equivalence

ISOGRAPHY AND THEMATIC TRANSFORMATION

The idea of equivalence, both as a strict mathematical relationship and a loose intuitive one, has historically been of great interest to composers and music theorists. Entire theoretical systems have been developed for the purpose of relating and comparing disparate musical phenomena (most often sonorities and, in NRT's case, harmonic progressions). These equivalence relations are then used to link what, on the musical surface, might seem dissimilar or incommensurable objects normally hidden from view. The ability to determine musical equivalence helps composers and theorists demonstrate sophisticated, subtle, and elegant connections. Discovering equivalences between pitch structures has been a driving force behind much atonally oriented analysis, and it often seems to stimulate an intensely mathematical and formalistic perspective, as is epitomized by abstruse technologies like Generalized Interval Systems and Klumpenhouwer Networks.[22] The central analytical desideratum of these systems often seems to be **isography**—the property in which two passages containing dissimilar musical materials are shown to be powered by the same underlying set of transformations.[23]

One form of equivalence that requires less of a mathematical mindset to apprehend is *thematic* equivalence: the discovery of connections between musical ideas with melodic, associative, or symbolic content. Thematic equivalence may take two shapes. The most common form is change or development that affects a single recurrent musical idea. More sophisticated is the form of equivalence that involves linkage of distinct musical ideas through a shared motivic common ancestor. Matthew Bribitzer-Stull, employing an apt genetic metaphor, dubs these two dynamic forms of musical equivalence thematic mutation and evolution respectively (2015: 170–194).

Both thematic mutation and evolution are widely analyzed and sought-after aspects of leitmotivic compositional practices. Not surprisingly, they have also enjoyed a privileged status within film music analysis, where melody is often the easiest musical parameter to grasp.[24] But as by the multi-cue network of progressions in Herrmann's *Mysterious Island* proves, harmony may also serve a motivic function in film music, independently from its connection to melody. Harmonic motivism can take a number of guises. Very often, a nonstandard scale, sonority, or progression will be used to provide a distinctive tint to a score, like the dorian ambiance of Thomas Newman's *American Beauty* (1999), or the ♭VII⇨V half-cadences that suffuse Jerome Moross's *The Proud Rebel* (1958), *The Big Country* (1958), and many other Westerns. The most thoroughly deployed harmonic motifs may rise to the level of full-blown *leitharmonie*, developed methodically over the soundtrack, shifting in outward form and accumulating meaning in exactly the ways we expect of melodic themes.

Locating thematic and leitharmonic equivalences has been of central importance of the project transformation theory since its inception. David Lewin's discovery of an isographic relationship between two seemingly unrelated ideas in Wagner's *Das Rheingold* is the classic instance of transformation theory revealing (or asserting) connections not immediately apparent in the score.[25] However, the true value of Lewin's analysis is not that it demonstrates a recherché structural connection between Wagner's materials. Rather, it is the way that the observation opens up a variety of *interpretive* possibilities—in the case of *Rheingold*, concerning the dramatically significant corruption of one leitmotif by another—that makes it a worthy model for analysis. Demonstrating musical equivalence is, at its core, a means of establishing compositional unity, which, given certain widespread but by no means unquestionable assumptions, entails compositional value. As I argued in Chapter 1, unity—and by extension equivalence—is not of *automatic* interest to film music analysis. Indeed, the discovery of leitharmonic similarity across a score matters at least as much for what it makes possible for hermeneutic investigation as for what it has to say about textual unity. In the short case studies to follow, I entertain both purely formalistic and interpretive forms of harmonic equivalence. An incidental but intentional focus on the leitharmonic value of **Slide** throughout each case study provides its own form of unity on this section.

THE GOONIES

Dave Grusin's score to *The Goonies* (1985) contains a beautifully realized example of harmonic motivicism. The score is eclectic and highly referential in its deployment of tonal idioms, which range from Baroque-pop for the opening chase sequence to scrambling atonality during frightening scenes. Grusin leans heavily on pantriadic chromaticism for plot elements concerning the film's central quest, which revolves around a group of children seeking out a pirate treasure horde (hidden away somewhere on the coast of modern Oregon, of all places). One way in which the composer ties these diverse tonal styles together is with a recurrent multi-triad progression, encapsulated by the transformational cell **L·S**. This transformational germ exemplifies Bribitzer-Stull's evolutionary paradigm, arising in a number of expressively and thematically dissimilar contexts over the course of the film.

Figure 4.10 summarizes three iterations of this harmonic motif as it emerges within a trio of very different cues (▶). Upon its first iteration (18:11), the **L·S** progression falls near the end of a quietly enigmatic cue, "Map and Willy" (Figure 4.10a). In this context, the succession of A♭m⇨EM⇨Fm brings to a close an otherwise thoroughly hexatonic succession of triads and polychords. All are orchestrated with what will become a recurrent timbral figure, a downward arpeggio on a Rhodes keyboard. The setting in which these chords appear is essentially tonic free, but the leitharmonic cell really does stand out, with the **S**-progression

Figure 4.10 Grusin, *The Goonies*, recurrences of transformational motif: (a) "Map and Willy"; (b) "The Goondocks"; (c) "Pirate Ship."

in particular forming a striking contrast against the overall hexatonic organization of the cue.

A second instance of **L·S** occurs not as a floating progression like in "Map and Willy," but *intra*-thematically, nestled squarely within a theme. It provides a dash of pantriadic piquancy to Grusin's wistful cue "The Goondocks" (21:30, Figure 4.10b), which showcases a lyrical melody that comes to attach to the titular group of misfits. Unlike the earlier case, here the progression can be heard as a chromatic digression within the global context of a conventionally articulated tonic (A major). In prolongational terms, **L·S** helps sustain and recolor the theme's leading tone, G♯. Significantly, the pitch A♭/G♯ serves, as it did in the "Map and Willy," as both a conspicuous common tone and a short-range pedal point in the bass.

Also like "Map and Willy," the **L·S** cell within is flanked by two major-third progressions, which are also indicated in Figure 4.10b. However, the reader should note a certain degree of transformational inexactitude due to the dissonant structure of some of the adjacent chords. This additional resemblance nevertheless strengthens and expands the leitharmonie into an **LP·L·S·L** progression five chords long. The equivalence relation happens to be dualistic. Where the "Willy" progression (Cm⇨A♭m⇨EM⇨Fm⇨D♭M) had major chords, the "Goondocks" (AM⇨C♯M⇨Fm⇨EM⇨G♯m) has minor ones. Yet despite its emergence within two wholly different thematic and expressive contexts, the linkage is eminently audible. A host of corroborating features—pitch level, voicing, texture, and temporal proximity—ensure that an associative bond is formed between these mirror-image passages.

After several subsequent cues that employ this progression, Grusin summons the **L·S** motif for one last statement (1:47:40, Figure 4.10c) during the film's closing image of a pirate ship miraculously piloting itself across the Pacific. To accompany this astounding sight, Grusin integrates the leitharmonic progression into yet another theme, this one of a heroic, seafaring character.[26] The functional role of **L·S** within this context is straightforward compared to its earlier iterations: it facilitates a prolongation of the submediant of C major, producing both modal flavors of the scale step after a statement of the subdominant, IV⇨vi⇨♭VI. As before, Grusin aids the filmgoer in making this film-spanning harmonic association through orchestrational details; again, he colors the magical **S**-progression (Am⇨A♭M) with that characteristic downward Rhodes piano arpeggio. The ultimate effect is one of film-spanning unity, yes, but also—and primarily—of associative consistency. In *The Goonies*, feelings of mystery and adventure, friendship and family are tied up with one another, even in a sense mutually implicative, all connected to a basic quest narrative, that, unlike other aspects of this quintessential 1980s film, will never feel out of date.

KING KONG

A less overt but more dramatically interesting instance of transformational recurrence may be found in James Newton Howard's score to Peter Jackson's

King Kong (2005) remake.[27] Like the hidden connections that Lewin unearthed from Wagner's *Ring*, the leitharmonic developments in *Kong* rely not on a literal identity between compositional details, but rather on a subtle equivalence that can be made apparent through transformational analysis. Unlike the relationships at work in *The Goonies*, Newton Howard's leitharmonic connection involves progressions in their purest form, irrespective of chronological ordering or tonal function. The two relevant ideas, which I label as "Threat" and "Dignity," come from early and midway through the film, respectively, and represent a critical shift in attitude (from protagonist and audience alike) toward the titular beast.

Figure 4.11 shows two versions the "Threat" motif (▶). It makes its first appearance at the moment the movie's title appears on screen (Figure 4.11a). The audiovisual accent, along with the motif's growling tone, renders its intended monstrous referent unmistakable. At this nascent stage, "Threat" lacks triadic thirds, making its modality ill-defined. The two vertical dyads E-B and E♭-B♭ contain hints of both modes, while the bass motion falls in pairs of ominously descending minor thirds (G2⇨E2, E♭2⇨C2). The motif's aggressive guise and placement within a larger G-minor cue lend it the negative valence of the minor mode without literal scalar confirmation. This is Newton Howard's representation of Kong as a monster, a primitive threat born of Western civilization's deepest fears.

Figure 4.11b portrays a fleshed-out form of the motif as it occurs during the action set-piece cue "Tooth and Claw." Newton Howard's music accompanies a bravura action scene in which Kong does battle with three giant theropod dinosaurs—all while attempting to protect the luckless heroine Anne Darrow (Naomi Watts). There is now enough contextual information to confidently analyze "Kong's Threat" in terms of the key of C. Furthermore, its functional succession [i⇨♭vi⇨♭VI⇨IV] embeds a host of triadic transformations that will soon be rearranged and repurposed. The m3-paired dyads of the initial "Threat" motif are here now treated as **RP/PR**-related chromatic mediants with respect to each other. Meanwhile, the pivot around ♯6̂/♭6̂ from the original, unharmonized motif

Figure 4.11 Newton Howard, *King Kong*, "Kong's Threat" motif: (a) main title; (b) "Tooth and Claw."

now plays host to a Slide, one of Newton Howard's favorite progressions. The overall motion from Cm to FM is encapsulated by the ever-functionally allusive **F**, while two phantom **L**-relations connect the non-adjacent chords in the passage. Every one of these individual transformations revolves around the same fixed point: a C♯ common tone, providing the chordal root, third, and fifth of C-, A/A♭-, and F-triads respectively.

Soon after introducing this more robust version of the "Threat" motif, Newton Howard begins assembling a new theme, one that will come to connote Kong's wild—but sad and ultimately tragic—grandeur. The dinosaur battle culminates with a definitive pronouncement of this new idea, a "Dignity" theme (1:53:58, ▶). At the moment of full annunciation (Figure 4.12), the theme marks Kong's defeat of the last of his adversaries, a feat witnessed by Darrow with a combination of awe, fear, and gratitude. "Dignity" is subject to continuous and rapid chromatic modulations both on its outskirts and, more distinctively, *within* its phrasal boundaries. It is sufficiently pantriadic so as to discourage definitive tonic assignment except for the asserted (but prolongationally unearned) reference chords of Dm and AM. Each individual transformation lends a distinctive affective quality to the theme as a whole. The emblematic progression is **S**, which steers its first phrase (Dm⇨D♭M) and guides chord-to-chord motion in its second (Gm⇨G♭M and B♭m⇨AM). **S** has the effect of shifting the tonal ground under the melody's feet, ensuring that the arpeggio-based theme is always struggling to remain tonally balanced. It is not a poor harmonic analog to Kong's attempt to grapple with his reptilian assailant, who eventually succumbs to the giant ape's superior strength.

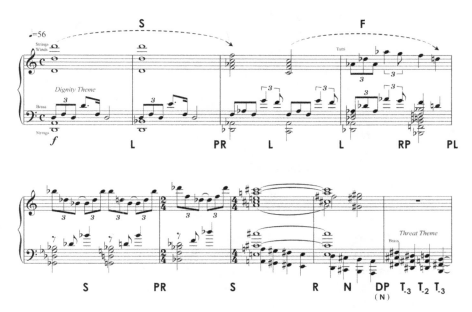

Figure 4.12 Newton Howard, *King Kong*, "Kong's Dignity" motif.

The theme's mode-mirroring **L** transformations tap that progression's twin cinematic associations with sentimentality and epic import, in the process lending to the scene a sense of sonic pathos that contrasts nicely with its visual ferocity. The **RP** that draws the music to B♭ major suggests heroism, while the **F** that does so indirectly taps that progression's connotation of amazement. Together, **RP** and **F** signal the long-awaited turning of the tide in Kong's favor. In general, like-moded third progressions serve intensificatory purposes in "Dignity." This is particularly clear with the Gm⇨B♭m motion that precedes the passage's climactic discharge of tension onto a triumphal chord of A major at the excerpt's end.

S, F, L, and **RP/PR** . . . If these transformations sound familiar, it is because viewers of *King Kong* have heard them before, and shall hear many times more as the movie progresses. Though the long, arching contours of "Dignity" have little in common melodically with the terse "Threat" motif, the former's first phrase (which is motivically detachable) shares with it exactly and exclusively the same transformational vocabulary. The easiest way to depict this equivalence—what amounts to transformational isography—is by recourse to the *Tonnetz*. Figure 4.13 displays the *Tonnetz* "slices" occupied by both themes. The identical tonal geometry implied by these leitmotifs is unmistakable. Both hinge on a single common tone (C♯ for "Threat," F♯ for "Dignity"), though in neither case is that retained pitch prominently emphasized on the musical surface. The space constitutes what Cohn (2012: 113) calls a common tone "neighborhood": a loop of six triads—some diatonic kinsfolk, some chromatically estranged—that can be created and traversed by twice iterating an ordering of **L**, **P**, and **R** that uses each NRO once and only once. In neither theme does Newton Howard visit all six triads in the neighborhood. Rather, he leaves unsounded the **N**-related pair of triads (FM and B♭m for "Threat," CM and Fm for "Dignity"). This shared omission further strengthens the association of the two motifs, and accounts for their conspicuous non-reliance on dominant⇨tonic functional articulation.

In the four-chord segments of the *Tonnetz* that comprise the *Kong* neighborhood, there are six possible generic moves between triads: two **L**s, two **RP/PR**s, an **S**, and an **F**. But while Figure 4.13 models the equivalence of triadic interrelationships across the two motifs, there is nothing in the graph that mandates hierarchy or chronological ordering. This omission is deliberate; while Newton Howard's themes share the same harmonic DNA, they differ markedly in their formal and temporal characteristics. In Kong's "Threat," **S** shifts between modally mixed submediant triads, while **F** stands in as a quasi-cadential means of returning the subdominant to the local tonic. In Kong's "Dignity," these two progressions are more or less set free of any specific tonal mooring, and only occur between non-adjacent chords. Conversely, the **L** relation is explicit in "Dignity," as befits the theme's more pathetic tenor, while it lurks only implicitly in "Threat."

These divergences amount to a difference in the way shared harmonic genetic material is expressed. Over time, Newton Howard allows the embryonic, naively fearful "Threat" motif to metamorphose into the mature, humane "Dignity" theme. By virtue of a clever transformational equivalence, then, Kong's "Threat"

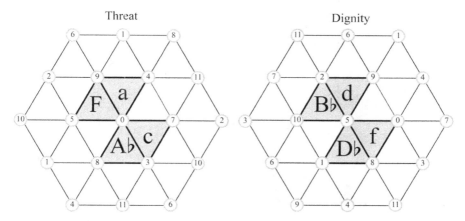

Figure 4.13 Newton Howard, *King Kong*, motifs in the *Tonnetz*.

transforms right alongside the audience's relation to the titular beast. We shift from viewing him unfairly as an antagonist at film's beginning to potential protagonist at its midpoint, and by the tragic ending, by far the most sympathetic character, human or simian.

INCEPTION AND VERTIGO

In keeping with the spirit of Babbitt's idea of contextuality, most readings of transformational equivalence stick to single musical texts—in our case, individual films and film franchises. But while evidence of authorial intentionality or audience perceptibility necessarily drops off when we begin discussing harmonic equivalences *across* ostensibly unrelated films, there is something to be gained by comparing tonal materials from disparate films. Film musicologist Tom Schneller, for example, has located a number of harmonic quirks within John Williams's film music that appear to signify clearly and consistently. For example, he peels back a few layers of surface dissimilarity to show a structural I⇨ii$^{\varnothing7}$⇨♭II⇨I progression at the heart of several of Williams's themes for female protagonists in *Star Wars* and *Indiana Jones* franchises (2013: 64–67).[28] Schneller's approach, while not transformational per se (he is primarily focused on diatonic mode mixture), nevertheless exemplifies the proper rationale for locating cross-film harmonic equivalences: associativity. It is not compositional influence, but associative cachet that makes locating harmonic equivalences across multiple films a worthwhile task.

Consider two very different psychological thrillers: Christopher Nolan's *Inception* (2010) and Alfred Hitchcock's *Vertigo* (1958), the themes of which are reduced and analyzed in Figure 4.14 (▶). As I observed in this book's introduction, Hans Zimmer's motto for *Inception* has to it a curious harmonic structure.[29] The theme (Figure 4.14a) compulsively shifts the ground under a doggedly retained B♭ common tone, beginning on Gm, flexing then to G♭M, and inevitably curving back via E♭M and C♭M^{Ma7}. Over the course of *Inception*, Zimmer's theme

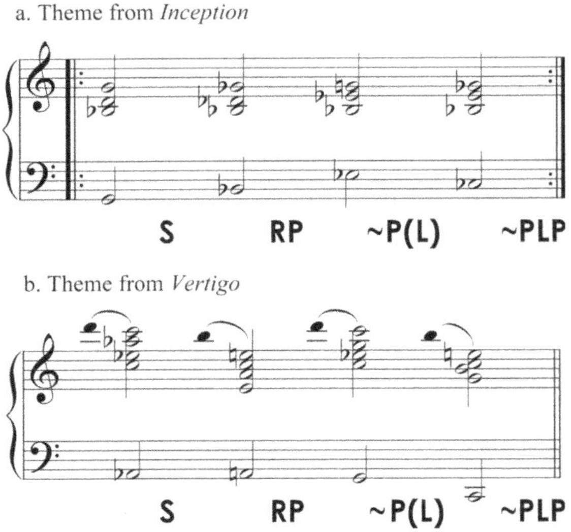

a. Theme from *Inception*

S   RP   ~P(L)   ~PLP

b. Theme from *Vertigo*

S   RP   ~P(L)   ~PLP

Figure 4.14 Zimmer and Herrmann, transformational analogues: (a) *Inception* theme; (b) *Vertigo* theme.

becomes a musical metaphor for the film's warped landscapes and recursively nested dream narratives.[30]

The progressions that power this motif thrum with harmonic ambivalence and distortion. **S**lide gets things off to a confusing enough start, instantly putting into question the tonicity of the phrase-initiating Gm. This motion is followed by a more unambiguously distant transformation, an octatonic **RP** that lands on E♭M, and after those, two further hexatonic rotations. The presence of a chordal seventh in the fourth step of the progression, C♭M^{Ma7}, requires some transformational massaging. The transformation that acts on the upper pitches alone is indicated outside parentheses, while the transformation that would then produce the more salient C♭M is enclosed within parentheses. Thus, E♭M⇨C♭M^{Ma7} is analyzed as ~P(L), with **P** yielding an E♭ minor triad that is retained, followed by **L** to generate C♭M.

Herrmann's score to Hitchcock's *Vertigo* is a similarly **S**lide-obsessed. The film's iconic sonority, heard prominently during point-of-view shots of acrophobia-inspiring heights, has been dubbed the "Vertigo Chord" (Cooper 2001: 29–30). The sonority is hardly composed of a bitonal juxtaposition of "unrelated triads," as Cooke, echoing many commentators, notes (2008: 208). Rather, the Vertigo Chord is a verticalization of the leitharmonic **S**-progression. The result is a polychordal clash between E♭ minor and D major, voiced as a throbbingly dissonant (and cannily symmetrical) E♭m$^{7(♭9,♯11)}$ chord.[31] This emblematic sonority is itself derived from *Vertigo*'s tonally queasy "Prelude." An eerie presentiment of the chord arises out of the first presentation of the movie's dreamy love theme, the harmonic outlines of which are reproduced in Figure 4.14b. Herrmann's added-note chords contribute color but do not conceal the underlying **S** between the phrase's opening A♭M⇨Am shift. And the presence of non-<037> pitches if anything *strengthens* the hexatonic orientation of the theme's concluding sweep of Cm$_4^6$⇨CM^{Ma7}. The final chord of the phrase can be thought of as a fusion of Em and CM, its formation therefore described once again by the fuzzy compound ~**P(L)**.

Remarkably, the transformational structure of *Vertigo*'s love theme is identical that of Zimmer's *Inception* theme. Though the mode of their initially inputted triad differs, the transformational succession is perfectly isomorphic: in both cases, **S·RP·~P(L)·~PLP**. In the case of *Vertigo*, the common tone that gives the theme a contrapuntal through-line is a texturally unemphasized C5, compared to the similarly inconspicuous B♭4 in *Inception*. Even the ~**P(L)** that accounts for polychordal mixture for the fourth chord achieves the same end and in the same fashion for both themes. A conscious intertextual reference on Zimmer's part is extremely unlikely—in no interview has Zimmer ever so much as mentioned Herrmann as an influence, much less one particular moment from a film scored half a century prior. Nevertheless, the way in which both themes share this underlying transformational plan is fitting and not altogether surprising. Continuing Bribitzer-Stull's hereditary metaphor, the *Vertigo/Inception* similarity is a case of convergent motivic evolution. Herrmann and Zimmer independently discovered separate but analogous ways in which to interweave hexatonic and **S**lide-based transformations into memorable thematic materials. The choice of those individual progressions, it is clear, was informed by their strong extramusical connotations—ambivalence, dream, wonder, paradox. The result in both cases is a riddle four chords long, unnerving the listener early on and suggesting the films' respective narratives are not to be taken at face value.

Patterning

SYMMETRY AND SYMMETRY BREAKS

Try out one more experiment on the piano. Pick any triad and with it any (non-involuting) triadic transformation. Apply that transformation once. With the resulting new triad, apply that same transformation again. And again. Notice how the expressive impact of the initial transformation is redoubled. And notice too how successive repetitions of the same triadic shift can make even the most "incoherent"-sounding initial motion start to sound purposeful, even inevitable. Now try the same experiment with a cell of two (or three, or four) transformations instead of one. Do the expressive and syntactic aspects get reinforced, or are they diluted?

Because pantriadic harmony tends to disrupt centric modes of hearing, composers who employ this style often turn to alternative principles for organizing harmony. The creation of methodically patterned progressions is a common tactic, especially when realized through symmetrical processes like sequences and interval cycles. The dramatic potential of patterns and regular routines is high, as is their ability to lend otherwise disruptive chromaticism a form of regularity. This capability is particularly true of symmetries that are spawned through long discursive progressions, such as generated by repeated iterations of NRO compounds. The most filmically familiar of these are hexatonic and octatonic sequences, though other more exotic cycles find their way into underscore as well. While symmetrical tonal processes will, by definition resist the stabilizing force of a single prolonged key, they can impose affective uniformities and long-range expectations of their own.

Affective intensification is often the goal of chaining together multiple instances of the same progression; if one transposition makes a scene feel more urgent, imagine how much more dire three or four feel. But the expressive impact of transformational patterning also inheres in the way symmetry divides tonal space up differently from the way conventional functional tonality does. Asymmetries within the diatonic collection help the listener orient him or herself. Without those built-in signposts of difference, symmetrical progressions can easily suggest ambiguity, disorientation, lack of direction, chaos. At the same time, a sequence is defined by a predictable, internally consistent pattern and thus can evoke order, meticulousness, and—if sequential or cyclical completion is telegraphed—teleology. We are rarely truly "lost" within a clearly maintained chromatic sequence: we remember where we begin and can anticipate where we are heading. This is not as contradictory as it sounds. Distinguishing between symmetry-as-tonal-antigravity and symmetry-as-tonal-hyper-logic typically depends on contextual details outside the sphere of harmony proper—matters like phrase rhythm, motivic relations, and progression-spanning dynamics and orchestration.

Like equivalence and isography, tonal patterning is a fervently sought-after feature of many transformational analyses. However, film scoring is not about producing patterns for their own sake, and composers are under no obligation to follow through with what in a concert work could be a systematic or form-generative symmetry. It is for this reason that film music stands as an ideal repertoire in which to inspect how and why transformational patterns not only arise, but change, break down, or are forgotten. As we will see, symmetry-breakage can be an expressive device of comparable dramatic value compared to the original procedure itself.

ABOVE AND BEYOND

More than even Bernard Herrmann, Hugo Friedhofer was a cunning synthesizer of musical styles, able to blend the rich symphonic canvases of Classical Hollywood with a sometimes startlingly bold harmonic language. Figure 4.15 provides a reduction of a sequence in Friedhofer's score to the 1952 military drama *Above and Beyond* (1952, 1:45:25, ⓟ). The film has a weighty subject matter: it tells the story of the American pilots involved in dropping the atomic bomb on Hiroshima. Pantriadicism is reserved for moments of wonder and dread throughout Friedhofer's works, and in *Above and Beyond*, it becomes associated with the terrible power of the nuclear weapon. This particularly brooding sequence stems from a scene in which *Enola Gay* pilot Paul Tibbets (Robert Taylor) informs his crew that they will be arming the bomb themselves once airborne. Friedhofer's harmony is tritone-driven, with four successive oscillations between T_6-related minor triads. The infernal connotations of the "devil's interval" are in full force here, insinuating that the weapon is a kind of primal evil about to be unleashed on the world.[32]

The passage is orderly to an almost rigid degree. The Tonnetz slice in Figure 4.16 illustrates the systematic manner in which the music visits each

Figure 4.15 Friedhofer, *Above and Beyond*, "Hiroshima Run."

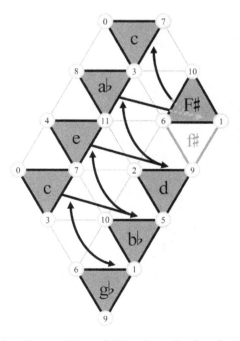

Figure 4.16 Friedhofer, *Above and Beyond*, "Hiroshima Run" in the *Tonnetz*.

tritonal oscillation. Friedhofer introduces new oscillations by repeatedly shifting down by major second, from Cm to B♭m, Em to Dm and so on. Doing so allows the progression to eventually return to its starting point of C minor. In the process, the chordal roots of the sequence form a little whole-tone scale, C-D-E-F♯-G♯-B♭. As is typical with symmetrical music, one pattern gives rise to another: the metrically emphasized triads (Cm⇨Em⇨A♭m⇨Cm) of the progression also form an implicit hexatonic cycle, inserting yet more anxiety and murk into the already pitch-black cue.

As elegant as the zipper-like structure of Figure 4.16 is, Friedhofer's sequence does not adhere to a *perfect* transformational symmetry. One small detail—the way in which C minor is recaptured—falls outside the governing pattern. A♭ does not transit to F♯minor on its way to C, but rather hits F♯ major. This is the first and only major-mode triad in the sequence. Admittedly, the basic transpositional scheme is not compromised—the roots of all triads are still related by T_6 or T_{10}. But the modal symmetry is disrupted, if just for a moment. It is impossible to know the exact compositional justification for such a small incongruity. We might speculate that Friedhofer wished to emphasize the return to C minor by slightly recoloring this progression, by that point in the cue heard seventeen times. Triads of differing mode related by tritone actually involve shorter neo-Riemannian compounds than like-moded pairings (the difference between the ternary **RPR** and quaternary **RPRP/PRPR**). Yet considering the modal uniformity of the rest of the cue, the impact here is actually of *greater* distance, or at least greater contrast. Habituation breeds decreased attention, even with as strange a transformation as T_6. The more unyielding a composer's adherence to a predictable pattern, the more easily a strategic disruption can prick the listener's ears.

BATMAN

Friedhofer's triadic symmetries emerge on the musical surface, but patterning has its uses on a cue or even score-based level as well.[33] Such is the case with the cue "Flowers" from Danny Elfman's career-making score to *Batman* (1989, 47:35, ▶). During this sequence, Bruce Wayne (Michael Keaton) is tailed surreptitiously by the reporter Vicki Vale (Kim Basinger). At the end of her pursuit, Vale discovers the millionaire placing a bouquet down in a dingy alleyway. The main portion of the cue is represented in an annotated harmonic reduction in Figure 4.17. Elfman's harmony is densely pantriadic, skirting speedily (and without cadential reinforcement) across chromatically related regions in a manner characteristic of much of the composer's scoring. The surface is enriched by more than a few nonresolving dominant sevenths, augmented triads, and added-sixth chords—for the sake of clarity, most, if not all, of these extra-triadic materials are reduced out in the diagram. The result is harmonically tentative and perhaps a little morose, instantly calling to mind the sound world of Herrmann, one of Elfman's avowed idols.[34]

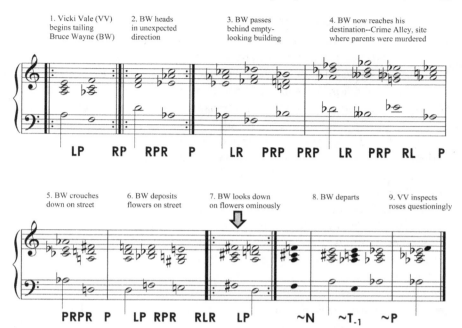

Figure 4.17 Elfman, *Batman*, "Flowers."

Over the span of nine harmonic modules, Elfman spins out a series of developing variations on *Batman*'s main leitmotif.[35] Consequently, the majority of chord-to-chord transformations reflect the harmonic makeup of that germinal theme. Upon its first appearance in the film's splendidly Herrmannesque main title, the Batman motif emphasizes progressions by chromatic minor and major third (E♭M⇨F♯m, F♯m⇨Dm), major second (Bm⇨C♯M), and tritone (Gm⇨E♯M). All of these are represented in "Flowers," though not always in the same phrasal situation as in their initial utterances. The sense of tonal center is in flux throughout, and even progressions stemming from the same transformation can take on different tonal weightings as a result of local context. The **LP/PL** loop that steers the first module, for example, is metrically and melodically weighted in such a way that the higher triad, Am rather than Fm, sounds more stable. Later, in module 7, an identical **LP/PL** loop emphases the lower of the two triads, Dm instead of F♯M—the result of the former's longer duration and recent emphasis in prior modules.

There is much worth remarking upon in this atmospheric cue, but what interests us here is the way its overall tonal trajectory is governed by a symmetrical transformational plan. Short of a few looping progression in modules 1, 2, and 7, there is little direct transformational symmetry on the musical surface. Certain transformations, however, are repeated in characteristic places—**LP**s within modules, **P**s across them, for instance—and this repetition helps engender a different kind of patterning. Peel a layer back from the chord-to-chord surface and one discovers a neatly balanced transpositional succession of tonal regions. This pattern results from the cue's gravitation toward to a limited number of triadic roots—A, A♭, D, and D♭. Figure 4.18 summarizes the near-palindromic structure of Elfman's music. The network makes apparent how the various modules (defined in terms of most salient triadic root, not key) are transposed according to short range $T_{+/-5}$ or T_6 transplantations while being simultaneously related to one another on a grosser scale by $T_{+/-1}$ global transformations. Module 4, which begins with D♭, falls in the middle of the pattern. Its onset marks Wayne's arrival at his destination, and thus serves as an effective hinge about which both the scene and Elfman's tonal plan pivot.

Figure 4.18 features a single wayward module—the brief, isolated A♭m^{add6} chord that effectively concludes the cue with a tonal "symmetry break." The more one studies film music, the more one realizes that even the most mechanically patterned sequences and cycles almost invariably contain such discrepancies. Broken patterns should not be a cause for analytical frustration. Rupturing a regular, orderly process like the "Flowers" palindrome can serve as a neat way to suggest that the narrative is moving on to other matters, similarly to how otherwise monotonal cues might end on a non-tonic chord or trail off on an unresolved dissonance. In "Flowers," the difference in global transformational strategy is echoed through a distinction in local voice leading. Elfman links the last few chords not through direct shifts between triads, but via a sequence that passes through augmented coupling chords, necessitating the use of fuzzy transformations.[36] Yet, even in this case, the symmetry break borrows from the cue's larger transpositional plan, adopting the T_{-1} from earlier and now applying it (almost) directly to A to yield A♭.

Though the overall transformational pattern of "Flowers" does play out directly on the musical surface, it is perfectly easy to hear. It occurs over a short (one minute) span and is conveyed through a consistent, cumulative course of modular variation. Its expressive implications are perhaps a little less obvious, arising, as I suspect the palindrome does, as a bottom-up process—the result of the peculiar ordering of surface triadic transformations that are overtly and intensely expressive on their own. Despite this higher significance placed on the musical foreground for expressive meaning, Elfman's symmetrical design nevertheless

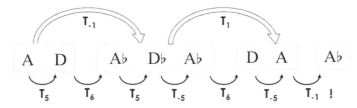

Figure 4.18 Elfman, *Batman*, "Flowers" transformational plan.

does fittingly reflect a certain perplexity that lingers after the scene. The audience, along with our surrogate Vicki Vale, does learn something about Wayne, and this process of discovery seems encapsulated in the forward-driving thrust of the first few modular transpositions. However, by the end of the sequence, the plot significance of those flowers remains (for a naive viewer, at least) obscure. It is thus appropriate that Elfman's tonal trajectory doubles back on itself, leading the listener back to tonal "square one."

CONTACT

One of the most common forms of pantriadic symmetry in film music is the interval cycle, especially interval cycles that spin out of iterated major or minor thirds. Triadic interval cycles have an uncanny capacity to simultaneously suggest continual forward momentum and harmonic stasis. This "barbershop pole" effect is the result of two factors: (1) the symmetrical division of the octave, which weakens, without necessarily eradicating, a sense of return to an already trod cyclic peg and (2) the illusion of constant ascent or descent in frequency. Nowhere is the power for endless intensification more thoroughly exploited in film music than in minor-third (**RP/PR**, or $\mathbf{T}_{+/-3}$)–derived material. Ascending ic 3 cycles acting on minor triads are, along with simple stepwise modulation, among the most common stock generators of chromatic tension in Hollywood. **RP**(m) is an especially expressively potent progression because of the way it transforms the negative valence inherent within the minor triad-as-a-sonority into a dynamic root motion. Upward moving cycles on this transformational generator magnify the darkening effect while adding another perverse twist. Each step along the path of, say, Cm⇨E♭m⇨F♯m⇨. . . has the potential to sound like an escape to the relative major, a chord that, in normal diatonic contexts would serve as a kind of major safe haven away from the minor tonic. Yet the minor tinting of each successive peg along an **RP**(m) cycle denies the listener entry to that major oasis. And, repeated enough times, **RP**(m) arpeggiates a fully diminished seventh bass—a sonority long linked with stress, fear, and abjection.

Examples of downward minor-third cycles are comparatively less common, lacking as they do the steady rise in frequency of their triadic roots that is so historically important in the operation of Bailey-style "expressive tonality." However, they are every bit as capable of installing tension as their up-shifting cousins. Where ascending **RP**(m) cycles "break" the normal progression from i⇨♭III, descending **PR**(m) cycles channel the negative valence of their triadic inputs themselves into a musical motion. When Cm is taken to Am, the chordal root ($\hat{1}$)of the initial triad is turned into the affect-bearing modal scale degree (♭$\hat{3}$)of the next chord. If we put it crudely, with a **PR**(m)-cycle, everything is always getting "more" minor.

For some composers—notably Rózsa, Goldsmith, and Silvestri—octatonicism is a recurrent stylistic signature, even a default way of organizing triadic harmony. Though Silvestri's music to *Contact* (1997) bears considerably less m3-driven material than his veritably Stravinskian scores for *Back to the Future* or *Who Framed Roger Rabbit*, the climactic cue "Good to Go" exploits a downward minor-third cycle to maximum effect. The scene that the octatonic spiral accompanies (1:49:50, ▶) is essentially a lengthy countdown sequence. We see the protagonist Ellie (Jodie Foster) strapped into an untested space-travel vessel while mission control awaits the precise moment to drop the craft into a massive gyroscopic structure. Figure 4.19 displays the complete harmonic trajectory of this cue, with the relative durations of each tonal center conveyed through horizontal extent. Because the various chromatic steps of this cue take place between prolonged regions rather than pure triads (and thus negate parsimonious voice leading to an extent), the transformation T_{-3} is employed instead of **PR**.

Against a series of ceaselessly pulsing ostinati, Silvestri embarks upon two full trips through an $oct_{1,2}$ triadic cycle, beginning on G minor. Regular and predictable as it is, each twist of the cycle seems to bring us closer to the scene's goal of interstellar takeoff. With every slide down the m3-barbershop pole, Ellie's gyroscope speeds up, its whirling energies triggering increasingly strange visual phenomena. The second time Silvestri hits C♯ minor, a significant change of texture grips the orchestra: the ostinato drops away, with more sustained strings and ominous brass counterpoint taking over. This sonic shift coincides with a huge electromagnetic burst on screen, and continues through the following B♭ peg of the cycle.

Desperately concerned that the energy surge has put Ellie's life in danger, mission control ponders aborting the drop entirely. That choice is marked by the first change of trajectory within the T_{-3} cycle—the sequence "backs up," returning to the previous peg on C♯. This harmonic jolt breaks Silvestri's pattern and threatens to undo the inexorable forward motion of the cycle, just as aborting would undo all the narratival momentum that has built up in the film and has come to a head at this decisive moment.

Thankfully, another surprise follows on the heels of mission control's reevaluation. Foster's blind colleague Kent (William Fichtner) exclaims, "I hear her" over the radio, and the option to cancel the drop is summarily taken off the table. Though the launch is now back on track, Silvestri does not use the moment to shore up the deteriorating $oct_{1,2}$ cycle. Rather, he effects a palpable

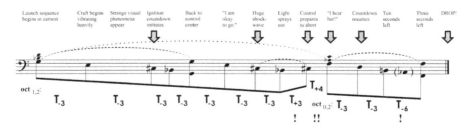

Figure 4.19 Silvestri, *Contact*, "Good to Go."

transformational "modulation," hurling C♯ to F minor. This constitutes a break *out* of the prevailing octatonic space by means of a qualitatively different M3 motion, T_4. The wholesale shift opens up a whole new octatonic sphere ($oct_{0,2}$), which comes to host its own, considerably sped-up T_3 cycle. A crucial narrative stumbling block has been overcome, and the music is now truly "good to go." Silvestri has one more trick up his sleeve, compressing the space between D and F minor down to a single transposition ($T_{-6} = T_{-3}(\times 2)$), one last harmonic acceleration that corresponds exactly to the moment the drop successfully takes place and Ellie is whisked off to a wondrous new part of the universe.

5

Pantriadic Wonder

The Art of Amazement

Pantriadic harmony aims to amaze us. Whether heard in short bursts or lengthy paragraphs, in subtle andantes or stereo-throttling fortissimos, nonfunctional, noncentric chromaticism has helped suggest—and sometimes inspire—wonderment for as long as music has accompanied the moving image. This "sense of wonder" is, at least in part, the response that all the music we examined in the previous chapter strives to evoke. Countless other cues make use of similar progressions to push the limits of our diatonically accustomed ears. Film composers, of course, did not invent this association of musical material and affect. Pantriadicism was linked with an aesthetic of astonishment throughout the "long" nineteenth century. The connection with Cohn's "altered and heightened realities" is evident across the entire spectrum of Romantic compositional schools, styles, and forms. Even after the advent of musical modernism at the *fin de siècle*, an extensive segment of post-Romantic art music continued (and continues) to cling to the affiliation of chromaticism and what Illario Meandri (2014) calls "the Marvelous."[1] Before they were opening the floodgates to emancipatory dissonance, composers on the atonal vanguard like Schoenberg, Stravinsky, and Bartok cavorted in pantriadic playgrounds (see, for example, *Gurrelieder*, *The Firebird*, and *Bluebeard's Castle*). Indeed, no matter how much they tried to suppress set class 3-11, the mature works of these modernists often still betray allusions of the earlier triadic practice, as with the constant (and still expressively potent) employment of the hexatonic and octatonic collections. The tenacity of triadic chromaticism amid stylistic upheaval is particularly evident in figures like Debussy and Ravel, Vaughan Williams and Holst, and Prokofiev and Shostakovich. These are composers who, even at their most adventurous—and, indeed, atonal—rarely fully abandoned the consonant triad. Small surprise, then, that they had an especially strong influence on Hollywood's tonal palette—and that several became accomplished composers of film music in their own right.

The continuity of style between concert hall and cinema meant that chromatic wonder was virtually assured a place in the associative vocabulary of early film composition. It came along for the ride, as it were, right alongside a panoply of other indispensible style topics that signal the otherworldly: heavenly wordless choirs, buzzing *ex nihilo* introductions, granitic pillars of sound, and so on. Classical Hollywood scoring thoroughly absorbed late Romantic aesthetics, and as a result, the bond between chromatic harmony and the fantastic became a powerfully established convention within twentieth-century mass culture. In many ways, film provided a laboratory for pantriadic experimentation that was even better equipped for wonderment than the previous century's stages and concert halls. I have already noted the difficulty that film scores have in propping up lengthy tonal structures and intricate designs. But this impatience has a happy consequence: any inclusion of pantriadic harmony, no matter how disruptive, cannot truly run afoul of listener expectations for long-range musical coherence. Even the wildest chromaticism is unlikely to pose a threat to the overall structural integrity of a film's soundtrack.

The formal amenability of the moving picture to pantriadic harmony is complemented by a friendly set of filmic aesthetics. Cinema has historically lent itself to wonder, emphasizing the fantastic through a variety of means like visual spectacle and imaginative narrative. Film also fosters amazement on a broader ecological level. As audience members, we find ourselves placed in darkened and carefully temperature-controlled theaters. We recline back in our plush seats, gazing upon impossible images projected on huge screens, all while being submerged in a bath of immersive audio. Altogether, this confluence of structure, style, and setting make the movies a uniquely welcoming place for the consonant triad to run free.

Representative examples of cinematic chromaticism connoting wonder are not difficult to come by. Consider the passage reproduced in Figure 5.1, from Howard

Figure 5.1 Shore, *Fellowship of the Rings,* "Gandalf's Escape."

Shore's score to *The Fellowship of the Ring* (2001, 1:25:50, ▶), first entry in the *Lord of the Rings* trilogy. Shore's music accompanies a marvelous rescue sequence. The protagonist, Gandalf the wizard (Ian McKellan), has been imprisoned atop the fortress of Orthanc by his corrupted counterpart, Saruman (Christopher Lee). At the moment Gandalf's captor prepares to dispatch him, the gray wizard plunges off the tower's edge and onto the back of a colossal eagle. Gwaihir, as the raptor of legend is named, spirits Gandalf away from Isengard, and we see the two soar across an immense mountain range before the scene cuts away to another location.

Shore's music for the incident begins in D aeolian, a hard-edged mode lent dire urgency by rolling low drums and a throbbing, immobile D2 pedal. As a moth flutters across the screen, a chorus briefly punctuates the texture—the augur of something extraordinary to come. When Gandalf takes his fateful dive, an expansively orchestrated F-minor triad (m. 6) shifts the music's course dramatically. Like a tonal deus ex machina, the pc5 preserving transformation (**PR**) that powers this transition seems to instantly whisk away the tonal obstacle posed by D. This progression initiates a series of chromatic shifts, alternating minor (**PR**, **RP**) and major third (**PL**, **LP**) relationships, always between minor triads. The F♮-minor and F♯-minor triads are related by M3 (first upward, then downward) to the "diatonic" chords on A and D into which they resolve. The particular ordering of transformations (**RP·PL·PR·LP**) thus enables a very weak emphasis of D minor and its minor dominant, Am. The sight of Gwaihir flying across a mountainous landscape inspires a further digression at m. 10, by this point fully detached from the threat of D aeolian. The final four measures make use of the pitch B♭3 as a common tone, a parsimonious thread stringing together otherwise diatonically estranged chords, Bm⇒GM⇒G♯m⇒Em.

Shore's tonal rhetoric, his summary disposal of predictable monotonality in favor of noncentric chromaticism, is decisive in evoking the scene's intended feeling of astonishment. Certainly, dynamics, contour, and phrase structure also play a crucial role in the cue's ability to astound; the affective quality of the scene is particularly hard to imagine without Shore's muscular orchestration, especially the entrance of trumpet at m. 6 and roiling percussion throughout. I do not mean for this single case study to suggest that pantriadicism is the only tonal idiom that filmmakers use to intimate the incredible.[2] Indeed, both prosaic diatonicism and atonality have the potential to generate this affect (not to mention non-Western pitch resources).[3] But there is something special about chromaticism. Pantriadic harmony such as we hear in "Gandalf's Escape" occupies a privileged place among film music parameters *specifically* for its ability to connote altered and heightened realities. In fact, we can go further: chromaticism using triads is *the* primary agent for connoting astonishment in mainstream film scoring. And, inversely, a sense of wonder is the central aesthetic goal of filmic pantriadicism.

My goal in this chapter is to erect an aesthetics of wondrous pantriadicism, one that is grounded in filmic practice and supported by research in music theory, literary theory, and psychology. In order to restrict the chapter's purview, I draw examples primarily from the popular and influential *Lord of the Rings* (*LOTR*) trilogy. More so than contemporaneous fantastic franchises like *Pirates of the Caribbean* or *Star Wars*, these three movies trade in astonishment. Peter Jackson's take on Tolkien's saga is the *ne plus ultra* of spectacle-laden Hollywood blockbusters in the twenty-first century. Much of *LOTR*'s running time features some combination of ancient landscapes, staggeringly large battles, and impossible beasts; alongside these impressive sights are often heard patches of discursive pantriadic harmony like that which accompanied Gwaihir's unexpected intervention.

I begin with a general overview of the concept of wonderment. I include here a summary of David Huron's theory of musical expectation, which offers a useful model for the mechanisms through which the emotion of wonder arises *in time*, especially in terms of two distinct affects, frisson and awe. I then turn to Howard Shore's music, first exploring his idiosyncratic tonal language and then his strategies for manufacturing wonderment. The first of two extended analyses in this chapter, "Théoden Rides Forth," will deal with Huron's idea of frisson, specifically as it pertains to the dénouement to *The Two Towers* (*TTT*, 2002). Because awe and frisson can be differentiated by their approaches on musical time, I follow the first case study with an excursus into the idea of chromatic temporality, drawing on psychological perspectives on subjective time and musical processing. This prepares the way for my second case study on "The Argonath," a minute-long span of awe-inspiring music from near the end of *The Fellowship of the Rings* (*FOTR*). Throughout, I emphasize issues of spatiotemporal design in transformational analysis, as well as the interaction of neo-Riemannian and psychological models of musical understanding.

Wonder, Awe, and Frisson

Understanding how pantriadic chromaticism is able to map so readily onto a sense of wonder requires that we first investigate the cognitive and cultural foundations of wonderment. From this point forward, I treat wonder as an **affect**—that is, a mental state with a strong emotional and, in many situations, bodily component.[4] Provisionally, wonder is the pleasurable feeling one receives when experiencing a stimulus that is surprising and tricky to integrate with everyday experience. In cinematic contexts, this affect may assume three important-to-distinguish forms. Wonder may be *represented*, as in the case of characters whose dialogue and facial expressions indicate they are experiencing awe. Wonder may also be *cued* by the semiotic system that is set up by a film or filmic practice: for instance, when the soundtrack signifies "wonder" via an internal leitmotivic association, or by exploiting an arbitrary but intertextually clear wonder style topic through, say, orchestration. Finally, wonder may be *elicited*. Elicitation takes place when an audience member actually undergoes a set of specific psychological and physiological changes associated with the subjective feeling of wonder. These three modes of wonderment frequently coexist and overlap, but it is important to keep them differentiated when one is studying wondrous music, particularly when it comes to the sometimes large gap between cued and elicited affective states.[5]

No matter the guise, wonder always entails a sense of something outside of ourselves and our everyday frames of reference. Significantly, the objects to which wonder is directed do not pose a true physical or mental threat to the subject—and music rarely does! Compared to similar affects that involve confrontation with the unknown (for example, fear, shock, or confusion), wonderment is unalloyed in its positive valence.[6] It is a pleasurable and edifying state, apt for pairing with escapist media. We may think of cinematic wonder as a tamed and commercializable version of the sublime, Edmund Burke's "delightful horror," made palatable for the masses (2008 [1757]: 109). It can be poignant, but rarely existential, in line with Hollywood's ultimate aim to entertain and comfort, not challenge.

Wonder has a deep intellectual heritage. From its elevation by Plato as the very foundation of philosophy to present-day empirical research on the way artworks can inspire goosebumps, wonder has long been the object of veneration but also a degree of (potentially strategic) conceptual obscurity.[7] Philosopher and literary theorist Philip Fisher, in his monograph on the wondrous in Western culture, regards wonderment as "the pleasure of amazement," and one of the "primary aesthetic experiences within modernity" (1998: 2, 11). That cinema should seek to concoct wondrous experiences should surprise no one who appreciates the spectacle-delivering apparatus of American commercial film. The idea of wonder is embedded deeply within discourses on film and music, though not always by name. Various concepts that turn up frequently in both informal and scholarly film criticism assume an aesthetics of wonderment—special effects, the cinema of attractions, and the dream factory, to name a few.[8] Similarly in musicology, we have notions such as trance, formal breakthrough, and monumentality.[9] Of particular relevance to music theorists is the feeling of sudden insight one attains through careful analysis, that "eureka!" moment hunted so fervently in score study.[10]

Aesthetics and psychology provide two avenues into understanding wonderment that can lead to productive film musicological discussion.[11] Fisher, coming from the aesthetic perspective, is content to enumerate the attributes of wondrous encounter. For him, wonder is a constituent of "incomparable experiences," a rare and largely involuntary feeling of "radical singularity of means" induced by purposefully original or challenging art (6). It has a distinctive epistemological character, one based on an awareness of personal ignorance. Wonder is a "pleasure in the unexpected," particularly when it gives way to an "a-ha!" moment of well-earned discovery and understanding (26). Critically for Fisher, the absence of a clear or predictable progression from one experiential state to the next helps facilitate the effect. "Syntax and grammar are the enemies of wonder," he claims categorically (22) because syntax and grammar tend to militate against syntactical-expectancy violations. One might say the same thing of tonality: harmonic function and cadential logic are the enemies of pantriadicism, insofar as they impose a priori tonal regulations and temporal expectations on music.

Tellingly, Fisher uses the term "intelligibility" as a basis for a stimulus's capacity for eliciting wonderment. Just as Hugo Riemann locates intelligibility in the ability to derive complex harmonic maneuvers from more simple constituents, wonder comes from something that is *potentially* understandable, but whose nature is not immediately revealed.[12] As in Kant's mathematical sublime, a superfluity of juxtaposed stimuli leads to an enjoyable state of perplexity. In the most thoroughgoing instances of pantriadic harmony, one feels as though they are lost in an overabundance of musical stimuli, with few preordained or obvious relations to be immediately drawn within this surfeit of information.

For Fisher, wonderment has a spatiotemporal component in addition to its emotional and epistemic aspects. Wonder requires a suddenness of onset and an all-at-once apprehension of some object of perception. The more vast that object, the better. However, because of his requirement that the whole is *visually* grasped at a single moment, Fisher rules out many non-scopic aesthetic experiences that rely on chronological unfolding, notably, most music (ibid: 20–24). Fisher's emphasis on visuality and instantaneous apprehension leads to a prohibitively narrow conception of wonder. Music can instill a feeling of sudden totality; the poetically inclined might even claim for music the ability to convey a kind of universal confluence or plenitude, crammed into one infinitely dense moment. But it seems uncontroversial to claim that wondrous percepts may also be temporally extended, and as such allows artists to prolong that feeling of pleasurable confusion and oceanic connectedness.

Fisher's insight that wonder has to do with violations of syntax allows us to translate his aesthetical notion into a psychological one. Wonder in this more rigorous sense comprises a mental state with two notable subaffects, defined by virtue of how they interact with musical expectation. These forms of wonder are musical **awe** and **frisson**, a categorization developed by music theorist David Huron. In theorizing the cognitive foundations of musical surprise, Huron isolates three kinds of responses to a violation of musical expectation: laughter, frisson, and awe.[13] Laughter, which he connects with the involuntary *flight* response, is not so relevant to the present discussion (at least in an obvious way).[14] Awe and frisson, however, very much are, and both have garnered a small but growing body of literature in psychology and cognitive neuroscience.[15]

Huron links awe with the physiological *freeze* response, which is characterized by fixed attention and the holding of breath. It is associated with a sensation of self-diminishment and a high degree of focus on the stimulus that provokes the emotion.[16] Awe attaches to objects of dizzying size, power, venerability, and—with special relevance for tonality—complexity. Each of these qualities has to it the hazard of cognitive unassimilability, and it is up to the creative artist to suppress a genuine feeling of peril lest the experience mutate into something more negatively valenced, like dread.

For an example of musical awe, Huron (2006: 289) cites a memorable tableau from Don Davis's score to *The Matrix* (1999, 32:40, ⓟ) in which the expressive power of atonality is strategically overwhelmed by the simplest of triadic relationships. Figure 5.2 offers a rough representation of this sequence. Out of a boiling sea of dissonance, orchestra and wordless chorus erupt with a massive D-minor triad, quickly transformed into B♭ major in first inversion, before returning to non-triadic pandemonium. The narrative event that cues this dire annunciation? The protagonist's first glimpse at the mind-bendingly huge extent of Earth's post-apocalyptic ruination. Granted, the tonal shift itself is hardly complex or unassimilable; it is a simple **L** transformation, with a prominently placed F♮ common tone. Nevertheless, a i⇔VI shift like this one has become common currency for instant awe in millennial "epic" film scores.[17]

Although Huron's *Matrix* example involves a simple diatonic progression set in relief from atonal surroundings, more patently chromatic harmony also evokes awe under a number of circumstances. Three strategies are commonly employed by film composers. First is the use of absolute progressions that are coded "portentous" or "magical." These include $\mathbf{T_6}$(M), **PL**(M), **F**(M), and, in the case of *The Matrix*, **L**(m). Second is the use of chromatic transformations that take unusually large strides across tonal space; this technique is often but not always entailed by the aforementioned strategy of affective encodedness. Third—and potentially making use of both other strategies—is the exploitation of *multi*-chord progressions in ways that defy the listener's comprehension of any underlying logic of harmonic succession. The latter two techniques pose a challenge to long-range schematic organization. Sustained discursive pantriadicism blurs harmonic goals and flattens tonal hierarchies. It draws our attention from the musical background squarely onto the foreground, and prevents the generation of robust projections into the future. In terms of musical anticipation, the hypnotic awe of pantriadicism thus results from (a) **the frustration of global harmonic expectancies** and (b) **the sustaining of tonal tension,** either through ambiguity or associative intensity.

Huron contrasts awe with the affect of frisson. Sometimes also referred to as "chills," frisson amounts to an aestheticized *fight* response.[18] Unlike instinctual flight responses, however, frisson can be intensely gratifying and may involve deep, sometimes bittersweet emotions. In bodily terms, it resembles a physical

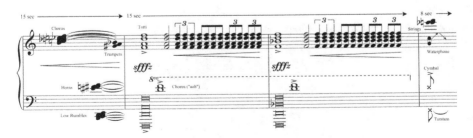

Figure 5.2 Davis, *The Matrix*, "Power Plant."

reaction to coldness: shivers up the spine, elevated skin conductance and heart rate, and gooseflesh (piloerection) are common manifestations. The physiological aspects of frisson are the product of an unusually heightened emotional state, typically brought on by an abrupt or transitory stimulus of profoundly unexpected character.[19] Interestingly, the physical setting of a temperature-controlled movie theater itself may play a role in facilitating a frisson response. Huron notes that colder ambient temperatures seem to assist the affect more than warm ones: "cinemas and concert halls with lots of air conditioning," he conjectures, "might well enhance the emotional experiences of patrons" (35).

In terms of tonality, frisson characteristically results from (a) **the violation of a local harmonic expectancy** and (b) **the build-up and discharge of tonal tension**.[20] Though Huron does not offer an example out of the cinematic repertoire, it is extremely common as a cued affect. For instance, in his score for *Wall-E* (2008, 35:05, ▶), Thomas Newman establishes a theme in D♭ major to accompany the titular robot's amazing journal through the solar system. The relevant portion of the cue is reproduced in Figure 5.3. Right when the melody seems to approach its anticipated plagal half-cadence (vi⇨V⇨IV), Newman lands on G♯ major (♯IV/♭V). This chord is a semitone away from the expected G♭M and a distant tritone away from the formerly governing tonic. The unexpected chord is immediately integrated back into conventional diatonic syntax, serving as the dominant within a perfect authentic cadence, where it guides the listener into the next, more expansive statement of the same theme in C major. Typical of such chromatically modulating cadences, the frisson-inducing shift is extremely disorienting when it first arrives, but is swiftly rationalized back into a perfectly normative tonal progression. (We will revisit these supremely cinematic cadences in the next chapter.)

As with awe, frisson is associated with a host of non-pitch parameters. It can be generated by unanticipated changes of dynamic level and by wide swings of frequency range or musical texture. The prototypical instance might be when the full orchestra suddenly gives way to an exposed solo instrument, as though a lone human voice were pleading in the darkness.[21] In film, separate musical parameters often work together and in concert with comparable visual techniques, producing passages of heavily overdetermined frisson. In *Wall-E*, for example, expectations for tonal and phrasal closure are aligned closely with the sequence's visual

Figure 5.3 Newman, *Wall-E*, "Sunburst."

grammar, with important musical events synchronizing with a quizzical advertisement on the moon and a shot of a solar prominence that further dwarfs the
robot's tiny spaceship. Delicate calibration of visual and editorial pacing like this
can significantly magnify the shock of an unexpected key change and the pleasurable release that comes with diatonic realignment.[22]

In practice, awe and frisson can be difficult to tease apart, with many musical
passages seamlessly moving from one to the other or evoking an affective blend.
This mix is true, for instance, of "Gandalf's Escape," which makes use of triadic
chromaticism for both its bolt-from-the-blue modulation and its subsequent
flight across tonal space. Wonderment as I conceive it effectively folds both awe
and frisson into a more holistic state of impressed surprise. Nevertheless, distinguishing the two subaffects can be quite useful for fine-grained inspection of
pantriadic passages. Most important for film music analysis is the fact that awe
and frisson have dissimilar temporal profiles. Frisson jolts us instantaneously but
soon subsides. Awe, conversely, is prolonged, sometimes setting in quickly but always striving to leave the listener immobilized and stupefied. This characteristic
will become quite important when we explore chromatic temporality.

Both awe and frisson involve what Huron calls "contrastive valence" in slightly
different ways. As Huron and Elizabeth Hellmuth Margulis write, "[emotional]
states appear to be strongly influenced by contrast. If we initially feel bad and
then feel good, the good feeling tends to be stronger than if the good experience occurred without the preceding bad feeling. Conversely, if we initially feel
good and then feel bad, the bad feeling tends to feel worse" (Huron and Margulis
2010: 598–599). With musical wonderment, an involuntarily negative reaction to
an unexpected or inexplicable stimulus gives way to a heightened positive emotion.[23] The preliminary object of shock is reappraised as strange but harmless,
something interesting and culturally-encoded as impressive.[24] In the case of awe,
the pleasure remains even after the initial contrast has dissipated, as we have already seen in some more discursively pantriadic passages from *Mysterious Island*,
Superman, and *King Kong*.

Despite the familiarity of chromatic progressions in film music—in many cases
exploited to the point of flagrant overuse—these harmonic gestures remain tremendously effective as objective correlatives for cinematic wonderment. Their
very conventionality is part of the reason for their success. Familiarity with how
these progressions tend to arise in dramatic contexts helps to telegraph the intended emotional response and can deepen its resonance.[25] Indeed, research suggests that prior exposure to music *enhances* the likelihood it will produce chills
(Panksepp 1995). Even filmgoers who are exhausted with surprise chromatic mediants might not be able to resist their sway! This is by no means to claim that all
listeners will experience these emotions in the same way, or indeed, at all. Perhaps
there are audience members who truly are emotionally immune to these well-
worn devices. Nevertheless, if we recall the distinction between represented,
cued, and elicited affects, it is easy to accept that, for minimally acculturated

filmgoers, certain chromatic progressions will still serve the *symbolic* function of evoking wonderment. After all, one does not need to experience piloerection for a tritonal transformation to direct one's attention pertinent new information, or feel shivers down the spine to receive instruction on how to interpret a narrative.

Tonal Strategies in *The Lord of the Rings*

Before we delve into the ways Shore specifically assembles musical awe and frisson in this series, it is worthwhile to consider the composer's general harmonic language, in particular the way his brand of leitmotivic scoring interacts with chromaticism and modulation.

In keeping with the *LOTR* saga's Wagnerian pretenses, Shore rarely misses an opportunity to conjure the "science of harmonic dread," as critic Alex Ross describes the composer's facility with late Romantic chromaticism (2003).[26] Shore is fundamentally a chordally oriented composer, and his avoidance of counterpoint and predilection for absolute progressions result in an emphasis on pure, rich sonority throughout the series. Uses of wondrous chromaticism in the *LOTR* trilogy range widely in scope and duration. Some of Shore's chromatic gestures are abrupt and clearly tailored to evoke chills and goosebumps. One such example is the dazzling shift from F_{phry} to $F\sharp_{lyd\text{-}\natural2}$ that accompanies an establishing shot of the tree city of Lothlorien in *FOTR*. Other uses of chromaticism are protracted over huge musical paragraphs, thereby cueing more of an awesome musical affect. This may be observed, for example, with the kaleidoscopic modulations that match the righteous siege of the Ents in *TTT*.

Standing out as a particularly expansive foray into pantriadic harmony is the beacon-lighting sequence in *The Return of the King* (*ROTK*, 46:09, ▶). This minute-long scene depicts a breathtaking spectacle: a montage of remote mountain outposts, communicating via huge pyres an urgent message across the vast ranges of Middle Earth. Figure 5.4 offers a pure harmonic reduction of the restless sequence, from the moment the hobbit Pippin (Billy Boyd) ignites the first pyre up through its harmonic and thematic telos—a broad and triumphal statement of the Gondor leitmotif, prepared by a modal cadence into D dorian.

Shore's heavily foregrounded music flings itself from one tonal vista to another, covering what seems like a tremendous amount of tonal ground. On closer inspection, however, one notices that the triadic itinerary is fairly limited, with only seven distinct major or minor triads, of which those rooted on D, E, and F are by far the most emphasized. In addition to those stations, a handful of diminished and augmented triads contribute to the harmonic flavor of the sequence, and in several cases facilitate tighter common-tone-preserving voice leadings

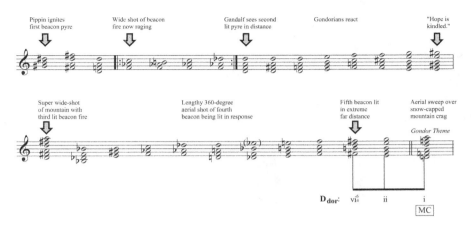

Figure 5.4 Shore, *ROTK*, "Lighting the Beacons."

between triads.[27] Of particular significance is the pitch class 5 (F♯), which serves as a unifying thread for many of the individual chords, to the extent that a common-tone neighborhood on the Tonnetz surrounding this note captures much (but not all) of the important transformational behavior of the sequence's surface. This space is displayed in Figure 5.5a, the first of two networks that illustrate differing but simultaneously operating levels of transformational organization in this cue. (The topic of reconciling competing ways of hearing pantriadic music will be considered in a sustained way in the next chapter.)

Though marked at times with conspicuous instances of parsimonious voice leading, the basic logic of the cue is one of stepwise transposition—especially of the "move all three notes of a triad at the same time by the same interval" style aptly described by T_n. This transpositional scheme is most apparent among triads within the aforementioned m3 range between Dm to Fm, with EM/m acting as a mediator between these two poles. The transpositional ladder presented in Figure 5.5b models this comparatively more blunt aspect of the cue's tonal organization, with only T_1 and **P** needed to convey the essential upward thrust of the cue.

Considering the importance of F and D triads (and their common pc 5) to both transformational readings of the cue, one might make an argument for a double-tonic complex between these chords over the short span of this passage. But despite the presence of these recurring points of reference, the overwhelming impression is of ceaseless motion and change. Throughout *LOTR*, Shore often communicates wonder through stepwise lines like those present in the "Lighting the Beacons" sequence, rising inexorably toward some lofty melodic peak. An easily graspable melodic pattern thus compensates for the fact that the pantriadic harmony in "Beacons," and many cues like it, are strictly non-thematic, not obviously based on any melodic particles already established in the film trilogy.

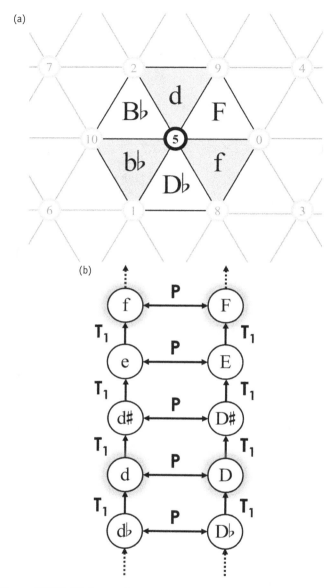

Figure 5.5 Shore, *ROTK*, "Lighting the Beacons" tonal spaces: (a) Common-tone neighborhood; (b) transpositional ladder.

Pantriadic harmony in *LOTR* tends to be coordinated with the disclosure of various leitmotifs. Shore is fond of preparing and exiting motivic statements with non-thematic chromatic progressions, especially for the most definitive annunciations of his themes—note how the jaunt through pantriadic space in "Beacons" built up to a broad statement of the "Gondor" leitmotif. Chromatic bookending helps to set a given theme in high relief, either by providing it a harmonically marked lead-in or an unexpected continuation. More rarely, Shore's themes themselves are constructed *through* chromatic progressions, though they still tend to revolve around a locally prolonged tonic. The motif for the Elvish tree city of Rivendell, for example, consists of little more than an oscillation between two arpeggiated major triads that are related by major third (e.g., CM⇔A♭M). The Rivendell motif is further embellished by major sevenths and augmented fifths on its musical surface, accentuating the hexatonic magic that underlies the **PL·LP**(M) harmonic cell. Opposite in affect but comparable in transformational structure is a seldom heard theme for the wretched creature Gollum. His motif is based entirely on a smooth major-third circuit (**LP·PL**) around a minor triad, sometimes with an added octatonic ladder at its tail (e.g., Cm⇨A♭m⇨Cm⇨E♭m⇨F♯m).[28]

The most thoroughly chromatic theme in *LOTR* is associated with the forces of righteousness in Middle Earth, especially as they reflect a connection with the natural world. This motif (Figure 5.6, ▶), which Doug Adams (2010: 118) calls "Nature's Reclamation," is harmonized in an extremely parsimonious fashion, with each chord connected to the next by incremental stepwise motion. Even the **S** between F major and F♯ minor, which already bears an emphasized common-tone of A3, is mediated by a diminished triad on F♯. Much of the theme's expressive quality derives from the impression of a steady upward motion, straining for an undefined harmonic goal. As with "Beacons," a sense of gradual elevation is assured by the transformational structure of "Nature's Reclamation"; from m. 2 to m. 9, the **S·P·N·L·R·LR** chain is realized through entirely upshifting voice leading. Individual voices inch back downward only at the end, where a small concession to contrary motion is required to clinch the weak modal cadence (**LR**, or **D**) back into A minor.

Not every passage of fantastic chromaticism is as aggressively foregrounded on the soundtrack as the examples we have surveyed thus far. There is, for example, the silkily alluring music that precedes Aragorn and Arwen's nocturnal tryst in *FOTR*, analyzed in the previous chapter. In that cue, the crossing of two hexatonic systems helps install a gentle feeling of magic and danger to the pair's confession of secret love. And while Shore frequently leans on chromaticism for the purposes of cueing wonder, he does not restrict himself inflexibly to nonfunctional, or even necessarily tertian, harmony when summoning this affect. The protagonists' entry into the great stone-hewn Dwarven city of Dwarrowdelf (*FOTR*, 2:09:40, ▶),

Figure 5.6 Shore, *TTT*, Nature's Reclamation Theme.

Figure 5.7 Shore, *FOTR*, "Entry into Dwarrowdelf."

for example, is accompanied by a paragraph of almost purely diatonic (aeolian) harmony. Figure 5.7 offers a transcription of this set-piece.

The columnesque triadic writing and wordless choir are responsible for much of the feeling of awe here. At the same time, Shore does manufacture two moments of frisson through harmony. The first is the tremendous sense of arrival that takes place at m. 9, with its newly unveiled root-position submediant supporting a melodic goal note of A4. The second chills-worthy moment comes with the perfect authentic cadence at m. 13, which sets the cue's foot down on the newly pivoted-to key of the mediant, C major. The former moment corresponds with a sweep of the camera that reveals the full extent of the subterranean marvel, while the latter matches a cut back to the adventurers, traversing the Dwarven hall.[29] The choice of tonal idiom here is thus more familiar, less mannered than that connected to the trilogy's magical races (fitting, perhaps, for the earthy directness of the dwarves). Yet despite the comparatively mundane diatonicism of the passage, a few well-placed harmonic and contrapuntal maneuvers prove amply capable of casting a wondrous spell over this subterranean voyage.

Frisson

Musical frisson is a natural companion for scenes of impossible rescues and miraculous reversals of fortune. In the cue that introduced this chapter, "Gandalf's Escape," the eagle Gwaihir intervenes unexpectedly to save a protagonist from an otherwise intractable situation. Moments of frisson in Shore's *LOTR* soundtracks often adhere to a tonal arc comparable in structure to this narrative device: the deus ex machina. Some aspect of a cue's pitch design comes to pose a problem. This musical issue could take any number of forms: a gradual shift into the minor mode, a quick swerve into a distantly related chromatic region, even a simple increase in dissonance and volume. The characteristic subjective aspects of chills emerge as that issue approaches an instant and thorough resolution. Shore's preferred method for "solving" these problems is to use a momentarily disruptive gesture that steers the music headlong into a bold and semantically unambiguous statement of a leitmotif.[30] By progressing into a clear-cut theme, the music reassures the listener that harmonic logic is still in operation, that monotonality and phrasal predictability has not been fundamentally tampered with. Awarding the listener with a recurring theme right after a chromatic jolt provides just the right payoff to a brief rash of musical disorder.

THÉODEN'S RIDE

A representative instance of such frisson-by-leitmotivic-preparation may be found in *TTT* (2:38:30, ▶). Throughout the cue "Théoden Rides Forth," Shore uses chromatic harmony to grind tonal progress to a standstill, unveiling predictable leitmotivic statements after these tonal about-faces. At the conclusion of the film's climactic battle, Aragorn (Viggo Mortensen) and King Théoden (Bernard Hill) mount an eleventh-hour charge against the army laying siege to the fortress Helm's Deep. Just as their desperate efforts seem lost, a narratival savior arrives in the form of wizard Gandalf (plus the cavalry he has rallied). Shore's music for Gandalf's miraculous entrance hits all the right music buttons to cue—and, for receptive filmgoers, potentially elicit—a frisson response.

Figure 5.8 displays a reduction of this sequence, beginning when Théoden's company rides into the battlefield and ending where the scene cuts away from Helm's Deep. T_n/P-type labels are given between staves to indicate the tonal relationship between each of the sequence's four subsections, all of which are located in a distinct key or mode. The broad path is from D in both its major and minor forms, modulating up two fifths to A and eventually E minor. The tonal scheme for "Théoden Rides Forth" is therefore not especially unconventional or wide ranging, as it involves progressive transposition across closely related keys—a means to increase intensity that would have been commonplace even in the eighteenth century.

What marks Shore's cue as being harmonically "Hollywood" is the insertion of pantriadic transitions between each of its four thematic subsections. These linking progressions instantly dilute the force of the erstwhile tonics, acting almost like anti-cadences, in that they dispel rather than confirm tonicity. Note the use of the operator D', the inverse of the **D**ominant transformation (i.e., "go to triad of same mode down a fourth). This is a convenient way of denoting *subdominant*-to-tonic relationships, the likes of which are rife in the modal sound

Figure 5.8 Shore, *TTT*, "Théoden Rides Forth."

world of Middle Earth, without overburdening ourselves with new nomenclature. Note as well the use of non-parsimonious tritonal motions as the penultimate progression-type before every new theme (i.e., at mm. 6–7, 14–15, and 20–21). Each of these tritonal shifts finds itself operating in a subtly different tonal and functional context; this disparity has the effect of generating continually new harmonic expectations even while the basic modulatory procedure remains essentially invariant. The tritonal root motions at mm. 6–7 and 21–22, for example, are between like-moded triads, minor to minor in the first case and major to major in the second. (The differing quaternary compounds of **PRPR** and **RPRP** help capture the smoothest voice leading specifically of upper voices). Meanwhile, the **RPR** shift at mm. 14–15 goes from a major to a minor triad. Notably, the Fellowship leitmotif it harmonizes is able to retain its diatonic melodic pitches, even landing on the former $\hat{1}$/D. We can think of **RPR** as being subdivisible into an **RP** (ushering us to the assumed normative D major), followed by an **R** that disrupts that expected tonic and enables the tritone between chordal roots F and B.

Each chromatic gesture paves the way for a more functionally referable "cadential" progression into the next section, and these cadences in turn accompany the disclosure of a new and inspiring visual event. In the first case (mm. 7–8), it is the unveiling of Gandalf's cavalry that is presaged by a tritonal spasm. In the second (mm. 15–16), the initiation of the cavalry's charge gains this special chromatic preparation, while the in third (mm. 22–23) it is coupled with the meeting of the two armies. This last progression is especially stirring, as it integrates the tritone progression for the first time with a conventional functional routine—namely a perfect authentic cadence prepared by the Neapolitan (♭II) chord. Because the cadential progression is far more customary here than the modified subdominant cadences at m. 7 and 15, the expectation of a significant dramatic event with which it will coincide is that much stronger. This newfound cadential resolve is reinforced by the most dramatic orchestrational shift, from a quiet solo-vocal passage to a huge, triumphant tutti. The cue thus adheres to a large-scale pattern of throwing a distant transformation like a monkey wrench into otherwise largely well-behaved diatonic functional progressions.

Each of the three tritonal swerves seems tailored to evoke frisson, and together, the piling on of harmonic elicitors of chills makes "Théoden Rides Forth" one of the most emotionally effective set pieces in the whole trilogy. In order to understand the exact psychological processes that encourage this affect, it is worthwhile to inspect the moment-to-moment structure of one of the sequence's subsections. Since it is the first and most shocking of the three modulations in the cue, I concentrate on mm. 1–8.

As Théoden's band of horsemen charges the enemy, Shore blasts out a defiant statement of the Rohan leitmotif in D dorian. The theme proceeds as accustomed for three measures, but what begins as an innocuous phrasal extension via an L-shift of Dm to B♭M (m. 5) increasingly starts to turn the modal tide against the heroes. At m. 6, **P**-driven conversion of the submediant sends B♭M to its dark minor (and contextually chromatic) twin. At this moment, in the heat of desperate battle, Aragorn's eyes affix on a distant wonder. As the camera cuts to a shot of Gandalf in the far distance, bathed in sunlight, Shore unleashes a dramatic transformation: the root-position B♭ minor is yanked to a root-position E minor with a tritonal **PRPR**, most distant and "roughest" of the octatonic transformations. Shore strengthens the latent alterity of the move to E minor by letting it ring for two extra beats. The swerve into unknown tonal territory intensifies the already darkened harmonic landscape and poses a critical harmonic "problem" that Shore's transformational deus ex machina needs to rapidly address.

In fact, there may be more problems than just one to wrestle with, given this chromatic transformation. On the original motion picture soundtrack, and in some later recordings by different orchestras, the only chord heard at m. 7 is E minor. However, in every consumer release of the film on DVD (both theatrical cut and extended editions), the overwhelming impression at this juncture is of a *full choir* belting out G minor. Though difficult to discern, one can still make out the "original" orchestral E minor too, meaning the Gm chord was most likely recorded separately and looped over a quieted-down version of the original, purely orchestral stinger chord. Thus, the vocal Gm chord creates a polychordal sonority against the Em bass chord. These sorts of small-scale revisions are routine in postproduction, particularly in the *LOTR* series, but in this case the harmonic modification creates an interesting wrinkle in our transformational analysis. Ultimately, however, it is a wrinkle that *reinforces* the carefully measured symmetry at the heart of the progression.

Regardless of which version the filmgoer hears, the result of the tonal and timbral veer at m. 7 is a quite literal "fight" response. E minor (plus or minus G minor) signals a potentially profound reversal of fortune for Théoden's army. Magnifying its contrastive valence is the audience's own realization that, as soon Gandalf is shown, the battle has instantaneously turned in the favor of the protagonists. Having served its purpose as a tonal jolt, Gm/Em leads directly to a statement of the heroic Fellowship Theme (retrospectively functioning as supertonic in the restored key of D major). No subsequent frisson-inducing gesture in this cue will quite match the hair-raising bombshell of the wizard's initial musical reveal.

MUSICAL EXPECTANCY

The chromatic strategy Shore uses in this scene and comparable ones leaves little ambiguity as to intended expressive effect. David Huron's cognitive model of musical expectation proves useful in situations such as these, in which cued emotional responses are overdetermined. Central to his theory is the temporal profile of musical expectation, named ITPRA after its five components: Imagination, Tension, Prediction, Reaction, and Appraisal (Huron, 2006: 8–15).[31] Figure 5.9 presents a schematic representation of the ITPRA model, in which those five components emerge in relation to a single generic musical event, flanked by a pre- and post-outcome phase. The pre-outcome phase begins with an imaginative mental state, wherein the listener unconsciously hypothesizes the end result of an ongoing musical process, often forming an intellectual as well as emotional investment in the expected outcome. As the event onset nears, a tension response sets in, with attendant increases in psychological and bodily activation. Moments *after* the event, two fast responses first take place. A prediction response evaluates if the listener's expectations are met or not (with corresponding positive valence if the listener is correct, or negative valence if wrong). At the same time, an involuntary reaction response reflects the instantaneous, superficial evaluation of the nature of that event; it is here where the chills of frisson and the stopped breath of awe are most likely to descend on the listener. Finally, a comparatively long-lasting appraisal response evaluates the event in light of more complex

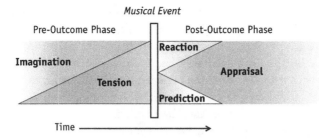

Figure 5.9 Expectancy profile of generic event.

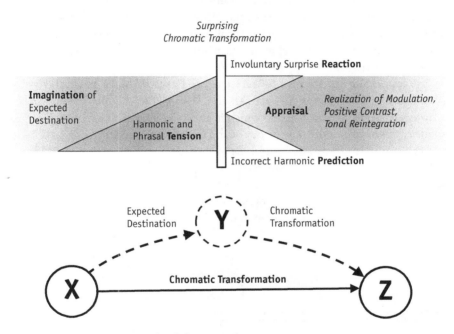

Figure 5.10 Expectancy profile of chromatic frisson.

context-sensitive knowledge. Through appraisal, the listener figures out what the musical event means in light of what has come before, and what it implies about that which is in store. Provided the musical event does not pose a real threat, appraisal also bestows some well-earned positive contrastive valence.

Huron's ITPRA model is an intuitive and versatile account of musical expectation. Though he does not offer a direct description of how frisson works within the scheme, we can use his model to explore the contours of musical chills more deeply. The expectancy profile of a frisson-inducing chromatic transformation is represented in Figure 5.10; for the time being, we will treat it as a pure musical stimulus, without important but complicating additional audiovisual factors.

Given a chord or harmonic region (X), the listener begins building expectations for some sort of normative tonal destination (Y). Y may be projected according to normal diatonic syntax, or other sort of regulative patterning, as with the nonfunctional but predictable chordal oscillations and cycles explored in earlier chapters. Note that the relationship between X to Y can be any kind of progression, even Identity, as long as it is predicted by previous tonal information. While harmonic or phrasal tension implies the imminent arrival of Y, in the case of a chromatic surprise, that projected event never comes. Instead, the music yields to an *unanticipated*, new chord or region, Z. Both X and Y are subjected to transformations, the former literally, the latter through implication and denial. The listener's immediate responses will thereby be of an incorrect harmonic prediction and an involuntary surprise reaction. However, as soon as Z is established or leads to a sturdily prolonged new key, a full appraisal of the event will bring about understanding, positive contrast, and (assuming a receptive auditor) a potential experience of frisson.

The applicability of Huron's ITPRA theory to Howard Shore's musical wonders should now be clear. Figure 5.11 renders mm. 1–8 of the "Théoden" sequence into a transformation network, above which is an account of an idealized frisson response spawned from the motion out of and back into D dorian/major. In order to be faithful to the two available versions of this cue, I include both E and G minor in the network and indicate their relationship with respect to each other and the larger transformational trajectory of the passage. An important aspect of the imagination phase is captured by implied—but never realized—triadic nodes that fan away from GM and B♭M: these nodes represent potential and plausible ways

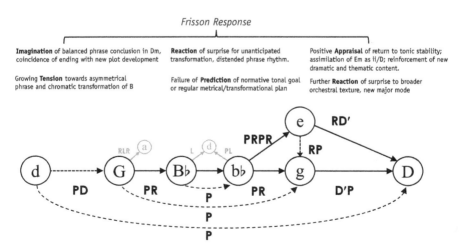

Figure 5.11 Shore, *TTT*, "Théoden Rides Forth" ITPRA/transformation network.

of getting back to D minor in a manner habituated from various earlier iterations of the Rohan theme.

The transformation network highlights the Em stinger chord's crucial role in two ways. First, it serves as the affective climax of the sequence, largely by virtue of its transformational estrangement from its immediate triadic predecessors, B♭ major and minor. Second, E minor acts as a pivot between the modal poles of D minor/dorian and D major (globally related by a **P** relation), and the keys' associated leitmotifs. In this sense, it is the progression *out* of E minor that is the harmonic deus ex machina, insofar as it makes possible the passage's ultimate positive appraisal. The step progression Em⇨DM instantly restores phrasal and harmonic order, allowing a safe monotonal rationalization of a chord that moments earlier threatened disruption and gloom. To anyone hearing across the central B♭ chords, it is evident that G major and E minor are related by simple **R** transformation, with both serving similar functions as sub/predominant progressions abutting D tonics. The retrospective appraisal of the stinger chord as functional within a D-major context is indicated with the rightmost arrow (**D′·P**) in the network. This analysis reflects, among other things, a neat near-symmetry with the **P·D** progression at the excerpt's onset.

If we treat the DVD version of the cue as "definitive," then we see another, even tighter kind of transformational mirroring that controls the musical and psychological trajectory this sequence. With G minor as the most audible component of the stinger chord, a strict bookending symmetry with its target chord (**D′·P**) is put in place, while the complexity of the move that introduces it is lessened slightly (**PR**, instead of the more dramatic **PRPR**). Though neither version is more "frisson-guaranteeing" than the other, the Gm-bearing one does have the advantage of creating a perfectly symmetrical journey through the major and minor versions of every chord present in the progression (not to mention contributing to a more hair-raisingly dissonant sonority). These multiple layers of symmetry are indicated below the main network with nested **P**-progressions starting at the midway point of the passage.

Huron notes experimental evidence that shows chromatic progressions, such as the tritonal modulations in "Théoden Rides Forth," are capable of generating intensely ambiguous and expressively potent emotions (2006: 270–275).[32] The foregoing analysis of "Théoden" indicates is that frisson is best evoked when the tonal contexts surrounding the surprise event are robustly centric and temporally well defined. The security of the key of D at either end of Figure 5.11 ensures that the move from B♭m to Em or Gm is understood *within* a recently formed harmonic context, even though its local structure is decidedly not permissible in either key. Frisson in chromatic film music relies on this kind of strictly *local* thwarting of expectation. To understand more sustained, more challenging chromatic stimuli, we must investigate how tonality and temporality interact.

Chromatic Temporality

Pantriadic harmony is suited to evoking wonderment in part because chromatic progressions so easily suggest distance or remoteness. Some of the longest spans of triadic chromaticism in Hollywood film music are to be found accompanying shots of impossibly massive or otherworldly visual spectacles. As we have already seen, one of the tasks given to Shore's music in *LOTR* is mirroring shifts in visual perspective. Harmony proves especially useful in underlining the disparity between the film's enormous geographical spectacles and the puny human (and demi-human) personae that bear witness to them.

But while tonal distance is an important factor in this juxtaposition of the immense and the intimate, the special quality of awe-inspiring chromaticism does not reside solely in the metaphorical cognitive spaces that it traverses. Just as relevant is the manipulation of subjective temporality.[33] As has been consistently argued by theorists of each medium, film and music are each an "art of time."[34] These media cannot be taken in all at once, but must be apprehended over time, at a predetermined pace and in a predetermined order. Both possess an ability to structure and influence temporal perception—and to present situations in which it is advantageous to interpret a text *as though* it were manipulating time.

This mutable attitude toward time is evident in much of *LOTR*. The franchise's complex plots often seem to take a back seat to action set pieces and special-effect showcases.[35] Sheer spectacle tends to deliver little new plot information and, in the case of scenic shots, may not be motivated by the narrative at all.[36] It is no accident that such plot-arresting scenes also tend to feature highly foregrounded music. Despite the difficulties involved in explaining music's elusive temporal nature, many scholars from a variety of disciplines have attempted to unearth the temporal peculiarities of the medium.[37] In order to ground my contention that pantriadic harmony can, under the right circumstances, play a part in constructing filmic temporality, I find it worth considering a few complementary approaches from music theorists and psychologists, particularly as they pertain the experience of wonderment.

Frisson is an event-oriented affect, rising and falling with the onset of some shocking or poignant musical transformation. Awe, by comparison, stretches out an amazing encounter. The psychological trajectory of awe does not center on a sudden jolt of strangeness (though it may be initiated in such a way), but rather on a protracted gaze or a dawning realization. We have seen that pantriadicism is a negation of the accustomed hierarchies of diatonic tonality. Its strongest forms, "triadic atonality" does away with the stable points of reference and concrete goals of tonality altogether. Tonality serves as theorist Jonathan Kramer's *sine qua non* for goal-directed "linear time," in which past events determine or imply subsequent developments within a piece. The ability for the past to impinge on the future is the basis for any ascription of causality to music and allows us to speak of progression in the strongest sense. Harmonic routines like scalar continuation and dominant⇒tonic resolution are the mainstays of linear musical time, imbuing common-practice music with a purposeful, forward-driving teleology. Tonal function enables listeners to form predictions and projections, and thereby invests music with a sense of its own future.[38]

Nonlinear time, by contrast, is "the determination of some characteristic(s) of music in accordance with implications that arise from principles or tendencies governing an entire piece or section" (Kramer 1988: 20). Large-scale contingency reigns, and non-local factors like gradual process or holistic affect come to replace musical inevitabilities at a measure-to-measure level. By abandoning or recontextualizing the progressions of diatonic tonality, pantriadicism can hinder the forward march of musical chronology. In place of harmony, other musical parameters like dynamics or rhythm rise in prominence for maintaining music's forward flow. In extreme cases, they too may subside.

Depending on the particularities of a progression and its narrative context, chromatic awe can suggest a number of temporal manipulations. It can alter the perceived pace of a scene or, more radically, unstick the listener from the normal flow of diachronic time. These changes correspond to several of the categories of unconventional musical temporality proposed by Kramer. Some kinds of pantriadic harmony may usher the listener into a "non-directed" sense of time, which preserves the feeling of forward momentum without any expectation of large-scale structural goals. Nondirected musical time "carries us along its continuum, but we do not really know where we are going in each phrase or section until we get there" (ibid.: 40). The "Beacons" sequence in *ROTK* falls into this category; the impression is of being escorted through a series of continuously surprising chords, their destinations unclear, that nevertheless collectively adhere to a global pattern of stepwise ascent and common-tone retention.

Alternatively, triadic chromaticism can facilitate what Kramer calls a *multiply* directed form of time. Here, vestiges of tonal implication are strongly present, but discontinuities and expectancy violations frustrate their realization, leaving the listener in a constant state of imaginative possibility (ibid.: 46–49). Especially impatient underscore, dense with motifs and modulatory digressions, is well suited to this kind of diffractive temporality. Steiner's coruscating music for *Now Voyager*, full of (often uncorroborated) functional progressions, and bound by editorial rather than tonal logic, seems to invite the listener into this state.

Most radically, Kramer introduces an idea of *vertical time*. This is the stretching out of a single "moment" over an entire section or composition (ibid.: 54–57). Vertical time is marked by extreme consistency of material and the absence of internally dictated expectations, with the instant-to-instant experience of music shorn of cause or effect, beginnings or endings, lulls or climaxes. Music that inhabits vertical time is almost by definition athematic, as any recognizable theme will come loaded with melodic expectations, and therefore a strong feeling of traversal forward through time. A ceaselessly rotating chromatic progression, dictated by nothing other than a need to visit new chords, might be the closest approximation of this extreme aesthetic. Some music by Bernard Herrmann comes close; the "Nautilus" from *Mysterious Island*, with its endless recombinations of a single transformational cell and virtually no change in texture or volume, may well approach Kramer's notion of a music outside time. Today, one is more likely to find this temporal archetype in ambient and electronic scores, which are more able to fully renounce the teleological expectations embedded into Western tonal systems.

Kramer is quick to caution that his categories are ideal types, only rarely occurring in unequivocal forms. Crucially, he notes that his notions of "linear" versus "vertical" time are not necessarily subjective states: the categories "apply variously to compositions, to listening modes, to performing modes, to philosophies of composition, and to time itself" (ibid.: 61). To that list we might add figurative analytical or interpretive perspectives as well. In our investigations of harmonic oscillations and cycles, we have already seen one manner in which chromaticism can symbolize, without necessarily eliciting, an idea of nondirected or "cyclical" time. This is not a power exclusive to chromatic harmony—a deceptive cadence, for example, might represent time "grinding to a halt"—but functional diatonicism in general lends itself less to radical manipulations of musical temporality.

It is for these reasons prudent not to treat symbolic aspects of music as though they automatically brought about the psychological states they represented. However, the manipulation of temporality in pantriadic passages is not necessarily metaphorical, only ever an abstract or descriptive musical quality that maps onto an affective condition without eliciting it. Musicologist Joan Widgery, in her study of the effects of music on film temporality, contends that stimuli with clearly defined rules of organization and "complex hierarchical relationships" help us form temporal expectations. These expectations in turn aid in positioning ourselves accurately within the flow of time (1990: 97–98). "The more a listener is able to anticipate what music will follow," Widgery notes, "whether through the preceding symmetries or familiarity with the genre or individual piece—the more three-dimensional the sense of temporal space in the music" (99). Time sense, it would seem, is implicated within the same syntax and hierarchy sensitive mental faculties that support wonder, as per Phillip Fisher's theorization.

A substantial psychological literature exists on the ways an individual's sense of time's passage can change, depending on a surprisingly large number of influences. To list just a few factors on which temporal perception may hinge: the intrinsic structure of a stimulus, particularly its relative eventfulness; its repetitiveness; its abruptness or novelty; the amount of attention devoted to perceiving it; the emotional disposition of the perceiver; the pulse rate of various neural internal clocks; and the perceiver's age and strength of memory.[39] The mutability of experienced time, particularly duration, leads cognitive scientists and philosophers to speak of *subjective temporality*. Time for an individual, research makes clear, is a function of a person's state of mind more than any intrinsic chronometric flow detected within a given stimulus, or indeed the universe at large.

Empirical evidence suggests that music can influence the way we judge time's passage, and pantriadic chromaticism appears to be one way to reliably accomplish subjective temporal manipulation. The ability to accurately predict music's path lies at the heart of such effects. Psychologist Marylin Boltz's expectancy contrast model holds that listeners use differing attentional strategies for differently structured musical stimuli (see Boltz 1989, 1991, and 1993). *Future attending* is a mode of cognition triggered by music that is organized in a coherent and systematic way. This is the normal strategy employed when acculturated listeners hear diatonic music organized around regular metrical and phrasal patterns. According to Boltz, "time estimates are influenced by structural characteristics of the events to be judged," and confusing events distort such evaluations insofar as they disrupt expected, predictable processes (1989: 416). Future attending turns out to be prone to misjudgments of elapsed time in cases in which there is a pointed violation of musical expectancy. For example, a leading tone that is left dangling can give the impression that a musical phrase is shorter than it actually is, while a tonic resolution that occurs a few beats later than predicted can lengthen its theme's subjective duration past its veridical length.

On the other hand, when musical stimuli lack a hierarchical structure, Boltz argues listeners enter into an *analytic attending* strategy. Pieces that feature a comparatively high degree of randomness, noise, or unfamiliarity (and correspondingly, little redundancy or obvious grouping structure) have more information for listeners to parse and store.[40] Boltz claims that instead of extrapolating underlying structures and projecting future expectations, listeners of non-hierarchical music focus on the local relationships between adjacent events. They may do so through small-scale grouping, counting, "associative labeling," and other change-attending strategies, none of which involve interpreting events within broader hierarchical structures (Boltz and Jones 1989: 474). *These are precisely the processes that neo-Riemannians argue listeners use to understand pantriadic music.* Absent functional prolongations and normative syntaxes, we focus on the quality of progressions themselves and any emergent patterns or symmetries that arise between them. With other musical dials like orchestration and dynamics turned in just the right way, such time-manipulating unpredictability can, I propose, lend itself to the impression of awe.

Figure 5.12 represents the expectancy profile of awe, presented as a chaining together of two (and potentially many more) ITPRA trajectories. Like the psychological trajectory for frisson, surprise events here involve chromatic transformations of both the immediately preceding chord (X) and an unrealized destination chord (Y). But because awe does not rely on one-off disruptions of forecast tonal goals, the strength of these projections is much lower (hence the label "possible" destination rather than "expected"). Also unlike frisson, the profile for awe is progressive, involving an iteration of the basic expectancy-violation process in which each chromatic destination (Z) provides the footing for the next unanticipated tonal turn. By allowing these trajectories to dovetail with one another, my model of awe integrates Boltz's mode of analytic attending with Huron's dynamic time course.

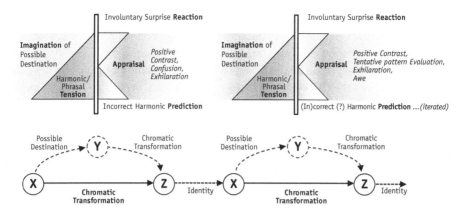

Figure 5.12 Expectancy profile of chromatic awe.

During passages of sustained pantriadic harmony, tonal expectations are initially constrained to the musical surface, with each transformation judged solely in relation to its immediate neighbors. A feeling of confusion is a more prominent affective component of the appraisal phase than in frisson. But so too is exhilaration, which can set in as the listener comes to realize that the music's logic is one of *predictable* unpredictability. And while pantriadic awe may remain limited to this moment-to-moment perceptual horizon, it is also possible to establish fairly robust contextual patterns after a few iterations of this model. Predictable unpredictability is the principle behind cycles of major and minor thirds, for example. In those cases, the imagination phases gradually become more assertive, while the prediction reactions trade their negative valence as tentative tonal patterns come to the fore. And, as we have seen again and again, other musical or filmic parameters like editing rhythms and dialogue can help to reinforce any gradually emergent logic of harmonic succession.

Boltz's analytic-attending mode concentrates on local detail and is more mentally effortful than future attending. She attributes the fact that listeners report greater time estimations in non-syntactical music to the higher cognitive load required in juggling of many micro-events. As stimuli shift along a continuum of coherence and incoherence, subjects will rely more or less on future-oriented and analytic modes. As Kramer puts it, "the more 'storage space' a passage requires, the longer its subjective duration. Thus a two-minute pop tune will probably seem shorter than a two-minute Webern movement. And a florid passage that prolongs one harmony will seem shorter . . . than one with a rapid harmonic rhythm" (ibid.: 337).

Boltz's distinction between analytic and future attending is not useful for understanding musical awe; it also helps explain divergent experiences of subjective time in cases of *sudden* and harmless unpredictability (and thus frisson). The ability for triadic chromaticism to play with our sense of duration is given

empirical support by studies by the research team led by Érico Firmino, who locates a relationship between tonal distance and subjective time experience.[41]
Using Fred Lerdahl's tonal-pitch-space metrics to quantify their claims of harmonic surprise, Firmino et al. considered the effects on time estimation made by
distant chromatic modulations within otherwise fully functional tonal contexts.
Though subtle, the influences they found proved statistically significant. The researchers determined that remote trajectories (e.g., CM⇨GbM) correlated with
shorter retrospective time estimations than familiar diatonic ones (e.g., CM⇨CM
or CM⇨FM⇨CM). Mediated chromatic paths (e.g., CM⇨EbM⇨GbM) yielded
more modest temporal underestimations; this result could be explained at least in
part by a habituation effect on listeners after they heard multiple similar modulations. These results contradicted the researchers' own hypothesis, that the longer
the path through pitch space, the greater time *overestimation* would be observed.
The intuition was that distant modulations would be felt to be inherently more
time consuming, a sensible prediction, since one might expect greater musical
durations to be required for remote keys to be properly set up. However, because
Firmino's experiment showed the opposite, it follows that a simple proportional
mapping of harmonic distance to temporal contraction/dilation is insufficient to
account for a distinctive temporality of chromaticism.

In accordance with Boltz's findings for future-based attending, Firmino et al.
suggested that abrupt chromatic modulations give the impression of coming too
quickly or ending too soon—that is, occurring before normal predictive expectancies would have them do so. Listeners were ostensibly not fooled by sheer distance
in tonal space into overcompensating in their judgments of elapsed duration.
Given what we have already seen of musical frisson, this response makes sense. It
is clear that a "coming too quickly" temporal compression effect is mixed in with
the other affective markers of frisson for pantriadic transformations.[42] Chromatic
frisson exploits our preference for future attending. It enables the magnification
of musical impact, the kind that film composers concoct by, say, flanking a chromatic jolt on either side by more traditional harmony. This result is precisely what
we have seen in "Théoden Rides Forth," and it also plays a role in the chromatically
modulating cadences we will explore in greater detail in Chapter 6.

Combining the insights of Kramer, Boltz, and Firmino et al. leads to the conclusion that, in certain situations, moving to a distant key or through an unpredictable progression can change the tempo of subjective temporality. It is necessary
not to overrate the correlations found in these studies. Importantly, the experimental stimuli in this research are highly end weighted; Boltz's and Firmino's
tests relied on working memory and retrospection, without inspecting the much
harder to evaluate *at-the-time*, situated phenomenology of time's passage.[43]
Nevertheless, their findings provide ample grounds for thinking about a dynamic
sense of temporality in conjunction with the specific aesthetic goals of musical
wonder.[44] Where shocking harmonies disrupt the flow of functional expectations
(and thus temporarily interfere with future attending), we might expect a frisson

response, one that—for some listeners—could genuinely speed up the rate of time's passage. Where lengthy pantriadic passages provoke Boltz's analytic mode of attending, we may find that a filmgoer's experience of temporality is stretched out far, far longer than normal. And what, ultimately, could be more wondrous than the alteration of such basic parameter of the fabric of reality as time itself— and by nothing more than pitch design?

Awe

The ability for chromaticism to warp time opens some intriguing doors for the inter- pretation of "awesome" film music. Of particular interest for this study, it suggests ways of integrating the spatial visualizations of NRT with the ebb and flow of cine- matic temporality.[45] Consider a textbook instance of Huron's awe paradigm in music, "The Argonath" sequence in FOTR (2:56:39, ▶). Late in the film, shortly before its climactic battle, Peter Jackson offers audiences the most longingly lingered upon of the movie's many locational marvels. The scene intercuts footage of the fellowship traveling down the River Anduin and a pair of centuries-old stone statues, easily hun- dreds of feet tall, flanking a narrow pass. These gigantic figures prompt a reaction of muted astonishment from the protagonists—a clear instance of awe in its repre- sented form. Aragorn is the only one to break the silence, murmuring softly to him- self: "Long have I desired to look upon the kings of old . . . my kin." Besides moving from a fairly arbitrary geographical point A to point B, nothing happens here beyond the stunning spectacle. Yet despite its apparent cessation of forward narrative mo- mentum, the sequence lasts a surprisingly short seventy seconds.

Shore's music takes the form of a sustained crescendo, starting out hushed and ending completely foregrounded on the soundtrack. Figure 5.13 offers a reduction and initial analysis. Beginning at m. 8, the cue is impelled by a steadily ascending melody, undergirded by vigorously nonfunctional harmony.[46] In an unsurprising but effective orchestrational choice, Shore entrusts the phrase to the chorus, intoning obscure words in one of Tolkien's invented tongues.[47] As listeners have by this point become accustomed, the non-thematic pantriadic section prepares a definitive statement of an important leitmotif. Here, it is a grand rendition of the "History of the Ring" theme at two successive transpositional levels. In this context, the "Ring" motif acts as a vivid sonic memory, an ominous but also sad reminder of the unthinkably deep history behind every aspect of Middle Earth.

The Argonath sequence plays with scope and perspective on both visual and musical levels. The audience is afforded different views of the duoliths and their spatial relation with respect to the band of protagonists. First we see the statues at a great distance (m. 8). Then the camera shifts to close-ups on the members of the Fellowship, as the full extent of the effigies begins to dawn on them (m. 9). This moment is followed by a spatially orienting establishing shot of both statues,

Figure 5.13 Shore, *FOTR*, "The Argonath."

now occupying the majority of the frame, with the Fellowship's boats situated in the foreground (mm. 11–17). More facial close-ups follow, and then, as the heroes navigate directly past the Argonath, only partial views. The gigantic foot of the left statue is shown to completely dwarf the protagonists' skiffs when they are juxtaposed in the same image. This last shot provides the definitive establishment of visual scale, and Shore tellingly uses the moment (m. 18) to commence the cue's next section on a surer footing, thanks to leitmotivic and harmonic familiarity. [48]

Like the visuals, the musical score engages the sense of scale, playing with tonal distance and metrical emphasis before fixing the music's spatial dimensions definitively. Several important perspectival manipulations are apparent on the surface. The steady climb in tessitura across different octaves of G♯ (G3⇨G4⇨G5) and its chromatic neighbors conveys an impression of effortful craning. The heptatonic scale to which the melody clings (F♯-G-A♭-B-C♯-D-E♭) effectively flanks the root and fifth of an (extremely weakly asserted) G-major reference chord with double neighbor tones. The combination of these two linear effects is an impression of simultaneous constriction and expansion.[49] The effect is akin to tunnel vision, a stare fixed on an impossibly large object that starts off small and steadily comes to fill up one's perceptual field.

Transformational features enhance this sense of spectacular envelopment. The sequence's primary synch points—the visual reveal of the Argonath and the cutaway to its feet—are framed by mirror transformations, first **RP** and then **PR**. Together, they erect the harmonic arena in which the rest of the passage plays out. The flow of harmonic novelty here is constant. With the exception of **S**, no single transformation is repeated in precisely the same way. Each step of the process from mm. 5 through 16 provides a new harmonic vista, and no sooner is one transformation established than musical perspective is widened by the introduction of another. No more than a single motion (a singular **L** between E♭m and BM) is diatonic. The paucity of functional footholds and the constant revising of transformations cannot help frustrating the listener's tonal position-finding abilities. Compounding the feeling of disorientation is the hierarchically undifferentiated metrical structure, consisting of little more than a chained succession of two-measure subphrases. Within these subphrases, the first chord tends to sound as if it led into the second, by dint of smooth semitonal connections resembling leading-tone resolutions in effect if not hierarchical function. While not enough to set up a sturdy framework of hypermetrical stresses, it does create at least a fragile tension-release pattern, a feeling of steady exhalation that comprises the progression's only real element of predictability.

If syntax and grammar are the foes of wonder, as Fisher claims, then Shore seems have aligned himself with the enemy here. He has built a musical phrase coursing with a kind of carefully managed tonal irregularity. By loosening the predictable temporality of functional tonality, Shore forces listeners to attend to the phrase analytically in Boltz's sense. Whatever aspects of future attending are made available are driven by non-harmonic parameters, like the rise of register and volume. The Argonath's pantriadic progression is suitably brief that short-term memory should suffice to render G major a familiar sonority upon its reappearance at m. 14 (strengthened, perhaps, by the repetition of the **S** into A♭/G♯ at m.15). Yet even this element of recurrence manages to wriggle away from the grip of robust musical expectancy. Because G major appears as the *first* chord within a two-measure unit, rather than the second (as it did at m. 6), the harmonic way station cannot claim "tonicity" by virtue of the tense-to-relaxed micropattern established in the previous measures. Instead, G♯m at m. 12 becomes the newly stronger locale, and, in classic **S** behavior, it summarily dislodges any vestigial stability existing in the passage's tonal structure.

As a strictly blow-by-blow neo-Riemannian account of the passage, Figure 5.13 does an adequate job of accounting for the diachronic unfolding of the cue. Yet it also leaves out and misrepresents some important transformational and expressive aspects, particularly the sequence's distinctive temporal quality. The scoring and the scene it inhabits both seem tailored to remove us from the irresistible sense of time's forward passage. The continuously ascending nonatonic melody hints at Kramer's nondirected linear time, while the sea of possibilities that opens with each subsequent chord calls to mind the multiply directed framework. The combination of novelty and non-orientability makes a strong case for Boltz's analytic attentional mode, and with it, the possibility of a distension of the scene's subjective duration. Analytic attending impedes our ability to accurately judge elapsed durations, and in light of the profuse, non-hierarchical information content of this sequence, it is plausible that filmgoers will experience an elongated sense of time's passage while watching the Fellowship sail down the River Anduin. Put more poetically, the huge and complex tonal distances covered make it seem as though eons of forgotten history were somehow embedded within the twelve-chord-long progression. True, there is a visual and musical telos: the authoritative establishment of scale and the annunciation of the "Ring" motif. However, the essential task of the music is to evoke a distinctive frame of mind, rather than to punctuate specific actions or to usher the narrative along. Addressing this need should not require wholesale abandonment of musical chronology; rather, an analysis of "The Argonath" should strive to integrate the aspects of the cue's harmonic design that push it forward toward a goal with those that meander in a more suspended time frame.

Figure 5.14 presents a transformational network that synthesizes the spatial/perspectival and temporal/affective aspects of this cue. On the outer fringes of the diagram lie C and F minor, the two keys that serve as a chronometric frame for the sequence. These chords connect to E♭m and G♯m with mirroring minor-third progressions. C and F exist both in and outside the harmonic universe of "The Argonath," serving at once as constituents of prolonged keys and as portals into the more devotedly pantriadic syntax of the cue's core. Together with the regions that lead into C and out of F at the cue's edges, these chords form something like a diachronic spine to the cue, the start, middle, and endpoints of its very loosely directed tonal design. This organization is indicated by placing them on the same horizontal plane, which one could compare with the x-axis of a standard timeline.

Sandwiched between those bookends is another kind of space entirely, a frozen slice of the Tonnetz, in which normative future-attending principles of musical time are held in temporary abeyance. No matter how it is devised, any possible transformation network will necessarily downplay some potentially relevant aspects of the cue's tonal construction (for example, Figure 5.14 does not deal with the inversion of chords or the location of some nodes at alternative enharmonic locations on the Tonnetz). Nevertheless, the way this particular graphical arena is arrayed is meant to provide a visual analogy to the manner in which Shore resists propelling the music forward in time. Instead, he allows the tonal space itself to dilate and contract, with the triads within it seeming to move neither backward nor forward.

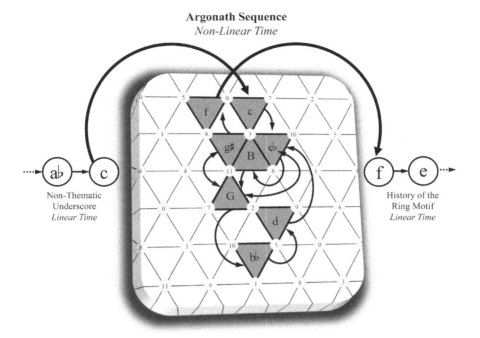

Figure 5.14 Shore, *FOTR*, "The Argonath" in tonal space.

Though one may trace the progress of the cue's roving chordal "Klang" step by step through this graph, the directed arrows do not specify a strict order. This is another analytical choice made to distinguish the linear temporality of the cue's surroundings with the nonlinear temporality encountered at its core. Spatial extent, rather than tonal directedness, is what this graph strives to translate into visual terms. We can see, for example, how G major is the most connected chord, with three inputs and two outputs. This structure makes it sound like a hinge about which the cue pivots (notably with use of the "uncanny" **S** and **H** progressions)—even though G is not directly attached to either C or F-minor bookending nodes. Note too, how the shift from Gm to B♭m (**PRP**) spans not only three chords, but also two implicit hexatonic systems. This minor-third progression occurs slightly after the cut to the first wide-angle shot of the statues, just as the Argonath's staggering size truly sinks in. Time effectively comes to a halt with entry to the hex$_{1,2}$-diagonal containing Dm and B♭m, and the diachronic impetus is only fully regained once G♯ minor is revisited the second time. And from there, it is off to the stony foundations of the "Ring" motif. . . .[50]

Wondrous chromaticism enables the filmgoer to move seamlessly in and out of directed narrative chronology. The foregoing analysis of "The Argonath" asks that we hear music as projecting a sempiternal, "out-of-time" quality through its harmonic language, just as the film's protagonists (and movie theater audiences) are asked to muse, bewildered, on the lost-to-the-ages monumentality of these statues. My hybridized directed/vertical-time network emphasizes the different ways in which harmonic spatiotemporal perspective is established in this specific sequence. Yet it might also serve as an illustration of the more general ways in which different kinds of transformational networks can be operationalized to represent different forms of time's passage within pantriadic music. As we turn our attention in the next chapter to mixtures of diatonic and chromatic syntaxes, these same sorts of questions will steer us to yet more enchanting, even miraculous uses of triadic chromaticism in film.

6

Harmonious Interactions

The Cadence of Film Music

Part of every film composer's job is to provide musical punctuation to stress and structure the unfolding narrative. There are many techniques that can accomplish this task—stingers, crescendi, and silences, to name a few. One particularly efficient form of dramatic punctuation occurs when an onscreen event is coordinated with the beginning or ending of a musical phrase, especially when that phrase is framed by a cadence.[1] Cadences are the least idiosyncratic and most predictable parts of a musical thought, involving stereotypical harmonic progressions, voice-leading patterns, and melodic routines. The perfect authentic cadence (PAC) is the most decisive type of cadence, bringing together a number of factors that project finality: a V⇨I progression with root-position triads, the proper resolution of tendency tones, and a melodic $\hat{1}$ adorning the final tonic chord. Because they signal closure so unequivocally, PACs are actually quite rare in film underscore, being reserved for moments that warrant truly emphatic underlining. Half-cadences (HC), by contrast, are quite common in some styles. Because they close a musical phrase on a resolution-demanding chord (usually, but not exclusively, V), HCs have an inherent open-endedness, a kind of question-mark effect that commends them to moving dramatic action along. Many other species of cadences can be found in film music—such as plagal, modal, and chromatic. But despite their diversity, all cadences proceed in stylistically predictable ways, making them excellent tools for marking time and funneling expectation.

Cadences are an important ingredient in the "Hollywood Sound," inasmuch as composers have developed a host of cadential tropes that reliably serve certain filmic contexts and appear infrequently in other musical genres.[2] The mixed plagal cadence (e.g., iv⁶³⇨I or ii⁰⁷⇨I), for example, seems so emblematic of Classical filmmaking-era grand finales that theorist Steven Laitz dubs it the "Hollywood Cadence" (2012: 429–430). More recent usages of mixed plagal cadences such as at the end of Hans Zimmer's score to *The Lion King* (1994) proves it retains cachet in New Hollywood as well.[3] A related progression, ♭VI⇨ii⁰⁷⇨I, finds its way into numerous scores by Max Steiner like the finale to *The Fountainhead* (1949). Meanwhile, its cadential cousins, ♭VI⇨IV⇨I and ♭III⇨IV⇨I, are far more common in contemporary movies, in which uses such as the end of the "Semantics" scene in Jerry Goldsmith's score to *The Thirteenth Warrior* (1999) and the "Shawshank Redemption" in Thomas Newman's score for the film of the same name (1993) exemplify cadential mode mixture's linkage with heroism and hard-won triumph. Another keenly "filmic"-sounding progression, the aeolian cadence (e.g., ♭VI⇨♭VII⇨i), is more of a marker of contemporary scoring practices than those of cinema's Golden Age, employed as recently as *Star Wars: Episode VII* (2015) to close out John Williams's "Rey's Theme." A special "Picardy" version of this cadence, ♭VI⇨♭VII⇨I♯³, was a favorite of Goldsmith's, used perhaps most famously at the conclusion of his theme for *Star Trek: The Motion Picture* (1979). And no discussion of cinematic cadences would be complete without mention of the "Cowboy Half-Cadence" (♭VII⇨V), an absolute *de rigueur* signifier of the American frontier in countless Westerns ever since Jerome Moross's *The Big Country* (1958) and Elmer Bernstein's *The Magnificent Seven* (1960).[4]

In what way can these time-marking, expectation-structuring little musical particles contribute to the dynamic unfolding of film underscore?[5] Two cinematic cadences, one diatonic, one chromatic, are excerpted in Figure 6.1a and 6.1b (▶). Figure 6.1a is a moment of teenage romance scored by Leonard Rosenman—the second we have now encountered, this time from his score to *East of Eden* (1955, 1:17:00). Rosenman times his love theme so that it hits a PAC in C major right as Caleb (James Dean) and Abra (Julie Harris) pull in to kiss each other. The instant their lips lock, the orchestra surges and the theme's next phrase begins, which similarly stresses the tonic triad. Rosenman's musical ploy is hardly subtle. Not all instances of this type of audiovisual synchronization—what could be called

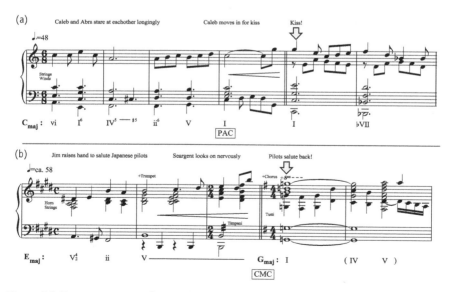

Figure 6.1 Two cinematic cadences: (a) Rosenman, *East of Eden*, "Kiss"; (b) Williams, *Empire of the Sun*, "Jim's Salute."

cadential mickey-mousing—are so unabashedly melodramatic. But there is an unavoidable forcefulness to this technique that, depending on the context, may be read as affectively exaggerated, emotionally earnest, and/or self-consciously "old-fashioned."

The second excerpt, Figure 6.1b, likewise indulges in calculated cadential overstatement. The passage, from John Williams's score to the World War II drama *Empire of the Sun* (1987, 1:08:02), is similar to Rosenman's cue from *East of Eden* in several respects. Its phrase boundaries are aligned to coincide with dramatic events; it builds anticipation with an ostensibly nondescript diatonic cadence; and it releases tonal tension with the arrival of a visual event of deep emotional resonance—this time childlike wonderment rather than amorous fulfillment. The scene finds Jim (Christian Bale) standing in front of a group of Japanese fighter pilots. The young protagonist, infatuated with the romance of flight, raises his hand to salute the servicemen; this is an audacious move, given that Jim is technically their prisoner. Jim's salute coincides squarely with the phrase's arrival on a cadential dominant in E major. The onset of the next phrase, which includes an orchestral and choral swell, synchronizes with the pilots lifting their hands to return Jim's salute. The result is a cinematic "holy moment," a spectacle of almost spiritual communion that crosses language barriers and the captor/captured divide.

And herein lies a crucial difference with the cadential mickey-mousing of *East of Eden*: the cadential dominant (B^7) in Williams's first phrase does not proceed to its expected key, but rather discharges onto a distantly related region of G major, which is then immediately treated as tonic of the new phrase. G major is doubly chromatic relative to its tonal surroundings—it stands in a chromatic major-third relationship (**PL**) to the erstwhile dominant, BM, and a chromatic minor-third (**PR**) relationship to the implied but never realized tonic, EM. When the cadence lands on G instead of E major, it feels as if a completely new world had been opened up. This is textbook contrastive valence—the intensification of an emotion by strategically violating a powerful musical expectation. Williams has exploited the cadential expectations laid down by diatonic tonality, and in doing so massively he has expanded the expressive impact of a *nondiatonic* progression.

The startling career from E to G major in *Empire of the Sun* is an example of a harmonic procedure endemic to film music: the **chromatically modulating cadence** (CMC). Chromatically modulating cadences occur when a standard diatonic cadence is set up, only to modulate immediately to a distantly related key, rather than settling on the expected tonic. We have seen a few other examples of this procedure, including passages from *Wall-E* and *The Two Towers*, that involve reorientations of tonal and visual perspective not unlike that in *Empire*. Chromatically modulating cadences resemble deceptive cadences (DC) in the way they pull the rug out from underneath the listener at the instant of highest formal and harmonic predictability. But unlike the more classically accustomed DC, which creates a purely temporary detour to be corrected in a subsequent phrase, a CMC asserts the tonicity of its new destination; it never "looks back," as DCs so often do (Schmalfeldt 1992).

CMCs impart a sense of both surprise and release in rapid succession, closely in line with the criteria for frisson outlined in the previous chapter. The shivers-inducing surprise is the product of deep structural tonal expectations. We assume that cadential chords—especially resolution-craving dominants—proceed to their implied tonics; it is a profound violation of tonal syntax when the actual destination of a cadence cannot be predicted by the logic of diatonic functionality. The element of release, on the other hand, arises from letting go of a tension-laden cadential chord like V^7 and settling on a definitive new tonic, a tonic whose stability is unquestioned, regardless of its initial sense of foreignness. CMCs thus shatter local expectancies concerning diatonic resolution, while fulfilling arguably deeper, more satisfying expectations for the *feeling* of tonal and phrasal closure.

Chromatically modulating cadences, these quintessential representatives of the "Hollywood sound," represent a flashy instance of a more general aspect of film music that has thus far occupied the outskirts of our discussions. Chromaticism, and pantriadicism in particular, exist alongside and often are influenced by other tonal paradigms. The meaning of a CMC depends on an interaction of chromatic and diatonic procedures. Pantriadic passages that are completely modeled by neo-Riemannian transformations, and that have zero functional or centric ramifications, are exceedingly rare, even in the most fantastic genres of film. As I argued earlier, film music is inherently eclectic, and part of this eclecticism occurs at the level of tonal idiom, of which pantriadicism is but one particularly vibrant flavor. If we are to properly understand cinematic chromaticism, we must consider its place within a much wider tonal universe.

In this chapter, I pull back from my earlier focus on pantriadic procedures and aesthetics and consider for the first time the issue of interactivity. My earlier emphasis has been on harmonic expressivity as a product of either individual transformations (as with absolute progressions) or certain ways of writing longer spans of nonfunctional chromaticism (as with awe and frisson paradigms). The thrust of this chapter concerns the sorts of expressivity that lie not innately within a given tonal style, but in the combination and overlap of styles. Crucially, the relationship between idioms—such as functional diatonicism, modality, and pantriadicism—is *dialectical* in character, and capable of generating wondrous affects little theorized in film, or indeed any other musical repertoire.

In order to make sense of tonal dialectics, we must first sort out what exactly these various forms of pitch organization are and what determines their differences. To that end, I begin by introducing a conceptual arena—triadic tonality space—that provides a rigorous way of defining idioms and showing their interrelationships. With this space fully mapped out, we can move onto the topic of intraphrasal chromaticism, in which nondiatonic procedures encroach *within* the boundaries of a theme. Intraphrasal chromaticism is a tricky phenomenon, analytically speaking, but becomes easier to understand with a working notion of triadic tonality space, and a more precise concept of centricity and function-ality. The analysis of well-defined, well-formed themes leads to an important question: to what extent does triadic chromaticism comprise a musical *syntax*? This is an issue that divides music theorists, and I strive to provide a balanced account of both sides in my formulation of tonal monism and dualism. In the section that follows, I formalize the dialectical aspects of syntactic combina-tion, developing three modes of tonal interaction—segregation, conversion, and interpenetration—and a way of treating motions between styles as stylistic trans-formations, not so different from the chordal transformations that have occupied us since Chapter 2.

By way of conclusion, I introduce a subspecies of the wondrous aesthetics broached in the previous chapter, the "beatific sublime." This aesthetic category is the product of an alchemy of diatonic, modal, and chromatic triadic processes, and is closely associated with scenes of religious revelation. Composers draw on the beatific sublime in order to give musical voice to a spectacle that might be considered unrepresentable, and they do so by milking the affective and historical connotations of certain tonal idioms for all they are worth. A set-piece cue from 1943's *The Song of Bernadette* serves as capstone analysis for this project. Alfred Newman's music for the film's vision scene engages almost all the analytical and theoretical technologies developed over the past six chapters. It also provides an unadulterated demonstration of the power of harmony to manufacture a sense of cinematic wonder.

Triadic Tonality Space

In Chapter 2, I described pantriadic chromaticism as a form of triadic harmony that is nondiatonic, nonfunctional, and noncentric. But pantriadicism is hardly the only tonal idiom of interest in film music, and there is no reason to assume the criteria that define it remain fixed, even in contexts in which chromaticism is pervasive. The work of Dmitri Tymoczko (2011a, esp. 181–191) points to a way of nuancing our conception of the triadic world. Tymoczko's central insight is that tonality is not an on/off phenomenon, but instead the convergence of multiple separate and changeable factors. Following Tymoczko's lead, we can isolate the three features that define pantriadic harmony and treat them as independent parameters, together capable of delineating a multitude of tonal practices. Each one of these parameters—diatonicity, functionality, and centricity—defines a dimension within a conceptual arena, a "triadic tonality space" that echoes Tymoczko's notion of tonality space, but here restricted to music where [037] dominates the musical surface.

Figure 6.2 charts out the basic skeleton of triadic tonality space, converting the three parameters into dimensional axes. The x-axis represents diatonicity, which is a function of what Tymoczko calls "macroharmony," or the collection of distinct

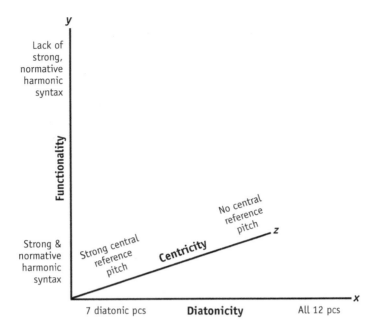

Figure 6.2 Three axes of triadic tonality.

pitch classes present over a given span of music. Complete chromatic saturation, in which every pitch class (pc) occurs with equal frequency, occupies one extreme pole along the macroharmonic continuum, the opposite side of which houses the limited pitch universe of the standard diatonic collection. The y-axis is given to functionality, which measures how strongly music adheres to the norms of a given tonal syntax: these norms include matters of chord succession, dissonance regulation, cadence placement, enharmonic (non)equivalence, and harmonic rhythm. On one end sits the heavily regulated, fifth-based harmonic grammar of common practice (CP) tonality; on the other, the ad hoc flux characteristic of the most discursive forms of pantriadicism. Finally, the z-axis captures centricity, which pertains to the presence of a stable pitch or chord of reference, and the richness of the resultant tonal hierarchy it erects. The most firmly monotonal music, in which tonal "home" is never in doubt, occupies one side of the centricity spectrum, the most uncompromisingly equalized atonality the other.

Connecting these axes in three dimensions generates a cube of tonal possibilities (Figure 6.3), with each vertex representing one of eight distinct states of triadic harmony. Each corner possesses its own deep expressive resonances, though, as we will soon see, film music often spends as much time moving around the space between idioms as it does securely ensconced within this or that corner.[6] Not every possible triadic idiom can be neatly located within the space—triadic pentatonicism, for example, sits outside the cube, even further to the left than pure

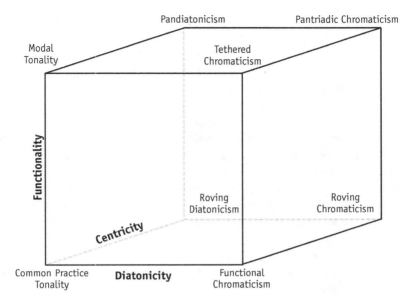

Figure 6.3 Triadic tonality space.

diatonicism. But overall, the space models all commonly encountered styles based on the consonant triad, and a few that are not so common.[7] The entire right face of the cube comprises what before now I have loosely described as "triadic chromaticism." Pantriadicism is now recognizable as the harmonic style at furthest remove from CP tonality. The other corners of the cube describe tonal idioms that have received comparatively less attention thus far in this study, and they warrant elaboration.

Common-practice tonality: Music in which tonal functionality, centricity, and diatonic macroharmony are all active. Throughout film history, CP tonality has served as a musical shorthand for normality and normalcy, though this is not to downplay the expressive richness that can be wrung out of even the most conservatively conceived white-note harmony. If described by the basic neo-Riemannian operators, diatonic progressions involve combinations of **L** and **R** but not **P** (except for the parallel transformation necessary to obtain the V$\sharp^3$ in minor). John Barry's film music tends to be more devoted to functional diatonicism than that of many of his contemporaries, and this devotion pays expressive dividends with his lyrical, easily remembered themes for dramas like *Out of Africa* (1985) and *Dances with Wolves* (1990).

Modal tonality: Music that maintains a single tonic and adheres locally to a single diatonic collection, but that lacks a strong sense of tonal function, particularly because of the absence of familiar dominant-driven cadential formulae. Modal tonality includes music that uses church scales (dorian, phrygian, etc.) instead of the usual major/minor system. Additionally, pentatonic scales and melodies derived from them are often harmonized through modal, rather than functional, means. Modal tonality encompasses pop and folk idioms that emphasize nonfunctional oscillations like I⇔vi over more directed progressions. This lack of the forward drive of functionality, coupled with a potential to evoke antique or folk associations, makes modal tonality well suited for scenes of stasis, placidity, and general emotional opacity. Much of Thomas Newman's film music exists in this category, such as the variously dorian, lydian, and mixolydian themes he wrote for *American Beauty* (1998). Sometimes Newman allows modes to overlap or interpenetrate, creating an ambiguous and expressively charged kind of modal chromaticism (Oden 2016).

Functional chromaticism: Music that adheres to CP syntax and sticks to one tonic while expanding its macroharmonic scope to accommodate nondiatonic pitches. This is an extremely broad category. Any music that is enriched with secondary dominants, tritone substitutions, altered predominants, modally mixed chords, and brief tonicizations fits into this category. Functional chromaticism, which is emblematic of nineteenth-century Romanticism as well as pre-1950s jazz and theater music, is more of a feature of Classical Hollywood than New Hollywood scoring practices. Many compositions that went on to become jazz standards, like David Raksin's theme from *Laura* (1944) and Victor Young's from *My Foolish Heart* (1949), fit into this versatile but still rule-bound tonal style.

Roving diatonicism and roving chromaticism: Music in which tonal syntax is operative but a sense of stable key is mutable or fleeting. Roving diatonicism captures harmony that moves between multiple keys in conventional ways, such as by diatonic sequences, deceptive cadences, or pivot-chord modulations.[8] Much of Korngold's underscore, which is tonally digressive while being firmly anchored by CP surface routines, fits this category. Roving chromaticism, on the other hand, explores more remote tonal areas, spins out chromatic sequences, and relies upon abrupt or exotic means of navigating tonal space. It may also may employ diatonic routines like fifth progressions, but leave the keys those routines imply unstated or underdetermined. The constantly shifting and chromatically kaleidoscopic music James Horner uses to intimate the workings of genius in movies like *Sneakers* (1992), *Searching for Bobby Fisher* (1993), *A Beautiful Mind* (2001), and *The Amazing Spiderman* (2012) belongs to this idiom (Eaton 2008, Lehman 2013a). A great deal of Classical Hollywood dramatic underscoring, with its reliance on extended tonal techniques, sits somewhere along the continuum between roving diatonicism and chromaticism. Steiner's style, as discussed in Chapter One, exemplifies the roving style, and the famous "Paris Flashback" from Steiner's *Casablanca* (1942) is particularly demonstrative.[9]

Pandiatonicism: Music that uses the notes of the diatonic scale in equal proportion, while avoiding a sense of key or functionality (Slonimsky 1994 [1937]: xxii). This style is easier to define than it is to locate in practice, since the familiarity of the diatonic scale—and especially its internal asymmetries—make it difficult to avoid echoes of tonal syntax or centricity. The sorts of music that pandiatonicism was coined to describe (stretches of Stravinsky's *Petrushka*, for instance) generally rely upon extended tertian chords or dissonant, non-triadic sonorities. Specifically triadic guises are rare, particularly in film music, though the scores of Copland and his many imitators sometimes hint at this idiom. "Grandfather's Story" from *The Red Pony* (1949), for example, is in D major overall; but except for moments when a low D occurs in the bass, this key is underarticulated amid a series of drifting but resolutely diatonic progressions.

Tethered chromaticism: Music with a strong sense of tonicity but without the predictable routines of functional syntax or the limitations of a single diatonic collection. The "tethered" adjective describes the way in which chromatic progressions that would be destabilizing in other contexts are tied down to a fixed point of reference. In order to counter the disruptive potential of nondiatonic progressions, tethered chromaticism makes use of a handful of compensatory tricks: maintaining a straightforwardly structured melody; frequently restating the tonic; and finding ways of mimicking cadential procedures without using dominants or dominant substitutes. Tethered chromaticism offers a way to exploit the expressive otherness of chromaticism while preserving the formal constraints of centric music—constraints that can facilitate followability and memorability. A not-insignificant number of film themes from fantasy genres belong to this category. A few particularly famous examples are the *Harry Potter* theme and the "Imperial March," both by John Williams. A good way to determine whether a passage exhibits tethered chromaticism is to attempt a Roman numeral analysis on it. If a tonic chord clearly emerges, but is found to be surrounded by nondiatonic triads (e.g., ♭ii, ♭iii, ♯IV, etc.), tethered chromaticism is in operation.

Intraphrasal Chromaticism

A good proving ground for this more expansive theory of triadic tonality space is in the analysis of themes—or, more specifically, the analysis of themes featuring *intraphrasal chromaticism*. While themes of the tonal CP are almost always tonally centric and framed by clear functional cadences, the harmonic and formal norms governing thematic structure in film music are considerably more diverse, as established in a comprehensive study by music theorist Mark Richards (2016). In many of the examples analyzed in earlier chapters, instances of triadic chromaticism have been relegated to the outskirts of thematic units or have fallen within non-thematic or developmental musical modules. And while chromaticism at the edges of phrases is often expressively impactful—think CMCs—it is not tonally *integral* in the same way that chromaticism strictly within the boundaries of a phrase can be.[10] Over the course of this study, we have become accustomed to treating chromatic transformations as special effects, not part of normal tonal discourse. Yet when incorporated fully into a theme, such daubs of harmonic color can be, if not completely normalized, then at least rendered less marked, less intrinsically disruptive.[11]

With intraphrasal chromaticism, pantriadic procedures are sewn into the fabric of otherwise formally straightforward themes. Chromatic transformations interact with and potentially replace the elements of diatonic syntax we expect in well-formed melodies. Suffused thus with chromaticism, film themes are naturally prone to harmonic ambiguity, but they need not sound structurally disjointed. Phrasal regularity, motivic repetition, and other aspects of thematic "four-squareness" help offset the loss of coherence normally vouchsafed by centricity and cadences. So can transformational strategies such as oscillation, transposition, and the occasional pseudo-functional operator like F or N. These stabilizing devices, which tend to focus the tonal spotlight onto certain chords or referential progressions, can bestow something of an ersatz centric quality, such that even compulsively nondiatonic themes rarely make the leap into pure pantriadicism without other parametric interventions. More typically, we find intraphrasally chromatic themes inhabiting and moving about multiple regions of triadic tonality space. With the following three short analyses, I illustrate how intraphrasal chromaticism can function within (and between) functional, roving, and tethered styles, respectively.

DR. STRANGE

With the ascendency of minimalist, modal, and electronic styles in modern film scoring, it can sometimes seem as though today's filmmakers were slightly embarrassed to employ dominant-driven functional tonality. Of prominent composers currently working in Hollywood, Michael Giacchino is perhaps the most unafraid to mine the resources of good old-fashioned CP harmony. His scores for *Ratatouille* (2007), *Up* (2009), *Super 8* (2011), and *John Carter* (2012), for example, revolve around sturdily functional themes tailored to stir up nostalgia for bygone time periods and musical practices. But Giacchino's knack for "traditional" styles goes beyond rote imitation and includes an instinct for cleverly inflecting or warping the well-trod grounds of diatonic tonality.

Figure 6.4 displays the leitmotif for *Dr. Strange*'s (2016, ⊙) titular superhero, a man able to traverse dimensions and to bend time and space at will. Giacchino injects only a small dose of functional chromaticism into the theme, but it is enough to lend it a suitably mind-bending quality. As with many of Giacchino's melodies, its formal structure is simple and singable: an eight-measure phrase, subdivided into a series of rhythmically similar two-measure ideas, starting on the tonic (D minor) and, in an act rare in modern superhero films, ending with an unmistakable half-cadence in the same key. The forcefulness of the cadential dominant is indispensible to the theme's overall effect. The V/Dm chord serves as a reclamation of tonal clarity in light of the chromatic swerve taken in the foregoing five measures. The theme is thus a model of functional tonality at its edges, with D being established at the onset and confirmed by way of A^7 at its conclusion.

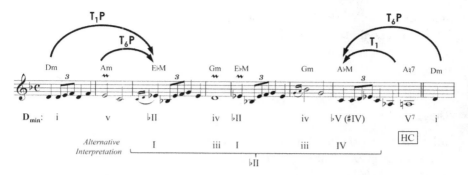

Figure 6.4 Giacchino, *Dr Strange*, theme.

But elsewhere, it occupies a boundary space, with one foot dipping into a weirder chromatic realm.

A sense of tonal self-alienation is already apparent with m. 2's minor dominant, but the strangeness really asserts itself with next chord, E♭M—related by tritone (T_6P) to its predecessor and semitone (T_1P) to the global tonic. Giacchino initiates a brief oscillation between E♭M and its L-partner, Gm, before heading to the second chromatic chord of the theme A♭M—the leitmotif's harmonic far-out point and a tritonal double (T_6P) of the home key. This penultimate triad is then transposed up by semitone (T_1), straight into the welcoming arms of the cadential dominant. There are therefore aspects of the middle six measures that appear to be playing by transformational rules: the break from a diatonic collection, the undulation of Gm and E♭M, and the loose symmetry of tritonal and semitonal relations flanking the pillars of D-minor tonality. Yet the theme is hardly pantriadic. It includes only two chromatic pcs relative to D minor (3 and 10), it is hierarchically organized, and it is functional where it counts most.

Giacchino's *Dr. Strange* theme thus presents a case of functional chromaticism pushing in the direction of pantriadicism but not taking the full plunge. With a bit of finessing, Roman numerals still work here. Even if prepared in a nonstandard way, E♭ major sits on a familiar scale step, the Neapolitan (♭II). E♭'s role, along with Gm, is to provide a larger prolongation of predominant function—though it is an unusually early and lengthy predominant prolongation, and one that comes on the heels of a disruptive tritonal motion. This leaves A♭ major unaccounted for. I concede that "♭V" does not offer much illumination, though its enharmonic doppelgänger ♯IV (G♯M) makes a certain amount of sense as a chromatic lead-in chord to the dominant—a super-chromaticized version of V⁶/V, perhaps. (This interpretation also accords with the melodic line's behavior, which from mm. 6–8 implies a $\hat{4}$-♯$\hat{4}$-$\hat{5}$ line, with octave displacements).

A more satisfying explanation, one that does not involve weirdly inflected scale steps, is to treat the theme's interior not only as a generic predominant prolongation, but also as a tonicization specifically of the Neapolitan triad. In this case, Gm takes on mediant function (iii/E♭), and A♭M absorbs subdominant function (IV/E♭). Critically, this tonicized parallel universe is not meant for an extended stay: no sooner are we allowed to gain footing in E♭ than Giacchino teleports us back to the prime-material plane of D minor, keys and psyches basically still intact.

BASIC INSTINCT

Although roving chromaticism is pervasive in through-composed underscore, it is less common as a feature of well-defined themes, which tend to stick to one key within their boundaries. A memorable incarnation of this style within an intraphrasal context may be found in Jerry Goldsmith's score for the thriller *Basic Instinct* (1992, ▶). Figure 6.5 reproduces and analyzes the theme as it appears during the film's sexually suggestive opening credits, which the composer described as sounding "erotic and evil at the same time."[12]

Goldsmith's theme throbs with libidinous energy. Its serpentine contours are thickened throughout with parallel thirds, while a profusion of common-tone-preserving transformations provides further harmonic sinew. A pattern of octave displacements masks the extreme semitonal continuity of the melody, which never moves but by step (including octave displacements). The theme falls into four equally long subphrases, each with a distinct tonal profile. Nods to tonal functionality begin to accumulate once the second phrase is under way. In particular, the **N** transformation powers several undeniable (if strictly local) dominant/tonic motions such as BM⇨Em and GM⇨Dm. The second phrase marks the initiation of a lengthy downshift pattern, with the bass sagging from A2 to D2 over the course of nineteen measures. Beginning at m. 13, Goldsmith also begins

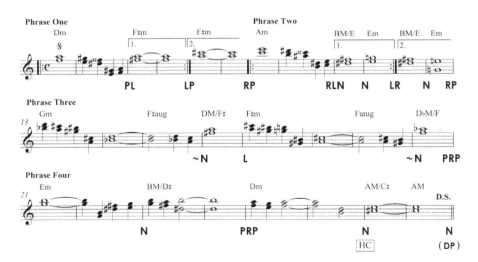

Figure 6.5 Goldsmith, *Basic Instinct*, theme.

a parsimonious sequence that utilizes augmented triads to smoothly bridge **N**-related triads. The pattern starts covering more ground at m. 21, with consecutive root-position triads related by whole step rather than semitone (although the bass line continues to inch down by half step). The entire theme thereby gives the impression of continual descent, of slipping ever more deeply and quickly into dubious territory.[13]

While the bulk of the *Basic Instinct* theme occupies a chromatically roving realm, the theme's opening eight measures exhibit a tethered aspect. Goldsmith sets up an oscillation between Dm and F♯m, a triadic pair seemingly bonded, not exactly polytonal but hardly traditionally monotonal, either. Neither chord in the **PL/LP** loop appears to have an automatic or overriding claim to tonicity. Scott Murphy's notion of stylistic disambiguation, introduced in Chapter 3, is relevant here. Faced with locally underdetermined progressions, Murphy argues that listeners fall back on already established patterns and disparities of triadic weighting. He observes that major-third motions between minor triads have a greater tendency to tonicize the upper triad (as in i⇔♭vi) than the lower triad (as in the considerably rarer i⇔iii♯). For this reason, he argues that F♯m assumes tonic status in the *Basic Instinct* theme, with Dm constituting an off-tonic opening (2014a: 490–491). Murphy's contention is corroborated by the behavior of the next phrase (mm. 7–12), which houses an unequivocal auxiliary motion into E minor—that is, another off-tonic beginning, this time prepared by diatonic chords (iv and V) rather than the more exotic minor flat-submediant (♭vi).[14]

It would not be fair to decide upon F♯m's hierarchical priority without considering the case for its competitor. Murphy concedes that Dm has the privilege of temporal priority, allowing it to initially sound as tonic by "fiat" simply by coming first. But D minor also has more structural priority over the cue as a whole, given the remote but potent dominant resolution from AM to Dm that occurs when the theme restarts itself (mm. 24–29). Of course, a purely neo-Riemannian analysis remains uncommitted. While a diatonic functional interpretation forces the question—and an answer—the neo-Riemannian interpretation **PL/LP** leaves the issue open. The theme's expressive tanginess resides in no small part in Dm⇒F♯m's harmonic multistability. An analogy with the famous Necker cube optical illusion, in which one can squint to see either (or neither) of the faces as "front," is not inapt. In the case of this progression, one can plausibly hear either (or neither) of the respective triads as occupying the hierarchical foreground. There are, undoubtedly, factors in place that can disambiguate the opening six measures' hierarchical disposition—"opposing perceptions [in multistable figures] are not equally likely," as Candace Brower notes of both chromatic third relationships and the Necker cube (2008: 58–59, 98). Yet it is important to acknowledge that, in *Basic Instinct*'s case, those disambiguating factors are imposed from outside and do not inhere within the odoriferous measures in question.

VIOLENT CITY

There is something deeply uneasy about the opening oscillation in *Basic Instinct* that exceeds theoretical explanation, a kind of polymorphous perversity of pitch design. More than other sectors of triadic tonality space, tethered chromaticism produces music that feels intrinsically tense. One can understand this idiom in terms of competing physical forces.[15] On one hand, chromatic transformations act centrifugally, constantly swinging the ear away from all points of stability. On the other hand, the local tonic—along with those non-harmonic parameters that assert its presence—provides an opposing centripetal tug on the listener, dragging down to earth what might otherwise fly off into tonal outer space. Inspecting the Emperor's leitmotif from *Star Wars*, Buhler hears something phantasmagorical in its harmonic disquietude: "The music gives the impression that only a very powerful sorcerer, perhaps even a god could animate the chords [Cm⇨E♭m$^6_4$⇨Cm⇨F♯m] thus, could make them progress against their tonal nature" (2000: 47). The triads in tethered themes and passages like these move "against their tonal will," and find themselves forced into one another's proximity by unnatural (e.g., nondiatonic, nonfunctional) processes. Themes composed in this style must maintain a fragile equilibrium. Venture too far from the tonic, and those tethers risk snapping, sending the music off into pantriadic free-for-all. Hew too closely to the tonic and everything might revert to a distorted "wrong-note" sort of functional diatonicism.

Ennio Morricone's main theme for the pulpy revenge thriller *Violent City* (1970, also known as *The Family* and *Città Violenta*) offers an illustration of the mechanics and nervous expressive potential of tethered chromaticism. The theme, analyzed in Figure 6.6 (▶) is supported exclusively by minor triads and contains not a single fifth motion or traditional cadence. Yet despite bearing all the trappings of intensified minor chromaticism, Morricone's melody is also stubbornly monotonal. It begins and ends in A minor, and with each of its four subphrases it projects a key in an unambiguous—if rather twisted—fashion. Tonicity is determined not through syntactical dependency relations, but rather sheer persistence. In the first phrase, for example, every other chord is an unbudging A-minor triad until m. 4, marked by the intrusion of a surprising and functionally ambiguous A♭m (or is it G♯m?). Morricone eventually "corrects" this vagrant A♭m in the fourth and final phrase, cadencing chromatically onto the global tonic of A♮ minor at m. 19.

On a chord-to-chord level, the behavior of Morricone's theme is wholly transpositional in nature. This means that, despite every one of the theme's twenty-seven individual harmonic motions being nondiatonic, it is not particularly well suited to analysis by the **LPR** family of transformations: Morricone progresses from one triad to the next not by exploiting common-tone relationships or emphasizing smooth voice leading, but by picking up each chord in its entirety and placing it down elsewhere. This technique contributes to the theme's spasmodic, off-kilter

Figure 6.6 Morricone, *Violent City*, theme.

quality, an effect also aided by pervasive syncopation and magnified by an active percussion part. These musical factors all help construct the thriller's seedy tone, a world in which no one can be trusted and plot twists are meted out with cynical regularity.

The overall tonal design of the *Violent City* theme—as opposed to its surface construction—is governed by a functionally allusive brand of transposition. Phrase two, which is "in" B minor, is a direct copy of the first five measures, transposed by a major second (T_2). The same goes for phrase three, "in" D minor, a minor third (T_3) from its immediate predecessor and a perfect fifth (T_5) from the opening and closing phrase. The final five measures present an unaltered copy of the first phrase, the cadentially corrected final two measures notwithstanding. The theme's superstructure is thus akin to a large-scale plagal progression: i⇨ii⇨iv⇨i, a perfectly coherent if somewhat weak means of articulating a tonic. Morricone thus coordinates his intraphrasal chromaticism with a judicious dose of *inter*phrasal diatonicism. But is this background diatonic plan enough to tame the theme's surface transformational energies? I suspect not. The chromatic triads at the end of the first three phrases, A♭m, B♭m, and D♭m are estranged enough from these diatonic pillars to render the underlying i⇨ii⇨iv⇨i plan basically inaudible to a casual listener. As is often the case with tethered chromaticism, the bonds keeping everything from flying apart (here diatonic transpositions) are hidden away from view, a fact that only adds to the impression of tonal phantasmagoria.

Tonal Monism and Dualism

It is one thing to claim that triadic tonality assumes numerous distinct and independent forms; it is quite another to contend that these forms entail distinct and independent listening strategies. Theories of chromaticism have long wrestled with this question: do listeners switch between qualitatively different modes of tonal understanding when music involves both diatonic and chromatic processes? What I propose here is an interactive model of chromatic tonality, one that allows for a flexible, quasi–ad hoc interfacing of theoretical perspectives, sometimes in a perfectly complementary way, sometimes without the possibility of reconciliation.[16] For us to understand this dialectic, it is necessary to introduce the two schools of thought that have coalesced around the issue of the diatonic/chromatic interface: what we might call tonal monism and dualism (not to be confused with the largely discredited *harmonic* dualism of Hugo Riemann). The monistic perspective holds that a single unified theory can account for the behavior of triadic chromaticism. The dualistic perspective, by contrast, asserts that triadic chromaticism involves fundamentally different procedures from those of diatonicism, and is thus owed a conceptually and methodologically unique approach. Thus far, I have implicitly endorsed the dualistic stance, inasmuch as I have analyzed cinematic chromaticism with NRT—a tonally agnostic theory—rather than adapting or extending theories of monotonality. The implications of this decision, both perceptual and aesthetic, deserve an airing, and a case for monism is overdue.

Monists view chromatic procedures to be outgrowths of diatonic ones, compatible with, and ultimately subsumable under, CP tonality. There exist several theoretical strategies for assimilating triadic chromaticism under the rubric of diatonic tonality. Some are reductive in character, while others are expansionary. Schenkerians, for example, are able to rationalize chromaticism as the byproduct of linear processes—contrapuntal exfoliations and chromatic excursions ultimately in service of an underlying diatonic prolongation. Riemannians, on the other hand, tend to focus on enlarging the universe of harmonic functions, so that chromatic chords are granted similar intentional capabilities to those of the paradigmatic tonal pillars of diatonic tonality. Why not accept, say, ♭vi as a perfectly coherent scale step, if its function can be understood clearly, as a substitute subdominant (or is it a dominant . . .)?

Consider again the *Basic Instinct* theme, now imagining it from a monist's point of view. A Schenkerian might explain the passage as a circuitous prolongation of D minor, involving an initial bass arpeggiation up to $\hat{5}$ (mm. 1–7), a lengthy chromatic expansion of the predominant E minor (mm. 8–24), and an eventual securing of the structural dominant at theme's end. A Riemannian function theorist, meanwhile, might focus on more local tonal energies, like the gravitational implications of Dm⇔F♯m at the theme's opening. Depending on the particular stripe of function theory, this oscillation might be considered either a contorted subdominant-to-tonic motion (emphasizing ♭$\hat{6}$⇔$\hat{5}$) or a mangled dominant-to-tonic motion (emphasizing ♮$\hat{7}$⇔$\hat{1}$). If one is open to enharmonic contradictions, the progression might entail both simultaneously. Ultimately, what matters to a monist is that the majority of chromatic phenomena can be adequately understood by using the core principles of functional diatonic monotonality, even if those principles require a little room to wiggle.

Charles Smith, whose theory of chromatic tonality incorporates both linear and functional considerations, makes a forceful claim for monism:

> . . . chromatic tonality utilizes the same central notions of functional direction as does diatonic tonality, and . . . the functional categories that define directionality remain constant—even when represented by some extraordinary chords. In these terms, the space traversed by chromatic music, no matter how complex, is always viewed through diatonic collections with their provocatively asymmetrical functions, rather than through the symmetrical. and therefore functionally neutral, chromatic scale (1986: 109).

In addition to his affirmative case for monistic consistency, Smith argues that the dualist position is untenable on two grounds: lack of simplicity and lack of unity. He suggests that any bifurcated view of tonality will be theoretically unparsimonious, necessitating an explosion of labels and competing explanations for apparently singular musical phenomena. Parsimony is, of course, a highly desirable trait for any explanatory framework, but it is not an obligatory one. More important than the diversity or complexity of a theory's tools is the soundness of conceptual foundations. In the case of chromatic tonality, transformation can serve as a keystone concept, shouldering similar theoretical duties as prolongation or function do for other approaches.

Smith's second objection is more difficult to dismiss: that theorizing chromaticism in a way detached from diatonicism foists a fundamental aesthetic and perceptual disunity upon the repertoire. "I cannot believe," Smith avers, "that any chromatic master conceived of his musical terrain as so partitioned [between different tonal languages]; I hear no grinding of gears as one area is left and the other entered" (109).[17] One might point to an ambiguous chromatic sonority, such as the infamous Tristan chord, as an example where these "tonal gears" do start encountering friction. Yet moments of harmonic multivalence do not pose an insuperable challenge to monistic models, particularly for Smith's wide-reaching theory of "extravagant" chromaticism. In fact, nondiatonic problem patches *affirm* tonality precisely *because* they suppose an underlying (if absent or divergent) set of functional expectations. For monists like Smith, it is preferable to patiently bring chromatic puzzles into the embrace of CP tonality than to throw up one's hands and devise a new system from full cloth.

Still, we should not prematurely abandon Smith's idea of gear grinding, as it is theoretically and aesthetically underrated by monists and dualists alike. Before recuperating this notion, we must first entertain the perceptual dualist's perspective. Most triadic transformation theorists work under an assumption of some version of dualism, but only Richard Cohn has made it an explicit and carefully developed aspect of his theory. Cohn's case for dualistic hearing hinges on two factors, structural and cognitive: (1) the inherent double nature of the consonant triad, and (2) the ability for listeners to switch between distinct modes of understanding music that uses the same basic materials in different ways. The internal structure of the consonant triad, Cohn claims, spawns two fundamentally dissimilar forms of pitch organization that listeners parse in an entirely dissimilar way. On one hand, the acoustic consonance and rootedness of the triad gives rise to the norms of eighteenth-century-style functional diatonicism. Tonal hierarchy, dissonance regulation, fifth-based cadences and modulations—all these norms are claimed to originate from the simple harmonic ratios built into set class 3-11. On the other hand, the way in which the triad divides the octave into a near-even trichord grants it unique powers of self-duplication, with only semitonal displacements needed to transform one set class 3-11 into another. Cohn maintains that the Romantic practice that eventually exploited this second potential of the triad is, contra monists, *not* an outgrowth or disturbance of more basic diatonic principles. Rather, it constitutes a true musical syntax, every bit as rich and internally consistent as functional tonality.

Cohn's case for what he calls "double syntax" rests on the plausibility of listeners swiftly and smoothly shifting between different ways of understanding musical stimuli (2012: 199–210).[18] He compares the change from diatonic to pantriadic hearing to the code-switching that occurs when bilingual speakers shift from one tongue to another, usually a seamless and cognitively opaque process. This argument for a kind of musical multilingualism is compelling, as code shifting does appear to be a natural capability of the human mind. It is the *syntactical* aspect of Cohn's argument that warrants closer scrutiny. For a term that does a great deal of work in his theory, syntax remains somewhat diffusely defined—perhaps necessarily so, given the immense structural differences between music and language, in which the concept has been most vigorously theorized. Cohn does invoke a standard linguistic sense of syntax, which concerns formal rules of temporal ordering and progression among discrete discursive units—in the case of music, chords (2012: 12–15). But he invests more theoretical weight in a generalized conception of musical syntax as a framework of pitch relationships that exists over and above any one piece. Cohn emphasizes the important role coherence plays, whereby some utterances (e.g., harmonic progressions) sound logical and well formed within the norms of a given musical style, while others that are less syntactically organized seem out of place, or "go down hard."

The autonomous syntax Cohn proposes for pantriadic harmony results from the triad's propensity for smooth voice leading. Unlike diatonic tonality, where the ultimate object of reference is the tonic triad or pitch, every note in pantriadicism points back to the entire chromatic collection. And while diatonicism occupies a hierarchically stratified conceptual space, pantriadic harmony exists within a flatter, function-free realm driven by voice leading and/or group structure. On a local level (and perhaps not much higher than that), pantriadic harmony is organized through symmetrical cycles, pitch retention loops, continuous up/downshifting, and other noncentric procedures. These are the routines that guide triads within pantriadic space and that guide the ears of the stylistically conversant when they are parsing pantriadic music.

But is it fair to characterize this as a syntax? And does labeling it as such accord with, or undermine, Fisher's dictum that "syntax and grammar are the enemies of wonder"? It is undeniable that certain forms of musical organization, including most of Western classical harmony, share many characteristics with the linguistic syntax. As summarized by Patel (2008: 267), these traits include combinatorial organization; hierarchical and recursive structures; a structural/ornamental distinction; and interdependent functional categories that are contextual and amenable to substitution. Judged by these criteria, pantriadic harmony comes up short. As we have seen, true pantriadicism unequivocally exhibits only combinatorial organization and recursivity. The most essential element of linguistic syntax—hierarchy—is notably missing. While certain relations, routines, and even reference pitches/chords may assume structural significance in pantriadic music, the dependency relations that are part and parcel of functional tonality struggle mightily to assert themselves. Therefore, if we follow Cohn and accept that pantriadicism has syntactical features, we must admit they are weaker than the robust and ramified syntax of CP diatonic tonality.

A form of hierarchy can be injected back into the mix, if one wishes, by incorporating Murphy's statistical hypothesis of intra-triadic weighting. As detailed earlier, Murphian harmonic stability is not so much determined by the constraints of an overarching tonal system as it is tentatively disambiguated by reference to informal patterns of frequency across an entire repertoire. Robust and ramified Murphy's transformational syntax is not, and it describes something closer to tethered chromaticism than pure pantriadicism. Nevertheless, considering that these stylistic categories are porous (recall again the opening of *Basic Instinct*), Murphy's circumstantial form of hierarchy *plus* Cohn's well-developed models of pantriadic organization do point to something that is, if not genuine syntax, at least syntax-like enough to validate what really matters in Cohn's theory: his notion of dual modes of listening. And this, I claim, is crucial in understanding the very "cinematic" aesthetics of tonal interactivity.

Tonal Dialectics

Regardless of where we place the borders around the moving target that is "tonal syntax," Cohn's case for code switching between harmonic idioms is intuitively plausible and grounded in well-understood and well-studied psychological principles. Yet in defending double syntax from monistic objections, we should be cautious not to simultaneously neglect the aesthetics of syntactic clash. There is compositional value in bringing idioms into uncomfortable proximity, letting them bleed into one another, even occasionally allowing them to spiral into moments of incoherency.[19] Even if code switching is a completely cognitively opaque process, that does not mean a switch in modes of tonal understanding does not register in other psychologically impactful ways. Like many other musical parameters—phrase rhythm, metrical hierarchy, chord voicing, etc.—harmonic idiom is usually not the focus of conscious listener attention. This lack of prominence is especially true with musical multimedia. In film, even the most violent stylistic shifts rarely precipitate instantaneous aesthetic decoherence, any more than the machinery of film editing, even at its most convoluted and mentally taxing, yanks a sufficiently experienced viewer out of the story. Yet, just as moving between editing styles has enormous formal and emotional consequences, the use of multiple tonal idioms—the *collision* of tonal idioms—is artistically constructive in many circumstances.

THREE FORMS OF TONAL INTERACTION

The degree to which tonal gears will grind depends heavily on context. Differing modes of contextual interaction can be sorted into three categories: segregation, conversion, and interpenetration. All three forms of idiomatic interaction are expressive, and, particularly in the case of syntactical interpenetration, that expressivity is dialectical in character. This is to say, musical meaning emerges not only from the implications of one or another idiom taken on its own; it also inheres in the way that these different idioms, by coming into contact, influence and transform one another. It is an expressivity that is dynamic and fluid, prone to change and ambiguity, and always more than the sum of its stylistic parts. Theories of harmony—either monist or dualistic—that reify the borders of their idioms and downplay the possibility for productive friction therefore risk missing out the artistic centrality of this dialectic

Some passages of film music play up the disjunction between modes of tonal understanding quite vividly, in which case **syntactical segregation** takes place. The separation of idioms is at work, for example, in chromatically modulating cadences, in which diatonic syntax suddenly gives way to a surprise chromatic transformation. The "Argonath" sequence from *LOTR* also exhibits syntactical segregation, as it features cleanly defined boundaries between initial modal diatonicism, central pantriadicism, and closing tethered chromaticism. When tonal syntaxes are clearly demarcated and placed in direct juxtaposition, dual hearing is almost certainly in operation. For example, with a CMC, the listener starts and ends by applying the rules of diatonic syntax, in between quickly judging a chromatic event in terms of its transformational qualities. The cognitive process underlying this alternation may be likened to that of a bilingual speaker hearing one sentence in English, the next in Spanish, and a third back in English. As an expressive aesthetic, syntactical segregation evokes incompatibility, irreconcilability, and rupture; it is a dialectic whose conflicting terms are not meant to synthesize, but rather to intensify the unique and opposed affective qualities of one another.

Musical passages may instead conceal the gaps between tonal idioms, in what can be termed **syntactical conversion**. By masking fissures and disjunctions, syntactical conversion is phantasmagorical by nature and thus suited to music of magical, bewildering, or insinuating character. If we continue the linguistic analogy, conversion is like utilizing a word or phrase similar in sound and meaning, such as "chromatic/cromático" in English and Spanish, to provide a mid-sentence pivot from one tongue to another.[20] In music, a bridge idiom is one means of accomplishing this task. For example, functional diatonicism might visit functional chromaticism en route to tethered chromaticism, something that happens more than once in the *Basic Instinct* theme. A single transformation that can be interpreted in two tonal systems might also serve as such a bridge—a task Cohn observes is not unlike the role pivot chords assume in powering modulations between keys. This "pivot-transformation" phenomenon can be observed in the "Whale Poacher" cue from *Free Willy* from Chapter 2, in which a digressive chromatic sequence terminates with an **RL** motion that is retrospectively heard as a functional iv⇨i motion.

Just as easily, one can imagine *anti*-pivot transformations, involving chords that *cannot* be reconciled with ease between adjoining syntaxes. Here, Smithian gear grinding is very much part of the desired affective response: recall the anti-pivot progression from the *Dr. Strange* theme (A♭M⇨A♮M = V/D), or what amounts to essentially the same trick played in reverse in *Wall-E*'s "Axiom" (A♭M⇨G♮M=V/C). These cases highlight the *lack* of syntactical conversion—a lack that, as should now be apparent, is another way in which chromatic surprise may contribute to an aesthetic of shock and reorientation (i.e., frisson).

Finally, there are those pieces of music that fuse together diatonic and chromatic impulses. **Syntactical interpenetration** blends harmonic organizing principles from different syntaxes such that they are difficult to extricate from one another. An example in spoken language would be a conversation that freely intersperses elements of both English and Spanish vocabulary and grammar. This sort of hybridization is a marker of mixed dialects, which, with a large enough community of speakers, can become a full-blown Creole or pidgin language. And like mixed dialects, syntactical interpenetration in music might be disorienting for unaccustomed listeners, though more experienced "bilingual" auditors will still be able to parse it without huge difficulty.

The choice of analytical lens for cases of syntactical interpenetration can be a tricky one. If one idiom evidently operates at higher hierarchical level than the other, an "extended" form of the analytical lens for the dominant idiom is probably sufficient (e.g., Smith's chromaticized functions, Cohn's functional hexatonic cycles, and Bailey's expressive tonality). As theorist Yosef Goldenberg (2007) notes, some passages in nineteenth-century harmony embed small-scale neo-Riemannian procedures within larger diatonically prolonged spans; in those cases, orthodox Schenkerian tools still offer the best overarching approach, while **LPR** and company can populate sketches of the surface or shallow middle ground. Alternatively, prolongational routines can be nested within chromatic cycles or sequences, in which case NRT becomes the optimal global methodology. Adjudicating the line between transformational and prolongational syntax is often more difficult than simply deciding which is nestled within the other. We must keep in mind that, just like the eight idioms of triadic tonality space, these three syntactical categories are ideal types that only rarely appear in completely pure or rigid guises in real film music. In cases in which hierarchical determinations are difficult, the best approach may be what Rings (2007: 39) calls a "two-track" methodology, in which differing analytical perspectives are offered simultaneously, describing theoretically immiscible but perceptually complementary aspects of a musical passage.

THE X-FILES

As a way of illustrating the expressive potential of syntactical interpenetration, let us turn to a piece drawn not from the movies, but television. A short but ingenious cue by Mark Snow from an episode of *The X-Files*, "This Is Not Happening" (2001, ▶)) is reproduced in reduced form in Figure 6.7. Stylistically, Snow's music sits squarely within the Hollywood harmonic practice, the only major difference being its highly minimalistic textures and orchestrational austerity—a common aspect

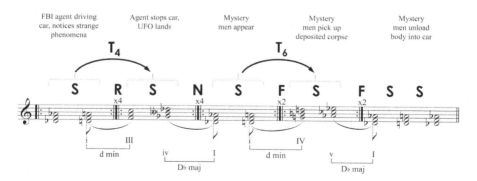

Figure 6.7 Snow, *The X-Files* (Season 8, Episode 14), "Alien Encounter."

of television, with its tighter deadlines than film and its emphasis on musical atmosphere over thematic design. The scene it accompanies sees Agent Monica Reyes (Annabeth Gish) stumbling upon an unidentified flying object while out on a night drive. Two mysterious men appear by the roadside, picking up what seems to be human body deposited by the alien ship, which turns out to be the corpse of the long-missing Agent Mulder (David Duchovny). Reyes confronts the two men, at which point Snow's cue stops. My analysis uses a Ringsian "two-track" methodology, describing both transformational and functional aspects of the cue's tonal organization without one asserting structural primacy over the other.

Rather than using dissonance or harmonic unpredictability to play up the potential terror of Reyes's encounter, Snow establishes a simple oscillation of **S**-related triads. This motif persists through the entire cue, instilling the scene with a sense of hushed uncertainty rather than extraterrestrial menace. In the absence of cadential confirmation, either member of the five **S** pairs has equal claim to local tonicity. Yet while there is no traditionally operating tonic, the pair D♭M⇔D♯m does fulfill a *referential* function, acting as a point of departure and return amid two tonally and rhythmically contrasting episodes. The first of these episodes, dwelling on FM⇔G♭m (related by overall T_4 to the initial cell), occurs once the alien spacecraft has come into sight. The second, a GM⇔A♭m pair (related by T_6 to the initial cell), accompanies the exploits of the mysterious men. The cue concludes with one last oscillation of D♭M⇔D♯m, with D♭ ultimately getting the final say.

The overall tonal idiom that results from these **S** oscillations appears at first glance to be strongly chromatic, nonfunctional, and (at best) only pseudo-centric. However, the surface of the cue is not uniformly pantriadic; recurrent hints of tonal functionality are in fact an essential component of the cue's air of uncanniness. While each of the two-chord cells is related globally to its neighbors by a chromatic transformation, the progressions that stitch successive episodes are diatonic and functionally allusive. D minor is ushered to F major by a **R**elative shift that sounds suspiciously like i⇒III/Dm in context. Even more suggestive are the fifth relations that connect subsequent episodes: G♭m to D♭M smacks of iv⇒I/D♭M; Dm to GM recalls i⇒IV/Dm; and, most potent of all, A♭m to D♭M brings to mind v⇒I/D♭M. Though these shards of functionality are fleeting and not sufficiently corroborated to establish true keys, they nevertheless evoke the logic of diatonicism as they snake through and inflect the prevailing chromatic weirdness. Indeed, considering the way D♭M "wins out" at the cue's conclusion, these diatonic transformations can be seen to cast a shadow I⇒iv⇒v⇒I progression over the proceedings. Weakly substantiated though these diatonic allusions are, they do provide a dim sense of musical familiarity throughout—a hint, perhaps, at the benevolent intentions of those mysterious men, and to the secret identity of their apparently deceased cargo.

We can visualize the interpenetration of chromatic and diatonic pitch design by representing Snow's cue within triadic tonality space. Instead of resting within one idiom, Figure 6.8 portrays "Alien Encounter" as transiting between nonfunctional chromaticism (embodied by the recurrent **S** oscillations) and functional tonality

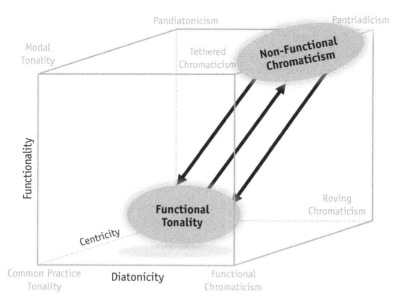

Figure 6.8 Snow, "Alien Encounter" in triadic tonality space.

(embodied by the allusive **R**, **N**, and **F** motions). There is a chronological aspect to this interaction, encoded through the directed black arrows: we hear nonfunctional chromaticism first, then a diatonic pivot, then more nonfunctional chromaticism, and so on. However, it is equally useful to imagine these spatial connections as more abstract transformations, not unlike the algebraic operations we have been using to describe triadic relationships, only here acting on whole *styles* rather than sonorities. Though I see no need to devise a mathematical group to formally encapsulate all the ways of moving (and combining moves) within this space, I continue to rely on these kinds of diagrams for the remainder of this chapter.[21]

The virtue of graphical visualization of triadic tonality space, even in this extremely schematic fashion, is that it provides a way to illustrate an idea broached back in Chapter 1—*meta-tonal design*. As indicated by the reciprocal relationship between functional and nonfunctional zones in Figure 6.8, the picture of meta-tonal design that emerges is neither strictly monistic (different syntactical principles are truly at play with each corner of the space) nor strictly dualistic (the continuity of styles is clear, and hybrid or transitional idioms are easily captured). The "transformation networks" that inhabit triadic tonality space are meant to bring the expressive dialectics of meta-tonal design into plain view.

Throughout this study, I have contended that pantriadic chromaticism and the (pseudo)syntax it gives rise to is associated in film with the aesthetics of amazement. To conclude, I propose that motion *through* triadic tonality space is just as conducive to harmonic wonderment, perhaps even more so, than unadulterated nonfunctional, noncentric chromaticism.

The Beatific Sublime

Over the course of *Hollywood Harmony*, we have examined music for aliens, ghosts, monsters, and superheroes. Triadic chromaticism being as it is a musical shorthand for the fantastic, this supernatural emphasis should come as no great surprise. With the possible exception of an excursus in Chapter 3 into *The Da Vinci Code*, the majority of studied films have drawn from completely invented mythologies, fictions that few would claim have any purchase on reality at all. And yet films revolving around religious stories—those understood by some believers to be true—are just as likely to feature colorful harmony as those with secular subjects. Indeed, film music that is enlisted to evoke "real-life" spirituality is somewhat *more* apt to play upon the diatonic/chromatic polarity than music for less theologically motivated flights of fancy.

JOAN OF ARC

Hugo Friedhofer's score to *Joan of Arc* (1948, 33:45, ▶) includes a vivid demonstration of the tonal-triadic dialectic in action. In a scene in which Joan (Ingrid Bergman) intuits the identity of a disguised Charles VII hidden within the Dauphin's crowded court, Friedhofer juxtaposes two contrasting tonal styles, which, along with a wordless chorus, impart a distinctly "holy" air to the soundtrack.[22] The cue falls in three parts, analyzed in Figure 6.9, with a series of neo-Riemannian transformations nested within a superordinate Schenkerian edifice. The sequence's first and longest section, which follows Joan as she navigates a throng of courtiers, sits in an unvarying G dorian, explored through imitative and increasingly dense counterpoint. The final section, following her realization, begins in D mixolydian and ends back in G, supported by another short span of elegant modal counterpoint. The overall trajectory of the cue is thus a perfectly

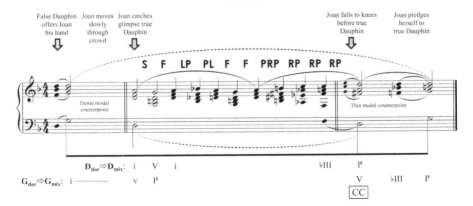

Figure 6.9 Friedhofer, *Joan of Arc*, "Joan's Test."

functional double-fifth progression, i⇨V⇨i, although this harmonic blueprint is not conveyed on the musical surface through conventional diatonic cadences.

In between these diatonic paragraphs lies a chromatic outburst that accompanies the moment of Joan's mystical discovery. First, Friedhofer introduces the new tonal focal point, tethering a D-minor triad to neighbor chords both modal (GM) and hexatonic (B♭m) in flavor. At this point in the cue, however, there is ambiguity over which member of the F-related pair, D or G, is the more weighty triad. Ultimately, it is a chromatic cadence, coming on the heels of a complete octatonic cycle, that settles the debate in D's favor and (temporarily) erases the memory of the erstwhile G tonic. The cue manages to settle on a definitive D3 bass through a chain of sequential minor thirds (**RP**) and a melodic D5 by a brief but symbolically apposite stepwise ascent. Though the chromatic interpolation does have some belated pseudo-functional power, taken as a whole it is an example of syntactic segregation, bracketed off in structure and meaning from its modal surroundings.

Over the course of just four measures, Friedhofer skates from modal diatonicism to tethered chromaticism to pantriadicism and back. Figure 6.10 provides a synopsis of the cue's path through triadic tonality space, a loop which begins and ends in modality and never leaves the top (nonfunctional) face of the cube. Diatonic pitch organization remains the overriding idiom through the course of the scene, which projects a solid prolongation of a G-tonic through stretches of modal polyphony and well-behaved points of tonal departure and arrival. But the chromatic digression at its core is transformative, even if it ultimately is a "mere" surface occurrence. It is as though the brief abandonment of tonal gravity was itself necessary to lift the listener to the telic key and mode of D mixolydian. With

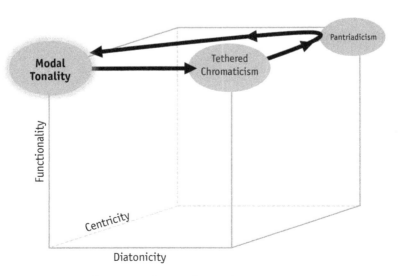

Figure 6.10 Friedhofer, "Joan's Test" in triadic tonality space.

little more than this chromatic diversion, Friedhofer can suggest that Joan of Arc is not just a lucky guesser, but a mouthpiece for the divine.

MODAL MOODS

The commingling of idioms observed in *Joan of Arc* is commonplace in scenes that dramatize revelatory visions and visitations. It is not a coincidence that the association of mixed tonalities with religious marvels is strongest in movies that draw from the history of Christianity (and even more specifically, Roman Catholic Christianity). The origins of this "beatific sublime" can be traced back to the nineteenth century, and a handful of programmatic compositions with Christian sacred themes in particular, with Wagner looming large, as ever.[23] Of special importance is the role *modal* harmony plays in this aesthetic. Just as we have seen that chromatic transformations are connoted with the supernatural and otherworldly, distinctively modal transformations being linked to ecclesiastical and archaic topics. Specific procedures used to conjure this modal sound include, but are not limited to the following:

- Plagal progressions
- Cadences with stepwise motion in outer voices
- Motion down, instead of up, the circle of fifths
- Interchangeability of major and minor forms of tonic
- Emphasis of subtonic scale degree ($\flat\hat{7}$) instead of raised leading tone
- Oscillations between diatonically related chords
- Parallel voice leading (organum)
- Progressions and linear schemata drawn from non-ionian church scales
- General weakening of tonal teleology

Importantly, film composers only rarely replicate the *actual* harmonic practice of pretonal composers, partaking instead of an imagined or reconstructed modal ethos of far more recent vintage. The modal counterpoint in Friedhofer's *Joan of Arc* cue resembles the pastiche modality of Vaughan Williams's 1921 *Mass in G Minor*, not liturgical music of a historically appropriate composer like Guillaume Dufay.[24] Many historically "authentic" modal procedures are not even triadic in orientation, but rather purely contrapuntal; hence, they do not easily lend themselves to the triad-based tonal practices of Hollywood. Thus, while Renaissance composers may have been fastidious in using *musica ficta* to avoid cross-relations and ensure raised leading tones at cadences, film composers are likely to milk cross-relations and flattened leading tones for all they are worth, so long as audiences continue to understand the larger sound world as a signifier of the old and the godly.[25]

Within the beatific sublime, diatonic/modal transformations supply connotations of the sacred, ecclesiastical, and ritualistic or purely earthbound aspects of spirituality. Chromatic moves, conversely, signify the numinous and incomprehensible, to the extent that such is ever possible through a representative (or pseudo-representative) medium. With these simple idiomatic associations in place, it is possible for the alternation of, say, a chromatic mediant and diatonic fifth transformation to suggest both piety and transcendence, humble faith and the mysteries of a kingdom beyond mortal knowledge. This heaven/earth dichotomy may be blurred (or intensified) by dancing along the centrifugal/centripetal boundary. The chromatic mediant might double as an applied dominant; the fifth progression might leave open which of its two components is the more hierarchically privileged. Indeed, this functional blur is precisely what happens with the initial Gm⇔DM⇔B♭m oscillation in *Joan of Arc*. In general, the admixture of modal and chromatic idioms in beatifically sublime music is dialectical in a metaphysically suggestive way, implying as it does the union of opposites and the bridging of incommensurable realms of experience.

OUR LADY OF FATIMA

Max Steiner's score for *Our Lady of Fatima* (1953, ▶) embarks upon a more complex voyage into the beatific sublime, wherein syntactic conversion is more the rule than the syntactic segregation observed in *Joan of Arc*. The film revolves around four apparitions of the Virgin Mary that are alleged to have occurred in 1917 Portugal. The first three visions are revealed to a trio of peasant children, while the last—the so-called miracle of the sun—is witnessed by thousands of devotees. Figure 6.11 provides a musical analysis of the first visitation scene (11:30), from the moment a rumble of thunder catches the children's attention to the point at which the Virgin begins explaining herself. (The second half of the cue, while containing a few chromatic splashes, is for the most part conventionally monotonal within E major). Once again, the analytical sketch employs both transformational and Schenkerian graphical techniques, but here they operate on more equal footing than in *Joan of Arc*, as befits the less stable, more syntactically varied harmonic makeup.

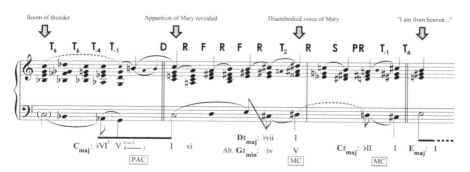

Figure 6.11 Steiner, *Our Lady of Fatima*, "First Vision."

Steiner's cue follows a formal scheme for beatific sublimity that was nearly standardized by the 1950s: begin with inchoate, tonally unfocused music; progressively achieve harmonic clarity; and finally coalesce on a big major triad, announced in a blaze of tutti orchestral refulgence. At the same time he draws from the models of earlier film scores, Steiner is also channeling Wagner's *Parsifal* in the measure-to-measure details of his cue. The sequence's central paragraph is a clear emulation of the great sequential trek at the end of *Parsifal*'s third act (beginning at m. 1109). Steiner borrows Wagner's angelic orchestration without replicating, his harmonic procedures: the section is based on a gradually ascending **R·F** pattern, comparable to Wagner's "Amen"-maximizing **R·L** sequence. Steiner's progression, which starts unspooling the moment the Virgin Mary appears, quickly begins accumulating sharps, as every second chord rises by a whole step above its predecessor, reaching skyward from C to E major by its third iteration. Whereas Wagner's **R·L** sequence submerged the end of his opera in an ocean of plagal serenity, Steiner's **R·F** alternation fills its scene with increasing brightness and energy.

Despite its overall chromatic trajectory, this Wagnerian sequence is everywhere locally diatonic and gives an impression more of modal perambulation than pantriadic discombobulation. The phrygian-style cadence that occurs the moment Mary speaks reinforces this modal atmosphere—although whether that cadence establishes I/D♯ or V/G♯ is left tantalizingly open. A similar cadence, now unambiguous in function (♭II⇒I/C♯), closes out the second half of the musical paragraph, which, in contrast to the adjacent **R·L** sequence, adheres to a less rigidly patterned **R·S·PR** progression. Figure 6.12, which tracks the traversal of triadic idioms over the course of the cue, depicts Steiner's cue as shifting back and forth between centrically

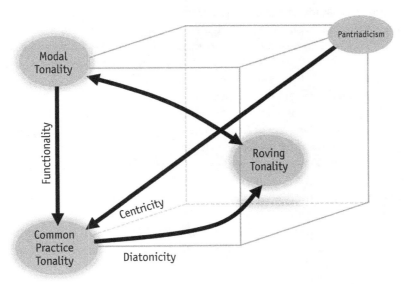

Figure 6.12 Steiner, "First Vision" in triadic tonality space.

modal and sequentially roving tonality; this trading relationship is indicated by the double-sided arrow reaching from the back face to top-left corner of the cube.

The central slice of Parsifalian harmony is prefaced by an introductory section that converts, in phantasmagoric fashion, a feeling of pantriadic weightlessness into a brief but emphatic affirmation of CP tonality. In synchrony with a booming thunderclap, Steiner opens the cue with a tritonal oscillation (T_6) of inverted C^7 and $G\flat^7$ chords. These two sevenths are lent harmonic intelligibility by a pair of common tones ($B\flat3$ and $E/F\flat4$), but at this stage the chords are not privy to any differentiation in terms of hierarchical priority. This taste of harmonic fear and confusion is only fleeting, however, as the chromatic oscillation yields to a "pivot" chord of sorts, $A\flat^{Ma7}$. The major-seventh sonority maintains an element of the transformational strategy from the earlier tritonal oscillation—namely its double common-tone preservation (now C5 and G4) with the preceding chord. However, it also serves as a functioning predominant for what is soon revealed to be a drawn-out PAC in C major. This unabashed use of cadential mickey-mousing proves a suitably portentous way to annunciate Mary's arrival. Like many other examples of functional routines mingling with passages of nonfunctional syntax, there is an element of overstatement to this cadence—note, for example, the stereotypically "churchy" $\hat{1}$-$\hat{7}$-$\hat{6}$-$\hat{7}$ suspension figure that Steiner lays over the dominant pedal bass. Here, at least, the rhetorical inflation of this tonal gesture appears commensurate to the gravity of the event it accompanies on screen.

"The Vision"

For a final case study in the beatific sublime, one that ties together threads not only from the current chapter, but this entire book, I turn to the 1943 religious drama, *The Song of Bernadette*. The score by Alfred Newman (with substantial contributions from arranger Edward Powell) was enormously popular and well regarded in its time.[26] It garnered Newman the first of his two Academy Awards, and it was only the second ever orchestral score, following Rózsa's *The Jungle Book* (1942), for which a commercial recording was released. The film, which is structured similarly to *Our Lady of Fatima*, chronicles a series of Marian apparitions supposedly witnessed by a teenage visionary, Bernadette Soubirous (Jennifer Jones), in mid-nineteenth-century Lourdes. Newman indulges heavily in the fulsome Romantic sound that by the early 1940s was second nature to Hollywood composers, but he cannily hybridizes it with tonal archaisms; this results in a unique, Tomás Luis de Victoria-meets-Mahler, musical aesthetic.

The score's biggest set piece, "The Vision," occurs during the title character's first encounter with the Virgin Mary within a secluded grotto (17:13).[27] Almost entirely free of dialogue, the scene relies on Jennifer Jones's expressive face and the exceptionally foregrounded score for its *wow*-factor. Figure 6.13 provides an analysis of the entire 4:17-minute-long cue, which falls in six sections demarcated by texture,

Figure 6.13 Newman, *Song of Bernadette*, "The Vision."

cadences, theme, and tonal idiom. To safeguard against over-cluttering the already busy diagram, I have limited my reduction to describing linear/prolongational structure and key areas/cadences. Transformational and neo-Riemannian aspects, while important, will be described in prose and subsequent diagrams.

Newman's music for Bernadette's reverie exhibits everything we have come to associate with the beatific sublime: a mixture of tonal syntaxes; a play of transformational distance and proximity; a tendency toward both inter- and intraphrasal chromaticism; the careful distribution of cadences; an abundance of allusions to nineteenth-century dramatic music; and a reliance on both frisson (local) and awe (global) paradigms for generating an affect of wonderment. Yet besides simply being a more thematically and tonally complex cue, "The Vision" differs in two ways from examples we have already investigated. First, while elsewhere the score does feature some nods to early European liturgical music, in this particular cue Newman relies far less on modality as a significatory resource than what we observed in *Joan of Arc* and *Our Lady of Fatima*. A single phrygian cadence ($\flat II_4^6 \Rightarrow I$) notwithstanding, the tonal dichotomy here is between functional diatonicism and nonfunctional chromaticism. The other significant difference is in the way "The Vision" mixes not only tonal syntaxes but also syntactical interaction strategies. Over the course of the cue, Newman plots a course through tonality space with abrupt transitions, smooth conversions, and thoroughly entangled interpenetrations. Figure 6.14 displays the convoluted path navigated in "The Vision." For aid in following the graph, labels for each of the cue's six sections, A through F, are also provided.

From the very beginning of the set piece, Newman situates the listener in a blended space, one in which three differing tonal styles—non-triadic atonality, pantriadicism, and CP tonality—are allowed to mix with one another through direct overlap and interfusion. The A-section features a dense tangle of essentially atonal string and woodwind activity meant to evoke gusts of wind, rushes of water, and random snatches of birdsong—a quietly busy backdrop for Bernadette's outdoor solitude. Against this buzz of "environmental" music, two additional layers of triadic activity gradually come into focus, presaging tonal developments later in the cue. In one layer, high strings offer a wispy and truncated reference to Bernadette's theme, first in G minor and later A major. Shortly thereafter, a wordless chorus begins providing its own harmonic commentary: first a polychordal clash of T_4 (E♭m vs. Gm) and T_6 (E♭M versus AM), then a more autonomous [vi$\Rightarrow$V$\Rightarrow$I] cadential progression in D major. These triadic layers are always sonically obscured to some degree by the persistent murmur of atonal environmental music. To the extent that it can be discerned, then, the dialectic between diatonic and chromatic idioms is at this point but a whisper, a hint of what is soon to come.

The glowing specter of Mary is revealed first to Bernadette, then the audience, during the second (B-section) leg of the cue, labeled "Emotional Prelude" in the conductor's score (Jackson 2010: 114). This eight-measure span is reproduced in

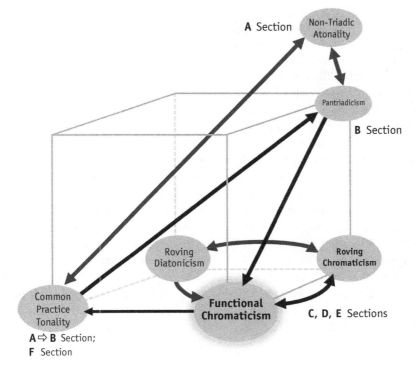

Figure 6.14 Newman, "The Vision" in triadic tonality space.

Figure 6.15 Newman, "The Vision," B-section.

Figure 6.15 (▶). The visual disclosure of the figure of the Virgin is synchronized with a triple forte B-major triad, the ecstatic objective of the music's mounting volume and orchestral tessitura. Indirect though it is, the overall tonal progression of the phrase is from F♯ to B and thus bears the faint residue of a customary dominant⇨tonic motion. Nonetheless, following an imperfect authentic cadence [F♯: iv⇨V⇨I] during its first three measures, the remainder of the succession is driven by a heaven-striving melodic line (from C♯6 to B6) and the alternation of chromatic and diatonic moves—not any inborn need to resolve F♯ to its tonic B. Indeed, B major's capture, which corresponds to the only truly strong audiovisual accent in the entire cue, is better explained as the product of a purely chromatic cadence. In this instance it is a cadence powered by the prototypically nonfunctional (**RPRP**) transformation, hurling FM headlong into BM.

The "Emotional Prelude" is vivid, poignant music, its effect stemming from the way it embodies a kind of musical split, a sundering of high and low, base and empyrean. Much of this impression owes to the bass line, always somehow out of phase tonally and rhythmically with the chorale-like progression in the higher reaches of the orchestra. Yet despite its wonderfully picturesque quality, the bass is harmonically ornamental, adorning more fundamental triadic pitches with piquantly unresolved neighbors and sometimes polychordal filigree.

The division of earthly and divine musical parameters plays out on a more structural level as well, as the transformational analysis in Figure 6.15 illustrates. With two **PL**s and that mighty **RPRP**, the first, third, and fifth transformations following the IAC/F♯ tug the tonal field away from any stable diatonic collection. Transformations two and four, by contrast, are feasible diatonic motions, and thereby point back toward the CP, even if the keys they specify are left beguilingly underdetermined. The latent functional energy inherent in the **LRLR** and **RL** compounds is captured with a suite of three Roman-numeral interpretations—all of which would be plausible in another context, but are here left floating and uncorroborated.

Following the climactic B-major triad, "The Vision" spends most of its time in a heady and changeable idiom somewhere between functional and roving chromaticism, always skirting around the bottom right edge of the triadic tonality cube (▶). It is here, in the C-section, where Newman's cue sounds most conspicuously

Figure 6.16 Newman, "The Vision," C-section.

late Romantic—indeed, we have not witnessed such luxurious harmonic schmaltz since *The Adventures of Robin Hood* back in Chapter 1. In particular, the material from "The Vision" theme, beginning in the fourth measure of Figure 6.16, calls to mind the stratospheric string orchestration of the *Lohengrin* Act I Prelude, stirred together with the superheated harmonies of *Tristan und Isolde*'s Act II love scene (especially Brangäne's Watch Song). The theme is pervasively chromatic, especially in its second half, and the cue loosens its grip on B major not long after the key is established. From mm. 9 through19, one may catch whiffs of no fewer than six independent reference chords ("key" is too strong to describe them): BM, Em, D♯M, CM, DM, and finally GM. These harmonic waypoints are connected directly by a variety of parsimonious (**RP, PL**) and extravagant (**T**$_{+/-1, 2}$, **H, RPR**) transformations, keeping the cue's tonal progress ever fresh and blithely unpredictable. The camera's fixation on Bernadette's wordless face strengthens the out-of-time quality already implied by Newman's meandering, tonally uninhibited *unendliche Melodie*.

On a constructive level, this is pure, plot-free spectacle. In terms of what is being portrayed on screen, we are witnessing Bernadette's temporary break from the physical world, with its measurable spaces and linear temporalities. Even with a number of internal cadences of varying kinds, Newman's churning musical prose hardly stops modulating until the instant the vision is over; it seems to inhabit a form of Kramer's "non-directed linear time," constantly moving but never telegraphing its destinations.

At the point at which the vision concludes, which coincides with the onset of the F-section, Newman supplies a closing rendition of Bernadette's theme; the leitmotif is housed within a diatonic and functional sanctum, replete with a structural dominant V/F resolving obediently to tonic. This late return to the CP is a necessary tonal "come-down" after the chromatic fervidity of the rest of the cue. The intense—even titillating—Tristanesque idiom that dominates Bernadette's trance might seem an odd choice to color this ingenuous teenager's perfectly innocent communion with the Virgin Mary. But if the cue is a bit sexier than expected, it is in keeping with Newman's understanding of the central character's journey, which he viewed as a kind of "unique . . . love story—the love of Bernadette for her Lady" (quoted in Burlingame [1999]). For Newman, devotional ardor is imagined as being no less rapturous than the most erotic tableaus in nineteenth-century music.

When we turn to the structure of "The Vision" as a whole, it is apparent that the cue is based on a pattern of alternation between chromatic and diatonic transformations, an extension of the principle observed more locally in the B-section. Instead of sequestering chromaticism to the most fantastical of moments, Newman allows it to burrow deeply into the structure of the sequence. As we have seen, this characteristic interaction between tonal realms is set in place from the beginning of Bernadette's encounter. The tonally hazy material in the A-section, with its adumbration of G and later D major, spans a diatonically reconcilable downward fifth (**T**$_{-5}$) interval. By contrast, the next large-scale tonal transition, from A- to B-section, traverses a chromatic mediant (T_4) in its leap from D to F♯ major. Once under way, the B-section navigates another perfect fifth, T_5, from F♯ to B. And so the pattern continues.

This transformational background, which exists on a different syntactical plane from that of the linear plot described by the earlier Schenkerian diagram, is depicted schematically in Figure 6.17. Every locally established key area is granted a triadic node, and every modulation a transpositional operator. Transposition rather than the **LPR** group is used to describe these shifts, because every modulation is strictly interphrasal and indirect, unable and uninterested in exploiting common tones or incremental voice leading. While the network is oriented chronologically, it is not "to scale," as durations and relative strengths of these key areas are not accounted for.

For visualizing the central (diatonic = earthly, chromatic = heavenly) tonal dichotomy, the relevant transpositions are arranged high or low on the basis of their diatonicity. (Admittedly, were it not for the unsubtle nature of the cue's overriding tonal metaphor, such a representation would rightly seem over-literal.) The three instances of a M3 transformation (T_4) are placed above the chain of keys, while three P5 progressions (T_5) sit below it. There are two transformations that disrupt this T_5/T_4 pattern: the first a chromatically modulating cadence from V/G to I/A♭ (T_1), the second a direct move up from I/G to I/F (T_{-2}). These key changes, both of which are based in stepwise transposition, suggest a tentative mediation of the underlying tonal dichotomy—chromatic in pitch content but diatonic with regard to common functional routines (V⇨♭VI and ♭VII⇨I, respectively). On the grossest transformational level, then, Newman moves from stratification to synthesis of differing tonal impulses. The music of the heavens is, figuratively speaking at least, brought down to earth.

***

Throughout this book, I have presented a case for the intensely expressive nature of harmony in film music, and in particular the expressivity borne of chromaticism's innate opposition to the unmarked, rule-bound diatonic style. As I have argued in this chapter, the diatonic/chromatic distinction is not a firm one, and few composers are content to sit still within their definitional containers. Pure pantriadicism may be the most structurally and expressively pure form of triadic chromaticism, but by finding ways to blend and merge chromatic and tonal impulses, film composers are able to open many new doors to wondrous

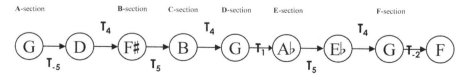

Figure 6.17 Newman, "The Vision," transformational background.

affects. Triadic tonality involves three independent parameters (functionality, diatonicity, and centricity) that combine into a number of separate tonal idioms; these parameters are slidable and dynamic, meaning that music always has the option of moving around triadic tonality space and, if it chooses, to occupy the undefined areas in between idioms. Whether by exploiting subidioms like tethered chromaticism in which certain aspects of monotonality are still operative, or by enabling a dynamic interaction of many different harmonic syntaxes, a composer can only intensify a sense of musical wonder when the weird logic of chromaticism is placed in contrast to the accustomed habits of diatonic tonality.

It is all, ultimately, a composer's trick; all this harmonic strangeness is manufactured, meticulously crafted to represent a state of spiritual communion. Whether or not filmgoers in 1943 (much less 2018) are cued into Bernadette's state of mind depends on their conversancy with the musical codes for the beatific sublime that Newman—rather thickly, perhaps even cynically—applies here. Actually *eliciting* an emotion of mystical ecstasy is an entirely different matter, and hardly one a major production from Classical Hollywood, even with its "Dream Factory" pretensions, can be expected to generate. One of the ironies of mainstream film music is that, when it comes to exploring experiences as private and mysterious as Bernadette's vision, composers tend to fall back on the some of the most conventionalized musical routines at their disposal. This is not meant to undersell Newman's (and Powell's) achievement: the music is gorgeous, impeccably crafted, ingeniously timed with the drama, memorable and haunting. Yet it is undeniable that Newman is not reinventing the wheel: his evocation of the beatific sublime is *conventional*, in the best possible sense of the word: it operates through a common set of strategies that audiences are well versed in and that requires little to no effort to understand emotionally (though, as I hope to have proven, it does take *analytical* ingenuity to plumb its depths).

Conventionality does not entail inefficacy. For all their (over)familiarity, the tonal devices employed in scores like *The Song of Bernadette* and *Joan of Arc* remain, I believe, inherently and genuinely wondrous—provided a listener is versed in the basic principles of Western musical pitch organization. There is something intrinsically fascinating about symmetry, something automatically bewildering about unpredictability, something involuntarily arresting about distance and difference. No amount of prior exposure or cliché-fatigue can entirely dull the effectiveness of these deeply rooted psychological responses.[28] Again and again, Hollywood harmony has proven to composers and audiences alike to be irresistible.

Afterword

Figure A.1 Shore, *Return of the King*, final cadence.

This book began with an examination of music that always comes before a feature film, so it seems fitting to conclude with a glimpse at some music that comes at the end of things. The figure above reproduces the final fifteen measures of Howard Shore's score to *The Return of the King*, heard at the conclusion of the film's lengthy end credits sequence. This music carries a heavy burden: it is the last word, so to speak, after a nine-and-a-half-hour stroll across Middle Earth (eleven hours for the "Extended Editions")—at least until Shore returned to the series with the *Hobbit* trilogy. In a film famous for its parade of multiple endings, this coda is also the last among many, being preceded in the credits by three earlier sections with their own satisfying musical closes: a song "Into the West" in C major; a small symphonic suite showcasing the "Shire" and "Gondor" themes in C and D major, respectively; and an ethereal vocalise, "The Evening Star," in E minor.

Unlike its immediate predecessors, this *final* final coda bears no thematic or motivic ties to the rest of the series. Its melody, such that it is, hardly concerns itself with anything other than a serene $\hat{1} \Rightarrow \hat{2} \Rightarrow \hat{1}$ neighbor figure. More salient are the sixteenth-note arpeggios in the high violins—a manifest allusion to Wagner's Rhine music and an apt musical rendering of the blissful ocean imagery of the film's last scene. Like so much of Shore's music, the passage is "chordy," and those arpeggios are the sole dynamic element in an otherwise very gradual, very placid succession of pure triads that culminates with a thirty-second-long sustained E-major triad. Harmony, not melody, not rhythm, not text, is the main attraction here. At this terminal stage, harmony is completely static, providing at last the firm tonal footing needed after a three-film-long excursion in which key was almost never stable. Fixity of key lends clarity and coherence to filmic form, even if in this case the prolonged E major is not necessarily earned, not the culmination of any long-range, deliberate process established earlier. The wholeness felt with this unbroken chord is different from that of the parallel tonal bookend that initiated the trilogy, the equally static F-phrygian drone that supplies the ground for *The Fellowship of the Ring*'s prologue. The coda's EM ending could hardly be more affectively unlike the mysterious, remote tenor of that progenitive tonal space. E major is a reclamation of familiarity, lulling the listener who sticks around for the end credits back into the undifferentiated ether in which we began, but now warm and comforting where initially it was mysterious and other.

Before settling in that dreamy sea of E major, Shore devises a simple but nevertheless effective chord progression, one that usefully summarizes some of the tonal strands of the *Lord of the Rings* series and, by extension, some important threads within the Hollywood harmonic practice(s) we have been examining. The three-chord succession is based on a light dose of chromaticism, with the tonic being flanked by its flattened subtonic (♭VII) and half-diminished supertonic (ii^{ø7}), both being products of the semi-exotic-sounding mixolydian-♭6 scale. There is nothing in the progression that suggests a tonally agnostic reading; the chords are plainly functional within the key of E and their transformational character is transpositional. (The simplistic voice leading between closed-position triads in the reduction is not an idealization, but how Shore actually moves from triad to triad.) These perhaps naive-sounding touches are, in fact, idiomatically appropriate: the parallel fifths, the lack of dominant articulation, the stepwise bass motion, the absence of any systematic tonal teleology or key symbolisms—these are not negative aspects, but rather distinctive, telltale procedures that differentiate the way movie music is written from its stylistic antecedents.

The harmonic content may not be particularly innovative or complex, but it does not need to be. Even without visuals or leitmotifs to clarify it, the chord progression is overflowing with expressive content. With the flattened subtonic, Shore conjures up the antique and folk associations that have accumulated around modal harmony throughout the *LOTR* series. With the diminished supertonic and the modally mixed cadence that it launches, he alludes to another set of connotations: the linkage of minor plagal motions in major mode to transcendence and bittersweet sentimentality. As noted in the last chapter, moves like iv⇨I and ii^{ø7}⇨I form a harmonic style topic that has a venerable lineage, and was so seemingly widespread in Classical American cinema that its label, the "Hollywood Cadence," feels intuitively right even if its true provenance was nineteenth-century Germany rather than twentieth-century Los Angeles. Brought into contact in this fashion, the two non-tonic chords in this coda evoke two different sorts of oldness, both imagined—the fantastic cultural agedness of Middle Earth and the more prosaic (but no less powerful) agedness of old Hollywood, where heroes always triumphed, big stars always got their big moments, and epic storytelling united filmgoers into a shared community, if just for a few hours. A tall order, perhaps, for two innocuous, even commonplace chords. But as I hope to have proven in this book, simple sounds rarely entail simplistic effects, and even the most familiar harmony can take us to some amazing places.

***

Stasis and motion, expression and transformation, familiarity and otherness— these are the tonal parameters at play in Shore's farewell to the *LOTR* trilogy, and the axes of meaning we have studied throughout *Hollywood Harmony*. The diversity of meanings elicited by the harmonic choices a film composer makes is an exciting aspect of this musical genre, and a feature that exposure to various music theoretical tools—transformational analysis in particular—can elucidate and enrich. The seeming familiarity of film musical tropes if anything *increases* the analytic payoff of approaching the genre in this fashion, as it makes intersubjectively plausible readings more readily available, without diminishing the "aha!" factor that arrives when a good musical interpretation does its job of revealing rather than describing. Analyzing musical wonder does not detract from the feeling of wonder; it deepens it.

This book has only scratched the surface of a small region within the immense film music repertoire. Despite being all about harmony, my investigations have been largely limited to the very simplest pitch object—the consonant triad; this focus has meant that short shrift has been given to the sometimes astonishingly rich and complex sonorities found in mainstream film scores, especially those with modernist and/or jazz influences; audiences are more likely to hear advanced tonal materials in the movie theater than in any other venue, as has been true for a long time. And although *Hollywood Harmony* has striven to be eclectic in its selection of case studies, decades' worth of culturally significant and finely crafted scores remain largely unexplored. It will take the efforts of many analytically minded composers, musicologists, and other close listeners to develop a full theory of musical design and semiosis in film. Further study in this area could easily progress to research into the stylistic roots of the pantriadic practice observed mostly in post-1970s scores within this book. It may also lead to a closer evaluation of the uses of—and potential tools for understanding—the atonal, ambient, and percussive styles whose prominence has grown markedly in the twenty-first century. These sites for future theoretical investigation, and many more, deserve fuller treatment in projects of different scope. The rise of public music analysis, as practiced with sometimes remarkable insight and systematicity on YouTube, Internet forums, podcasts, and other "open-access" platforms, signals where much of this sort of study will likely take place; at best, popular discourse on film music will continue to be informed by—and recognized by—more traditionally scholarly routes. Regardless of where this investigation occurs, I am confident that the prospect of delving into such a rewarding repertoire, so deeply meaningful for so many, means that we are witnessing only the beginnings of what film music theory can be.

Notes

Introduction

1. Paraphrasing Adorno and Eisler's 1947 critique of studio logos, James Buhler notes that "the title sequence . . . is a microcosm of the film, which celebrates and claims ownership over the illusion of reality that it creates. And the ownership and profits are the real story, the social truth, that the myth, music, and fiction of the film itself serve only to conceal" (2016: 6–7). Buhler's own analysis takes stock of the increased fluidity between corporate logos, film titles, and diegetic action in post-2000s cinema, in which music and other filmic devices conspire to "obscure the corporate origin of [a] franchise" by entangling it with the imaginary film world being conjured up (ibid.: 8–16).

2. For deeper analysis of this musical icon, see Buhler 2000 and Lehman 2013a.

3. Bordwell et al. note of the early association of branding with film advertisement, "For filmmakers, the purpose of brands was to spread the value of each film to all the films, hoping to entice repeated consumption of the manufacturer's offerings" (1985: 99).

4. Longer themes, such as Columbia Pictures (comp. Suzanne Ciani, 1976), United Artists (Josh Harnell, 1982), and Tristar Pictures (Dave Grusin, 1984), typically bear tiny bipartite structures: the first half opens with melodic fragments that begin quietly but grow in volume, and the second half (often following a modulatory "breakthrough") features fuller, more stereotypically fanfaric orchestration. Some exceptionally long and developed logo themes include the ABA′ form of John Williams's music for DreamWorks (1997), and Dave Metzger and Mark Mancina's music for Walt Disney Pictures (2006), which includes a short introductory passage before a full statement of Leigh Harline's "When You Wish upon a Star."

5. One hears only B♭ major for the original 20th Century Pictures logo (Alfred Newman, 1933); G major, along with the requisite lion's roar, for the sometimes heard MGM Fanfare (Franz Waxman, 1940); and a thirdless D♯ for Touchstone Pictures (John Debney, 1985). For short themes in which more than one chord is used, simple cadential progressions are employed, as with the straightforward IV⇨V⇨I of Selznick International (Newman, 1936), the plagal IV⇨I of the Universal Fanfare (Jimmy McHugh, 1936), or the drawn-out ii⁷⇨I of Castle Rock Entertainment (Marc Shaiman, 1989).

6. Not all movies feature musically accompanied logos, and those that do may recruit material written specially for the film rather than pre-composed musical signatures: this choice depends on many variables, including genre, studio, format, and filmmaking era. Especially during the height of the studio era, production houses were known for delivering certain kinds of films, an element of corporate branding that could be subtly reinforced by sound. The "Big Five" logos bore starkly differentiated sonic accompaniments, ranging from simple Morse code beeps for RKO to a lush symphonic fragment for Warner Brothers. The upbeat snippet of "Paramount on Parade" (Elsie Janis and Jack King, 1930) may have signaled to

241

audiences Paramount Pictures' reputation for comedies, revues, and musicals, while the lion's roar (and sometimes heraldic fanfare from Franz Waxman) may point toward MGM's reputation for prestige and all-star vehicles. By contrast, musical differences in contemporary Hollywood logos are much greater between types of studios (big conglomerates vs. independent outfits) than between directly competing companies.

7. Among the studios whose logos host lydian inflections are Columbia, Columbia Tristar, Davis Entertainment, Hollywood Pictures, Lionsgate, Phoenix Pictures, Samuel Goldwyn Films, Sony Pictures Home, and Walt Disney Pictures.

8. Some logos are substantially more chromatic than this one. Examples include Paramount Vistavision, Ladd Studios, Constantin Pictures, and DreamWorks Animation. One highly atypical example, Regency Pictures, draws its somber progression, Dm⇨B♭M⇨Fm⇨D♭M, from an already existing source: Danny Elfman's score to *Sommersby* (1993). Truly pantriadic logos are rare, though contemporary sound-system and theater-chain advertisements, which tend to be lengthy, sometimes bear them. The most thoroughgoing example from the early twenty-first century is AMC Theaters' "Magic Chairs" logo , whose music by Jay Lifton is based on a wild but affectively dead-on progression of CM⇨Fm⇨Cm/G⇨A♭m⇨E♭m⇨A♯M⇨G♭m7⇨D♭M.

9. Jerry Goldsmith's contrastingly martial theme for Universal Studios, a logo that supplanted Horner's in 1999, performs the same subtonic authentic cadence, although without modulating.

10. Because the advent of music theory as an autonomous discipline in the American academy began only in the late 1950s and was not completely established until several decades later (McCreless, 1997), early milestones in what might be called "film music theory" came from a diverse assortment of sources: these included music critics (Lawrence Morton and Hans Keller), musicologists (Frederick Sternfeld, Alfred Cochran, Graham Bruce), and, of particular interest, filmmakers and composers (Sergei Eisenstein, Fred Steiner). From an intradisciplinary perspective, perhaps the most noteworthy efforts to develop an autonomous field of "film music theory" were two issues of *Indiana Theory Review* (1990 and 1998, ed. Ralph Lorenz) dedicated to the analysis of this corpus.

11. The term *Leitharmonie* appears to have been coined by Rimsky-Korsakov in reference to his own music and later adopted for similar purposes by Stravinsky. See Taruskin (1996: 472).

12. I borrow this distinction from Lerdahl (1988). Complication involves a high degree of event non-redundancy, while complexity requires the operation of hierarchical structures and general cognitive richness.

13. I make a handful of exceptions to this constraint: the Israeli film *Waltz with Bashir*, the British film *Scott of the Antarctic*, and the American television shows *The X-Files* and *Twin Peaks*. I justify these jaunts outside Hollywood by their vividness in illustrating various analytical topics.

14. Rosar is less interested in the stylistic markers of film music's sound (which he ascribes mostly to its nineteenth-century inheritance) than in providing a definition of film music in the first place. For further investigation of film music's ontology, see J. Smith (2009), and Carroll and Moore (2011).

15. We will have many more opportunities to explore this ubiquitous progression (equivalently **LP**[m]), which has been dubbed by Matthew Bribitzer-Stull (2015) the "Tarnhelm progression" after its Wagnerian origins.

16. See Bordwell et al. (1985) for the definitive accounting of the various habits and techniques of narrative construction and continuity editing for this period.

17. The idea of "New Hollywood" can refer to different time frames and cinematic trends, depending on the theorist being asked. For some it delineates the edgy, auteurist, and decidedly non-high-concept films of the late 1960s through mid-1970s, such as *Bonnie and Clyde* and *The Graduate*. For others, it is the quite distinct Hollywood landscape that produced *Jaws* and *Star Wars* years later. For our purposes, we will retain the latter, blockbuster-driven sense of the term. For a thorough discussion of these varying stylistic, industrial, and social meanings of "New Hollywood," see King (2002).

18. I do not mean to imply the pre-1970s examples I include are somehow aberrations or tokens, either; for the most part, they are perfectly "mainstream" in their own right, and worth analyzing on their own merits. What the reader should take away from my analyses of Steiner, Friedhofer, Newman and company is (a) an aesthetic continuity with fantastical chromaticism in both 19th-century art repertoires and New Hollywood; and (b) a formal amenability to transformational analysis, albeit sometimes in a less facile or straightforward manner than contemporary movie music.

19. On the use of quartal harmony in film, particularly in the fantastic scores of Leith Stevens, see Rosar 2006. Stevens also uses pantriadic chromaticism (particularly tritonal oscillations) to good effect; Rosar argues that this approach, along with the penchant for quartal constructions, derives from Stevens's studies with the composer-theorist Joseph Schillinger.

20. See Buhler (2014: 198–207) for the connections between film music studies and neoformalist thought. It should be noted that the neoformalism of Bordwell, Thompson, Carroll and their associates was heavily inspired by musical scholarship, and takes as its object of study the film as such, eschewing those assorted methodological lenses typical of other film theoretical schools that are drawn from external critical theories, like psychoanalysis or Marxist criticism. At the same time, their project was less invested in hermeneutics than my own, and it is my hope that any formalist tools developed within this book are equally useful for furnishing interpretations as they are for describing "neutral" aspects of musical structure.

21. While sometimes estranged from the larger musicological discipline by artificially imposed departmental walls, the fields of music psychology and cognition are, it can be argued, music theoretical pursuits in principle. Music psychology in particular has made some significant strides in understanding the "how" of film music, as in the work of Annabel Cohen (see summaries in Cohen 2010, 2013, and 2014).

Chapter 1

1. I use the term 'practice' in the sense of "common practice" or "second practice." The former was established in music theoretical discourses by Walter Piston (1941) and refers roughly to the era of Bach through Wagner. For Piston, it emphasizes both a universality of tonal materials and the fact that some techniques were more or less frequently utilized. For a more recent discussion on tonal practice in this expansive sense, see Harrison 2016. "Second Practice" is the coinage of more recent theorists (see Kinderman and Krebs [1996]) and describes aspects of functional tonality's dissolution in the nineteenth century. Useful though such labels may be for periodization, the dates and theoretical underpinnings both are quite problematic. "Common practice," in particular, is a fraught term, because the functional tonality it purports to capture persists to this day in most commercial and some art repertoires, and was never so straightforwardly regulative even in its presumed heyday. On this issue, see, for example, Rothstein (2008). Because the "Second Practice" proposes a manner of composition and hearing independent of well-established tonal norms, it too has been subjected to vigorous critique, especially in Morgan (1999), who questions the extricability of functional harmonic patterns from much chromatic music.

2. See Bordwell et al. (1985: xii–11, *passim*). This is also the sense in which Claudia Gorbman uses the term "practice" in her distillation of Classical film scoring principles (1987: 7, 70–91).

3. The complexities of the authorial process in film composition have been given increased attention in recent scholarship, such as Nathan Platte's research on Rózsa's score to *Spellbound*. Despite its now canonical status, Platte finds that the soundtrack "represented not a single or even shared vision, but an intricate conglomeration of ideas, revisions, and interpolations" in a way fully typical of Hollywood collaborative practice (2011: 457).

4. Examples are too numerous to list thoroughly. For noteworthy expressions of this claim in influential music historiography, see Taruskin (2005: Book 4, 549–533) and Cooke (2008: 78–80). More extended discussions of Romanticism's imprint in Hollywood can be found in Flinn (1992) and Kalinak (1992).

5. Though she stops short of offering concrete musical comparisons, Caryl Flinn argues that "romanticism has done far more than simply determine the compositional shape of Hollywood film scores. In addition to giving Hollywood a formal and stylistic model, it provided ideological directives as well"—meaning a nostalgizing and idealistic outlook. (1992: 18).

6. One might also add the descriptor "neo-Romanticism" to this discursive field, which describes some music from more contemporary composers like John Williams and James Horner. For an account of neo-Romanticism in the work of American composers whose music is often said to "sound like film music" such as Hanson and Barber, see Simmons (2004, esp. 13–14).

7. Crucial in establishing the oft-neglected connection between film music and melodrama is foundational work from Anne Dhu McLucas (1984 and 2012) and David Neumeyer (1995 and 2010). See also Pisani (2014).

8. These styles remain under-theorized, though important groundwork is laid by Van der Merwe (1989) and Forte (1995).

9. This list includes Hanns Eisler, Friedrich Holländer, Erich Wolfgang Korngold, Miklós Rózsa, Hans Salter, Max Steiner, Dimitri Tiomkin, and Franz Waxman.

10. Composers with backgrounds in popular styles, especially Broadway and radio, dominated Classical Hollywood. A partial list includes David Buttolph, Adolph Deutsch, Leigh Harline, Alfred Newman, Frank Skinner, Roy Webb, Victor Young, and Max Steiner himself.

11. Some exceptional Studio Era scores did feature a tonal language far more modern than the norm. Lerner (2015) analyzes one such case, Waxman's music for *Pride of the Marines* (1945) that was leaps and bounds more experimental than heard in the typical war film, or any genre for that matter.

12. A useful critique of the value judgments often implicit in characterizing Hollywood as conventionally "Romantic" may be found in Whitesell (2005), specifically in reference to the music of Bernard Herrmann. On this issue, see also Buhler and Neumeyer (1994).

13. Flinn argues that the nostalgizing strain in classical Hollywood scoring serves "a kind of conduit to connect listeners . . . to an idealized past, offering . . . the promise of a retrieval of lost utopian coherence" (1992: 50).

14. Ben Winters (2007: 28) lends the name "pitch plateau" to the common method of using a sustained, unembellished note to generate tonal tension without interfering with dialogue.

15. On some of these practical justifications for Romantic melodiousness, see Hubbert (2011: 169–207) and Neumeyer (2010: 126–127).

16. Much of the language of harmonic sensuousness comes from German theorist Ernst Kurth, an important figure particularly in the reception of Wagner and Bruckner. Kurth's idea of the "absolute progression," in which pitch relations are justified by their "sonic appeal as such," will be explored more thoroughly in Chapter 2.

17. Pitch structures more in line with modernist developments begin finding their way into film music in the 1940s. See, for example, the kaleidoscopic profusion of dissonant sonorities in the famous cellar sequence in Roy Webb's *Notorious* (1946); these range from quartal trichords to consonant triads undergirded by dissonant pedals to unalloyed atonal counterpoint. Webb's style is notable for its careful control of relative tension and relaxation, through manipulation of intrinsic dissonance level, as well as the more conventional thinning and thickening of orchestral texture.

18. Neumeyer and Buhler (2001: 19–23) caution against the tendency to conflate consonance and dissonance with other harmonic parameters such as diatonic/chromatic and tonal/atonal that have potentially divergent associations. This is indeed a false equivalence, and one I will assiduously attempt to avoid.

19. For discussion of harmony in these particular films, see Rosar (2006) on *War of the Worlds*; Meyer (2015) on *Ben Hur* and *The Robe*; Rodman (2000) on *Maytime*; and Neumeyer (1990) on *Mildred Pierce* and (1998) on *The Trouble with Harry*.

20. Much of the theoretical background of Categories 8, 9, and 10 comes from Robert Bailey's foundational work (1969, 1977) on the music dramas of Richard Wagner. Directional

tonality is formulated in George (1970) and Krebs (1981). Tonal pairing is also sometimes called a "double tonic complex." For theoretical treatments, see Bailey (1985) and BaileyShea (2007).

21. Neumeyer's article "Tonal Design and Narrative in Film Music" (1998) is a particularly important milestone in the rigorous scholarly engagement with issues of long-range harmonic structure in film music. Neumeyer concludes that film-spanning tonality cannot be assumed to operate in the functional fashion that it does in common practice art music. Rodman (1998, 2010) has also theorized associative tonal procedures in film extensively, noting symbolic schemes in scores including *The Wizard of Oz* and the television show *The Rifleman*.

22. Musical markedness is, to paraphrase Robert Hatten (1994), a result of the significant asymmetries that exist between many paired elements in a musical discourse. In common-practice tonality, two familiar pairs are major versus minor or diatonic vs. chromatic. One of the terms in a relationship is a normative element of musical discourse (major, diatonic) while the other (minor, chromatic) is defined by difference or deviation, and is thus more receptive to absorbing and projecting meaningfulness.

23. On Korngold's nonconformist scoring regimen, see Winters (2007) and Hubbert (2011: 231–233).

24. The closest the composer ever came to sustained incorporation of jazz harmony is the night-club scene in his opera *Die Kathrin* (1937), in which instrumentation and some harmonic touches approximate the sound of a cabaret band. Yet it is in its every detail unmistakably Korngold. Modernistic harmony makes more frequent appearances, as with his tonal-center-free (if still conservative in terms of reliance on whole-tone collection) cue for Thorpe's pet monkey in *The Sea Hawk* (1940). Korngold's score to *The Sea Wolf* (1941) at times dabbles its toes in musical modernism with its expressionistic tone, but never fully takes the plunge.

25. This connection is further examined in Winters (2007: 97–102). Interestingly, *The Adventures of Robin Hood* was one of the few of Korngold's movie scores not to appear within a subsequent major concert work, though portions were it was reworked into a less official suite, meaning music that originated in *Sursum Corda* eventually reappeared, transformed by film, in the concert hall.

26. Interestingly, both appearances of this theme in *Sursum Corda* have more chromatic inner-voice counterpoint than the *Robin Hood* version. This difference suggests that Korngold felt a need to tone down the erotic chromaticism present in the source for this cue.

27. See also Rosenman (1968) for a more extended but similarly functionalist assessment of the structure of film music.

28. As Robynn Stilwell (2000: 222) observes, "Film music is perhaps the only predominantly instrumental musical genre which comes with no formal expectations; to the extent that conventionalized forms are a ramification of absolute music, expecting to find them in the dramatic or narrative context of film is slightly absurd."

29. The confusing ontology of "non-music" may be clarified by comparison with ideas of "filler," "furniture," or "wallpaper music" (the latter two coinages of Eric Satie). These notions are defined by their expressive neutrality and simple space-filling function. This idea of music's unobtrusive, utilitarian purpose finds its way into the discourse of film musicology in a number of sources and is closely linked with theories that regard underscore as somehow ideally "inaudible." See, for example Gorbman (1987: 56–60; 76–79) and Audissino (2014: xxiv). A useful critique of the idea of inaudibility and its supposed indispensability for suture theorists like Gorbman is offered by Jeff Smith (1996: 230–247).

30. See Hepokoski (1989) on Verdi's *Otello* for a look at the complications that transposition poses to analysis. Powers (1995), continuing the Hepokoski line of inquiry, argues that such shifts do not necessarily obviate meaningful key schemes or preclude symbolic tonal hermeneutics. Other studies of tonal design in Verdi include Levarie (1978), Marcozzi (1992), and Balthazar (1996).

31. Opera composers were not oblivious to the licenses that drama could afford to musical coherence. Wagner, for example, tended to rationalize certain musical transformations in his Ring Cycle as dramatically justified, even though they sounded "audacious" and "inconceivable" in a symphonic context. See Wagner, Ellis trans. (1994: 175–191). The changes to which Williams's music is subjected in *Star Wars* are different in kind, many being unintended by the composer, some even putting in question what counts as the definitive, analysis-worthy musical cue in the first place. Nevertheless, the processes yield similarly "audacious" harmonic content. It is no coincidence that those passages Wagner singles out in his own musical prose (specifically permutations of the Valhalla, Rheingold, and Tarnhelm leitmotifs) are among the materials most discussed by today's transformation theorists, as in Lewin (1992) and Hunt (2007).

32. For example, Bribitzer-Stull (2015: 292) proposes G minor to be "the key of the Empire" in *The Empire Strikes Back*. This claim can be supported by the fact that it is the key of the concert arrangement of the "Imperial March" (which provides the first, tracked instance of the theme in the film), and a handful of dramatic incidents involving the Empire make reference to G minor. These moments include the beginning of the carbon freezing sequence in *Empire*, the Emperor's arrival in *Return of the Jedi*, and Palpatine's declaration of the Galactic Empire in *Revenge of the Sith*. However, any linkage of (1) the Empire as a narrative force, (2) the "Imperial March" as a theme, and (3) G minor as a key breaks down as soon as one begins to keep close track of Williams's key areas in the franchise. He presents the "Imperial March," for example, in a kaleidoscopic and inconsistent variety of keys almost immediately after its introduction in *The Empire Strikes Back*. This mix makes robust claims of associative transposition somewhat dubious—especially across multiple films—and points toward a different kind of process, one more affectively opportunistic and structurally local, that guides tonal design in Williams's neo-Wagnerian scores.

33. Chloé Huvet (2014) has explored many of the issues on compositional coherence and leitmotivic development in light of editorial tinkering in the *Star Wars* prequels.

34. See Daniel Goldmark (2005: 6) for an account of the origins of this phrase in the 1930s, as a (then derogatory) term for precise, frequent, and literal-minded musical-visual synchronization, originally in live-action scoring.

35. Steiner dubbed this paradigm, rather dismissively, as "over-all" composing. Quoted in Buhler et. al. (2000: 15).

36. Cochran's work, problematic though it is, offers an instructive and occasionally penetrating picture of the nontraditional scoring approach taken by concert composers Aaron Copland, Gail Kubik, and Virgil Thompson. See Cochran (1986).

37. The most thorough theorization of audiovisual synch-points is Chion (1994: esp. 35–65). On the analysis of film musical accent, see also Burt (1994: 80–87).

38. George Burt (1994: 185–203) sees Rosenman's style—darkly psychological and suffused with knotty counterpoint and motivicism—as belonging to an expressionist tradition, informed by his studies with Schoenberg. Burt's analysis of the climactic scene from *East of Eden* grapples with Rosenman's linear, melodic-cell-driven compositional style. See also Missiras (1998) for in-depth analyses of Rosenman's scores.

39. Nelson contrasts color with musical line, which he characterizes as the "intellectual side" of music. He claims that "color is immediate in its effect, unlike thematic development, which makes definite time demands; infinitely flexible, color can be turned on and off as easily as water from a tap . . . color is easier to achieve than musical design—an important consideration when a composer writes against time" (1946: 57).

40. On modular form in film music, especially that of Herrmann, see Schneller (2012).

41. I import the adjective "impatient" from composer for screen and concert hall Irwin Bazelon, who draws a connection between immediacy of effect and the formal instability of the score. He claims that "[film music] has a function to perform and must make its presence felt without procrastination. It has to be extremely flexible and capable of immediate alteration, for music and picture must coincide and fit each other perfectly" (1975: 51). Scott Murphy

(2014a: 484) invokes Bazelon's imperative to justify a transformational and absolute-progression-driven analytic methodology.

42. Tonal expressivity may also originate from processes that build and release tension continually, like pedals, ostinati, and additive textures. On the power of striking sonorities, Bernard Herrmann notes that the composer "seldom has more than 30 seconds to gain his effect . . . and often a discord will make a quicker impression than a snatch of beautiful melody. Dissonant harmonies also express unpleasant emotions like fear, hatred, melancholy and the like much more effectively than do diatonic chords or square-cut melodies" Cited in Palmer (1993: 248).

43. According to Gorbman (1987: 90–91), "classical cinema, predicated as it is on formal and narrative unity, deploys music to reinforce this unity . . . the repetition, interaction, and variation of musical themes throughout a film contributes much to the clarify of its dramaturgy and to the clarity of its formal structures." On structural coherence in film scoring, see also Copland (1957).

44. Joseph Breil, composer for *Birth of a Nation* (1915), deplored disunity and endorsed tonal consistency across cues: "Just as in a great picture play the many scenes are all correlated, so too must its score be a collection of logical and correlative musical sequences that melt into each other." (Cited and discussed in Marks (1997: 159–160, 198–218). Local connections between the fifty-nine cues in *Birth* tend to be fairly close in terms of key signatures, but long-range tonal connections are much more tenuous. Act I, for example, begins in D minor and ends in A♭ major. Nor are any of Breil's many themes wedded to a single key, but rather appear in whatever tonal region the cue they occupy happens to be in.

45. This insight calls to mind what Waxman claimed about what makes effective film music: "it should have simplicity and directness. It must make its point immediately and strongly. The emotional impact must come all at once. It's not like concert music which is full of secrets that are learned from long acquaintance and many hearings" (1950: 135). One suspects Waxman is selling his own music, often long-breathed and calculated for cumulative effect, somewhat short.

46. Though this cue is "closely" related to the C major and E minor of its neighbors on the soundtrack—if we take its loose occupation with E♮ to comprise a governing pitch center—those proximal cues are both minutes away, rendering the fifteen-second rule moot.

47. On the uses of musical prose at the fin-de-siècle European art music, and its implications for musical narrative and temporality, see Rigbi (2013).

48. On the other hand, sustained, symmetrical lyricism tends to be a marked or foregrounded element of scores in which it occurs. Cases in which lyricism is normalized, as in the styles of Michel Legrand, Ennio Morricone, and John Barry, may be sufficiently different from Hollywood norms as to in fact constitute an alternative practice.

49. Theme labels are adopted from Daubney (2000).

50. Charles Leinberger (2002) shows that a degree of tonal diffusion is structured right into the score's symbolic key scheme. Steiner's panoply of associative keys produces a sprawling associative network, esthetically rich but potentially overwhelming to the average listener.

51. In her study of gender representation in 1940s film melodrama, Heather Laing observes that women are often treated differently from the way men are in tonal terms: "the music may surge and overtake the dialogue and wash over huge expanses of diegetic silence. It will rarely, however, leave the safe overall 'control' of the tonal system or the pleasurable familiarity of the symphonic sound. The use of chromaticism tends to remain within the—albeit generous—boundaries of late Romantic idiom, without too much evidence of the developments into atonalism that had long since happened in classical concert music" (2007: 143). Male characters, on the other hand, may garner more experimental or avant-garde musical treatment. Laing's observation is supported by a comprehensive analysis of the *Now Voyager* score (ibid.: 25–65).

52. See Schenker (2001 [1935], esp. 25–52). Notable adumbrations and adaptations of "prolongation" can be found in Salzer (1962 [1952]), Larson (1997), and Lerdahl (2001).

53. Neumeyer and Buhler (2001) note that "prolongation" is sometimes used in film musico-logical literature in a way that does not resemble Schenker's linearly driven conception, such as when invoked for passages in which the tonic is established through sheer asser-tion (e.g., by duration, emphasis, rhetoric, and other factors besides diatonic/contrapuntal composing out).

54. Stilwell smartly critiques the Schenkerian impulse in film music analysis, questioning whether the approach "based on voice-leading, is really appropriate for the discontinu-ities of film music, broken up as it is into many small cues separated by silence" (2002: 37). Notably, however, she does not weigh in on linear analysis *within* cues, which I take as a viable method, if hardly a universally applicable one.

55. For readers unfamiliar with this style of analysis: stemmed note heads represent pitches of structural significance; open note heads are of the highest importance, and small note heads of the lowest priority; slurs connect pitches related by prolongation or progression; beams connect essential melodic trajectories; flagged notes indicate pitches of special interest, often cadential predominants. The analytical orthography used here is based on Forte and Gilbert 1982, and ultimately, Schenker 2001 [1935].

56. Neumeyer's distinction arises from his differentiation of tonality in a well-behaved work by Chopin and tonality in a radically discontinuous score such as for *His Girl Friday* (1940).

57. Motazedian (2016: 172–173) observes that Morricone's score to *A Few Dollars More* is en-tirely within the key of D minor, and furthermore that the composer himself has claimed that "when I begin a theme in a certain key . . . I never depart from this original key."

58. The cognitive need for long-range tonal closure in art music has been challenged by music psychologists (see Cook 1987 and Marvin and Brinkman 1999). The limitations on struc-tural listening can be more profound only in the average film score.

59. For an example of tonality serving this "meta-diegetic" end, see Neumeyer's (1990: 19–20) analysis of Fumio Hayasaka's score for *Rashōmon*. In an analysis of the television show *The Rifleman*, "The Outlaw's Inheritance," Rodman (2010, 159–160) discerns a referential differ-entiation of keys, depending on dramatic purpose, in addition to tonal areas that provide an extra-narrative frame for the entire episode.

60. Another shrewd exploitation of the atavistic overtones of the octatonic collection is Williams's score for *Jaws* (1975). While rarely as unadulterated as Goldsmith's uses, Williams's score is shot through with varied deployments of the scale, notably a Stravinskian 5-31-set class harmonization of the main semitonal motif and a tritone-crisscrossing ar-peggio theme ($E\flat^7 \Rightarrow A^7$), which together contribute to the film's oppressive, primal horror.

61. Schifrin was himself no stranger to the octatonic scale, using it to good effect in his score to *Mission: Impossible*, for example. The composer cites his studies with Messaien as inspiration for usage of modes of limited transposition like the octatonic scale (Brown 1994: 316).

62. This average duration is trivially shortened to eight seconds if a largely monotonal (if still completely nondiatonic) parenthesis in D minor at 52:34–53:03 is excised.

Chapter 2

1. Although the vocabulary of opera analysis has many uses for film musicology, it should be acknowledged that its influence also reflects the long-standing privileging among music the-orists of opera over other dramatic repertoires. As noted in the previous chapter, melodrama, incidental music, and musical theater contributed just as much to the practices of silent and classical film, yet they remain deeply under-theorized compared to opera to this day.

2. The key texts here are Bailey (1969) and (1985: 113–146) on *Tristan* and Bailey (1977) on the *Ring*. See McCreless (1982) for the most thorough analysis of a Wagner opera (*Siegfried*) that uses Bailey's categories.

3. This maxim is meant to evoke Edward Latham's monograph *Tonality as Drama*, wherein the author examines the intersection of narrative and linear-prolongational structure in twen-tieth-century opera. While Latham's approach is explicitly Schenkerian, rather than asso-ciative like Bailey's, it stakes a similarly strong claim for the power of pitch relations: "the

unfolding of tonal musical structure—with all its detours, roadblocks, dead ends, and arrivals—is a roadmap for an inherently dramatic journey" (2008: 1).

4. For variations on this observation, see Taruskin (1985 and 2005), and Cohn (1999 and especially 2004 and 2006).

5. There also exists a handful of celebrated if isolated pantriadic experiments in the music of the Renaissance madrigalists, most notably from Maurenzio and Gesualdo. See Lowinsky (1961), Watkins (2010), and Chung (2013: 83–122) on this topic. An amusing "restoration" of this style may be heard in the music associated with Cardinal Richelieu in Michael Kamen's score for *The Three Musketeers* (1993), which appropriates triadic progressions straight out of Gesualdo's "Moro Lasso" at several junctures. The irony is that, with just a little orchestral titivation, these Gesualdian progressions could not sound more up to date or cinematic, despite being on loan from the early seventeenth century.

6. The glow of Wagnerian pantriadicism was especially entrancing to Ernst Kurth, the first in a long line to theorize this style, and what he called its "harmonic progressions whose colors diffract into the most glaring spectrum" (Kurth, in Rothfarb [trans.], 1991: 124). Notable neo-Riemannian efforts at elucidating the repertoire include Lewin (1984, 1992), Hyer (1989), Darcy (2005), Cohn (2006), and Hunt (2007).

7. Other examples of whole-tone harmony being linked to dream states include Korngold's *Devotion*; Roy Webb's *Cat People*, Leo Erdody's *Detour*; and Maurice Jarre's *Dreamscapes*. The associative tenacity of the whole-tone scale in film is discussed in Rosar (1983) and Halfyard (2010).

8. Though most closely associated with dream states, whole-tone harmony has also been used in Hollywood to suggest the uncanny, wildness, and portals and mirrors. For uncanny usages, see, for example, Steiner's *The Informer,* Waxman's *The Bride of Frankenstein*; Elmer Bernstein's *Ghostbusters* (1984); Elfman's *Edward Scissorhands* (1990); and Williams's *Harry Potter and the Chamber of Secrets* (2002). For feral states, see Steiner's *King Kong* (1933) and *They Died with Their Boots On* (1942); and Korngold's *The Sea Hawk* (1940). For mirrors, see Tiomkin's *Alice in Wonderland* (1933) and *A Tale of Two Cities* (1935).

9. Bailey's conception of expressive intensification resembles the notion of intensification (*Steigerung*) in wide currency in early-twentieth-century German music theory, particularly in Halm and Kurth. See Rothfarb (1991: 107–207). For systematic takes on the role of transposition and semitonal relations in nineteenth-century music, see Proctor (1978) and McCreless (1996: 87–113), respectively.

10. See, for example, Rothstein (2008) on Verdi; Buchler (2008) on Loesser; Doll (2011) on popular music; and Sayrs (2003) on a song by Jerry Livingston for the main titles of the film *The Hanging Tree*.

11. Doll (2011, fn. 18) provides an inventory of nicknames for this tonal phenomenon.

12. Michael Long, in discussing the technique in The Supremes' "I Hear a Symphony," links the technique to both cinematic and symphonic modes of hearing. He observes that a string of such modulations can invoke "a sense of symphonic proportions in an incredibly compressed space" (2008, 210–211).

13. Saint-Saëns bridges these two keys with a wrenching pivot chord (D♭M=♭VI/FM and V/F♯m) whose tonal ambivalence effectively telegraphs the arrival of bad news in the narrative. For an extensive discussion of *L'Assassinat*'s carefully constructed tonal design, see Marks (1997: 50–61).

14. Bashwiner (2015) provides an extensive analysis of this cue.

15. Interestingly, most intensificatory modulations in Arnold's score are by T_3 rather than T_2 or T_1, making it representative of a persistent side trend toward octatonicism for action sequences, a trend that maximizes the negative/dangerous sound of minor thirds.

16. Intensified transpositional chromaticism in its most cartoonish form can be observed in the "Bug Tunnel/Death Trap" sequence in *Indiana Jones and the Temple of Doom* (1985). In this cue, incremental stepwise modulations (up from A to B♭ minor, a full minor ninth!) combine with persistent tempo accelerations to create an effect so over the top in its exaggeration of tension that the whole scene veers into self-parody.

17. The notion of musical expressivity routinely provokes debates over the nature of emotion *in* music and the nature of emotion *in* the listener of music. (Davies 2001). The first dispute concerns whether emotion is somehow present within music or merely represented, mimicked, or indexed by it. The second asks whether listeners assume the emotional state of the music, or if they understand in an abstract way the state being expressed; it is the difference between emotional induction and representation. The former debate is ultimately immaterial to our study, but the latter does have ramifications that we will explore in Chapter 5. For now, it is sufficient to acknowledge that film music is tasked with both inducing and representing emotions (Cohen 2000).

18. My formulation of a bifurcated meaning-delivery apparatus is inspired by Scott Murphy's (2006) theorization of triadic transformational semiotics in Hollywood.

19. See Cook (2001) and Zbikowski (2002) for application of a model of cross-domain mapping specifically to multimedia, and Zbikowski (2002–2003: 77–95) for an in-depth treatment of the topic. Bribitzer-Stull (2015: 11–14) recruits Zbikowski's model to assess leitmotivic meaning. Readers familiar with Zbikowski's conceptual integration networks will note a few divergences from my own diagram, which relabels some categories and omits others for clarity's sake. Implicit in my schematic is a generic space that facilitates mapping of extrinsic and intrinsic harmonic features onto one another; this is effectively the audiovisual contract, the thing that conditions filmgoers to seek out meaningful connections between sensorial streams in the first place.

20. Knowledgeable filmgoers may pick out another extrinsic reference: James Horner's similarly wondrous music for *Brainstorm* (1983), which serves as a model for Silvestri's theme. Another "motivic" use of harmony in *The Abyss* is the association of a I⇔♭VI undulation with the protagonists' initial encounters with non-terrestrial intelligences, playing on the **LP(M)**-transformation's connotations of wonderment.

21. On the idea of musical register, see Long (2008). On stylistic competency, see Hatten (1994).

22. Matthew Bribitzer-Stull's work (Bribitzer-Stull [2015]: 79–108) on the mechanisms of leitmotivic association is particularly instructive, and much of his discussion is applicable to harmonic transformations just as well as melodic themes (n.b. his treatment of the "Tarnhelm" progression, ibid.: 131–155).

23. Murphy (2014b) adapts Cohn (2012: 22) by calling this same relationship a "homology."

24. Any claims to musical universals should be taken with a grain of salt, but research in music psychology does appear to establish consistent, albeit not inviolable, cross-cultural responses on issues of pitch height. See Eitan (2013) and Gabrielson (2016). For an exhaustive and comparatively critical treatment of the pitch height metaphor, see Cox (2016: 87–108).

25. Familiar melodic routines in Western music bear this theory out, such as suspension and "sigh" gestures signaling the expunging of tension, or even the contrast of major ($\hat{3}$ being relatively high) to minor (♭$\hat{3}$ relatively low).

26. See Krumhansl (1990) for a seminal treatment of tonal consonance and dissonance. Williams's theme for *Jaws*, likely the most recognizable motif in all film music, is a kind of atomic-level distillation of expressive tonality: a single semitone (E2⇔F2; eventually [E minor: $\hat{1}$⇔♭$\hat{2}$), sending out constant ripples of tension and deceptive release.

27. Cohen's description of congruency and reinforcement nicely supports Michel Chion's (1994: 5) notion of "added value" in his theory of audiovision.

28. On this point, see Agawu (1991: 24).

29. For example, Hefling and Tartakoff (2004, 135n150) explain an atypical modulation in a piece by Schubert as the product of different affective vectors than tension and release. They call the modulation a case of "expressive" tonality, in the sense that upward step motions express rising energy and brightness, and downward motions express darker, more depressed affects.

30. Another temptation that analysts should be cautious of is ascribing specific and localized meaningfulness to cues in which music's effect is more holistic. For an analysis of a cue by Phillip Glass that achieves its effect as a gestalt, see McClary (2007: 48–65).

31. I adapt this term from Cohn (2012: xiv), who himself borrows it from Evan Copley (1991). In previous essays, I have referred to the style as "triadic chromaticism." Following Cohn (1998: 168), I now recognize triadic chromaticism as a more general category that encompasses pantriadicism along with functional, tethered, and roving forms of chromatic pitch design.

32. See Harrison (1994: 1–2) for a discussion of this famous phrase from composer Max Reger.

33. Though obviously writing without cinematic analogies in mind, Kurth described chromatic absolute progressions, "the unmediated collision of two chords," in exactly this way, "as a special effect in itself" (Kurth, in Rothfarb [trans.] 1991: 120).

34. Interestingly, this particular third progression, **RP**(m), was adapted from the *Free Willy* score and remixed to become a villain leitmotif in the computer role-playing game, *Planescape: Torment* (1999, comp. Mark Morgan).

35. A paradigmatic example of tonality-by-assertion may be found in the move from B♭ to G♭ at the beginning of Schubert's D960, I. David Kopp (2002: 31) claims of the passage that "sheer duration leads us to hear and accept this chromatic mediant as an independent harmonic area."

36. See Cohn 2012: 12n12 for bibliographic litany of loose references to "coloristic" harmony. Schoenberg points to Debussy as a pioneer in this effect: "his harmonies, without constructive meaning, often served the coloristic purpose of expressing moods and pictures. Moods and pictures, though extra-musical, thus became constructive elements, incorporated in the musical functions; they produced a sort of emotional comprehensibility" ([1941] 2010: 216).

37. Nelson's (1946: 59–62) discussion of color in Classical Hollywood centers on various guises of chromaticism, which he locates in a diverse set of scores from Deutsch, Friedhofer, Rózsa, Toch, Waxman, and Webb. From these various uses, Nelson infers that "whatever the manner of its use, chromaticism tends in general to increase indefiniteness of key feeling and, by so doing, intensify unrest and tension" (60).

38. Adorno employs "phantasmagoria" to describe aspects of Wagner's music, including chromaticism, that seem mysteriously self-generating, masking their origination in human labor (2005: 74–85).

39. Tzvetan Todorov's (1970) influential formulation of the literary "fantastic" is nicely transferable to such usages of chromaticism in music. The fantastic, according to Todorov, requires a sense of liminality and a clash of undecidable alternatives, such as after one is presented with competing realistic and impossible explanations for unusual phenomena.

40. Another film with an association of intellection and chromaticism cited by Rebecca Eaton is *Proof* (2005), with music by Steve Warbeck. Music in a similar style and for similar purposes may be found in Murray Gold's score for *Hawking* (2004), Harry Gregson-Williams's score for *The Martian* (2015), and Hans Zimmer, Pharrell Williams, and Benjamin Wallfisch's score for *Hidden Figures* (2016).

41. See, for example, the "Cube Dance" tonal space devised by Douthett and Steinbach (1998: 253–254), and the affiliated "Weitzmann region" developed by Cohn (2000) and (2012). For an application to film music analysis, see Lehman 2012 (276–304).

42. Cohn (1998: 168) makes a similar point as part of his rationale for a neo-Riemannian approach, observing that diatonic models in particular were already considered "notoriously unresponsive" by music theorists of the early twentieth century. Methods devised for atonal music are of similarly dubious value, though in rare and special cases, may prove of some use, such as with David Shire's scores to *2010: The Year We Make Contact* and *Zodiac*, which both feature dodecaphonic principles applied to progressions among consonant triads

43. For variations of this point, see Clark (2011a: 317–318), Rehding (2011: 240–241), and Rings (2011a: 498–506).

44. Though he does not touch on transformational theories, Fink's deconstruction (1999: 73–137) of the musical surface speaks to many of the analytical values that underscore neo-Riemannian analysis. He concludes that "hierarchic music theorists ask us to renounce the pleasures of the surface for the defensive security of the depths. We may not all want to

make the exchange. Perhaps, after all, beauty is only skin-deep" (137). See also an essay in the same volume by Fred Maus (1999: 171–192) for a critique of closely related notions of musical unity and heterogeneity.

45. For a thoughtful treatment of musical organization across entire films, with a focus on the filmography of the Coen brothers, see Jarvis (2015).

46. Kurth had in mind assertively atypical progressions such as the hexatonic pole relation near the conclusion of *Parsifal*, shown back in Figure 2.1c, but also longer strings of chromatic harmony such as the same opera's chromaticized variations of the "Grail" motif.

47. See Cohn (1996: 21–22), once again centering on the moment of Kundry's chromatic expiry in *Parsifal*.

48. The notion of an "interval cycle" comes from George Perle (1977: 1–30), who recruited it for analysis of twelve-tone music, chiefly to describe intervals between pitches (rather than chords, as in NRT).

49. See Lehman (2012: 255–305) for a transformational analysis of the "The Cloud" in its entirety. See also Patrick (1986) and Buschmann (2015) for more sustained theoretical investigations into this remarkable cue, and chromatic materials in other *Star Trek* scores.

50. Planing adds another wrinkle to the chord/key issue. Sonorities generated through parallel voice leading, especially when it is quick and involves numerous stages, may fail to register even as autonomous chords, reverting instead to a condition of thickened melody.

51. The genre-establishing example here may be the wall-to-wall major chords that greet the listener behind door number five in Bártok's *Bluebeard's Castle* (a moment adapted, and then readapted, by Ralph Vaughan Williams in *Scott of the Antarctic* and *Sinfonia Antartica*/III, respectively). These passages treat the orchestra like a massive pipe organ, an instrument whose reputation as "king of the instruments" (and concomitant connection with the sublime) was firmly established in the nineteenth century.

Chapter 3

1. Rings (2011a) raises this question in his examination of the value system underlying NRT. He notes that the system, which was devised to understand the most remarkable and strange moments in nineteenth-century music, has often been applied in a way that dryly rationalizes them. "It is not the remarkable sound of those passages that is analyzed," he observes with some irony, "it is their coherence" (499).

2. A number of important articles by Lewin (1977, 1980, 1982) lay the groundwork for his transformational dichotomy, but its definitive treatment is in his seminal 1987 monograph, *Generalized Intervals and Transformations*.

3. In contrast to intervallic thinking, the transformational attitude is much less Cartesian. In Lewin's words, "given locations s and t in our space, this attitude does not ask for some observed measure of extension between reified 'points'; rather it asks: 'If I am *at* s and wish to get to t, what characteristic gesture . . . should I perform in order to get there?' The question generalizes in several important respects: 'If I want to change Gestalt 1 [a musical object or coherently associated group of objects] into Gestalt 2 (as regards content, or location, or anything else), what sorts of admissible transformations in my space . . . will do the best job?'" (1987: 153). The anti-Cartesian background is further explored in Klumpenhouwer (2006). Klumpenhouwer finds that the Lewinian transformational attitude enshrines a sense of interpretive openness for the listener, while rejecting the "single explanation is correct" approach to musical phenomena.

4. For a fuller theorization of the dynamical nature of music specifically in film, see Hazelwood (2014). Hazelwood comes at the topic from the perspective of musical energetics, rather than transformation theory, though there are points of contact between his work and the current study, particularly in the influence of Ernst Kurth.

5. Alex Rehding (2003: esp. 36–112, 186–198) provides an approachable introduction to Riemann's thought, as well as its assets and inconsistencies. He stresses that Riemann's functions are *not* strictly chords, but more abstract conceptual entities, since they are

subject to both literal alterations and contextual redefinition. For a comprehensive overview of Riemann's theories of function and chromatic tonality, see also Kopp (2002: 61–102).

6. As a harmonic dualist, Riemann insisted that major and minor triads were mirror images of each other, with minor triads counterintuitively rooted on their fifth. Inversion for Riemann was therefore a transference between chords with the same dualistic "root" but different mode. For example, inverting CM yields Fm, which has the same triadic structure of the original chord, except the major and minor thirds are built down rather than up from C. See the pertinent essays in Gollin and Rehding (2011: 165–267) for more on this now largely discredited idea.

7. Riemann's *Harmonieschritte* were themselves something of an adaptation of Arthur von Oettingen's *Schritte/Wechsel* system. This connection is described, along with the general combinatorial and transformational properties of the *Harmonieschritte*, in Engebretsen 2011.

8. Following most neo-Riemannians, I use the terms "operation," "operator," and "transformation" interchangeably in this study, though this may be a cause for minor irritation for mathematicians. A transformation, following Lewin, is a function from S into S itself—that is, a procedure (function *f*) applied to one music object *x* (argument) from a certain family or class (S) to reliably yield a unique *y* (value) within the same family. An *operation* carries the further refinement of being a transformation with the property that every potential *y* of a function has exactly one *x* that can produce it (in other words, it is a bijection, having the properties of being *one-to-one* and *onto* with regard to S). A *group* is the collection of moves: it consists of all the transformations that, when combined, yield the objects within a family S, including identity and inverse transformations. When an entire group has the property that each and every object is relatable to one another one through one and only one transformation, it has the property of *simple transitivity*. While simple transitivity is an elegant feature, it will not be a feature of all of my analyses, which mix and match transformations from various families according to my analytical discretion. A concise explication of the neo-Riemannian group in these more mathematical terms is given in Crans et al. (2009).

9. See Hyer (1989) and (1995); Klumpenhouwer (1994); and Cohn (1996), (1997), and (1998).

10. Cohn (1997: 1–2) requires triads to share two pcs in order to be parsimoniously related, though I recognize parsimony as a more relative property that may also obtain between chords with only one common tone, as in an **S** transformation. Maximal smoothness, after Cohn 1996, involves displacement of a single pitch by only a single semitone. It is a stronger property than simple parsimony, and possessed only by **L** and **P**.

11. Some theorists, including most vocally Tymoczko (2011a and 2011b), have criticized NRT for this aspect, which they argue is an anachronistic theoretical holdover from discredited dualist thinking. Following most current neo-Riemannian theorists, I usually jettison the dualist implications of NRT, though a few uses of major/minor equivalence for film music analysis will be demonstrated in Chapter 4.

12. In Lewin's memorable formulation, "the nature and logic of [neo-] Riemannian space are not isomorphic with the nature and logic of scale-degree space" (1984: 345).

13. Despite the nuance of much of his discussion of chromatic harmony in film, Robert Nelson cannot help falling into this trap on occasion. This lapse is particularly on display in his reliance on a highly under-theorized notion of "polytonal" music, which involves "contradictory chords" that "lack significant tonal relationships among themselves" (1946: 60).

14. The following sentence, from an otherwise sensitive appraisal of Danny Elfman's discography, is characteristic in its misuse of the term "unrelated": "Elfman's theme [for *Pee Wee's Big Adventure*] emphasizes repeated notes, perhaps reflecting the narrowly-focused obsessions of the Pee-Wee character; they veer off into unrelated keys, only to return abruptly to the home key" (Wright 2006: 1030).

15. The original German term, still used by many neo-Riemannian theorists, is *Leittonwechsel*. The fact that **L**'s label invokes the idea of a leading tone, even though the transformation moves a minor chord's *fifth* scale degree, is another vestige of nineteenth-century German dualism that need not overly concern us here.

16. See Capuzzo 2004 (181–183) for a useful explanation of abstract versus realized voice-leading efficiency.
17. The **S** transformation can be decomposed into ternary compounds of the form **LPR** or **RPL**. Similarly, **N** decomposes into **PLR** or **RLP**; **F** into **PRL** or **LRP**; **H** into **PLP** or **LPL**; and **D** into **RL** or **LR**, depending on the mode of the input triad.
18. This property was first observed in Morris (1998: 184–185).
19. Slide was introduced by Lewin (1987).
20. My names for these two transformations are new to this book and are meant to highlight their similarity to each other as fifth-relating progressions. However, the transformational labels **N** and **F** have theoretical precedent. The **N** relation was first described by Carl Friedrich Weizmann as *Nebenverwandt* (neighbor relation) and was later reintroduced by Cohn (2000). The **F** relation is an adaptation of David Kopp's (2002) "Fifth Change," though here it acts as an involution, as opposed to Kopp's non-involuting transformation F, which effectively conflates my **N** and **F**.
21. Cohn (1996) named the progression "hexatonic pole" and later (2004) provided an archaeology of the relation.
22. One should take care here not to confuse **D** with **N** and **F**, which connote fundamentally different kinds of operations. While **N** and **F** are undoubtedly functionally *allusive* in many of their guises, only **D**, **D·P**, and their inverses convey the intentional, cadential sense of the dominant interacting with its tonic within a hierarchical monotonal context. Conversely, fifth progressions between triads of the same mode that *do not* have functional implications may be communicated by using the **LR** and **RL** transformations (or, more outlandishly, **NP** and **FP**),
23. Other such diatonic functional operators have been employed by transformation theorists, including the author in earlier analyses, but these additional transformations tend to be tricky to define and even trickier to integrate into predominantly nonfunctional analyses without a great deal of careful explanation.
24. By allowing dualistic and transpositional transformations to freely intermix, I sometimes violate the "path consistency condition" (through which networks produce the same result for major and minor inputs) in some of my analyses. As per Hook (2007), path consistency is not a crucial desideratum for transformational analysis and is better suited to interpretations that place more value on dualistic and inversional network properties than the current study.
25. Methods have been developed for accounting for transformations among seventh chords—for example, Childs (1998).
26. I borrow the nomenclature and conceit of fuzziness from Straus (1997, *inter alia*), whose more formalized notion of fuzziness requires sets of the same-cardinality. Lewin 1998 has a similar method for relating close but not exact relationships. My own approach admittedly represents a sacrifice in algebraic rigor, but I believe it works no worse for our purposes as would an additional bulky system of transformations between and across non-<037> sonorities.
27. See also, for example, Julian Hook's (2002) uniform triadic transformations.
28. Murphy's labeling system involves three elements: the mode of a relatively stable triad, the interval of transposition, and the mode of a relatively unstable related triad. One of two TTPCs for hexatonic poles, for example, is m4M, which denotes progressions of the type Cm⇨EM and EM⇨Cm; both are instances of the same progression class because of a contextual determination that Cm is more stable than EM. If the opposite were the case, the TTPC would be M8m.
29. Gollin (2000: 6–10) makes a similar point with regard to the retrograde-inversion operation. The assumption here is perfectly reasonable: we should not allow our formal labeling system to forcibly commit us to counterintuitive hearings. Unfortunately, the machinery of triadic transformation theory makes devising unary labels trickier to do for non-involuting and mode-flipping progressions, though it is not impossible (see, for example, Hook 2002).
30. This nomenclature is suggested by Charles Smith's (2001) study of the connections between functional scale steps and neo-Riemannian transformations.

31. There are, to my mind, two possible ways to make Identity an analytical interesting transformation. First is to draw attention to noteworthy, perhaps unexpected continuations or recurrences. If we stick with the Goldenthal repertoire, there is an I-worthy passage in *In Dreams* (1999, 8:00) in which an otherwise pregnant change in texture and instrumentation does not interfere with a prolongation of D minor. The other situation in which **I** can be useful is for "near" identity relations, to show how *literally* dissimilar harmonic regions might nevertheless be heard as occupying the same tonal role.

32. For a discussion of expressive qualities of inter-*key* relationships in film, rather than interchordal relationships, see Motazedian (2016: 184–186).

33. Additionally, **L(m)** is sometimes associated with grief and rituals of mourning, as exemplified by the i⇔VI undulation throughout Chopin's famous funeral march. In his study of the musical semiotics of death, Phillip Tagg (1993) calls this progression the "aeolian pendulum" and observes its presence in a large body of mournful popular music. See also Björnberg (2007). On the expressive connotations of aeolian harmony in film music more generally, see Collins 2004 and Lehman 2016.

34. An additional "wondrous" wellspring for **F** in film music is Ravel's *Daphnis and Chloe*, in which a closely related oscillatory progression (e.g., Fm$^{7(\flat5)}$⇔D♭M^6) serves a motivic function. The influence of this work in general—and harmonic trope in particular—is evident throughout the oeuvre of Jerry Goldsmith.

35. For three characteristically "dreamy" examples from the 2000s, see the main theme from *Tomorrowland* (Giacchino), the Rivendell theme from the *Lord of the Rings* trilogy (Shore), and the main theme to *Cosmos* (Silvestri). A closely related harmonic trope is the I$^{(\text{add},6)}$ chord, which if anything is more prevalent than its triadic counterpart: for prominent examples, see, for instance, the Marvel Fanfare (Tyler), and numerous cues and themes from Zimmer (*Through the Wormhole, Interstellar*, etc.).

36. The associative power of Tarnhelm progressions may be doubled when iterated; see, for example, the "Prophecy Theme" from Toto's score for *Dune* (1984), which begins with an i⇔♭vi motion that is balanced by a mirror image i⇒iii♯ progression, thereby rounding out a single hexatonic cycle.

37. See Murphy 2006 on the tritone progression in general, and Murphy 2012 in *Final Fantasy: The Spirits Within* specifically.

38. For example, the same suite's "Neptune," which is suffused by **LP(m)** motions and polychords, is an important post-Wagnerian reference point for film composers using the "Tarnhelm" progression (Lehman 2014b).

39. This paradox is examined at length in Brown et al. (1997). It is worth noting that, with a sufficiently articulated tonic, even a tritonal motion can be accommodated within what I come to describe as "tethered chromaticism." (Williams's "Ark Theme" from *Raiders of the Lost Ark* provides a nice demonstration of this motion.)

40. This newfound preference among film composers owes perhaps to what Murphy (2014a) has suggested amounts to untapped unfamiliarity: **S**, he argues, has not yet sufficiently solidified its presence or expressive associations to attain the status of cliché.

41. The cue is particularly reminiscent of music from Glass's *The Hours*, notably the harmonic pattern in "Morning Passages" [Gm⇒F♯+⇒B♭M/F⇒AM/E⇒ . . .], with which it shares a similar chromatic descent. Another reference might be Carter Burwell's theme to the *Being John Malkovich*, which also turns on an initial i⇒♭vi^6⇒III$^6_4$ progression.

42. Walker, comparing her score to the example laid out by Danny Elfman in his score to *Batman* (1989), notes, "On a purely musical level, I went in places Danny wouldn't necessarily go as a composer . . . I felt like I had complete musical freedom, especially in a chromatic way. And not just in harmonic changes, I mean the real chromaticism that's in some of those cues . . . I felt like I was getting to do what I wanted with the character" (quoted in Schelle 1999: 373).

43. The most sophisticated model along these lines is Fred Lerdahl's tonal pitch space theory, which offers a number of hierarchical stratifications to differentiate between pitch, chord, and key spaces. Lerdahl (2001: 83–86) has offered some critiques of neo-Riemannian

models of tonal space in comparison to his own approach, some of which I address in an informal way in Chapter 4, "Distance."

44. On the cognitive structures implied by neo-Riemannian theory, see Krumhansl (1998) and Lerdahl and Krumhansl (2007).

45. A full historical genealogy of this tonal network and its role within Riemannian theory is provided by Mooney (1996).

46. Tymoczko (2011a: 412–414) correctly notes that the Tonnetz does not model smooth voice leading per se. He observes that an FM⇨CM progression involves fewer steps through the grid than the more parsimonious Fm⇨CM. Cohn (2012: 65–67) acknowledges this as a shortcoming, though he goes on to present a convincing case for continued use of the Tonnetz as an analytical resource, if not the final arbiter of inter-triadic distance.

47. The theoretical underpinnings of transformational network analysis are provided in Lewin 1987 (157–244) and 2007.

48. See Heine (2001) for a full comparison of the symphony and film score.

Chapter 4

1. Expressive parameters like these may sometimes be strategically misaligned. Jonathan Berger (1994: 308), invoking Eisenstein's theory of cinematic counterpoint, notes this combinatorial potential of style topics in general. An example of topical admixture involving harmony may be found in a theme in Williams's score to *Memoirs of a Geisha*. "The Chairman's Waltz" mixes a graceful, alluring dance topic with a dark, mysterious harmonic topic (a stereotypically malignant undulation of i and ♭vi).

2. The interactivity between different forms of musical meaning is hardly a unique capacity of chromatic film music. In developing a semiotics of eighteenth-century Classical era instrumental music, Kofi Agawu argues that the "play" of matters of structure (for him things like sonata form or prolongational counterpoint) and matters of extramusical connotation (like style topics) is the very foundation of musical drama. And it is "the elucidation of that drama," Agawu claims, that "should form the highest goal of analysis" (1991:79). If there is a meaningful distinction between Agawu's repertoire and ours, it is that in film music, we are less likely to underrate the contribution of those outward-directed systems of meaning than we might for a Mozart string quintet.

3. William O'Hara (2012) offers an argument for what he calls "inherent *playfulness* of many approaches to music analysis," notably for him the Lewinian style of phenomenologically refractive analysis that developed into transformational theory. O'Hara advocates for an analytical sense of play that cracks open "the hermetically sealed 'work,' into something infinitely malleable and thoroughly non-linear."

4. This stance is articulated elegantly by Steven Rings (2011b: 43). Borrowing a distinction from David Temperley (1999), Rings advocates for a "suggestive," rather than purely "descriptive," style of transformational analysis, that is, one that seeks to "stimulate new (or perhaps more sharply focused) hearings of musical phenomena."

5. If the three separate chords belong to a single diatonic collection, the process investing one of them with tonic status is made considerably easier, by virtue of characteristic asymmetries within the diatonic scale. On this process of tonic "position finding" in diatonic music, and a highly pertinent variety of alternative *rhetorical* means for establishing tonicity in chromatic music, see Harrison (1994: 73–90). For a survey of different psychological theories of key finding, see Schmuckler (2016: 145–165).

6. A third experiment would be to place two additional *arbitrary* triads (not C majors) around the original two, and determine how this added context informs the way we hear the central two.

7. This notion of contextuality was first articulated in transformation theory by Lewin (2007 [1993]: 7) and laid out in neo-Riemannian theory by Cohn (1998: 170). See Kochavi (1998) and Lambert (2000) for more in-depth explorations. See also Straus (2016a) for an introduction to the topic.

8. See also Straus (2016b: 689–692) on the implications of Babbitt's terminology, and Cook (2011: 516–517) for a consideration of its ramifications in NRT.

9. The idea of intelligibility—how we make sense of a transformation, simple or complex—is central to the neo-Riemannian project. As Nora Engebretsen explains, it is the combinatorial potential of triadic transformations that enables us to talk about what tonal relations are intelligible and why (2011: 351–366).

10. The **LP**(m) progression is a prominent feature of many other "Batman themes," including those from Elfman, Walker, and Goldenthal, as well as Zimmer's motif for the hero in *Batman v Superman: Dawn of Justice* (2016).

11. It can be difficult to gauge what is actually innovative in Herrmann's style, given the way in which his canonization and "auteur-ization" in musicological discourse tend to warp analyses around issues of the stylistic composer's originality and uniqueness. Rosar (2003: 133–142), for example, notes that there are ample precedents for Herrmannesque chromaticism, both in earlier film music (Heinz Roemheld, James Dietrich) and concert music (Wagner, Holst, Vaughan Williams).

12. Some of Herrmann's music for *The Kentuckian* (1955) approaches intensified major chromaticism (as in the cue "Morning and Night," around 14:54), though a local tonic can be discerned behind the pantriadic surface.

13. See Schneller (2012: 127–151) for a revealing study in the dramatic and structural implications of Herrmann's modular technique. While pantriadic harmony tends to be coordinated with Herrmann's non-thematic modules, examples of it occurring within phrases that are conventionally lyrical are not altogether uncommon. A handful of Herrmann's pastorales from *The Trouble with Harry*, for example, contain notable instances of triadic chromaticism operating within an intraphrasal context.

14. Interestingly, the distinctive EM⇨Dm motion is presaged by a reversed variant of that transformation in the immediately preceding module, steered by [G$^{\varnothing 7}$⇨CM] and [F$^{\sharp\varnothing 7}$⇨BM] shifts. The rest of the progression meanwhile is guided by an accumulation of downward third motions. One can hear Herrmann first outlining an augmented triad (D-B♭-G♭), then a diminished triad (G♭-E♭-C), before reversing course with the first upward motion, back to E major.

15. The effect is not unlike that of a deceptive cadence (i.e., V⇨vi), which we could represent transformationally as **D·R**. That compound captures the way in which an unexpected dominant resolution requires mentally passing through the tonic—more so, at least, than T_2, which tells us nothing about tonal context.

16. These three metrics can easily be developed into a more rigorous numerical measure of distance in the manner of Lerdahl (2001), but for the purposes of the current study they can usefully remain as more informal gauges rather than systematically quantized mathematical values.

17. Tymoczko (2009: 264–267) points to divergences in voice-leading work and word length for the **N** (or **RLP**) transformation, citing this incommensurability as a formal deficiency of NRT. I prefer to see it as a secret asset, as it suggests that multiple metrics are actually *necessary* to judge complex tonal phenomena outside the bubbles provided by monolithic theories of distance. Cohn (2012, 6–8) also explores this important misalignment.

18. The viability of these three operations (plus **D**) as measures of subjectively felt harmonic distance is lent empirical support by a study by Carol Krumhansl (1998). Interestingly, Krumhansl observes that less musically trained listeners are more likely to fall back on **LPR**-based (pitch-proximity) understandings of triadic distance. Lerdahl (2001: 80–86) cites this fact as a shortcomings of NRT, given that experienced musicians are better at picking out deep hierarchical structure, which surface-oriented **LP** and **R** fail to capture. But in actuality, this seeming limitation only commends NRT the more for truly pantriadic passages. In "robust" triadic chromaticism, every listener is in a sense a beginner, since the music eschews functional relationships actively thwarts recourse to "rich" diatonic syntax.

19. An analogous pantriadic squall occurs slightly earlier in the film (1:21:00) to accompany a similar nautical spectacle.

20. This tonal effect can also be explained leitmotivically. The preponderance of M3-related chords betray the passage's motivic derivation from the "Rivendell" theme, which is comprised of little more than two **LP**-related chords, each of which is internally ornamented by a $\hat{5}\Leftrightarrow\flat\hat{6}$ pattern.

21. David Kopp (2002: 166–169) takes the unary route in devising chromatic mediant transformations that rely on no intervening chords to garner their intelligibility. For example, Kopp's **M** relation links triads that may share only one common tone together (example: CM to A♭M). On the uses of non-parsimonious voice leading in general, see Robert Cook (2005).

22. See Lewin (1987 and 1990, respectively). On background of equivalence in atonal theory, both from a formal and meta-disciplinary perspective, see Schuijer (2008, esp. 84–129).

23. Lewin's definition of isography is more complex and mathematically oriented than is necessary to understand the concept, but those curious are invited to consult *Generalized Musical Intervals and Transformations* (1987: 198–200).

24. For an example of thematic evolution in film music, Bribitzer-Stull (2015: 290–291) refers to a constellation of motifs from the *Harry Potter* series that seem to spring from an originary source of the "Mischief" theme from the first film in the franchise (particularly its double-chromatic neighbor figure around m. 5). To the list of leitmotifs with this common feature, we might add the "Voldemort," "Chamber of Secrets," and even principal "Harry Potter" theme, suggesting that $\flat\hat{6}\Leftrightarrow\hat{5}\Leftrightarrow\sharp\hat{4}$ is the true motivic binding agent in this series. It is, of course, easy got get carried away with this style of interpretation, which contains the seeds for a totalizing sort of organicism, the kind of which Ruth Solie (1980) diagnoses running through much music theory

25. See Lewin (1987: xiii–xv, 178–179), Lewin (1992), and further development in Hunt (2007). Since the linkage in question involves the "Tarnhelm" progression, Bribitzer-Stull's archaeology (2015, 131–155) of that move as an associative progression is instructive.

26. The **F** transformation makes a notable appearance early on in this theme (CM⇔Gm), and with it something of a nautical association. Other instances of **F** being tied to adventure on (or under) the high seas include the themes from Debney's *Cutthroat Island* and *Seaquest DSV*, Newton Howard's *Waterworld*, Silvestri's *The Abyss*, and Zimmer's *Muppet Treasure Island*, as well as smaller-scale non-thematic moments in Doyle's score to *Shipwrecked*, Williams's for *Hook*, and Newton Howard's for *Treasure Planet*.

27. On the subject of Newton Howard's use of chromaticism in another, even more pervasively pantriadic score, see Heine 2016 on *Signs*.

28. Transformationally, this progression hinges on a kind of modified **N** operation that activates $\flat\hat{6}$ within a major context, and a subsequent fuzzy **L** to produce $\flat\hat{2}$.

29. The *Inception* progression proved to be of sufficient interest to generate a discussion thread for the Society of Music Theory's official online listserv in 2010. Theorist Stephen Taylor began the discussion by pointing out that three of its four chords fall within Richard Cohn's "Western Hexatonic System.").

30. Even when Zimmer's harmonic motif modulates, it does so on an **S**-based axis. For example, in the track "Dream within a Dream," the progression initially begins in G minor only to modulate up to C minor. This global $\mathbf{T_7}$ transposition is cleverly accomplished by connecting the last chord of the G-centered progression (B^{Ma7}) with the tonic of the new progression Cm), in effect transferring the **S** progression from an intraphrasal to a temporarily *inter*phrasal function.

31. On mirror symmetries in general in Herrmann's score to *Vertigo*, see Blim (2013).

32. The music that accompanies the moment of detonation over Hiroshima contains similarly apocalyptic pantriadicism. Rosar (2002b: 13) notes that Dante's *Inferno* came to mind when the pilot Tibbets recalled the desolation wrought by this atomic bomb. Friedhofer's tritone-heaving chromaticism recalls, among other things, the conclusion of the "Inferno" movement of Liszt's *Dante Symphony* and the Satan-associated music in Vaughan Williams's ballet *Job* (the latter composer being an avowed influence for this score). Strauss's *Die Frau ohne Schatten* also seems to lurk in the background.

33. Rodman's analysis (1998) of Herbert Stothart's score to *The Wizard of Oz* is a particularly ingenious demonstration of score-spanning patterning. Arguing that the film's there-and-back narrative is reflected in tonal design, Rodman extracts a score-spanning symmetrical pattern of key selections, in which an underlying symmetrical (and, indeed rainbow-shaped!) *Ursatz* is disrupted in its middle by foreign chromatic elements—themselves aptly representing the fantastic or wicked forces within *Oz*'s plot. Rodman argues that the liquidation of this chromaticism is necessary for the score to properly return to its wholesome diatonic home key, just as Dorothy must thwart the Witch if she is ever to get back to Kansas.

34. "Herrmann was always my god," Elfman claimed in an interview (Florino, 2010).

35. See Halfyard 2004 (126–128) on Elfman's approach to motives and modules.

36. The resulting progression, Dm⇨C♯⁺⇨AM⇨C⁺⇨A♭M can be neatly accounted for by recourse to the Cube Dance, a chromatic tonal space developed by Douthett and Steinbach (1998) and Cohn (2012) that emphasizes the power of augmented triads to link consonant triads. The way in which voice-leading strategy changes at the end of the cue is mirrored by the cue's first thirty seconds (not pictured in Fig 4.17), which moves from chord to chord by parallel planing while prolonging the same A minor that prepares the portion of the cue analyzed here.

Chapter 5

1. Meandri (2014) notes the employment of mostly chromatic harmonic formulas to denote the Marvelous in film music, which he associates closely with rhetorics of discovery and revelation. Interestingly, Meandri, who comes from a European theoretical background, uses a functional/paleo-Riemannian instead of non-tonal/neo-Riemannian apparatus to analyze passages from *The Abyss, Stargate*, and *The Fellowship of the Rings*.

2. The availability of alternative musical strategies for the evocation of wonder is amply demonstrated by a number of (admittedly exceptional) soundtracks for experimental science-fiction films. A few canonical examples include the weird "electronic tonalities" that Bebe and Louis Barron use to paint the extraterrestrial sights of *Forbidden Planet* (1956); the expressionistic atonality of Leonard Rosenman's *Fantastic Voyage* (1966); and the adaptation of Györgi Ligeti's dissonant micropolyphony in *2001: A Space Odyssey* (1968). Jeremy Barham (2008) provides a useful overview of some stylistic markers of amazement, as well as an analysis of why romantic tropes continually make themselves present in the genre, reaching as far back as Gottfried Huppertz's symphonic score to *Metropolis* (1927).

3. Use of post-tonal idioms to elicit wonder may be found in many sci-fi films like *Close Encounters of the Third Kind* and *Arrival*. Non-western materials used for this purpose may be found across genres. Consider, for example, the dabblings with Southeast Asian scales for spiritual moments in Mychael Danna's soundtrack for *Life of Pi* (2012). The score's success suggests that Western audiences are perfectly responsive to affective cuing by less familiar tonal resources (in this instance made possible in part by a degree of topical otherness).

4. Affect theory is a growing if currently amorphous field of inquiry. See Gregg and Siegworth (2010) for a summarization and contextualization.

5. My effort to draw these distinctions clearly at the outset is an attempt to bypass a vein of deep and often unproductive controversy in the study of music and emotion. The problem boils down to how a non-sentient and non-linguistic form of art could either have or express emotions (particularly specific or negative ones). See Davies (2010) for a summary of the issues in this area, and Robinson (2011), Matravers (2011), and Trivedi (2011) for accounts of three leading philosophical theories on musical emotion. See Cohen (2010) for theorization of musical emotion specifically in filmic contexts.

6. In psychology, valence describes the relative pleasurability or offensiveness of a given emotion, and is linked with related issues of motivation and the adaptive and social values of emotion. See Brosch and Moors (2009: 401–402).

7. For a more specifically neurological and psychoanalytic perspective on wonder, see Johnston and Malabou (2013).

8. See Gunning (1986) and (1989), and Strauven (2006).

9. See Rouget (1985) and Buhler (1996). With respect to the latter category, Rehding (2009) explores musical wonder and the related aesthetic of monumentality in the context of nineteenth-century German concert music and its (sometimes unsavory) political uses in the twentieth century.

10. On the psychological foundations of the "eureka effect," see Topolinksi and Reber (2010).

11. Tzvetan Todorov's (1970) notion of the "fantastic" provides some precedent to the study of wonder in the literary arts.

12. On the notion of intelligibility in (neo-)Riemannian theory, see Engebretsen (2011: 362–366).

13. The majority of this discussion is drawn from Huron's *Sweet Anticipation* (2006: 25–39 and 269–295).

14. Derisive or skeptical laughter may result from attempts at generating wonder that, for one reason or another, go awry. One plausible scenario might be a filmgoer who is aware of film musical tropes but is intentionally emotionally closed off to them. For that person, hearing a sweeping chromatic modulation may inspire a chuckle of recognition, almost like a preemptory defense mechanism against psychological manipulation.

15. Reviewing the growing scholarly and cultural discourse on awe, Keltner and Heidt (2003) propose that its essential features of are (1) a perception of vastness and (2) the need for— if not necessarily realization of—Piagetian intellectual accommodation. They identify five further factors that "flavor" the awe-inspiring experience: exceptional threat, beauty, talent, virtue, and supernatural causality.

16. See Shiota et al. (2007: 951–954).

17. An instance from Shore's *LOTR* scores very similar to *The Matrix*'s in construction and affect may be found in *TTT* (3:20–23:35). As we see the distant Gandalf and his foe, the Balrog, plummet into an immense subterranean lake, Shore initiates an Em⇔CM oscillation, conveyed by tutti orchestra and full choir. For more examples, see "Lost in the Wild" from Jerry Goldsmith's *The Edge*, "Buckbeak's Flight" from John Williams's *Harry Potter and the Prisoner of Azkaban*, and the main theme from Patrick Doyle's *Frankenstein*. A wellspring for the associativity of the L(m)-transformation in this guise may be the music of American minimalists, particularly Phillip Glass (esp. the much-imitated "Pruitt Igoe" from *Koyaanisqatsi*) and John Coolidge Adams (esp. the much-imitated first movement of *Harmonielehre*). One may track its semiotic value much further back, however, at least as far as Siegfried's main leitmotif from Wagner's *Ring* cycle.

18. See Goldstein (1980) for the foundational study on chills in music, and Slobada (1991) and Panksepp (1995) for influential contributions (the former informing Huron's formulation). See also Hunter and Schellenberg (2010: 147–149) for a summary of current research on music and the frisson response, and Levinson (2006) for an aesthetic overview.

19. Panksepp (1995) notes that frisson is also linked to impressions of musical sadness and loss, especially among female listeners. He proposes a Separation Distress theory of frisson, which conjectures the origin of frisson as an evolutionarily based sensitivity to the sound of distress calls from threatened loved ones. Using clips from film scores, Benedek and Kaernbach (2011) corroborate the gendered aspects of frisson responses, and their linkage with ambivalent emotions, like vulnerability and "being moved." Huron and Margulis (2010) usefully contrast Panksepp's model with Huron's own Contrastive Valence theory (which is adopted here).

20. William Benjamin (2007) suggests the manipulation of expectation itself may not be a necessary component for the elicitation of frisson, and he emphasizes the role of memory and engagement in ushering in musical pleasure such as frisson. These factors often are inextricably linked, as for example, in the leitmotivically driven sequences of this chapter. However, the well-supported empirical studies Huron draws from in describing this phenomenon, and the palpable and self-evidently calibrated effect of chills in film music, mean we need not dilute Huron's formulation to incorporate "non-expectational" frisson here.

21. See Panksepp (1998: 278–279). A good example of this effect happening in the *LOTR* series is Gandalf's apparent death in *FOTR*, during which dense action music cuts away to a solo boy soprano singing against soft string chords.

22. Elizabeth Margulis's (2005) theory of melodic expectation proposes a trio of musical tension types (surprise, denial, and expectancy), each of which has a distinctive phenomenal character. With denial tension, for example, a highly predicted event is substituted with an unpredictable one, in the process projecting a "sense of will, intention, or determinedness" onto the music (693). This substitution has interesting implications for chromatic surprises in film music like *Wall-E*'s modulation. If Margulis is correct, then certain types of tonal realignment might be able to impart something akin to agency and even raw power to the soundtrack. It would be as though the *music* were what was actively steering visual and/or narratival changes, and not the other way around.

23. In this way, contrastive valence is very close to the "benign violation" theory put forth for explaining humor, a fit already suggested by Huron's linkage of the flight response and laughter. See Veatch (1998) for the hypothesis's formulation and McGraw and Warren (2010) for an expansion.

24. Huron's work (2006: 270–274) suggests of another form of contrast that film composers understand intuitively. In an experiment, Huron asked listeners to describe their emotions after hearing a diatonic progression followed by a chromatic third-related chord. Unsurprisingly, the subjects used words indicative of weirdness or difference for many of the progressions. But Huron was struck by how much more intensely the listeners described the relative emotional valence of the chords compared to diatonic chords of the same mode within the key. Given the low probability with which most listeners expect chromatic chords, Huron hypothesized that "in light of poor statistical linkage to the preceding and following chords, the qualities of 'major' and 'minor' come to the fore. Major chromatic chords tend to sound more distinctly 'major,' and so are somehow 'brighter' or more 'positive' than major chords within the key. [And equivalently for minor chords]" (274). Pantriadic music lacks the contextual markers of monotonality, and thus with it we lose the capacity for contrastive heightening with respect to a diatonic norm. However, because of the paucity of predictive syntax, every chord in a pantriadic passage may be judged *primarily* on its modal and transformation qualities, on its own and with respect to its immediate neighbors. This effect, I suspect, allows for a potentially even greater magnification of affective valence, and may account for the privileging of absolute progressions in film music.

25. On the matter of surprise from familiar musical stimuli, see Bharucha (1994) for a distinction between schematic and veridical expectations, which can be met and violated independently.

26. While Ross's comparison is for the most part quite apt (especially considering Shore's predilection for Bribitzer-Stull's "Tarnhelm" progressions), one crucial element of Wagner's harmonic idiolect is notably all but absent in the *LOTR* soundtrack: seventh chords—perhaps the single most important ingredient in "the dread mage" of Bayreuth's magical brew.

27. Interestingly, these augmented and diminished triads play a larger role in an earlier version of the cue, which Shore subsequently revised to "increase the dramatic tension and underscore Gandalf's dire situation" (Adams 2007: 10). The rewriting is to the final sequence's detriment as the original version (which can be heard on the OST and Shore's *LOTR Symphony*) is more harmonically and motivically cohesive.

28. "Gollum's Song," a non-leitmotivic theme that attaches to the same character at the end of *TTT*, bears a sinuous pantriadic progression with prominent common-tone connections. The underlying progression is, in full, $G\sharp m \Rightarrow B_3^6 m \Rightarrow Cm \Rightarrow DM \Rightarrow BM_3^6 \Rightarrow Bm_3^6 \Rightarrow Cm \Rightarrow DM \Rightarrow Gm_4^6 Bm_3^6 Cm \Rightarrow DM$.

29. Interestingly, the VI chord and the pan to the Great Hall are not perfectly synchronized. The chord is captured moments before the full extent of the landscape is revealed, while the Hall itself had been revealed visually before any notable points of musical arrival. Such cases of soundtrack-visual mismatch are fairly common with wonder-inspiring moments in fantasy

films. They form an effective means of building and layering expectation, not dissimilar to what Buhler et al. call a "sound advance" and "sound lag" (2010: 92–98).

30. A useful comparison can be drawn here with the Mahlerian formal strategy of *Durchbruch* ("breakthrough"). Paraphrasing Adorno (2002 [1963]), Buhler defines breakthrough as "a moment of structural re-orientation, a deflection or 'turning-aside' (*Ablenkung*) from the expected formal course of a piece . . . The opposite of tragic reversal or catastrophe, break-through is an unforeseen event, a sudden turn toward transcendence from an unexpected formal trajectory of tragedy" (1996: 129). Sudden musical transcendence easily verges on arbitrariness, and this result poses a significant problem for formal autonomy in absolute music. Buhler suggests that in programmatic music, "thematic integration may replace formal and tonal integration as the binding force of music" (128). Admittedly, the requirements of formal and tonal integration are much lower in film music than in sonata-form-bearing works like the *Titan* symphony. In *LOTR*, however, moments of tonal rupture sometimes do make use of a very local kind of breakthrough rhetoric, justifying themselves insofar as they facilitate the acquirement of a thematic telos.

31. Huron's ITPRA model has some precedents in Narmour's Implication-Realization theory of musical expectation. See Narmour 1990 (esp. the discussion of "cognitive exhilaration").

32. The example Huron himself uses to illustrate musical frisson involves exactly this sort of chromatic transformation, a stunning **S**(m) that bridges sections in Schoenberg's *Verklärte Nacht* (2006: 282).

33. Bribitzer-Stull (2015) relates Shore's expansive symphonic set pieces directly to the phantasmagoric preludes and transitions in Wagner's music dramas, the *Ring* in particular. With respect to chromatic temporality, one might recall how *Parsifal's* Gurnemanz claims "here, time becomes space," immediately before the incredible pantriadic peregrinations of Act I's "Transformation Music."

34. See, for example, Alperson (1980) and Chion (1994: 16). No less an authority than Bernard Herrmann made the following claim: "I feel that music on the screen can seek out and intensify the inner thoughts of the characters. It can invest a scene with terror, grandeur, gaiety or misery. It can propel narrative swiftly forward, or slow it down" (quoted in Palmer 1993: 253).

35. The temporal sense in the *LOTR* trilogy is in many ways itself more forward driven than the novels it is based on. On the conversion of Tolkien time into Hollywood time, see Langford (2006: 29–46).

36. Film theorist Geoff King identifies a tendency to regard this emphasis on spectacle as a detriment to narrative coherence: "Spectacle is seen as a source of distraction or interruption. Our focus on narrative development is halted while we sit back to contemplate with amazement/pleasure/horror (or whatever particular reaction) the sheer sensory richness of the audio-visual experience" (2002: 179). King counters that Hollywood set pieces are often tightly motivated by overall narrative, feature their own internal narrative logic, and even at their most episodic do not intrinsically detract from the intelligibility of the larger plot.

37. A few notable examples of the extensive literature on musical temporality from theorists include Kramer (1988), Epstein (1995), Hasty (1997), Tenzer (2011), London (2012), and Margulis (2014).

38. On this point, see Kramer's discussion of information theory and Markov chains (1988: 22–23, etc.) and Huron on harmonic schemata (2006: 239–268).

39. Kanai (2014) provides a useful categorization of various forms of distortion effects on subjective time perception. See also Wittmann and van Wassenhove (2009) for an overview of current cognitive neuroscientific perspectives on subjective temporality, several of which (esp. Eagleman and Pariyadath 2009) corroborate findings from the slightly older music psychological studies on which I base my observations here.

40. Information richness is one of the several psychological criteria for awe-inspiring stimuli that Bueno et al. (2002) and Shiota et al. (2007) confirm experimentally.

41. See Firmino et al. 2008a for the original study and 2008b for a summary.

42. Chromatic surprises are not the only way to produce this effect, nor do they need to generate positive affects like awe or frisson. Boltz (1989a) demonstrates that time underestimations can stem from ending music on the unstable leading tone or in the middle of
metric-phrasal groupings. A terrific example occurs in Philip Glass's score to *Kundun* (1997).
The final cue "Escape to India" ends abruptly, before the repeated harmonic-metrical cell
($\flat$VI⇨$\flat$VII⇨i) hits its tonic securing point. The sudden silence following an unresolved $\flat\hat{7}$ in
the bass coincides with an abrupt cut to the text "The Dalai Lama has not yet returned to
Tibet. He hopes one day to make the journey." The premature musical ending helps make
a political point: the Dalai Lama's tenure in his native country was cut short after he fled
to India in 1959 following the Chinese occupation of his country. Director Scorsese thus
uses unresolved music to induce frustration, even indignation, toward a continuing injus-
tice. Though less high minded, a similar premature-ending effect is achieved in Zimmer's
score to *Inception*, which concludes with the termination of a four-chord harmonic ostinato
(Am⇨Em⇨GM⇨DM) on its last, most unstable triad.

43. See Wearden et al. 2014 (287) on the decoupling of these two often conflated ideas in
subjective-time scholarship.

44. On audiovisual interactions see Wearden et al. (2006) who suggest that auditory stimuli
tend to get larger temporal overestimations than equivalently long visual ones.

45. David Lewin's own theories of musical temporality and its relationship to transformation
theory are of considerable interest. In general, his focus fell on abstract "out of time" relationships in music and did not require his transformation graphs to convey chronology (e.g.,
1987: 210–218). Elsewhere, he cites psychologist Jeanne Bamberger's (1986) distinction
between figural (chronological) and formal (abstract) modes of representing events (Lewin,
2007 [1993]: 45–53); this distinction has been picked up and developed by other transformation theorists, notably Rings (2011b: 140–144). The relationship of time perception to
Lewin's celebrated phenomenological approach to music is also fascinating, albeit too complex for adequate summarization here. See Lewin 1986, Moshaver 2012.

46. The opening six chords of the pantriadic portion of this cue are transformationally and pitch
identical to the theme from Vaughan Williams's score to *Scott of the Antarctic* and subse-
quent *Sinfonia antartica*. Though it is difficult to say whether Shore was directly alluding to
Vaughan Williams's work, the subject matters are not so different—imposing, unknowable,
timeless landscapes and the feeling of awe they inspire in those that traverse them. Joseph
Auner (2013: 154–155) notes the similarities in experience and outlook between Vaughan
Williams and J.R.R. Tolkien, suggesting that Shore may well have been influenced by the
English composer, his Pastoral Symphony in particular.

47. The text, in Quenya (Elvish), speaks of the arrival of an ancient king (Elendil) whose heirs
shall rein "unto the ending of the world." (Adams 2011: 191–192).

48. A remarkable alternate version of this cue exists. The pantriadic section from mm. 5–15
remains in place, but rather than the "History of the Ring" motif, the aftermath is given to
a muted statement of the Gondor theme in D major (in what would have been its first appearance in the trilogy). The harmonic makeup of this section is in closer keeping with the
transformational lexicon from the preceding chromatic passage. The Gondor theme is prepared by a short pantriadic progression [. . . A$\flat$m⇨GM⇨B$\flat$m$^6_4$⇨Dm . . .] and exited in similar fashion [. . . DM⇨E$\flat$m⇨C$\flat$M⇨A$\flat$m⇨D$^6_4$M⇨BM⇨Bm]. Note, among several similarities
with mm. 5–15, the redoubled emphasis on the S-transformation [A$\flat$m⇨GM, DM⇨E$\flat$m]
and repetition of several local transformations at the same pitch level.

49. A useful comparison may be drawn with the music of Anton Bruckner, whose particular
brand of musical monumentality is the clearest nineteenth-century precedent for Shore's
mammoth edifices. Bruckner's symphonies, with their hair-raising brass apotheoses and
tsunami-like codas, have long been felt to project a certain sort of pre-Christian or even
prehistoric timelessness. In some twentieth-century performances, Bruckner's works
were played in what might strike us as rather cinematic contexts, "in fully darkened concert halls, enveloping the audiences in cathedrals of sound, as a musical return into the
womb" (Rehding, 2009: 181). Bruckner's habit of building climaxes with chromatically

twisting sequences, mediant-based breakthroughs, and especially the L(m) progression are all echoed in Shore's own approach to composing awe.

50. The "Ring" motif has its own tonal complexities, not all of which are conveyed by the rather blunt $T_{1/-1}$ label. The leitmotif is not absent functional implications, but those implications are extraordinarily fragile, and the relative tonicity of either the first or second chord in each iteration can seem to shift back and forth. Associatively, this is apt—glimpses of an older, more balanced and orderly society, but in the present now fractured, without direction, in need of reassembly. To capture these curious tonal qualities, an alternative analysis might make use of **S**, **P**, and even **D** transformations.

Chapter 6

1. Many attempts have been made to provide a definitive definition of "cadence" (see, for example, Blombach 1987, Caplin 2004, and Harrison 2016). I define a cadence as a stereotyped harmonic and melodic process used to mark the conclusion of a musical phrase.

2. If we are willing to expand the definition of "cadence," then we should acknowledge less harmonically driven punctuational processes that increasingly populate contemporary scores, a few familiar varieties of which include "the rising crescendo on a dissonant cluster to an abrupt silence cadence"; the "accelerating pin drop leading to a big downbeat chord cadence"; and the "decelerating series of low thumps leading to brief silence, followed by a cleanly exposed leitmotif cadence." Notably, all of these routines are as much the products of sound design as music composition, and many are regularly occurring elements of film trailer music.

3. Laitz was most likely alluding to the way modern listeners *expect* big Studio Era films to conclude more than any actual models, such as *Rebecca, Captain Blood,* or *Key Largo,* that contain the gesture. Modally mixed plagal cadences are indeed a characteristic aspect of old Hollywood scoring but by no means obligatory, or even especially common in Laitz's 1920s–1950s time frame. (On this point, see also Lehman 2013a.)

4. Composer Frank Skinner notes another cadential archetype endemic to film Westerns: the melodic approach to the final tonic with a $\hat{2}⇒\hat{1}⇒\hat{6}⇒\hat{1}$ motion over a functional mixture of dominant and subdominant harmony (Skinner 1950: 199–200). The routine has a pentatonic character that clearly alludes to American and Western European folk song traditions. While earlier examples, such as the theme to *Stagecoach* (1939) are not difficult to locate, the paradigmatic example of Skinner's cadence is assuredly Victor Young's theme to *Shane* (1953), which includes both the $\hat{2}⇒\hat{1}⇒\hat{6}⇒\hat{1}$ pentatonic line and fused subdominant/dominant chord at its final cadence. See also van der Merwe (1989) on "horse opera modal" harmony, and Beckermann and Rosar (2009) on pentatonicism in film Westerns.

5. Some have suggested specific film studios have unique cadential signatures—Henry Mancini, for instance, alludes to an "over-used but definitely usable 'Paramount' ending" (1986: 232–234), by which he appears to mean a drawn-out, richly scored cadence in the major mode and $\hat{2}⇒\hat{3}$ in melody.

6. Neumeyer (1998: 113–115) proposes a similar continuum for describing tonal functionality and formal proportion, using the analogy of a computer slidebar as a way of adjusting these independent variables.

7. A similar taxonomy of tonal styles is developed in Everett (2004) specifically for rock music.

8. The idea of roving (alternatively "fluctuating" or "*schwebende*") tonality originates with Arnold Schoenberg (2010 [1947]; 1969 [1954]), though my definition is more inclusive than his, which is defined negatively, as the condition in which "no succession of three chords can unmistakably express a region or tonality" (3).

9. Steiner's tonal language in *Casablanca* is discussed in Marks (2000) and Neumeyer (2015: 99–180, with Buhler).

10. Tymoczko (2011a: 282) identifies Schubert as a composer who "liberated" chromatic transformations from their accustomed position at phrase boundaries. This decoupling of chromaticism from cadentially governed thematic structures, more than the distance

of modulations themselves, is something that Clark (2011b) points out was a key part of Schubert's problematic reception in the nineteenth century.

11. One of the clearest examples of intraphrasal chromaticism in the film repertoire is Korngold's theme for *The Sea Hawk* (1940), which embeds a series of hexatonic cycles at multiple levels of its structure. The model for Korngold's theme and others like it that contain full hex- or octatonic cycles is probably "Elsa's Dream" from *Lohengrin*, excerpted in Figure 2.1.

12. Quoted in Schweiger (1992). See Kreuzer (2003) for an extended analysis of the *Basic Instinct* score.

13. The enterprising reader is encouraged to map out this cue in the "Cube Dance."

14. This second phrase provides an illustration of Goldsmith's unmatched knack for motivic unity. One of the score's subsidiary themes, a sequential progression based on the harmonic module [Am⇨BM/E⇨Gm], is derived directly from the main title. But for its exclusion of E minor, this motif is identical to the harmonic content of the theme's second and third phrases, including, most strikingly, the BM/E slash chord.

15. The centripetal/centrifugal analogy is invoked by Schoenberg (1969 [1954]: 2–3) and developed by Dahlhaus (1980 [1974]: 65–78). Hazelwood (2014: 43–51) provides an in-depth analysis of the metaphor and applies it to film music analysis.

16. Rings (2007) argues that jockeying between Schenkerian and Riemannian functional theories is based on a false dilemma, with the two systems being complementary rather than in conflict, each providing different but equally valid perspectives. I follow Rings in advocating a dialogic, rather than competitive, analytical methodology; I also maintain that in some musical situations, prolongational and transformational processes really *are* in contest with each other, even to the extent of being analytically irreconcilable—to great expressive effect.

17. In a later study, Smith (2001) proposed a system for ascribing functional powers to the neo-Riemannian operators and the (nondiatonic) chords they generate.

18. Code switching is something we do in all sorts of music, not just pantriadic varieties. For instance, for some twentieth-century composers, atonal and tonal idioms were not always strictly segregated within a piece of music. The works of Alban Berg, with their aspects of both functional and twelve-tone organization, encourage and reward a dualistic mode of listening not so different from what Cohn advocates for split functional/pantriadic organization in nineteenth-century music.

19. The same is true for NRT as a system, as proving coherence in chromatic music appears in many analyses (including many within these pages) to be its methodological raison d'être. But as Rings (2011a) convincingly argues, to insist on coherence at the expense of musical idiosyncrasy, strangeness, and difference is to lose sight of the very things that makes this music interesting in the first place—and, Rings hastens to add—to disregard the lessons of New Musicology, with its critique of structural hearing and organicism. Against the backdrop of CP tonality, pantriadic routines are disruptive, often conspicuously *incoherent* gestures, and no amount of stress on the algebraic groups they form, the idealized voice-leading spaces they inhabit, or the common-tone relations they spin out should downplay this point. For variations on same, see Cohn (2012: 106–109) and Lehman (2015: 159–161).

20. Cohn (2012: 40), drawing from structural linguistics, calls the consonant triad itself one such "homophonous diamorph"—that is, a word that that can function in two languages (or here, tonal syntaxes). See also Clyne (2000) and Muysken (2000).

21. The symmetry group implied by triadic tonality space is quite easy to define, if one reimagines the three axes (functionality, centricity, and diatonicity) to be involuting transformations; whether this is a useful mathematization of tonal style I leave to the reader to determine.

22. Lawrence Morton, whose regular column "Film Music of the Quarter" in *Music Quarterly* featured some of the first sustained analysis of film scores in an English-language venue, singled out this cue from *Joan of Arc* as an instance of music worthy of admittance into a new film music canon. Morton notes that although Friedhofer's sonorities are for the most part simple triads, there is a play between modal and what he calls "modern" harmony.

The climactic section features some of this "modern" music, described by Morton as "alien" and even "polymodal" (Morton 1948: 396–399). The idea of polymodality stems from Béla Bártok, who described it as the use of harmonies drawn from two scales with the same tonic note (1976 [1943]: 367). It is questionable whether the bulk of the chromatic passage in *Joan of Arc* can actually be explained in terms of polymodality, as most its chords cannot be attributed to any traditional mode on either D or G.

23. The primary reference points are *Lohengrin* and *Parsifal*. On Wagnerian archaisms, see Richardson (2009). Additional pieces that supply precedents for the beatific sublime style include Schubert's and Liszt's late masses, Berlioz's and Fauré's requiems, Debussy's *Le martyre de Saint Sébastien*, and virtually all of Vaughan Williams's sacred and/or biblical works. Meyer (2015: 100–102) suggests a further precedent for ecclesiastical chromaticism in a trope he calls "ominous priests music" in nineteenth-century opera (*Les Huguenots, Samson et Dalila, Don Carlos*) that later appears in religious epic films like *The Robe, The Greatest Story Ever Told*, and *David and Bathsheba*. Compare also with the conclusion of Puccini's *Suor Angelica*.

24. In a gesture to historical fidelity, *Joan of Arc*'s filmmakers did include a modicum of more historically authentic music in various scenes; the most notable occurrence is the fifteenth-century Burgundian School–style choral music during the movie's coronation scene, music that Friedhofer identifies as Dufay (Danly 2002: 123).

25. On medievalism and historical authenticity in film music, see Haines (2014).

26. Somewhat incredibly, it was Igor Stravinsky who was initially signed to score the picture, but he parted ways with 20th Century Fox after the artistic mismatch became apparent (Walsh 2008). Stravinsky claimed to incorporate music he sketched for *Bernadette*'s first apparition scene into the second movement of his 1945 *Symphony in Three Movements*.

27. This cue is analyzed in detail in Jackson (2010), with a focus on intertextual references and the separate contributions of Newman and Powell.

28. James Newton Howard offers a telling confession with regard to his employment of such shopworn tropes as chromatic mediants in conjunction with spectacular imagery: "I resisted those kinds of chord progressions for years . . . I was in a kind of denial about [the efficacy of chromatic progressions], because audience, directors, producers—everyone watching the movie—has certain expectations. . . . When I did try to write something completely new, it ended up being, well, not quite right—too complicated, too notey—so I finally abandoned it. Actually, *Alive* is when I first started getting into a more conventional harmonic approach in some places. And doing that freed me. By giving myself over to certain harmonic progressions, I found a liberation. . . Any time you give yourself over to an existing device, it is going to inevitably open up some other doors for you that you just can't anticipate. It was just a matter of consciously bringing those chord progressions into my toolbox as just another place to think and another place to go" (quoted in Schelle 1999: 192–193).

Bibliography

Abbate, Carolyn. 2004. "Music: Drastic or Gnostic?" *Critical Inquiry* 30 (3): 505–536.

Adams, Doug. 2007. Liner Notes for *Lord of the Rings: Return of the King Complete Recordings* (Composed by Howard Shore). Reprise/Wea. B000V6BE6M.

———. 2011. *The Music of the Lord of the Rings Films*. Van Nuys, CA: Alfred.

Adorno, Theodor. (1963) 2002. *Quasi una Fantasia,* translated by Rodney Livingstone. London and New York: Verso.

———. 2005. *In Search of Wagner,* translated by Robert Livingstone. London: Verso.

Adorno, Theodor, and Hanns Eisler. (1947) 2007. *Composing for the Films.* Reprint, London: Continuum.

Agawu, Kofi. 1991. *Playing with Signs: A Semiotic Interpretation of Classic Music.* Princeton, NJ: Princeton University Press.

Alperson, Philip. 1980. "'Musical Time' and Music as an 'Art of Time.'" *Journal of Aesthetics and Art Criticism* 38 (4): 407–417.

Audissino, Emilio. 2014. "Overruling a Romantic Prejudice: Film Music in Concert Programs." In *Film in Concert: Film Scores and Their Relation to Classical Concert Music,* edited by Sebastian Stoppe, 25–43. Glückstadt, Germany: Verlag Werner Hülsbusch.

Auner, Joseph. 2013. *Music in the Twentieth and Twenty-First Centuries.* New York and London: W.W. Norton.

Babbitt, Milton. 1987. *Words about Music,* edited by Stephen Dembski and Joseph Straus. Madison: University of Wisconsin Press.

Bailey, Robert. 1969. "The Genesis of 'Tristan und Isolde' and a Study of Wagner's Sketches and Drafts for Act I." PhD Diss., Princeton University.

———. 1977. "The Structure of the "Ring" and Its Evolution." *Nineteenth Century Music* 1 (1): 48–61.

———.1985. "An Analytical Study of the Sketches and Drafts." In *Wagner: Prelude and 'Transfiguration' from Tristan und Isolde,* edited by Robert Bailey 113–146. New York: W.W. Norton

BaileyShea, Matthew. 2007. "Hexatonic and the Double Tonic: Wolf's 'Christmas Rose.'" *Journal of Music Theory* 51 (2): 187–210.

Balthazar, Scott. 1996. "Plot and Tonal Design as Compositional Constraints in *Il trovatore.*" *Current Musicology* 60–61: 51–77.

Bamberger, Jeanne. 1986. "Cognitive Issues in the Development of Musically Gifted Children." In *Conceptions of Giftedness,* edited by Robert Sternberg and Janet Davidson, 388–413. Cambridge and New York: Cambridge University Press.

Barham, Jeremy. 2008. "Scoring Incredible Futures: Science-Fiction Screen Music, and 'Postmodernism' as Romantic Epiphany." *Musical Quarterly* 9 (3–4): 240–274.

Bártok, Béla. (1943) 1976. *Béla Bártok Essays.* Selected and Edited by Benjamin Suchoff. Lincoln and London: University of Nebraska Press.

Bashwiner, David. 2015. "*Casino Royale's* First Chase Sequence in 'Multi-Score': Music, Drama, Camerawork." Paper presented at the Society for Music Theory Annual Conference, Film and Multimedia Interest Groups, St. Louis MO, October 30.

Bazelon, Irwin. 1975. *Knowing the Score*. New York: Van Nostrand Reinhold.

Beckermann, Michael, and William Rosar. 2009. "The Idyllic Sublime: A Dialog on the Pastoral Style in Westerns." *Journal of Film Music* 2 (2–4): 251–262.

Benedek, Mathias, and Christian Kaernbach. 2011. "Physiological Correlates and Emotional Specificity of Human Piloerection." *Biological Psychology* 86 (3): 320–329.

Benjamin, William. 2007. Review of *Sweet Anticipation* (David Huron). *Journal of Aesthetics and Art Criticism* 65 (3): 333–335.

Berger, Jonathan. 1994. Review of *Playing with Signs* (Kofi Agawu). *Journal of Music Theory* 38 (2): 293–313.

Bharucha, Jamshed. 1994. "Tonality and Expectation." In *Music Perceptions*. Edited by Rita Aiello, 213–239. Oxford: Oxford University Press.

Björnberg, Alf. 2007. "On Aeolian Harmony in Contemporary Popular Music." In *Critical Essays in Popular Musicology*, edited by Allan Moore, 275–282. Aldershot, UK: Ashgate.

Blim, Daniel. 2013. "Musical and Dramatic Design in Bernard Herrmann's Prelude to *Vertigo* (1958)." *Music and the Moving Image* 6 (2): 21–31.

Blombach, Ann. 1987. "Phrase and Cadence: A Study of Terminology and Definition." *Journal of Music Theory Pedagogy* 1: 225–251.

Boltz, Marylin. 1989. "Time Judgments of Musical Endings: Effects of Expectancies on the 'Filled Interval Effect.'" *Perception and Psychophysics* 46 (5): 409–418.

———. 1991. "Time Estimation and Attentional Perspective." *Perception and Psychophysics* 49: 422–433.

———. 1993. "The Generation of Temporal and Melodic Expectancies during Musical Listening." *Perception and Psychophysics* 53: 585–600.

Boltz, Marylin, and Mari Riess Jones. 1989. "Dynamic Attending and Responses to Time." *Psychological Review* 96 (3): 459–491.

Bordwell, David, Janet Staiger, and Kristen Thompson. 1985. *The Classical Hollywood Cinema: Film Style and Mode of Production until 1960*. New York: Columbia University Press.

Braudy, Leo. 2011. *The Hollywood Sign: Fantasy and Reality of an American Icon*. New Haven, CT: Yale University Press.

Bribitzer-Stull, Matthew. 2012. "From Nibelheim to Hollywood: The Associativity of Harmonic Progression." In *The Legacy of Richard Wagner*, edited by Luca Sala, 157–183. Turnhout, Belgium: Brepols

———. 2015. *Understanding the Leitmotif: From Wagner to Hollywood Film Music*. Cambridge: Cambridge University Press.

Brosch, Tobias, and Agnes Moors. 2009. "Valence." In *Oxford Companion to Emotion and the Affective Sciences*, edited by David Sander and Klaus Scherer, 401–402. Oxford: Oxford University Press.

Brower, Candace. 2008. "Paradoxes of Pitch Space." *Music Analysis* 27 (1): 51–106.

Brown, Matthew, Dave Headlam, and Douglas Dempster. 1997. "The ♯IV(♭V) Hypothesis: Testing the Limits of Schenker's Theory of Tonality." *Music Theory Spectrum* 19 (2): 155–183.

Brown, Royal. 1994. *Overtones and Undertones: Reading Film Music*. Berkeley: University of California Press.

Buchler, Michael. 2008. "Modulation as a Dramatic Agent in Frank Loesser's Broadway Songs." *Music Theory Spectrum* 30 (1): 35–60.

Bueno, Jóse, Érico Firmino, and Arno Engelmann. 2002. "Influence of Generalized Complexity of a Music Event on Subjective Time Estimation." *Perceptual and Motor Skills* 94: 541–547.

Buhler, James. 1996. "Breakthrough" as Critique of Form: The Finale of Mahler's First Symphony." *19th-Century Music* 20 (2): 125–143.

———. 2000. "Star Wars, Music and Myth." In *Music and Cinema*, edited by James Buhler, Caryl Flinn, and David Neumeyer, 33–57. Hanover, NH: Wesleyan University Press.

———. 2001. "Analytical and Interpretive Approaches to Film Music (II): Analyzing the Music." In *Film Music: Critical Approaches*, edited by Kevin Donnelly, 39–61. Edinburgh: Edinburgh University Press.

———. 2014. "Ontological, Formal, and Critical Theories of Film Music and Sound." In *The Oxford Handbook of Film Music Studies*, 188–225. New York: Oxford University Press.

———. 2016. "Branding the Franchise: Music, Opening Credits, and the (Corporate) Myth of Origin." In *Music in Epic Film: Listening to Spectacle*, edited by Stephen C. Meyer, 3–26. New York: Routledge.

Buhler, James, and David Neumeyer. 1994. Review article of *Strains of Utopia*, Flinn and *Settling the Score*. *Journal of the American Musicological Society* 47: 364–385.

Buhler, James, Carol Flinn, and David Neumeyer, eds. 2000. *Music and Cinema*. Hanover, NH: Wesleyan University Press.

Buhler, James, David Neumeyer, and Rob Deemer. 2010. *Hearing the Movies: Music and Sound in Film History*. New York: Oxford University Press.

Burke, Edmund. (1775) 2008. *A Philosophical Enquiry into the Sublime and Beautiful*. London: Taylor and Francis.

Burlingame, John. 1999. Liner notes for *Song of Bernadette* (Composed by Alfred Newman). Varèse Sarabande, 6025, compact disc.

Burt, George. 1994. *The Art of Film Music*. Boston: Northeastern University Press.

Buschmann, Carl-Henrik. 2015. "The Musical Conventions of Star Trek: A Search for Musical Syntax in Science Fiction." Master's thesis, Nesna University College.

Caplin, William E. 2004. "The Classical Cadence: Conceptions and Misconceptions." *Journal of the American Musicological Society* 57 (1): 51–118.

Capuzzo, Guy. 2004. "Neo-Riemannian Theory and the Analysis of Pop-Rock Music." *Music Theory Spectrum* 26 (2): 177–199.

Carroll, Noël, and Margaret Moore. 2011. "Music and Motion Pictures." In *The Routledge Companion to Philosophy and Music*, edited by Theodore Gracyk and Andrew Cania, 456–467. New York: Routledge.

Chattah, Juan. 2015. *David Shire's* The Conversation: *A Film Score Guide*. Lanham, MD: Rowman and Littlefield.

Childs, Adrian. 1998. "Moving beyond Neo-Riemannian Triads: Exploring a Transformational Model for Seventh Chords." *Journal of Music Theory* 42: 181–193.

Chion, Michel. 1994. *Audio-Vision: Sound on Screen*, translated by Claudia Gorbman. New York: Columbia University Press.

———. 2000. "Audio-Vision and Sound." In *Sound*, edited by Patricia Kruth and Henry Stobart, 201–220. Cambridge: Cambridge University Press.

Chung, Andrew. 2013. "Lewinian Transformations, Transformations of Transformations, Musical Hermeneutics." Honors thesis, Wesleyan University.

Clark, Suzannah. 2011a. "On the Imagination of Tone in Schubert's *Liedesend* (D473), *Trost* (D523), and *Gretchens Bitte* (D564)." In *The Oxford Handbook of Neo-Riemannian Theories*, edited by Edward Gollin and Alexander Rehding, 294–320. New York: Oxford University Press.

———. 2011b. *Analyzing Schubert*. Cambridge: Cambridge University Press.

Clyne, Michael. 2000. "Constraints on Code Switching: How Universal Are They?" In *Bilingualism Reader*, edited by Li Wei, 257–280. London: Routledge.

Cochran, Alfred. 1986. "Style, Structure, and Tonal Organization in the Early Film Scores of Aaron Copland." PhD diss., Catholic University of America.

———. 1990. "The Spear of Cephalus: Observations on Film Music Analysis." *Indiana Theory Review* 11 (1–2): 65–80.

Cohen, Annabel. 2000. "Film Music: Perspectives from Cognitive Psychology." In *Music and Cinema*, edited by James Buhler, Caryl Flinn, and David Neumeyer, 360–377. Hanover, NH: Wesleyan University Press.

———. 2010. "Music as a Source of Emotion in Film." In *Handbook of Music and Emotion: Theory, Research, Applications*, edited by Patrik Juslin and John Slobada, 879–908. New York: Oxford University Press.

———. 2013. "Congruence-Association Model of Music and Multimedia: Origin and Evolution." In *The Psychology of Music in Multimedia*, edited by Annabel Cohen, Roger Kendall, Scott Lipscomb, and Siu-Lin Tan, 17–47. Oxford: Oxford University Press.

———. 2014. "Film Music from the Perspective of Cognitive Science." In *The Oxford Handbook of Music in Film and Visual Media*, edited by David Neumeyer, 96–130. New York: Oxford University Press.

Cohn, Richard. 1996. "Maximally Smooth Cycles, Hexatonic Systems, and the Analysis of Late Romantic Triadic Progressions." *Music Analysis* 15 (1): 9–40.

———. 1997. "Neo-Riemannian Operations, Parsimonious Trichords, and Their *Tonnetz* Representations." *Journal of Music Theory* 41 (2): 1–66.

———. 1998. "An Introduction to Neo-Riemannian Theory: A Survey and Historical Perspective." *Journal of Music Theory* 42 (2): 167–180.

———. 1999. "As Wonderful as Star Clusters: Instruments for Gazing at Tonality in Schubert." *19th-Century Music* 2 (3): 213–232.

———. 2000. "Weitzmann's Regions, My Cycles, and Douthett's Dancing Cubes." *Music Theory Spectrum* 22 (1): 89–103.

———. 2004. "Uncanny Resemblances: Tonal Signification in the Freudian Age." *Journal of the American Musicological Society* 57 (2): 285–323.

———. 2006. "Hexatonic Poles and the Uncanny in *Parsifal.*" *Opera Quarterly* 22 (2): 208–229.

———. 2011. "Tonal Pitch Space and the (Neo)-Riemannian *Tonnetz.*" In *The Oxford Handbook of Neo-Riemannian Music Theories*, edited by Edward Gollin and Alexander Rehding, 322–348. Oxford and New York: Oxford University Press.

———. 2012. *Audacious Euphony: Chromaticism and the Consonant Triad's Second Nature*. New York: Oxford University Press.

Collins, Karen. 2004. "'I'll Be Back': Recurrent Sonic Motifs in James Cameron's *Terminator* Films." In *Off The Planet: Music, Sound, and Science Fiction Cinema*, edited by Philip Hayward, 165–175. New Barnet, UK: John Libbey.

Cook, Nicholas. 1987. "The Perception of Large-Scale Tonal Closure." *Music Perception: An Interdisciplinary Journal* 5 (2): 197–205.

———. 1998. *Analysing Musical Multimedia*. Oxford: Oxford University Press

———. 2001. "Theorizing Musical Meaning." *Music Theory Spectrum* 23 (1): 170–195.

Cook, Robert. 2005. "Parsimony and Extravagance." *Journal of Music Theory* 49 (1): 109–140.

———. 2011. "Tonal Interpretation, Tonal Models, and the Chromatic Calls to Repent in Franck's *Le Chasseur Maudit.*" In *The Oxford Handbook of Neo-Riemannian Theories*, edited by Edward Gollin and Alexander Rehding, 512–549. New York: Oxford University Press.

Cooke, Mervyn. 2008. *A History of Film Music*. Cambridge: Cambridge University Press.

Cooper, David. 2001. *Bernard Herrmann's* Vertigo: *A Film Score Handbook*. Westport, CT: Greenwood Press.

Copland, Aaron. 1957. *What to Listen For in Music*. 2nd ed. New York: McGraw-Hill.

Copley, Evan. 1991. *Harmony: Baroque to Contemporary, Part I*. Champaign, IL: Stipes.

Cox, Arnie. 2016. *Music & Embodied Cognition: Listening, Moving, Feeling, & Thinking*. Bloomington & Indianapolis: Indiana University Press.

Crans, Alissa, Thomas Fiore, and Ramon Satyendra. 2009. "Musical Actions of Dihedral Groups." *Atlantic Mathematical Monthly* 116 (6): 479–495.

Dahlhaus, Carl. (1974) 1980. *Between Romanticism and Modernism: Four Studies in the Music of the Later Nineteenth Century*, translated by Mary Whittall. Berkeley and Los Angeles: University of California Press.

Danly, Linda. 2002. *Hugo Friedhofer: The Best Years of His Life*. Lanham, MD and Oxford: Scarecrow Press.

Darcy, Warren. 2005. "'Die Zeit ist da': Rotational Form and Hexatonic Magic in Act 2, Scene 1 of *Parsifal.*" In *A Companion to Wagner's Parsifal*, edited by William Kinderman and Katherine Syer, 215–241. Rochester, NY: Camden House.

Daubney, Kate. 2000. *Max Steiner's* Now Voyager: *A Film Score Guide*. Westport, CT: Greenwood.

Davies, Stephen. 2001. "Philosophical Perspectives on Music's Expressiveness." In *Music and Emotion: Theory and Research*, edited by Patrik Juslin and John Sloboda, 23–44. New York: Oxford University Press

———. 2010. "Emotions Expressed and Aroused by Music: Philosophical Perspectives." In *Oxford Handbook of Music and Emotion: Theory, Research, Applications*, edited by Patrik Juslin and John Sloboda, 15–43. New York: Oxford University Press.

Doll, Christopher. 2011. "Rockin' Out: Expressive Modulation in Verse-Chorus Form." *Music Theory Online* 17 (3). http://www.mtosmt.org/issues/mto.11.17.3/mto.11.17.3.doll.html.

Douthett, Jack, and Peter Steinbach. 1998. "Parsimonious Graphs: A Study in Parsimony, Contextual Transformations, and Modes of Limited Transposition." *Journal of Music Theory* 42 (2): 241–263.

Eagleman, David, and Vani Pariyadath. 2009. "Is Subjective Duration a Signature of Coding Efficiency?" *Philosophical Transactions of the Royal Society of London B, Biological Sciences* 364: 1841–1851.

Eaton, Rebecca. 2008. "Unheard Minimalisms: The Functions of the Minimalist Technique in Film Scores." PhD diss., University of Texas at Austin.

———. 2014. "Marking Minimalism: Minimal Music as Sign of Machines and Mathematics in Multimedia." *Music and the Moving Image* 7 (1): 3–23.

Eitan, Zohar. 2013. "How Pitch and Loudness Shape Musical Space and Motion." In *The Psychology of Music in Multimedia*, edited by Annabel Cohen, Roger Kendall, Scott Lipscomb, and Siu-Lin Tan, 165–190. Oxford: Oxford University Press.

Engebretsen, Nora. 2011. "Neo-Riemannian Perspectives on the *Harmonieschritte*, With a Translation of Riemann's *Systematik der Harmonieschritte*." In *The Oxford Handbook of Neo-Riemannian Theories*, edited by Edward Gollin and Alexander Rehding, 351–381. New York: Oxford University Press.

Epstein, David. 1995. *Shaping Time: Music, the Brain, and Performance*. New York: Schirmer Books.

Evans, Mark. 1975. *Soundtrack: The Music of the Movies*. New York: Hopkinson and Blake.

Everett, Walter. 1997. "Swallowed by a Song: Paul Simon's Crisis of Chromaticism." In *Understanding Rock: Essays in Music Analysis*, edited by John Covach and Graeme M. Boone, 113–153. New York: Oxford University Press.

———. 2004. "Making Sense of Rock's Tonal Systems." *Music Theory Online* 10 (4). http://www.mtosmt.org/issues/mto.04.10.4/mto.04.10.4.w_everett.html.

Fink, Robert. 1999. "Going Flat: Post-Hierarchical Music Theory and the Musical Surface." In *Rethinking Music*, edited by Nicholas Cook and Mark Everist, 102–137. Oxford: Oxford University Press.

Firmino, Érico, José Bueno, and Emmanuel Bigand. 2008a. "Tonal Modulation and Subjective Time." *Journal of New Music Research* 37: 275–297.

———. 2008b. "Traveling through Pitch Space Speeds Up Musical Time." *Music Perception* 26 (3): 205–209.

Fisher, Philip. 1998. *Wonder, The Rainbow, and the Aesthetic of Rare Experiences*. Cambridge, MA: Harvard University Press.

Flinn, Caryl. 1992. *Strains of Utopia: Gender, Nostalgia, and Hollywood Film Music*. Princeton, NJ: Princeton University Press.

Florino, Rick. 2010. "Danny Elfman Talks Tim Burton Scores, Bernard Herrmann's Influence, and More." *Artist Direct* (Online News and Interviews). http://www.artistdirect.com/entertainment-news/article/danny-elfman-talks-tim-burton-scores-bernard-herrmann-s-influence-and-more/8196173

Forte, Allen. 1995. *The American Popular Ballad of the Golden Era, 1924–1950*. Princeton, NJ: Princeton University Press.

Forte, Allen, and Steven Gilbert. 1982. *Introduction to Schenkerian Analysis*. New York: W.W. Norton.

Freud, Sigmund. (1921) 2003. *The Uncanny*, translated by David McLintock. London: Penguin Books.

Friedman, Michael. 1990. *Ear Training for Twentieth Century Music*. New Haven: Yale University Press.

Frymoyer, Johanna. 2016. "Octatonic and Ombra: The Russian Supernatural as a Musical Topic." Paper presented at the annual meeting for the Society for Music Theory, Vancouver, Canada, November 3–6.

Gabrielsson, Alf. 2016. "The Relationship between Musical Structure and Perceived Expression." In *The Oxford Handbook of Music Psychology*, 2nd ed., edited by Susan Hallam, Ian Cross, and Michael Thaut, 215–232. Oxford: Oxford University Press.

Genette, Gerard. 1987. *Paratexts: Thresholds of Interpretation*. Translated by Jane E. Lewin. Cambridge: Cambridge University Press.

George, Graham. 1970. *Tonality and Musical Structure*. New York: Praeger.

Goldenberg, Yosef. 2007. "Schenkerian Voice Leading and Neo-Riemannian Operations: Analytical Integration without Theoretical Reconciliation." *Journal of Schenkerian Studies* 2: 65–84.

Goldmark, Daniel. 2005. *Tunes for Toons: Music and the Hollywood Cartoon*. London: Oxford University Press.

Goldstein Avram. 1980. "Thrills in Response to Music and Other Stimuli." *Physiological Psychology* 8 (1): 126–129.

Gollin, Edward. 2000. "Representations of Space and Conceptions of Distance in Transformational Music Theories." PhD diss., Harvard University.

Gollin, Edward, and Alexander Rehding, eds. 2011. *The Oxford Handbook of Neo-Riemannian Music Theories*. New York: Oxford University Press.

Gorbman, Claudia. 1987. *Unheard Melodies: Narrative Film Music*. Bloomington: University of Indiana Press.

Greg, Melissa, and Gregory Siegworth, eds. 2010. *The Affect Theory Reader*. Durham, NC and London: Duke University Press.

Gunning, Tom. 1986. "The Cinema of Attractions: Early Film, Its Spectator, and the Avant-garde." *Wide Angle* 8 (3–4): 63–70.

———. 1989. "An Aesthetic of Astonishment: Early Film and the [In]Credulous Spectator." *Art and Text* 34: 31–45.

Haines, John. 2014. *Music in Films on the Middle Ages: Authenticity vs. Fantasy*. New York: Routledge.

Halfyard, Janet. 2004. *Danny Elfman's* Batman: *A Film Score Guide*. Lanham, MD: Scarecrow Press.

———. 2010. "Music Afoot: Supernatural Horror-Comedies and the *Diabolus in Musica*." In *Music in the Horror Film: Listening to Fear*, edited by Neil Lerner. New York: Routledge, 206–223.

Harrison, Daniel. 1994. *Harmonic Function in Chromatic Music: A Renewed Dualist Theory and Account of Its Precedents*. Chicago: University of Chicago Press.

———. 2002. "Nonconformist Notions of Nineteenth-Century Enharmonicism." *Music Analysis* 21 (2): 115–160.

———. 2011. "Three Short Essays on Neo-Riemannian Theory." In *The Oxford Handbook of Neo-Riemannian Theories*, edited by Edward Gollin and Alexander Rehding, 548–577. New York: Oxford University Press.

———. 2016. *Pieces of Tradition: An Analysis of Contemporary Tonal Music*. New York: Oxford University Press.

Hasty, Christopher. 1997. *Meter as Rhythm*. New York and Oxford: Oxford University Press.

Hatten, Robert. 1994. *Musical Meaning in Beethoven: Markedness, Correlation, and Interpretation*. Bloomington: Indiana University Press.

Hazelwood, Zachary. 2014. "Music, Action, and Narrative in Film: An Energetic and Gestural Approach to Film Score Analysis." PhD diss., Louisiana State University.

Hefling, Stephen, and David Tartakoff. 2004. "Schubert's Chamber Music." In *Nineteenth-Century Chamber Music*, edited by Stephen Hefling, 39–139. New York: Routledge.

Heine, Erik. 2001. "Musical Recycling: A Study and Comparison of Ralph Vaughan Williams' Film Score for 'Scott of the Antarctic' with Sinfonia Antartica (Symphony No. 7)." Master's thesis, University of Arizona.

———. 2016. *James Newton Howard's Signs: A Film Score Guide*. Lanham, MD: Rowman and Littlefield.

Hepokoski, James. 1989. "Verdi's Composition of *Otello*: The Act II Quartet." In *Analyzing Opera: Verdi and Wagner*, edited by Carolyn Abbate and Roger Parker, 125–149. Berkeley: University of California Press.

Hook, Julian. 2002. "Uniform Triadic Transformations." *Journal of Music Theory* 46 (1–2): 57–126.

———. 2007. "Cross-Type Transformations and the Path Consistency Condition." *Music Theory Spectrum* 29 (1): 1–40.

Hubbert, Julie. 2011. *Celluloid Symphonies: Texts and Contexts in Film Music History*. Berkeley: University of California Press.

Hunt, Graham. 2007. "David Lewin and Valhalla Revisited: New Approaches to Motivic Corruption in Wagner's *Ring* Cycle." *Music Theory Spectrum* 29 (2): 177–196.

Hunter, Patrick, and E. Glenn Schellenberg. 2010. "Music and Emotion." In *Music Perception: Springer Handbook for Auditory Research*, edited by Mari Riess Jones, Richard Faye, and Arthur Popper, 129–164. New York: Springer Verlag.

Huron, David. 2006. *Sweet Anticipation: Music and the Psychology of Expectation*. Cambridge, MA: MIT Press.

Huron, David, and Elizabeth Margulis. 2010. "Musical Expectancy and Thrills." In *Handbook of Music and Emotion: Theory, Research, Applications*, edited by Patrik Juslin and John Sloboda, 575–604. New York: Oxford University Press.

Huvet, Chloé. 2014. "George Lucas et les partitions de John Williams pour Star Wars—Episodes I, II et III (1999–2005): Une réécriture musicale problématique?" Paper presented at the sixth meeting of the Music and Media Study Group, Dijon, France, July 1–2.

Hyer, Brian. 1989. "Tonal Intuitions in *Tristan und Isolde*." PhD diss., Yale University.

———. 1995. "Reimag(in)ing Riemann." *Journal of Music Theory* 39 (1): 101–138.

Jackson, Roland. 2010. "The Vision Scenes in 'Bernadette': Newman's and Powell's Contributions." *Journal of Film Music* 3 (2): 111–125.

Jarvis, Brian. 2015. "Analyzing Film Music across the Complete Filmic Structure: Three Coen and Burwell Collaborations." PhD diss., Florida State University.

Jentsch, Ernst. (1906) 1995. "On the Psychology of the Uncanny," translated by Roy Sellars. *Angelaki* 2 (1): 7–16.

Johnston, Adrian, and Malabou, Catherine. 2013. *Self and Emotional Life: Philosophy, Psychoanalysis, and Neuroscience*. New York: Columbia University Press.

Kalinak, Kathryn. 1992. *Settling the Score: Music and the Classical Hollywood Film*. Madison: University of Wisconsin Press.

Kanai, Ryota. 2014. "Illusory Distortion of Subjective Time Perception." In *Subjective Time: The Philosophy, Psychology, and Neuroscience of Temporality*, edited by Valtteri Arstilla and Dan Lloyd, 343–354. Cambridge, MA: MIT Press.

Karlin, Fred, and Rayburn Wright. 2004. *On the Track: A Guide to Contemporary Film Scoring*. New York: Routledge Press.

Keller, Hans. (1955) 2006. *Film Music and Beyond: Writings on Music and Screen, 1946–59*, edited by Christopher Wintle. London: Plumbago Books.

Keltner, Dacherr, and Jonathan Haidt. 2003. "Approaching Awe, a Moral, Spiritual, and Aesthetic Emotion." *Cognition and Emotion* 17 (2): 297–314.

Kinderman, William, and Harald Krebs, eds. 1996. *The Second Practice of Nineteenth-Century Tonality*. Lincoln: University of Nebraska Press.

King, Geoff. 2002. *New Hollywood Cinema: An Introduction*. New York: I.B. Tauris.

Klumpenhouwer, Henry. 1994. "Some Remarks on the Use of Riemann Transformations." *Music Theory Online* 0 (4). http://www.mtosmt.org/issues/mto.94.0.9/mto.94.0.9.klumpenhouwer.html

———. 2006. "In Order to Stay Asleep as Observers: The Nature and Origins of Anti-Cartesianism in Lewin's *Generalized Musical Intervals and Transformations*." *Music Theory Spectrum* 28 (2): 277–289.

Kochavi, Jonathan. 1998. "Some Structural Features of Contextually-Defined Inversion Operators." *Journal of Music Theory* 42 (2): 307–320.

Kopp, David. 2002. *Chromatic Transformations in the Nineteenth Century*. Cambridge: University of Cambridge Press.

Kramer, Jonathan. 1988. *The Time of Music: New Meanings, New Temporalities, New Listening Strategies*. New York: Schirmer Books.

Krebs, Harald. 1981. "Alternatives to Monotonality in Early Nineteenth-Century Music." *Journal of Music Theory* 25 (1): 1–16.

Kreuzer, Anselm. 2003. *Film Musik: Geschichte und Analyse*. Frankfurt: Peter Lang.

Krumhansl, Carol. 1990. "Tonal Hierarchies and Rare Intervals in Music Cognition." *Music Perception* 7: 309–324.

———. 1998. "Perceived Triad Distance: Evidence Supporting the Psychological Reality of Neo-Riemannian Transformations." *Journal of Music Theory* 42 (2): 265–281.

Laing, Heather. 2007. *The Gendered Score: Music in 1940s Melodrama and Woman's Film*. Aldershot, UK: Ashgate.

Laitz, Steven. 2012. *The Complete Musician: An Integrated Approach to Tonal Theory, Analysis, and Listening*. New York: Oxford University Press.

Lambert, Philip. 2000. "On Contextual Transformations." *Perspectives of New Music* 38 (1): 45–76

Langford, Barry. 2006. "Time." In *Reading The Lord of the Rings: New Writings on Tolkien's Classic*, edited by Robert Eaglestone, 29–46. London: Continuum Press.

Larson, Steven. 1997. "The Problem of Prolongation in Tonal Music: Terminology, Perception, and Expressive Meaning." *Journal of Music Theory* 41: 103–136.

Latham, Edward. 2008. *Tonality as Drama: Closure and Interruption in Four Twentieth-Century American Operas*. Denton: University of North Texas Press.

Lehman, Frank. 2012. "Reading Tonality through Film: Transformational Hermeneutics and the Music of Hollywood." PhD diss., Harvard University.

———. 2013a. "Hollywood Cadences: Music and the Structure of Cinematic Expectation." *Music Theory Online* 19 (4). http://www.mtosmt.org/issues/mto.13.19.4/mto.13.19.4.lehman.html

———. 2013b. "Transformational Analysis and the Representation of Genius in Film Music." *Music Theory Spectrum* 35 (1): 1–22.

———. 2014a. "Schubert's SLIDES: Tonal (Non)Integration of a Paradoxical Transformation." *Music Theory and Analysis* 1 (1): 61–101.

———. 2014b. "Hex Appeal: Transformation and Prolongation in Holst's Neptune." Paper presented at Annual Meeting of Music Theory Society of New York State, New York NY, April 5–6. https://www.academia.edu/28489596/Hex_Appeal_Prolongation_and_Transformation_in_Holsts_Neptune

———. 2015. Review of *The Oxford Handbook of Neo-Riemannian Music Theories* (edited by Edward Gollin and Alexander Rehding). *Music Theory Spectrum* 37 (1): 154–162.

———. 2016. "Manufacturing the Epic Score: Hans Zimmer and the Sounds of Significance." In *Music in Epic Film: Listening to Spectacle*, edited by Stephen C. Meyer, 27–56. New York and London: Routledge.

Leinberger, Charles. 2002. "Thematic Variation and Key Relationships: Charlotte's Theme in Max Steiner's Score for *Now, Voyager*." *Journal of Film Music Studies* 1: 63–77.

Lerdahl, Fred. 1988. "Cognitive Constraints on Compositional Systems." In *Generative Processes in Music: The Psychology of Performance, Improvisation, and Composition*, edited by John Sloboda, 231–259. Oxford: Oxford University Press.

———. 2001. *Tonal Pitch Space*. Oxford: Oxford University Press.

Lerdahl, Fred, and Carol Krumhansl. 2007. "Modeling Tonal Tension." *Music Perception* 24 (4): 326–366.

Lerner, Neil. 2015. "Hearing a Site of Masculinity in Franz Waxman's Score for *Pride of the Marines* (1945)." In *Oxford Handbook of Music and Disability Studies*, edited by Blake Howe, Stephanie Jensen-Moulton, Neil Lerner, and Joseph Straus, 856–890. Oxford: Oxford University Press.

Levarie, Siegmund. 1978. "Key Relations in Verdi's *Un ballo in maschera*." *19th-Century Music* 2: 143–147.

Levinson, Jerrold. 2006. *Contemplating Art: Essays in Aesthetics*. Oxford: Oxford University Press.

Lewin, David. 1977. "Forte's Interval Vector, My Interval Function, and Regener's Common-Note Function." *Journal of Music Theory* 21 (2): 197–237.

———. 1980. "On Generalized Intervals and Transformations." *Journal of Music Theory* 24 (2): 243–251.

———. 1982. "A Formal Theory of Generalized Tonal Functions." *Journal of Music Theory* 26: 23–60.

———. 1984. "Amfortas's Prayer to Titurel and the Role of D in *Parsifal*: The Tonal Spaces of the Drama and the Enharmonic C♭/B." *19th-Century Music* 7 (3): 336–349.

———. 1986. "Music Theory, Phenomenology, and Modes of Perception." *Music Perception* 3: 327–392.

———. 1987. *Generalized Musical Intervals and Transformations*. New Haven, CT: Yale University Press.

———. 1990. "Klumpenhouwer Networks and Some Isographies That Involve Them." *Music Theory Spectrum* 12: 83–120.

———. 1992. "Some Notes on Analyzing Wagner: *The Ring* and *Parsifal*." *19th-Century Music* 16 (1): 49–58.

———. 1998. "Some Ideas about Voice-Leading between PCSETS" *Journal of Music Theory* 42 (1): 15–72.

———. (1993) 2007. *Musical Form and Transformation: Four Analytical Essays*. New York: Oxford University Press.

London, Justin. 2012. *Hearing in Time*. Oxford and New York: Oxford University Press.

Long, Michael. 2008. *Beautiful Monsters: Imagining the Classic in Musical Media*. Berkeley: University of California Press.

Lowinsky, Edward. 1961. *Tonality and Atonality in Sixteenth-Century Music*. Berkeley: University of California Press.

Mancini, Henry. 1986. *Sounds and Scores: A Practical Guide to Professional Orchestration*. Van Nuys, CA: Alfred Publishing.

Marcozzi, Rudy. 1992. "The Interaction of Large Scale Harmonic and Dramatic Structure in the Verdi Operas Adapted from Shakespeare." PhD Diss., Indiana University.

Margulis, Elizabeth Hellmuth. 2005. "A Model of Melodic Expectation." *Music Perception* 22 (4): 663–714.

———. 2014. *On Repeat: How Music Plays the Mind*. Oxford and New York: Oxford University Press.

Marks, Martin. 1997. *Music and the Silent Film: Contexts and Case Studies 1895–1924*. New York: Oxford University Press.

———. 2000. "Music, Drama, Warner Brothers: The Cases of *The Maltese Falcon* and *Casablanca*." In *Music and Cinema*, edited by James Buhler, Caryln Flinn, and David Neumeyer, 161–186. Hanover, NH: Wesleyan University Press.

Marvin, Elizabeth West and Brinkman, Alexander. 1999. "The Effect of Modulation and Formal Manipulation on Perception of Tonal Closure by Expert Listeners." *Music Perception: An Interdisciplinary Journal* 16 (4): 389–407.

Matravers, Derek. 2011. "Arousal Theories." In *The Routledge Companion to Philosophy and Music*, edited by Theodore Gracyk and Andrew Kania, 212–222. New York: Routledge.

Maus, Fred 1999. "Concepts of Musical Unity." In *Rethinking Music*, edited by Nicholas Cook and Mark Everist, 171–192. Oxford: Oxford University Press.

McClary, Susan. 2007. "Minima Romantica." In *Beyond the Soundtrack: Representing Music in Cinema*, edited by Daniel Goldmark, Lawrence Kramer, and Richard Leppert, 48–65. Berkeley: University of California Press.

McCreless, Patrick. 1982. *Siegfried: Its Drama, History, and Music*. Anne Arbor: UMI Research Press.

———. 1996. "An Evolutionary Perspective on Nineteenth-Century Semitonal Relations." In *The Second Practice of Nineteenth-Century Tonality*, edited by William Kinderman and Harald Krebs, 87–113. Lincoln: University of Nebraska Press.

———. 1997. "Rethinking Contemporary Music Theory." In *Keeping Score: Music Disciplinarity, Culture*, edited by Anahid Kassabian and David Schwartz, 1–49. Charlottesville: University of Virginia Press.

McGraw, A. Peter, and Caleb Warren. 2010. "Benign Violations: Making Immoral Behavior Funny." *Psychological Science* 21 (8): 1141–1149.

McLucas, Anne Dhu. 1984. "Action Music in American Pantomime and Melodrama." *American Music* 2: 49–72.

——. 2012. "The Continuity of Melos: Beginnings to the Present Day." *Journal of Film Music* 5 (1–2): 15–28.

Meandri, Illario. 2014. "Dal Meraviglioso all' Antimusica: Su alcuni cliché del Fantastico nel mainstream musicale hollywoodiano." In *Suono/Immagine/Genre*, edited by Illario Meandri and Andrea Valle, 173–198. Torino, Italy: Edizioni Kaplan.

Meyer, Stephen C. 2015. *Epic Sound: Music in Postwar Hollywood Biblical Films*. Bloomington and Indianapolis: Indiana University Press.

Mirka, Danuta, ed. 2014. *The Oxford Handbook of Topic Theory*. New York: Oxford University Press.

Missiras, Michael. 1998. "Musical Reference, Syntax, and the Compositional Process in Film Music." PhD diss., New York University.

Mooney, Michael Kevin. 1996. "The 'Table of Relations' and Music Psychology in Hugo Riemann's Harmonic Theory." PhD diss., Columbia University.

Morgan, Robert. 1999. Review of *The Second Practice of Nineteenth-Century Tonality*, (edited by William Kinderman and Harald Krebs). *Journal of Music Theory* 43 (1): 135–163.

Morris, Robert. 1998. "Voice Leading Spaces." *Music Theory Spectrum* 20 (2): 175–208.

Morton, Lawrence. 1948. "Film Music of the Quarter." *Hollywood Quarterly* 3 (4): 395–402.

Moshaver, Maryam. 2012. "*Telos* and Temporality: Phenomenology and the Experience of Time in Lewin's Study of Perception." *Journal of the American Musicological Society* 65 (1): 179–214.

Motazedian, Tahirih. 2016. "To Key or Not to Key: Tonal Design in Film Music." PhD Diss., Yale University.

Murphy, Scott. 2006. "The Major Tritone Progression in Recent Hollywood Science Fiction Films." *Music Theory Online* 12 (2). http://www.mtosmt.org/issues/mto.06.12.2/mto.06.12.2.murphy.html

——. 2012. "The Tritone Within: Interpreting Harmony in Elliot Goldenthal's Score for *Final Fantasy: The Spirits Within*." In *The Music of Fantasy Cinema*, edited by Janet Halfyard: 148–174. London: Equinox.

——. 2014a. "Transformational Theory and the Analysis of Film Music." In *The Oxford Handbook of Film Music Studies*, edited by David Neumeyer, 471–497. New York: Oxford University Press.

——. 2014b. "Scoring Loss in Some Recent Film and Television." *Music Theory Spectrum* 36 (2): 295–314.

Muysken, Pieter. 2000. *Bilingual Speech: A Typology of Code-Mixing*. Cambridge: Cambridge University Press.

Narmour, Eugene. 1990. *The Analysis and Cognition of Basic Melodic Structures: The Implication-Realization Model*. Chicago: University of Chicago Press.

Nelson, Robert. 1946. "Film Music: Color or Line." *Music Quarterly* 2 (1): 57–65.

Neumeyer, David. 2015. *Meaning and Interpretation in Music for Cinema*. With contributions by James Buhler. Bloomington: Indiana University Press.

——. 1990. "Film Music Analysis and Pedagogy." *Indiana Theory Review* 11 (1–2): 1–27.

——. 1995. "Melodrama as a Compositional Resource in Early Hollywood Sound Cinema." *Current Musicology* 57: 61–94.

——. 1998. "Tonal Design and Narrative in Film Music: Bernard Herrmann's The Trouble With Harry and Portrait of Hitch." *Indiana Theory Review* 19 (1–2): 87–123.

——. 2010. "Wagnerian Opera and Nineteenth-Century Melodrama." In *Wagner and Cinema*, edited by Jeongwon Joe and Sander Gilman, 111–184. Bloomington: Indiana University Press.

Neumeyer, David, and James Buhler. 2001. "Analytical and Interpretive Approaches to Film Music (I): Analysing the Music." In *Film Music: Critical Approaches*, edited by K. J. Donnelly, 16–38. New York: Continuum International Publishing Group.

O'Hara, William. 2012. "Music Analysis and Play." Paper presented at New England Conference of Music Theorists Annual Meeting, New Harbor, CT, April 20–21.

Oden, Chelsea. 2016. "Reflection and Introspection in the Film Scores of Thomas Newman." Master's thesis, University of Oregon.

Palmer, Christopher. 1993. *The Composer in Hollywood*. London: Marion Boyars Publishing.

Panksepp, Jaak. 1995. "The Emotional Sources of 'Chills' Induced by Music." *Music Perception* 13 (2): 171–207.

——. 1998. *Affective Neuroscience: The Foundations of Human and Animal Emotions*. Oxford: Oxford University Press.

Patel, Aniruddh. 2008. *Music, Language, and the Brain*. Oxford and New York: Oxford University Press.

Patrick, Cameron. 1986. "Anatomy of A Film Score: Star Trek—The Motion Picture." Master's thesis, University of Queenslands.

Perle, George. 1977. *Twelve-Tone Tonality*. Berkeley: University of California Press.

Pisani, Michael. 2014. *Music for the Melodramatic Theater in Nineteenth Century New York and London*. Iowa City: University of Iowa Press.

Piston, Walter. (1941) 1987. *Harmony*. 5th ed. Revised by Mark DeVoto. New York: W.W. Norton.

Platte, Nathan. 2011. "Music for *Spellbound* (1945): A Contested Collaboration." *Journal of Musicology* 28 (4): 418–463.

Proctor, Gregory. 1978. *The Technical Bases of Nineteenth Century Chromatic Tonality: A Study in Chromaticism*. PhD diss., Princeton University.

Powers, Harold. 1995. "One Halfstep at a Time: Tonal Transposition and 'Split Association' in Italian Opera." *Cambridge Opera Journal* 7 (2): 135–164.

Rahn, Steven. 2016. "Elemental and Corruptible: The Sound of Empowerment and Moral Conflict in the *Dark Knight* Trilogy." Paper presented at Music and Moving Image Conference XI, New York, NY, May 27–29.

Rehding, Alexander. 2003. *Hugo Riemann and the Birth of Modern Musical Thought*. Cambridge: Cambridge University Press.

——. 2009. *Music and Monumentality: Commemoration and Wonderment in Nineteenth Century Germany*. New York: Oxford University Press.

——. 2011. "Dualistic Forms." In *The Oxford Handbook of Neo-Riemannian Theories*, edited by Edward Gollin and Alexander Rehding, 218–245. New York: Oxford University Press.

Richards, Mark. 2016. "Film Music Themes: Analysis and Corpus Study." *Music Theory Online* 22 (1). http://www.mtosmt.org/issues/mto.16.22.1/mto.16.22.1.richards.html.

Richardson, Michael Scott. 2009. "Evoking an Ancient Sound: Richard Wagner's Musical Medievalism." Master's thesis, Rice University.

Rigbi, Elisheva. 2013. "Musical Prose and Musical Narrativity in the *Fin de Siècle*." In *Music and Narrative since 1900*, edited by Michael Klein and Nicholas Reyland, 144–162. Bloomington: University of Indiana Press.

Rings, Steven. 2007. "Perspectives on Tonality and Transformation in Schubert's Impromptu in E-flat, D. 899." *Journal of Schenkerian Studies* 2: 33–63.

——. 2011a. "Riemannian Analytical Values, Paleo- and Neo-." In *The Oxford Handbook of Neo-Riemannian Theories*, edited by Edward Gollin and Alexander Rehding, 486–511. New York: Oxford University Press.

——. 2011b. *Tonality and Transformation*. New York: Oxford University Press.

Robinson, Jenefer. 2011. "Expression Theories." In *The Routledge Companion to Philosophy and Music*. Edited by Theodore Gracyk and Andrew Kania, 201–211. New York: Routledge.

Rodman, Ronald. 1998. "'There's No Place Like Home': Tonal Closure and Design in the Wizard of Oz." *Indiana Theory Review* 19 (1–2): 125–143.

——. 2000. "Tonal Design and the Aesthetic of Pastiche in Herbert Stothart's *Maytime*." In *Music and Cinema*, edited by James Buhler, Caryl Flinn, and David Neumeyer, 187–206. Hanover, NH: University of Wesleyan Press.

——. 2010. *Tuning In: American Narrative Television Music*. New York: Oxford University Press.

Rosar, William. 1983. "Music for the Monsters: Universal Pictures' Horror Film Scores of the Thirties." *Quarterly Journal of the Library of Congress* 40 (4): 391–421.

——. 2001. "The *Dies Irae* in *Citizen Kane*: Musical Hermeneutics Applied to Film Music." in *Film Music: Critical Approaches*, edited by K.J. Donnelly, 103–116. New York: Continuum International Publishing Group.

——. 2002a. "Film Music—What's in a Name?" *Journal of Film Music*, 1 (1): 1–18.

———. 2002b. Liner notes for *Above and Beyond* Original Motion Picture Soundtrack (Composed by Hugo Friedhofer). Film Score Golden Age Classics 5 (11), compact disc.

———. 2003. "Bernard Herrmann: The Beethoven of Film Music?" *Journal of Film Music* 1 (2/3): 121–150.

———. 2006. "Music for Martians: Schillinger's Two Tonics and Harmony of Fourths in Leith Steven's Score for *War of the Worlds* (1953)." *Journal of Film Music* 1 (4): 395–438.

Rosenman, Leonard. 1968. "Notes from a Subculture." *Perspectives of New Music*, 7 (1): 122–135.

Ross, Alex. 2003. "The Ring and the Rings: Wagner vs. Tolkien." *New Yorker* December 22, 2003. http://www.therestisnoise.com/2004/04/wagner_tolkien_1.html.

Rothfarb, Lee. 1991. *Ernst Kurth: Selected Writings*. Cambridge: Cambridge University Press.

Rothstein, William. 2008. "Common-Tone Tonality in Italian Romantic Opera: An Introduction." *Music Theory Online* 14 (1). http://www.mtosmt.org/issues/mto.08.14.1/mto.08.14.1.rothstein.html.

Rouget, Gilbert. 1985. *Music and Trance: A Theory of the Relations between Music and Possession*. Chicago and London: University of Chicago Press.

Sabaneev, Leonid. 1935. *Music for the Films: A Handbook for Composers and Conductors*. London: Sir Isaac Pitman and Sons.

Salzer, Felix. (1952) 1962. *Structural Hearing: Tonal Coherence in Music*. Mineola, NY: Dover Publications.

Sayrs, Elizabeth. 2003. "Narrative, Metaphor, and Conceptual Blending in 'The Hanging Tree.'" *Music Theory Online* 9 (1). http://www.mtosmt.org/issues/mto.03.9.1/mto.03.9.1.sayrs.html.

Schelle, Michael. 1999. *The Score: Interview with Film Composers*. Los Angeles: Silman-James Press.

Schenker, Heinrich. (1935) 2001. *Free Composition*. Translated and edited by Ernst Oster. Hillsdale, NY: Pendragon Press.

Schmalfeldt, Janet. 1992. "Cadential Processes: The Evaded Cadence and the 'One More Time' Technique." *Journal of Musicological Research*, 12: 1–52.

Schmuckler, Mark. 2016. "Tonality and Contour in Melodic Processing." In *Oxford Handbook of Music Psychology*, 2nd ed., edited by Susan Hallam, Ian Cross, and Michael Thaut, 143–165. Oxford: Oxford University Press.

Schneller, Tom. 2012. "Easy to Cut: Modular Forms in the Film Scores of Bernard Herrmann," *Journal of Film Music* 5 (1–2): 127–151.

———. 2013. "Modal Interchange and Semantic Resonance in Themes by John Williams." *Journal of Film Music* 6 (1): 49–74.

Schoenberg, Arnold. (1954) 1969. *Structural Functions of Harmony*, Revised Edition. New York, NY: W. W. Norton & Company.

———. (1947) 2010. *Style and Idea: Selected Writings*. Edited by Leonard Stein, translated by Leo Black, reprint. Berkeley: University of California Press.

Schuijer, Michiel. 2008. *Analyzing Atonal Music: Pitch-Class Set Theory and Its Contexts*. Rochester, NY: University of Rochester Press.

Schweiger, Daniel. 1992. "A Conversation with Jerry Goldsmith." *Soundtrack Magazine* 11 (42).

Segall, Christopher. 2011. "The Common Third Relation in Russian Music Theory." Paper presented at Society for Music Theory Annual Conference, Minneapolis MN, October 27–30.

Shiota, Michelle, Dacher Keltner, and Amanda Mossman. 2007. "The Nature of Awe: Elicitor, Appraisals, and Effects on Self-Concept." *Cognition and Emotion* 21 (5): 944–963.

Simmons, Walter. 2004. *Voices in the Wilderness: Six American Neo-Romantic Composers*. Lanham, MD: Scarecrow Press.

Skinner, Frank. 1950. *Underscore*. New York: Criterion Music.

Sloboda, John. 1991. "Music Structure and Emotional Response: Some Empirical Findings." *Psychology of Music* 19: 110–120.

Slonimsky, Nicholas. (1937) 1994. *Music since 1900*. New York: Maxwell MacMillan International.

Smith, Charles. 1986. "The Functional Extravagance of Chromatic Chords." *Music Theory Spectrum* 8: 94–139.

———. 2001. "Functional Fishing with *Tonnetz*: Towards a Grammar of Transformations and Progressions." Paper presented at the Third Symposium on Neo-Riemannian Theory, Buffalo, NY, July 20–21.

Smith, Jeff. 1996. "Unheard Melodies?: A Critique of Psychoanalytic Theories of Film Music," in *Post-Theory: Reconstructing Film Studies*, edited by David Bordwell and Noël Carroll, 230–247. Madison: University of Wisconsin Press.

———. 2009. "Bridging the Gap: Reconsidering the Boundary between Diegetic and Non-Diegetic Music." *Music and the Moving Image* 2 (1). http://mmi.press.uiuc.edu/2.1/index.html.

Smith, Stephen. (1991) 2002. *A Heart at Fire's Center: The Life and Music of Bernard Herrmann*. Berkeley and Los Angeles: University of California Press.

Solie, Ruth. 1980. "The Living Work: Organicism and Music Analysis." *19th-Century Music* 4 (2): 147–156.

Stilwell, Robynn. 2000. "Sense and Sensibility: Form, Genre, and Function in the Film Score." *Acta Musicologica* 72 (2): 219–240.

———. 2002. "Music in Films: A Critical Review of Literature, 1980–1996," *Journal of Film Music* 1 (1): 19–61.

Straus, Joseph. 1997. "Voice Leading in Atonal Music." In *Music Theory in Concept and Practice*, edited by James Baker, David Beach, and Jonathan Bernard, 237–274. Rochester, NY: University of Rochester Press.

———. 2016a. *Introduction to Post-Tonal Theory*, 4th ed. New York: W.W. Norton.

———. 2016b. "Autism and Postwar Serialism as Neurodiverse Forms of Cultural Modernism." In *The Oxford Handbook of Music and Disability Studies*, edited by Blake Howe, Stephanie Jensen-Moulton, Neil Lerner, and Joseph Straus, 684–706. Oxford: Oxford University Press.

Strauven, Wanda, ed. 2006. *The Cinema of Attractions Reloaded*. Amsterdam: Amsterdam University Press.

Tagg, Philip. 1993. "'Universal Music' and the Case of Death." *Critical Quarterly* 35 (2): 54–98.

Taruskin, Richard. 1985. "Chernomor to Kaschei: Harmonic Sorcery; or, Stravinsky's 'Angle..'" *Journal of the American Musicological Society* 38 (1): 72–142.

———. 1996. *Stravinsky and the Russian Traditions: Volume One*. Berkeley: University of California Press.

———. 2005. *The Oxford History of Western Music*. Oxford: Oxford University Press.

Taylor, Stephen. 2010. "Inception Chord Progression." Post to SMT-talk mailing list, 8/10/2010. http://lists.societymusictheory.org/pipermail/smt-talk-societymusictheory.org/2010-August/003520.html

Temperley, David. 1999. "The Question of Purpose in Music Theory." *Current Musicology* 66: 66–85.

Tenzer, Michael. 2011. "Generalized Representation of Musical Time and Periodic Structures." *Ethnomusicology* 55 (3): 369–386.

Thompson, Kristen. (1981) 2004. "The Concept of Cinematic Excess." In *Film Theory and Criticism: Introductory Readings*, 6th ed., edited by Leo Braudry and Marshall Cohen, 513–524. New York: Oxford University Press.

Todorov, Tzvetan. (1970) 1975. *The Fantastic: A Structural Approach to a Literary Genre*. Ithaca, NY: Cornell University Press.

Topolinski, Sascha, and Rolf Reber. 2010. "Gaining Insight into the 'Aha' Experience." *Current Directions in Psychological Science* 19 (6): 402–405.

Trivedi, Saam. 2011. "Music and Imagination." In *The Routledge Companion to Philosophy and Music*, edited by Theodore Gracyk and Andrew Kania, 113–122. New York: Routledge.

Tymoczko, Dmitri. 2009. "Three Conceptions of Musical Distance." In *Mathematics and Computation in Music*, edited by Elaine Chew, Adrian Childs, and Ching-Hua Chuan, 258–272. Heidelberg: Springer.

———. 2011a. *A Geometry of Music: Harmony and Counterpoint in the Extended Common Practice*. New York: Oxford University Press.

———. 2011b. "Dualism and the Beholder's Eye: Inversional Symmetry in Chromatic Tonal Music." In *The Oxford Handbook of Neo-Riemannian Music Theories*, edited by Edward Gollin and Alexander Rehding, 246–269. New York: Oxford University Press.

van der Lek, Robert, and Mick Swithinbank. 1994. "Concert Music as Reused Film Music: E.W. Korngold's Self-Arrangements." *Acta Musicologica* 66 (2): 78–112.

van der Merwe, Peter. 1989. *Origins of the Popular Style: The Antecedents of Twentieth-Century Popular Music*. Oxford: Clarendon Press.

Vasalou, Sophia. 2016. *Wonder: A Grammar*. Albany, NY: SUNY Press.

Veatch, Tom. 1998. "A Theory of Humor." *Humor: International Journal of Humor Research* 11: 161–215.

Wagner, Richard. (1879) 1994. "On the Application of Music to the Drama." In *Religion and Art*, translated by William Ashton Ellis, 175–191. Lincoln: University of Nebraska Press

Walsh, Stephen. 2008. *Stravinsky: The Second Exile: France and America, 1934–1971*. Berkeley and Los Angeles: University of California Press

Watkins, Glenn. 2010. *The Gesualdo Hex: Music, Myth, Memory*. New York: W.W. Norton.

Waxman, Franz. 1950. "'Music from the Films:' A CBC Broadcast." *Hollywood Quarterly* 5 (2): 132–137.

Wearden, John, Alan O'Donoghue, Ruth Ogden, and Catharine Montgomery. 2014. "Subjective Duration in the Laboratory and the World Outside." In *Subjective Time: The Philosophy, Psychology, and Neuroscience of Temporality*, edited by Valtteri Arstilla and Dan Lloyd, 287–306. Cambridge, MA: MIT Press.

Wearden, John, N.P.M. Todd, and L.A. Jones. 2006. "When Do Auditory/Visual Differences in Duration Judgments Occur?" *Quarterly Journal of Experimental Psychology* 59 (10): 1709–1724.

Wherry, Mark. 2003. Interview with Elliot Goldenthal. *Sound on Sound* March 2003. http://www.soundonsound.com/sos/Mar03/articles/elliotgoldenthal.asp?print=yes

Whitesell, Lloyd. 2005. "Concerto Macabre." *Music Quarterly* 88 (2): 167–203.

———. 2010. "Quieting the Ghosts in *The Sixth Sense* and *The Others*." In *Music in the Horror Film: Listening to Fear*, edited by Neil Lerner, 206–223. New York: Routledge.

Widgery, Claudia. 1990. "The Kinetic and Temporal Interaction of Music and Film: Three Documentaries of 1930's America." PhD diss., University of Maryland College Park.

Wierzbicki, James. 2009. *Film Music: A History*. New York: Routledge.

Winters, Ben. 2007. *Erich Wolfgang Korngold's* The Adventures of Robin Hood: *A Film Score Guide*. Latham, MD: Scarecrow Press.

Wittmann, Marc and Virginie van Wassenhove. 2009. "The Experience of Time: Neural Mechanisms and the Interplay of Emotion, Cognition, and Embodiment." *Philosophical Transaction of the Royal Society of London B, Biological Sciences* 364: 1809–1813.

Wright, Stephen. 2006. "The Film Music of Danny Elfman: A Selective Discography." *Notes* 62: 1030–1042.

Zbikowski, Lawrence. 2002. *Conceptualizing Music: Cognitive Structure, Theory, and Analysis*. Oxford: Oxford University Press.

———. 2002–2003. "Music Theory, Multimedia, and the Construction of Meaning." *Integrál* 16–17: 251–268.

Multimedia Index

Subject Index

Note: Tables and figures are indicated by t and f following the page number.

development of, 86–87
film musical applications of, 51, 141
methodological issues of, 13
transformations, 89–95, 202
Neumeyer, David, 5, 7, 22, 24, 39, 42, 45, 244n18,
245n21, 248n53, 254n6
Newman, Alfred, 2, 14, 20, 23, 34, 132, 203,
228–235
Newman, Thomas, 9, 146, 172, 200, 206, 219
New Musicology, 4, 265n19
Newton Howard, James, 104, 131, 149–152,
258n27, 266n28
noncentricity, 66–68, 75–77, 222
nondiatonicity, 66–68, 75–76, 212
"non-directed linear time," 187, 233
nonfunctionality, 66–68, 75–77, 80, 133, 140, 212,
222, 224
non-harmonic parameters, 8–9, 26, 71, 76, 106,
124, 138, 148, 231
and musical expectations, 187, 189–190, 194
wonderment and, 167
nostalgia, 1–2, 16, 20–21, 208, 225,
238–239, 244n5
NRT. *See* neo-Riemannian theory

Oden, Chelsea, 206
O'Hara, William, 256n3
oscillation, chordal, 3, 71, 76, 94–95, 130, 138,
145–146, 156, 206, 225
absolute progressions, 23
slide, 105
tritone, 68, 157, 228

pandiatonicism, 68, 205–207
pantriadic aesthetics, 51, 69–73, 165, 167, 174,
177–178, 196
atypical psychology, 71–72
fantasy, 70
intensification, 70
sublime, 72–73 (*see also* sublimity)
in *LOTR*, 174, 176–177
temporality of, 74, 186–187, 189, 191
pantriadic chromaticism, 11–13, 44–50, 65–73,
81–83, 129, 147, 203, 222–224, 230,
249n5, 251n31
as compositional style, 66, 132
expressivity of, 106–107, 136
in film, 85–86, 128
fixity of key, 68
guises of, 13
intensified minor modality, 47
normative features (*see* noncentricity;
nondiatonicity; nonfunctionality)
in Romantic era, 50–51, 165
structure of, 12, 106–107
syntactical features, 68–69, 211, 217
parallel transformation (P), 54, 77, 82,
91, 100, 205

parallel voice leading, 81–82, 143, 145,
225, 252n50
paratext, 1–2, 42
parsimony, 13, 88, 91, 107, 127, 141–142, 145,
175, 215, 253n10
patterning, 13, 127, 155–156, 158, 160,
162, 259n33
pentatonicism, 20, 25, 44, 204–206, 264n4
phantasmagoria, 70, 212–213, 219,
251n38, 262n33
pitch design, 8, 11–12, 15, 28, 129
authorial intentionality of, 12, 15–16
expressivity of, 59, 65
and subjective temporality, 190–192
planing. *See* parallel voice leading
play, 127–128, 138, 256nn2–3
playing-through paradigm, 29–30, 210
Poledouris, Basil, 66–68, 77, 219
polystylism, 7, 11–12, 17–18, 202, 204
Powell, Edward, 228, 235
Powell, John, 56–57, 58
practice, tonal, 8, 10, 15–48, 88, 203, 225, 243n1
progressions, third, 3, 66–67, 128, 134–135
Prokofiev, Sergei, 165
prolongation, 37, 40, 42, 133, 139, 150, 209, 248n53
and structure, 37
and syntax, 220
and teleology, 37
prose, musical, 34, 44, 233, 247n7
Puccini, Giacomo, 20, 266n23
"pump-up modulations." *See* expressive tonality

quartal harmony, 10, 243n19, 244n17

Rachmaninoff, Sergei, 20, 132
Ravel, Maurice, 165, 255n34
referentiality, 12, 19, 42–43, 47, 127, 135, 221
as analytical asset, 45
associative power of, 44
in film music, 59
vs. functionality, 45
relative transformation (R), 77, 90–92, 100, 115,
145, 155, 185, 205, 221
Richter, Max, 105–107, 108
Riemann, Hugo, 86–87, 253n6, 256n1
Rings, Steven, 58–59, 129–130, 135–136,
220–221, 252n1, 265n19
Rodman, Ronald, 5, 22, 27, 42, 245n21,
248n59, 259n33
Romanticism, 16, 18–19, 22, 24, 26, 31, 34, 39, 43,
81, 206
film music influence, 9, 165–166, 238
style topic, 12
Rosar, William, 7, 132, 242n14, 243n19, 244n19,
249n7, 257n11, 258n32
Rosenman, Leonard, 21, 27, 30–31, 34, 44,
200–201
compositional style, 246n38

"Tarnhelm" progression (LP(m)), 101–102, 132,
    177, 242n15, 255n36, 255n38
teleology, 46, 133, 145, 156, 186–187
temporality
    cinematic vs. musical, 31–32
    filmic, 10, 29
    subjective temporality, 186, 188, 192
        harmonic manipulation of, 189, 190–191,
            195, 263n42
        phenomenology of, 191, 263n45
        and visualizations of tonal space, 192–197
tension/release dichotomy, 62, 64–65, 202
tethered chromaticism, 207, 211–213, 217, 224
texture, 26, 133, 135, 140, 145
theme, 14, 21, 134, 150, 203, 207, 210
    harmonic grammar, 6
    preparation of, 176–177, 192
    See also cue; leitmotif
tonal agnosticism, 13, 74, 88
    and NROs, 91
tonal design, 27, 145, 159, 213
    and narrative synchronization, 159
    and pragmatism, 27
tonal idioms, 147, 202–205, 212, 218, 221, 235
    commingling of (interactivity?), 64–65, 68, 225
    inventory of, 205
tonal intentionality, 129–130, 135
tonality, 205
    cinematic, 17
    directional, 22
    as drama, 49–51
    excess, 29
    expressivity, 15, 19, 51, 24n42
    "fifteen second" rule, 32–34, 45
    filmic function of, 8, 15
    and gender, 247n51
    immediacy, 12, 19, 31, 127, 247n45
    meaning, 16, 27
    paired, 22
    subordination, 12, 19, 26–27, 129
        and expressivity, 27
        and harmonic coherence, 28
        and "mickey-mousing," 28
        of musical (tone) logic, 31
        as narrative asset, 31
    as a style topic, 44
    symbolic, 22
    triadic, 14
    Wagnerian, 50, 261n26
tonal monism and dualism, 203, 214
    definitions of, 214
    monism vs. dualism, 215–216, 221–222
tonal pairing, 23
tonal space, 89, 110–114, 134
    circle of fifths, 111, 114
    as conceptual space, 111
    definition of, 110
    measurement of, 137

navigation of, 89, 91, 110–111, 134
and subjective temporality, 191
visualizations of (see common-tone
    "neighborhood"; Tonnetz)
Tonnetz, 13, 111–112, 137, 151–152, 157, 256n46
    as analytical tool, 114, 116–119, 120, 124
    origins, 111
    visualizations of, 110, 112–113, 120–123,
        137, 196
T_n transformation, 54, 59, 91, 175, 179, 208,
    212, 234
trailers/previews, 1
transformation, 12, 45, 58–59, 85, 150, 220
    expressivity of, 59
    in film music, 59
    as listening strategy, 83
    as theoretical foundation, 215
    types of, 82
        displacement, 82
        inversion-based, 82
transformational analysis, 128, 149
    advantages of, 120
    multiplicity of, 128, 136
    orthography of, 55
transformational complexity word length, 137–140,
    143, 145
    subjectivity of, 137
transformational network, 135
transformational syntax, 220
transformation network, 13, 119–118, 222
    depictions of, 118f, 120f, 176f, 196f
    for inter-/intrafilmic analysis, 118
    pantriadic temporality, 197
transformation theory. See neo-Riemannian theory
triadic cycle, 162
    by leap, 64–65
    by step, 54, 59
"triadic tonality space," 202–204, 207–208,
    212, 235
    visualization of, 221–222
tritonal progression (T_6), 82, 140, 156, 243n19,
    248n60, 255n37, 255n39
    diabolism, 82, 156
    oscillation of, 68, 157, 228
    transposition by, 103–103
Tymoczko, Dmitri, 14, 111, 203–204, 253n11,
    256n46, 264n10

uncanny, the, 70–71, 100, 103–104, 196
Universal Studios, 1
    logo theme, 2–4, 15, 82, 242n9

Vaughan Williams, Ralph, 73, 118–124, 165, 225,
    252n51, 263n46
voice leading, 13, 77, 81, 88–89, 127, 134, 140–142,
    160, 217, 238
    for formal and expressive ends, 143
    parsimonious, 77, 80, 91, 142, 162

CPSIA information can be obtained
at www.ICGtesting.com
Printed in the USA
BVHW030858291120
594145BV00002B/7